Constructing

Constructing Place is a cutting-edge study exploring the nature of how we conceive, construct, perceive and interpret 'place'. It offers an important reading of the subject, since at its heart is an acceptance of the central role of the mind, rather than just analyses of the cultural content and physical manifestation of 'place'. The book uses the frameworks offered by Melanie Klein, Donald W. Winnicott, Arnold Berleant, Adrian Stokes and Luce Irigaray, and addresses the ideas of two leading writers on 'place': Amos Rapaport and Edward Casey.

The book is divided into two parts: Mind, looking at how we project a relationship on a place and the philosophy of place; and Matter, in which the essays examine more concrete examples of architectural places grouped under two headings – 'Modern mediation' and 'Considerate intervention'. Essays examine the attitudes to both nature and the built environment of the designer, the client and the society in which an intervention (be it architecture, landscape design or a piece of art) is made. The legacy of the modernist view of nature and the environment is also discussed, and the degree to which such ideas continue to impinge on contemporary interventions is assessed. These topics are addressed through the methodologies of history, theory, philosophy and psychology.

Constructing Place forges new collaborative ideas in an interdisciplinary way, including essays on architecture, planning, landscape and philosophy (particularly applied aesthetics). Written for and by those in both practice and academia across this range of fields, it is also useful for those interested in psychology and creativity, and those who are keen on issues about the value of engagement with the environment.

Sarah Menin studied architecture before researching a PhD on parallels between the creative works of Aalto and Sibelius. She is a Lecturer in the School of Architecture, Planning and Landscape at University of Newcastle upon Tyne, teaching architectural history and theory, and design. She has recently published *Nature and Space: Aalto and Le Corbusier* with Flora Samuel (Routledge). She also continues to practise architecture.

This book is dedicated to Anna Feige Menin,
my sweet and lovely daughter.

Constructing Place

Mind and Matter

Edited by Sarah Menin

LONDON AND NEW YORK

First published 2003 by Routledge
11 New Fetter Lane, London EC4P 4EE

Simultaneously published in the USA and Canada
by Routledge
29 West 35th Street, New York, NY 10001

Routledge is an imprint of the Taylor & Francis Group

Typeset in Univers by Bookcraft Ltd, Stroud, Gloucestershire
Printed and bound in Great Britain by T J International Ltd, Padstow, Cornwall

British Library Cataloguing in Publication Data
A catalogue record for this book is available from the British Library

Library of Congress Cataloging in Publication Data
Constructing place : mind and matter / edited by Sarah Menin.
p. cm.
Includes bibliographical references and index.
1. Architecture—Aesthetics—Congresses.
2. Architecture—Psychological aspects—Congresses. 3. Space (Architecture)—Congresses. 4. City planning—Psychological aspects—Congresses. 5. Spatial behavior—Congresses. 1. Menin, Sarah.
NA2500.C5985 2003
721'.01—dc2l
2003001260

ISBN 0-415-31465-8 (hbk)
ISBN 0-415-31466-6 (pbk)

Contents

Considerate intervention

Illustration credits

Adam Sharr ©, 9.1, 9.2, 9.3
Aldo van Eyck ©, I.13, Plate 6
Alvar Aalto Foundation ©, 17.1, 17.2, 17.4
Annette Condello ©, I.19, 22.1, 22.3, 22.4, 22.5
Balthazar Korab ©, 19.2, 19.3, 19.4
Camlin Lonsdale ©, 3.3
Clean, Naples ©, 22.2
David Messent ©, 18.2
Didem Kiliçkiran ©, I.11, 6.1, 6.2, 6.3, 6.4
Digne Meller Marcovicz ©, 9.4, 9.5
FLC/ADAGP ©, Paris and DACS ©, London, 2002, 16.2, 16.3, 16.4
Gabinetto Fotografico ©, Florence, Plate 4
General Motors ©, 19.1
Hélène Binet ©, 14.4
Ian Thompson ©, 3.1
Italo Martinero / Alvar Aalto Foundation ©, 17.5
J. Tiainen ©, 14.5
Jørn Utzon ©, 18.5
Kati Blom ©, I.14, 14.2, 14.3
Kunstmuseum & Museum für Gegenwartskunst ©, Basel, 14.1
Laboratorio Fotografico Soprintendenza per I Beni Ambientali e Architettonici Delle Marche ©, 13.3
Lindsey Black ©, I.9, Plate 3
Malcolm Menin ©, I.8
Mark Kirchner ©, I.18, 20.1, 20.2, 20.4
Martin Beattie ©, I.12, 11.1, 11.2, 11.3, 11.4
Max Robinson ©, 10.1, 10.2, 10.3, 10.4
Michael P.T. Linzey ©, 21.1
Nathaniel Coleman and FLC/ADAGP ©, Paris and DACS ©, 15.1, 15.2
Nathaniel Coleman ©, 15.3, 15.4
National Gallery ©, London, 13.4
Peter Cook / View ©, Plate 7

Peter Kellett ©, I.10, 5.1, 5.2, 5.3, 5.4
Richard Weston ©, I.16, 18.1, 18.3, 18.4
Rowan Newby ©, I.6
Sarah Menin ©, cover, I.2, I.3, I.4, I.5, I.7, I.15, I.17
Simon Unwin ©, 4.1, 4.2, 4.3, 4.4, Plate 2
Steph Lane ©, I.20
Stephen Kite / J. Tiptree ©, 13.1
Stephen Kite / P. Rotondi ©, 13.2
Suzanne Ewing ©, 23.2, 23.4
Sverre Fehn ©, 23.5
Teigan©, 23.1, 23.3
Turner, T., 3.2
University of Hawaii, School of Architecture Kenneth F. Brown Award Program Archive Photograph ©, I.1, 20.3
Unterlinden Museum ©, Colmar, France, 16.1
V.A. Walström / Museum of Finnish Architecture ©, Plate 5

Contributors

Andrew Ballantyne is Professor and Director of Architecture at the School of Architecture, Planning and Landscape, University of Newcastle upon Tyne. He has published a number of books, including *What is Architecture?* (Routledge), and *Architecture Landscape and Liberty* (Cambridge University Press).

Martin Beattie is a Lecturer at the School of Architecture, Planning and Landscape, University of Newcastle upon Tyne. After completing an MA in Critical Theory at Nottingham University, following his training in architecture, he began his PhD research into the Barabazaar in Kolkata.

Arnold Berleant is Emeritus Professor Long Island University and Chair of the International Applied Aesthetic Association. He is founder of the discipline of Environmental Aesthetics, and has written a number of highly acclaimed books on this subject, including *Art and Engagement*, and *Living in the Landscape: Towards an Aesthetic of Environment*.

Kati Blom is an architect and teacher. She is a teaching at the School of Architecture, Planning and Landscape, University of Newcastle upon Tyne, and is currently studying for a PhD which examines transparency in architecture. She has written for many years on contemporary Finnish architecture.

Brian Carter is Dean and Professor at the School of Architecture and Planning, at the School of Architecture and Planning, University of Buffalo. In addition to his work in practice he has written extensively and is the author of several books.

Nathaniel Coleman is a Lecturer, teaching design and architectural theory and history at the School of Architecture, Planning and Landscape, University of Newcastle upon Tyne. His doctoral thesis considered the role of utopia in the invention of exemplary architecture. Until recently Coleman taught at Washington State University.

Annette Condello teaches architecture at the University of Western Australia. She is currently studying for a PhD on Architecture and Luxury.

Suzanne Ewing is an architect and educator. She is currently Lecturer in Architecture at Edinburgh University, has published articles on a number of architectural subjects, and continues to practise.

Peter Kellett is a Senior Lecturer at the School of Architecture, Planning and Landscape at the University of Newcastle upon Tyne. His research interests focus on housing, particularly on understanding how disadvantaged households create, use and value dwelling environments in developing world cities. Much of his recent work focuses on how meanings of home are socially constructed and the application of ethnographic methodologies to housing research. He has published a large number of articles on housing in developing countries.

Didem Kiliçkiran is completing her PhD at the Bartlett School of Graduate Studies, University College London. Her research investigates the ways refugee and immigrant households construct a 'sense of place' within their new homes in a foreign country, focusing particularly on issues of gender and ethnicity. Her research includes an investigation of ethnicity, identity and domestic space culture among Kurdish, and Turkish refugee women in North London. She also teaches in Turkey, at the Middle East Technical University, Ankara/Turkey.

Stephen Kite is Senior Lecturer in Architecture at the School of Architecture, Planning and Landscape at the University of Newcastle upon Tyne. His PhD was on Adrian Stokes' critical writing and on the traditional architecture of Oman. He is currently writing *Reflective Practice: Colin St John Wilson* with Sarah Menin for Ashgate.

Michael P. T. Linzey is Senior Lecturer in Architecture at the University of Auckland. He taught previously at Melbourne University, where he received his PhD. His field of research is a study of the cultural logic of architecture, including questions relating to meaning, narrative, myth and metaphor, western and non-western cultural logics, and bicultural developments in New Zealand architecture.

Ali Madanipour is Professor of Urban Design at the School of Architecture, Planning and Landscape, University of Newcastle upon Tyne. He has studied, practised and taught architecture, urban design and town planning, winning design awards, conducting academic research, and publishing widely. His latest book is *Public and Private Spaces of the City* (Routledge, forthcoming).

Sarah Menin is Lecturer at the School of Architecture, Planning and Landscape at the University of Newcastle upon Tyne. Her PhD examined the lives and creativity of Alvar Aalto and Sibelius, from which she is now writing a book. She has recently held a Leverhulme Special Research Fellowship to examine the relationship between the ideas about nature held by Aalto and Le Corbusier, the results of which contributed to *Nature and Space: Aalto and Le Corbusier*, co-written with Flora Samuel. Menin is also co-writing a book on the architectural career of Colin St John Wilson with Stephen Kite.

Samia Rab is an architect and educator. Her research explores the timeless but place-specific role of indigenous knowledge in architectural production. She is currently teaching at the American University of Sharjah, UAE, where she is developing the region's first heritage management programme.

Simon Richards is a Research Fellow at the University of Essex. He has written, *Le Corbusier's Concept of Self*, (Yale), and is working on an AHRB-funded project into 'Concepts of "Self" in the theory and practice of architecture and town planning since 1945'.

Max Robinson has practised architecture for many years, and currently holds a position of Director of the School of Architecture at the University of Tennessee – Knoxville.

Flora Samuel is Lecturer and architect at the Welsh School of Architecture, Cardiff University. She has written *Nature and Space: Aalto and Le Corbusier* with Sarah Menin, and is currently writing *Le Corbusier Architect and Feminist* for Wiley.

Adam Sharr is an Lecturer and architect at the Welsh School of Architecture, University of Cardiff. His research concerns relationships between physical, social and intellectual structures in architecture.

Fran Speed, formerly a Lecturer in Visual Culture at the University of Central England in Birmingham, is currently a doctorate student researching in the field of environmental aesthetics at the Institute of Environment, Philosophy and Public Policy at Lancaster University UK, where she gained an MA in environmental philosophy. She holds a degree in Art and Design, having graduated as a fine artist. For a significant part of her professional life she worked in film, TV and the media.

Ian Thompson is Lecturer in Landscape Design at the School of Architecture, Planning and Landscape, University of Newcastle upon Tyne. He is author of a number of articles on landscape architecture and the book *Ecology, Community and Delight*, published by Spon.

Simon Unwin is a Senior Lecturer in the Welsh School of Architecture, Cardiff University. He has published a number of books on architectural theory, including *Analysing Architecture* and *An Architecture Notebook*: *Wall*, both published by Routledge.

Richard Weston is a Research Fellow at the Welsh School of Architecture, Cardiff University. He has written extensively on modern architecture, including *Alvar Aalto and Modernism* for Phaidon, and *Jørn Utzon* for Edition Blondal.

Acknowledgements

I would like to thank all the authors who have contributed to this book for their patience and the capacity to share in the process of creating this artefact. Special thanks are due to my colleagues Stephen Kite, Andrew Ballantyne, Nathaniel Coleman and Kati Blom for their critical reading, and their assistance in undertaking picture searches.

Many thanks are also due to all who attended the Constructing Place conference at Auckland Castle in April 2002, as keynote speakers and as delegates, without whom this book could not have been made. The conference was characterized by the strong intention to balance theoretical exploration with a demonstration of the practical outworking of place-making. I am most grateful to the practitioners for their cameo presentations, which were interwoven with the academic explorations – Steve Crister (Studio Granda, Iceland), Irena Bauman (Bauman Lyons, Leeds), Eric Parry (Eric Parry Architects, London), Ivor Richards, David Prichard (McCormac Jameson Prichard) and Wolfgang Weileder (Germany and Newcastle).

Very many papers could have been included, and in selecting I have had to put aside some most interesting, most learned, and most creative essays that did not fit the shape of the book that emerged. The conference attracted delegates from twenty-one countries, and a great variety of professions and therefore of methodologies was represented. Although the book includes nine essays that reflect some of the research undertaken at our Centre for Tectonic Cultures, School of Architecture, Planning and Landscape at the University of Newcastle upon Tyne, the remaining fourteen essays represent colleagues from elsewhere in England, Scotland, Wales, Australia, New Zealand, the United States, and the United Arab Emirates. Many of those writing herein are domiciled away from the places they consider their true homes, or the places with which they have very close relationships. This draws into the fabric of the book countries such as Finland, Turkey, Iran, France, Colombia, Chile and Italy. I am extremely grateful for the deep understanding that comes from experience and knowledge of this rich diversity of peoples, cultures and geographies, which has clearly inspired many of the essays included here.

I am indebted to the Leverhulme Trust for the Special Research Fellowship from which the idea for the conference grew. Thanks also to Steph Lane who assisted in the arrangements for the conference, and to the students who helped keep the electronic media moving. I am grateful, as ever, to Caroline Mallinder, Michelle Green, Laura Casban and their colleagues at Routledge and to Joan Hodsdon at Bookcraft for their help and guidance in the production of this book.

Deep thanks are due to Gerry O'Meara and Arthur Vincent, to whom I am indebted for helping to re-construct my place, and to Jeanne Hinton, Carolyn Reinhart, Ruth Vincent and Julia Waterfield for their friendships in so making it a place of sharing. Finally, special thanks are due in great measure to David Feige, and in particular to my Feigeles (Anna and Amos) for their patience, their love, and their enthusiasm for making great little places at home in which we can play together. I dedicate this book to Anna, my sweet and lovely daughter.

Foreword

I am delighted to enthusiastically endorse the publication of this book on a subject so crucial to the current debate about architecture and the environment. It is a debate that is too often confused by the propensity of critics to be trapped by the style wars of novelty and fashion. Few seem to appreciate the depth of design endeavour and understanding that it takes to create pleasure from constructed places. Our expectations are too low, the economic and programmatic goals are mismatched to cost in use and an understanding of the absolute importance of architectural, urban and landscape design as the framework for social interaction. Architecture is beyond all else the most profound mimetic adventure, one of artifice and nature; the utopian and the world of real possibilities; the sacred mirror and its secular reflection. In these chapters, this mimetic drama is played out repeatedly and on the whole is positively accumulative. As a participant in the conference that laid the ground for this book I am aware of the breadth of scholarship that it drew together and the depth of stimuli that it provoked, as a result of which it is entirely appropriate that, rather than remaining in the sphere of personal memory, its cumulative results should be shared.

The authors bring with them a rich diversity of comparative evidence through built precedent and philosophical speculation. Of the former, the creative possibilities of the environment of the workplace are well illustrated in the rather overlooked but seminal headquarters, campus and research and development centre for General Motors, with its echoes of the Finnish landscape and adoption of automotive technology and product design – particularly, externally, in the gasketed windows of the curtain walling and the glazed-brickwork gables. The modernist proto-dwelling is discussed in papers, firstly on Alvar Aalto's profound attempt to bridge the divide between the modern milieu and the natural environment in his Experimental or Play House at Muuratsalo, secondly in the paper on Le Corbusier's unbuilt scheme for La Sainte Baume in which he proposed housing alongside an underground basilica and museum.

The use of precedent also usefully draws on polarities that, juxtaposed, reinforce the case made by individual contributors. One such comparison is that of the empowerment and ensuing creativity illustrated by the freedom to build, evident in the squatter settlements of Colombia, with the meditation on the mediation of the terrestrial and celestial in the earth-bound platforms and floating roofs of the architecture of Jørn Utzon. Another is the comparison of the transient temporality of the beach shelter and the multi-layered associations conjured in the Architectural Spoils: Francesco Venezia and Sicily's *spogliatoia*. Under the rubric of Mind there are to be found a number of valuable discourses. Papers on the Aesthetics of Place, the Sacred Environment and the Genius Loci explore the importance of meaning and experience in the interpretation of the manifest quality of space in both the natural landscape and the artifice of object, enclosure and boundary. Understandably, several contributors emphasize the importance of orientation, for instance through Heidegger's concepts of horizons and *raum*, Jay Appleton's theory of Prospect and Refuge, and the catatonic qualities of transparency emergent from an interpretation of Julia Kristeva's theory of communication.

This is a book that will help to beat a path across the often frustrating barriers between theory and practice by bringing into focus projects, built and unbuilt, as precedents to be explored from divergent philosophical positions. They are on the whole fresh accounts of exemplars from the second half of the twentieth century. Broadly, the analysis that is offered shows how powerful the cultural resonances can be when site, programme and construction are mutually bound to create a memorable synthesis.

A departure has been created on at least two fronts for sequel publications. Firstly, the precedents for the section on Matter are almost exclusively taken from a landscape context and could be very usefully matched by the analysis of urban qualitative equivalents. Secondly, the question of construction and material, though touched on, remains an unrequited aspect of the Making.

Eric Parry, Architect
London, October 2002

Introduction

Sarah Menin

Place, progress and evolution

This book is an exploration of the processes, the histories and the impacts of constructing place. It accepts that the making of place is simultaneously a material construct and a construct of the mind.

Taking up the challenge laid down by Amos Rapoport's argument that 'place' has become a buzz word – being space plus 'something', where the something is never completely explained[1] – this collection of essays seeks to explicate this 'something', which may be both mental and, through detailed examples from a variety of specific contexts, material, or may, indeed, be only mental with little material manifestation. The contrary (a material context with little mental meaning) is more unlikely, since we invest material phenomena with meaning by engaging with them, and there can be little, if any, material that has no meaning. In his argument against the use of the term 'place', Rapoport notes that 'one person's place is another's non-place',[2] and that the meaning of 'place' can be so culturally and sub-culturally variable as to be indefinable, non-scientific and, he argues, therefore irrelevant. Rapoport's reason for dismissing the idea of 'place' (its multivalency and cultural determinancy)[3] is the very issue at the heart of this collection of essays. His scholarly thesis is 'not concerned with unique cases or with the multiplicity of examples', but has a main interest in 'general features'.[4] Here it is exactly the specificity of the particular that is studied, from which, as this introduction demonstrates, some general features and principles do emerge. As Anne Stenros argues 'most essential in this discussion is the experience of place, the feeling of place, and its origins, since place is the most unique experience of space, it is man's deepest experience of the environment.'[5]

Indeed, the discussions in this book seek to move to a reading of place that is not defensive against Rapoport's scepticism, but rather one that is confident of the inherent efficacy of place. Such confidence comes from the philosophical heritage of the notion of place, of the idea of 'being-in-place'; from Aristotle's

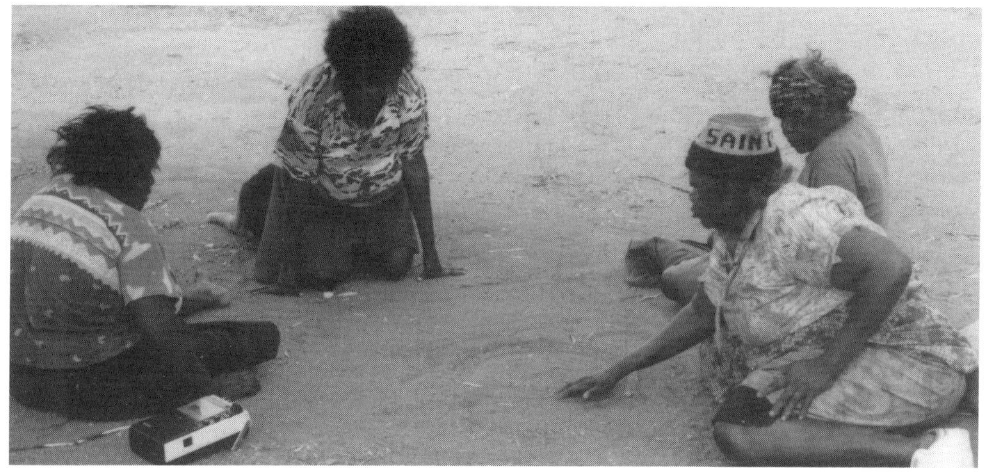

I.1
The elders of the Anangu tribe map and paint stories of Uluru. They are engaged in developing the programme brief and the precise citing of the Uluru-Kuta Tjuta Cultural Centre, Northern Territories, Australia
ANCA, with Gregory Burgess, c.1993

concern with 'where' in *Physics* (making it one of the ten indispensable categories of every substance) to Heidegger's noting, in *Being and Time*,[6] that 'all "where's" are discovered and circumspectively interpreted as we go our ways in everyday dealings; they are not ascertained and catalogued by the observational measurements of space', and to Luce Irigaray's important re-reading of *Physics* in which 'there is always more place'.[7]

Support for the psychological reality of 'being-in-place', comes from the research of Melanie Klein and Donald D. Winnicott, amongst others, who recognized the environment as isomorphic with the healthy life of the individual self. The assurance in the efficacy of the notion of place also derives from the experience of being in 'given' natural environments, be they conserved or wild, and from making built environments and being moved by, and seeing people effected by, places conceived, built or assembled by others.

In fact confidence in 'place' also comes from experience of the inverse of these positive encounters of the mind and of material place. It is the experience of *atopos* (literally meaning the 'no place'): of Auschwitz-Birkenau (Fig. I.2);[8] of inner-city nightmares; of Eliot's *Waste Land*; and also the *atopos* of the mind, which is a characteristic of an emotional, mental and physical nothingness that can accompany depression or sense of *Unheimlichkeit* – homesickness or not feeling at home, or a deep angst of unbearable emptiness. Edward Casey believes that *atopos* is something, or somewhere, that philosophers have sought to deny.[9] Yet atopia is a place familiar to psychiatrists and priests – and architects, landscape architects and planners have built it too. For the re-orientation, not to say correction, of these negatives we must refind place – even if we may be searching materially and mentally for something that can, in some cases, be found only spiritually.

I.2
Rails leading into Auschwitz-Birkenau

However, this book explores a number of ways in which this potential void can be addressed: by simply conceiving or building enclosure; by conceiving an outside environment that mediates between human life and the physical and metaphysical realities of nature; by revisiting a lost cultural identity by the placing of artefacts; by repositioning cultural spoils in the rebuilding of devastated towns, or ruined castles, or troubled lives (Fig. I.3). Yet we know from experience that from within *atopos* come new beginnings:

> We shall not cease from exploration,
> And the end of all exploring,
> Will be to arrive where we started,
> And know the place for the first time,
> Through the unknown remembered gate,
> When the last of earth left to discover,
> Is that which was the beginning.[10]

Indeed, central to the parallel examination of the material and the mental construction of place herein is the concomitant fact of the evolution of the mind during the process of creativity (be it artistic or psychological creativity).[11] In the case of the creation of a place there may be a great deal of mental creative

activity and/or cultural connotation, and yet only the slightest placing of a physical sign as the material evolution of the setting into the intentional place, such as that which Didem Kiliçkiran demonstrates in chapter 6 in her study of the placing of artefacts in the homes of Kurdish refugees in London. This book is as much concerned with such an evolution of place through the lives of people who are not professionally occupied in the fields of aesthetics, architecture, planning and landscape, as with those who are. Its central inquiry is thus the process of conceiving and then, in one way or another, constructing place, of living creatively in a context to which we want to reach out, and with which we want to engage.

Behind this idea of a relationship between the self and the context is the premise that before an engagement there is a self that needs to engage. As Winnicott has put it, being must come before doing.[12] This book is concerned both with the human being associated with constructing place, and the mental investment in the physical places then conceived. Winnicott's ideas strengthen the notion that there is a close link between the growth of the individual's psyche (i.e. their personal creativity) and the development of the wider environment (be it cultural, social or religious) by exploring the 'potential space' in which the creative mind lives. 'Cultural experience starts as play, and leads on to the whole area of man's inheritance, including the arts, the myths of history, the slow march of philosophical thought and the mysteries of mathematics, and of group management and of religion.'[13] From this postulation Winnicott offers a 'tentative' formulation that cultural experience is located, primarily, 'in the potential space between a child and the mother when experience has produced in the child a high degree of confidence in the mother, that she will not fail to be there if suddenly needed.'[14] From this grows a familiar behavioural pattern in which mental experiments, such as imaginative play and creative constructs, are the norm. This may then continue as a matter of course, through life, and thus into the mental experience of environments in which one lives and moves. From this the mental, and later physical, construction of place is forthcoming.

Personhood and the growth of place

I.3
Remu'h Cemetery, Krakow. Gravestones, dating from the sixteenth century, and desecrated by Nazis, have been rebuilt into a powerful wailing wall.

This book aims to broaden concern for creating place from the professional to the everyday engagement with both physical settings and mental meta-locations within a broader definition of creativity that incorporates both creative living, and the more traditional tropes of artistic creativity. It is also important to acknowledge the complex specificities of human engagement with innumerable settings, and that the commonest of everyday locations may, by the turning of the mind (i.e. a creative moment) become an experience of something new (Fig. I.4). It is as

I.4
An informal street 'ceiling' in Venice

much the individual mental 'take' on a space that determines its import – and all that goes to the creation of a state of mind: environmental, sociological, familial, spiritual or psychological impacts upon the self. As Simon Richards suggests, we should recognize that it is as much a process of creating selves as it is creating place. The inverse of this argument is also apparent. When the self is depressed, and cannot be creative in its 'being' in the world, how deadening are both beautiful and decrepit places alike. Italio Calvino has written:

> Beyond six rivers and three mountain ranges rises Zora, a city that no one, having seen it, can forget. […] Zora has the quality of remaining in your memory point by point, in its succession of streets, of houses along the streets, and of doors and windows in the houses, though nothing in them possesses a special beauty or rarity. Zora's secret lies in the way your gaze runs over patterns following one another as in a musical score where a note can be altered and displaced … This city which cannot be expunged from the mind is like an armature, a

> honeycomb in whose cells each of us can place the things he wants to remember.[15]

Atopos, that inner place of desolation, is extrapolated on to the environment around, and far from relationship, it is isolation that is projected. It is equally a sense one may have of an external, physical *atopos* that may be introjected into the self, as many contributors have suggested.

There should be as much a concern with what the self (both individual and collective) brings to the place as with the definition of the intrinsic character of that place – something explored in later parts of the book. Together the collection of essays demonstrates processes and phenomena that are extremely rich (and indeed complicated), but the explication of them enlightens us as to the process through which humans comprehend, mark and settle in both natural and man-made settings. This includes aspects of both the mental and material construction of place that are too often ignored, too easily missed, and too easily destroyed. Compare, for instance, the care taken in the slow construction of squatter shelters with the banality of vast unarticulated glass façades of some contemporary architecture, and the mindful mapping of indigenous concepts of place into modern architectural icons with the repeated mistakes made in professional conceptions of urban life that alienate those forced to inhabit these constructed concepts. In this way the essays comprise a number of different perspectives, definitions and descriptions of the process of place-making, but underlying their legion concerns is the understanding of the affective fecundity in the lives that conceive place, and the subsequent lives lived in and around these places.

Multivalent placings

The book is concerned with the process by which a setting becomes a place – a process in which the setting is loaded with mental constructs (the realms of psychological and philosophical, and even the metaphysical). This defines, in a limited way, the nature of constructing place with which the book concerns itself, and celebrates the diversity of experience and expertise that contribute to our understanding of place.

In acknowledgement of this the book is divided into two parts: Mind and Matter. The boundaries between these realms are recognized to be artificial in recognition of the interrelations between the areas of experience, understanding and making place – relations that have occupied philosophers since at least the time of Plato, and perhaps more importantly relations that allow the smallest of creative investments (in the psyche, or as a physical act) to be honoured. This explains the division of the book into two parts, since, although in part two many exemplary examples of modern architecture are analysed, in part one, essayists from a wide variety of backgrounds explore many different ways in which distinctive aspects of 'place' are constructs of the mind (and the self) first, and then how they becomes physical – even with the building of essential shelter the shack is shown to become a 'place' rather than a mere collection of reclaimed materials, because of an intention to make a 'home' which aspires to being like other homes in another, more stable, milieu.

Flexible boundaries between mind and matter

It is also important to note that, although many essays in part one address the relationship between self and place, they do not put aside nor do they deny the material impacts of this mental process of aspiration; indeed most papers are deeply rooted in the examples of physical actuality. Equally, in part two the essays mainly address the detailed material reality of modern places, but they also make profound enquires into aspects of the mind. In this way essays from 'Mind' and 'Matter' have in common a desire to explore the social, the psychological, or the philosophical roots of what has then become physical.

Indeed, in the essays the discussion moves, reciprocally, between examination of the very process of becoming sedentary and of building a psychological relationship to a place, before moving to an exploration of making tectonic, material settlements, and a process of developing philosophies about these settlements through which the place is mapped (Fig. I.5). As Arnold Berleant, the inventor of environmental aesthetics, has suggested elsewhere, places 'insinuate themselves in to our bodies, stirring up somatic and affective responses'.[16] There is a continuity between ourselves and the place in which we have our being.

The inquiry of this book is, therefore, concerned with what Plato defined in *Timaeus*, alongside Being (ratio or proportion) and Becoming (*physis* or nature), as *chōra*,[17] that which is both a cosmic place and abstract space, and is also 'the substance of the human crafts … an "invisible ground" … that can be grasped only with great difficulty, obliquely so to speak, through a kind of "bastard reasoning".'[18] It is that which Rapoport says cannot be identified, but which nevertheless is a central ingredient of the nature of what makes a physical space an experiential place. With Merleau-Ponty we might respond to Rapoport that 'To seek the essence of perception is to declare that perception is, not presumed true, but defined as

I.5
Niemilä Farmstead. This farm was moved from Konginkangas to the Folk Museum at Seurasaari, Helsinki

access to the truth',[19] accepting that perception is essential to being in the world. In her book *Socrates' Ancestor*, Indra Kagis McEwan examined *chôra* as a dance, the fluidity of which is a vital aspect of what comprises Daedalus' notion of architecture:[20] the weaving of recorded and unrecorded reality,[21] of the actualité and the imagined realms of experience. McEwan explains that the word *chōros* came to mean not only dance floor, or dancing place, but the process of the dance itself.[22] In other words, the *chōra* (the 'invisible ground') is a situation in which mental place is constructed in (and through) the experience of an activity. In this context we can extract the sense of a process of continuity between the activity in a place and the making of the place itself, that being in a setting creates the meaning of the setting in some way. This suggests that the activity in a setting and the setting itself are sometimes isomorphic. This is not always the case, but the idea does explain why in a depressed and squalid setting, or *atopos*, the lives of those inhabiting the place may be affected by the void or the negativity. Boundaries between the phenomenon of the people and the phenomenon of the place are crossed; both negatively and positively.

The correlation between globalization and the lack of a persistent sense of the locale is addressed by many contributors, and in fact the richness of both colloquial and professional sensitivities to the desire for local identity are demonstrated as rich examples of constructed places.[23] Indeed, the continual sense of upheaval and displacement that accompanies much of our contemporary lives need not mean there is an enduring sense of *atopos*, as Fran Speed in chapter three, Peter Kellett in chapter five and Didem Kiliçkiran in chapter 6 explicate herein, displacement may distil essences of a lost place, as the barest possessions are positioned in ways that define cultural identity and make possible the temporary settlement of mind as well as body.

In this way, throughout the book the themes and frameworks used in the essays interweave to form a complex matrix of understanding, seeking to explain the sometimes contradictory nature of these interrelationships, the edges between them, and in so doing to challenge the often rigidly delimited roles carved by the professions concerned with conceiving, planning and making human settings. The quality of richness that informal or 'other-than-designed' settings have is something that is sometimes missed or devalued by professionals involved in the 'design' of intentionally 'artful' or 'functional' environments of all sorts (Fig. I.6).

An unveiling place

By joining Luce Irigaray in defining the nature of place and the nature of self as being close together (in fact being isomorphic)[24] we ensure that the metaphysical agenda must surface in the dialectic herein. In this view our environmental chaos is 'our' chaos, and the crisis is in and through us, not something outside. It is personal as much as global, cultural as much as environmental. Here the argument visits that of Susannah Hagan in her book *Taking Shape: A New Contract between Architecture and Nature* which addresses how, amid our feelings of impotence about changing the meteorological climate, there is also a great need to change the cultural climate. Just as Hagan describes how the debate about sustainability is often polarized between an Arcadian view and a utilitarian rationalist view,[25] so the viewing of place as something within as well as something outside ourselves ensures a continuum that is filled with both optimism and dread. To unveil what Heidegger describes as the 'still veiled' nature of space and place[26] is part of the generating energy of this book. This demands a mental move towards the hidden and veiled aspects of self as much as the hidden character of place. Much supposed place-making in contemporary architecture involves the construction of what are often experienced as *atopoi*, as non-places and deadening placelessness, as Kati Blom examines in relation to new glass architecture in chapter 14, finding a close relationship between this deadening placelessness and catatonia. By eking out the nature of what is lacking in such environments Blom unveils the loss of place that is both external and internal (possibly reflecting some lack within ourselves).

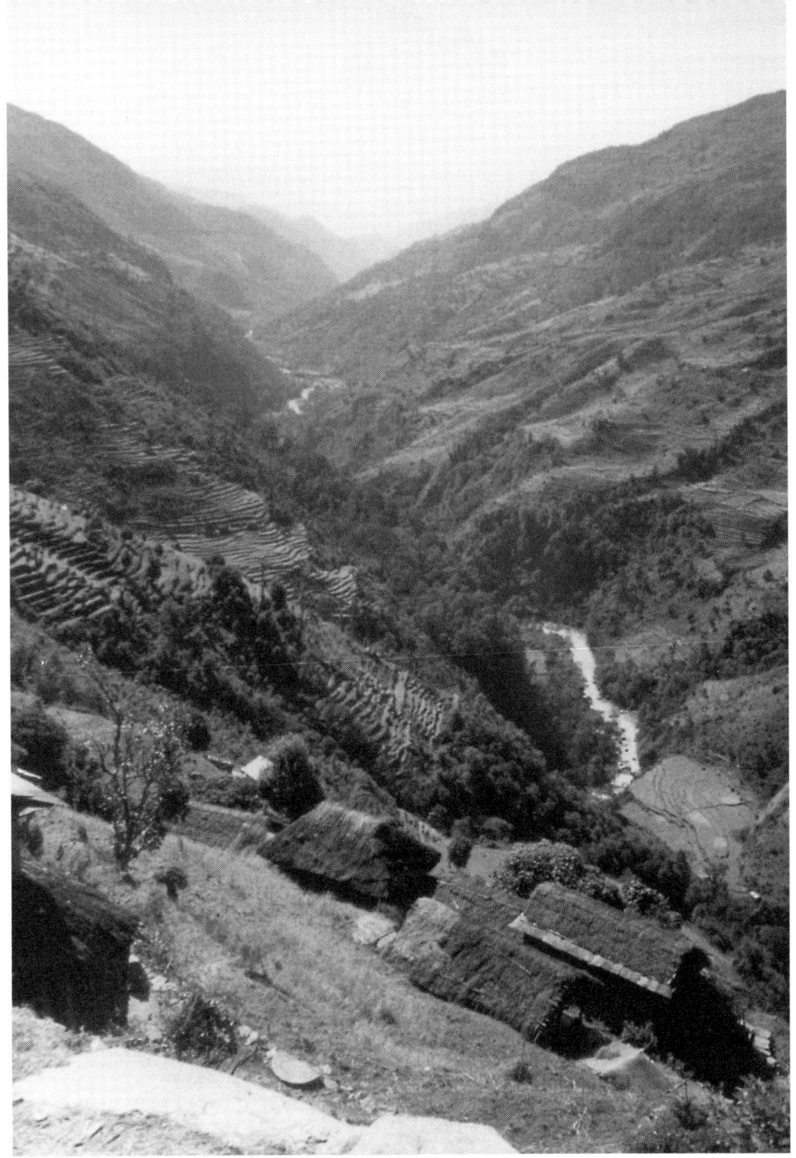

I.6
Agricultural terracing in a valley in Nepal

Mind

Mind, part one of the book, is largely concerned with the mental construction of place. This may be simply the completely intangible 'event' of a change of mood that occurs as we move in to a different environment (be it natural, designed or ruinously accidental),[27] around which we momentarily construct a sense of place, or it may be the experience of consciously seeking to make physical the settling of elements that may comprise a space and give it meaning. These essays demonstrate that the mental construction of place may be in the micro-context of personal home-making or in the making of cities, and may be both architectural and non-architectural, physical and metaphysical. Indeed, some essays address the process of constructing place from the initial realm of psychology wherein we relate in one way or another to place (including the often hidden, psycho-philosophical process of projecting a relationship on to that place), through the beginnings of conceiving a way of thinking about space and place (those processes of philosophizing about the significance of the realm of place, both natural and man-made).

Projecting a relationship

Under the sub-heading 'Projecting a relationship' eight essays explore the process by which place is conceived through a process in which something of oneself, one's beliefs or values, is ascribed to a setting one inhabits. This is accepted as a normal psychological reality of human life.[28] It also takes as read that one's interaction with an environment leaves neither party unaffected, and thus borrows from Winnicott theories about the fecundity of 'environment' in the development of the psyche in infancy (with mother) and, by projection, beyond, into and through adulthood.[29]

These essays share the notion of there being a common aesthetic realm, an 'other' reality beyond the specificity of the individual self, the needs of the group seeking to inhabit the space, or the conjectured brief of a proposed building or landscape. Winnicott's concern with the process of coming to terms with a reality beyond the self,[30] the 'other', may in this instance also refer to the rich palette of implications (both human and non-human) that the constructed physical place offers. It may even suggest that where there is a meeting between agents (any mix of interactions between people and natural or man-made phenomena) a 'place' may be constructed socially or psychologically that is the root of subsequent material modelling or construction. The relationship between the needs and expression of the 'self' and the reality of an 'otherness' recurs as a theme in part one, since the notion of an 'other' allows for discussions both of internalized 'others' within the self, and of the relationship of individual self to an external 'other', or settings of a shared reality. The 'other' may, for example, be the natural 'otherness' of the site and all ecologies associated with it, or it may refer to the metaphysical 'other' implied or conjured by a constructed intervention (be it social, spiritual or psychological in phenomenon).

There is, after all, a continual process of 'distinguishing between actual happenings and what goes on in the imagination', from infancy throughout life, as Winnicott identified.[31] The physical spaces we encounter are invested with symbolism and metaphor and are thus much enriched for this interplay between fantasy and reality – a process of enrichment of place that also enriches self, and offers to all who encounter a rich place the chance to live 'creatively'. Winnicott argues that there is a connection between living healthily and being able to be challenged by cultural experience.[32] Just as in infancy the child (and therefore the mother) lives creatively with whatever materials are available[33] – be it a cardboard box, a piece of wood or some Mozart – so this transition between reality and fantasy may continue into our contact with the physical environment; how we conceive it, how we shape it, how we construct it and how we experience it.

Body and place

In her re-reading of Aristotle's *Physics*, Irigaray reanimates the 'ancient (and very recent) question: How are body and place related?'[34] This is relevant here at a number of levels, not least the aspect of the physical place, but also the philosophical inquiry that encompasses the ethical, political, social and religious. The essays in 'Projecting a relationship' have in common, with Irigaray, an awareness that there should be a challenge to the Aristotelian notion of place as something contained. In general they arrive at a challenging acceptance that it is something that may be both closed and open in turns or simultaneously.

Elsewhere Irigaray suggests that woman may minister to her own psychological displacement (rooted, she implies, in social displacement) through her offspring. 'If she is unable to constitute, within herself the place that she is, she passes ceaselessly through the child in order to return to herself. This captures the other [i.e. the child] in her interiority.'[35] This process of capturing, or introjecting, something external into the interior is apt. In constructing a place mentally a person is both an actor in a situation (and a single kind of place for self), and is also in relation to others, in this case the child. Irigaray movingly suggests women are scattered in any number of places and selves, able to 'move within place as place. Within the availability of place. Given that her issue is how to trace the limits of place herself so as to be able to situate herself therein and welcome the other there.'[36] Woman is who she is 'across' and 'through' the others in the situation, a mechanism for relation to self through an-other person, situation or setting. Here woman is not just 'outside' thought (in Deleuze and Guattari's nomad space) but her body-place is a matter of inter-enveloping parts.[37] Kiliçkiran's study, in chapter 6, is interesting here, not just because it addresses women, but because its subject is the examination of external symbols to shore up identity and define a place.

Casey and Irigaray here challenge Aristotle's model of envelopment as something strictly contained, since body-place is porous, exhibiting 'the openness of the open' (Heidegger's phrase as requisitioned by Irigiray).[38] Here

too the argument visits Jay Appleton's prospect-refuge theory,[39] Adrian Stokes's ideas of envelopment and exposure,[40] examined further by Colin St John Wilson elsewhere.[41]

In this view there is a common move to turn Aristotle's cosmic view on its head and thereby, 'place as enclosure is reaffirmed', yet only insofar as the elements that make up place inhabit and suffuse the universe as a whole, now considered as 'a gigantic sieve-like vessel … which leaks.'[42] Casey suggests that 'the mirroring power of place is even more extensive than that of the body; as bodies expand into places, so places exfoliate through (built and given) things into (social and natural) regions, and regions expand in turn into worlds. From body and thing and region we come to world, but we do so only insofar as the event of place is active throughout.'[43]

In his essay 'The aesthetics in place' Berleant opens the discourse through an exploration of the engagement of the conscious body with a physical location, in this case 'Greasy Lake'.[44] In the essay he seeks to explore whether Greasy Lake is a place or not, arguing that the aesthetic is not only a factor in such

I.7
Open and closed balcony in Torun, Poland

I.8
A child's place

an experience of place, but is always present as one of its essential features. Berleant explores how the aesthetic has important implications for the construction of place, not just the understanding of it. He seeks to draw us from a purely biological or artistic understanding of place to an aesthetic one. Yet he offers an aesthetic broader than that offered by traditional artistic aesthetics, enveloping some territory of the psyche, and indeed the spirit, suggesting that the idea of the sacred place helps to identify place as an aesthetic field.

Berleant addresses the need to identify the human role in the search for the heart of place, citing Pauli Tapani Karjalainen, 'Palpable landscapes and impalpable mindscapes continually intermingle and form internal relations with each other',[45] but suggesting this does not go far enough. Berleant calls again on the metaphysical realm, and in particular on the question of the sacred, which comprises the signification people give to the physical location (Fig. I.9). He allows the sacred and the aesthetic to mingle, and borrowing from Hepburn promotes the idea of a realm in which, alongside a sense of awe, we find 'modes of being other than our own'.[46] Similarly, in Fran Speed's essay 'The sacred environment', aesthetic analysis is shown to have broader implications for place making than conventional analysis allows. She argues that perception of an environment as sacred is shown to be an emotional construction, constituted by a sense of meaningful relations, and examines how perception of an environment as 'sacred' influences our attitudes and behaviour towards it. She also argues that reality and invention in human experience are not rationally distinct, and illustrates the idea that perception of the sacred is not 'morally' determined, suggesting that it stems, not from rational motivation, but from emotional investment. Speed's ideas recall Jean-Luc Nancy: 'Divine places. Without gods, with no god, are spread out everywhere around us, open and offered to our coming, to our going or to our presence, given up or promised to our visitation, to frequentation by those who are not men either, but who are there, in these places; ourselves, alone, out to meet that which we are not, and which the gods for their part have never been … other tracks, other ways, other places for all who are there.'[47] Speed argues, however, to disassociate the sacred from religion, touching directly on the connections between the creation and the spirit of place, and that of the person creating or perceiving it; a subject that is revisited in many essays including Peter Kellett's exploration of squatter communities in Colombia, Flora Samuel's examination of Le Corbusier's La Sainte Baume project, my discussion of Aalto's retreat at Muuratsalo and Mike Linzey's exploration of Te Papa Tongarewa in New Zealand.

This discussion of the character of place is continued in Ian Thompson's essay 'What use is the *genius loci*?', in which he takes the discussion into the specific discipline of landscape architecture, suggesting that it is intrinsically concerned with *genius loci* through what he has identified elsewhere

I.9
Dendroglyph or incised tree, New South Wales, c.1940. The trees are marked with tribal totems to mark ceremonial grounds or graves
From Lindsey Black, *Burial Trees*, Melbourne: Robertson & Mullens, 1941

as the 'trivalent design' agendas (comprising concern for the aesthetic, the social and the environmental). Thompson suggests here that *genius loci* might be the keystone that locks trivalent design together, both in understanding landscape and creating it. He argues that *genius loci* is therefore useful in an instrumental sense, helping to defend 'valued' as opposed to 'damaging' forms of development; the creation of what are sometimes described as non-places or sites of placelessness.

Whether through built or given places the essays in this section then focus on examples of individual creation of place. 'Creativity, then, is the retention throughout life of something that belongs properly to infant experience: the ability to create the world ... Seeing everything afresh all the time ... apperception as opposed to perception'.[48] This positive, personal engagement with creativity is examined in the subsequent three essays in three diverse settings. The context that the three adopt for the discussion is a fascinating exposé of the primal human need to make sense of physical surroundings by organizing them into 'places'. Dealing with what at first may seem an ephemeral subject, Simon Unwin's essay 'Constructing place ... on the beach' reveals some fascinating examples of people's intuitive capacity for syntactic structure illustrated in the settlements they make when they spend a day on the beach, and in the ways they use those settlements to relate themselves to the context of sea, land, sun, wind and other people (see Plate 2). Finding parallels between the arrangement of beach settlements (composed of sand banks, towels, windbreaks, parasols ...) and those of ancient architectural forms (the megaron, for example), Unwin's essay touches on some primitive and apparently innate aspects of the ways people make and use places to mediate between themselves and the world they inhabit.

Temporary settlement in a more pressing context is demonstrated in Peter Kellett's essay 'Constructing informal places', in which the discussion moves from the rehearsing of anthropological settlement patterns in the leisure context of a beach in South Wales to those in the squatter settlements of Colombia. Here Kellett examines a situation, common in the majority of human experiences of settlement (Fig. I.10), where there is not a professional acting as protagonist in the act of making a home. Kellett demonstrates the profound pattern of defining a defensible space, the process of manifesting that defence, the joy of adorning the edifice, and the extraordinary capacity to move the whole construction, in a demonstration of a transient nature of place. This transience offers an important counter to the general understanding of the process of constructing place in which we requisition a space in our mind, investing it with relationship, and therefore meaning, and then manifest this in material form. Yet in this case, and in that examined by Didem Kiliçkiran in 'Migrant homes: ethnicity, identity and domestic space culture', we witness the way in which the reality of displacement in people's lives leads to a capacity to undertake place making in a more metaphysical realm. In both cases the material placing of certain iconic objects relative to each other offers a security and permanence, but actual physical siting is, perforce, much more transient (Fig. I.11). Although not because the force of the tide removes the place setting, the socio-political energy that controls lives acts against any desired permanence. Kellett identifies the process of the requisitioning of physical space for the making of richly symbolic home-places, and the manner in which illegal, often temporary, settlements again demonstrate the primary human need for group

I.10
A temporary dwelling erected in the early stages of a land invasion in Colombia. Such dwellings may be occupied for months (or even years) until a dwelling of solid materials can be constructed

settlement – but crucially the sense that, therein, the establishment of a series of 'signs' that may indicate to neighbours the status and achievements of those in the neighbourhood is as important as the physical protection offered by the fabric of the shacks. Kellett traces the paths of development from requisition of a plot, through the slow acquisition of basic building elements, to the elaboration of a system of culturally loaded visual metaphors that denote the relative 'establishment' of the family in their milieu. The process that Kiliçkiran examines is closer to an experience of creating a 'sense' of home through habitual, culturally informed ways of using domestic space, and through the construction of links with previous home environments in a multiplicity of ways. Most importantly, in her case, the display of consciously selected symbols of ethnicity and cultural identity fashions a 'sign' language that becomes a metaphor for a freedom of expression that Kurdish women lacked in their 'homelands', hence transforming the domestic setting to a sanctuary of ethnic and cultural identity. However, Kiliçkiran also directs our attention to the signs of change that she discovers in her analysis of the process of home-making, which are also interpreted by Kurdish women themselves with reference to their displacement and resettlement in their present milieu.

I.11
Kurdish hand-woven wall decorations in a flat in north London

A moral dimension runs through some of the essays, recognizing that any place-making involving professionals should realize 'a potentiality that already exists coiled within a given situation',[49] be it ergonomic human requirements, socio-religious tropes, cultural metaphors, psychological identities, or natural site specificities. This implies that there should be a certain humility on the part of those participating in the conception of a potential intervention, because it involves a dogged pursuit of the 'nature' of the place and the brief in all its legion selves. In pursuit of his mythical, 'higher' realm of architecture Louis Kahn called it the generating 'idea' or essence,[50] again highlighting, like Hugo Häring, 'what the building wants to be'.[51] This is inextricably linked, for example, to the needs of the user, be it human or bovine (in the case of the Gut Garkau cow shed), and the character of the site, as for example Hans Scharoun's Schminke House demonstrates.

The fact that the relationship of the self with the place is crucial, if the place is not to alienate, is a theme that many essays in this book expose. Yet, as Simon Richards argues in 'Communities of dread', the nature of 'self' in the realm of environmental design has rarely been explicated, though it has without such definition been used throughout history as a motivating force in the creation of human places. Richards suggests that an exploration of 'self' cuts to the ethical core of architecture and urbanism, and discusses this in relation to the issue of 'community'. Specifically, he provides a survey of a handful of influential American sociologists from the 1950s, all of whom were concerned with the question of urban and suburban community and the ways it impacted upon the individual human being. The concept of self was admitted as central at this time and, as a consequence, the debate was complex and circumspect. Richards then compares this with the unproblematic way in which architects and urbanists nowadays invoke community as a *cure-all*. But if 'community' is to be used in a more meaningful and responsible way, he concludes, the design community must begin to re-admit terms and questions comparable to those raised in the earlier debate. These terms address the realities of life and the construction of selves. Indeed, as Albert-Pérez-Gómez has put it, adapting from Octavio Paz, '[Architecture] opens up to us the possibility of being that is intrinsic in every birth; it re-creates man and makes him assume his true condition, which is not the dilemma: life or death, but a totality: life and death in a single instant of incandescence.'[52]

This argument is then developed by Ali Madanipour in his essay 'Design in the city: actors and contexts', in which there is an examination of the role of the architect (as self, citizen and expert), alongside many other players in the complex tapestry of meanings, possibilities and realities that constitute the urban context. Madanipour argues that perceiving the architects as 'actors' in the various frameworks that make up complex urban life may facilitate their professional role in making sense of this multiplicity of meaning, and avoid unintended consequences. Here his discussion of 'actors' and dialogue touches on issues that I touch on in my own essay on Aalto's understanding of the importance of play in the creative context. Madanipour incidentally strengthens the notion of the shared authorship of place by intimating the manner in which the expert actor must humble himself or herself, cooperating with other actors within the context. This accords with Nathaniel Coleman's argument in Chapter 15 regarding the characterization of modern architecture as altering rather than enhancing. In this way the architect is challenged to move beyond the artistic, to accommodate, for example, the geographic, social, psychological, spiritual and the cultural in the creative act of constructing place. Madanipour concludes that the interaction of actors and contexts ultimately shapes the city.

In 'Projecting a relationship' the essays explore the way in which the self projects a relationship on a setting to make a place for itself. The self thus invests the context with meaning, and it may then become a place for the self, with meaning for the self. The essays suggest that the construction of place for others may not be possible, since the place may mean nothing to me if I do not invest it with meaning myself. This is an important conclusion for architects and other professionals who, due to stylistic preoccupations and commercial pressures amongst other things, often offer disengaged artistic constructions about which users feel at best ambivalent and from which they may even feel alienated. In the interaction between the self and a place the relationship between the parts takes on the dimension of a player or protagonist in the whole, just as in personal relationships, where, for example, in addition to the two individuals there is the active factor of the relationship between them. Projecting a relationship explores this third phenomenon which exists between self and place – i.e. relationship. It is the realm of the 'in-between' explored by Merleau-Ponty[53] – that ground on which it is universally possible to bring things together, a subject also explored in the philosophical terms of, for example, Heidegger, Deleuze and Guattari, and the psychologizing terms of Klein, Winnicott and Stokes.

Philosophy of place

Under the subheading 'Philosophy of place', a collection of six essays takes a slightly different angle on the mental construction of place, examining the construction of human understanding about place – in physical, psychological and philosophical terms. Contemporary readings – or, in phenomenological terms, experiences – of place and dwelling cannot be divorced from the writing of the philosopher Martin Heidegger, which were influenced both by the philosopher's mountain 'hut' and his town house, built in Freiburg-im-Breisgau in 1928.[54] In 'The professor's house: Martin Heidegger's house at Freiburg-im-Breisgau', Adam Sharr examines how the philosopher sustained simultaneously quite different relationships with his hut and his house. The former appears closely aligned with his writings' emphasis on the philosophical and experiential potential of human situation. The latter was organized around domestic life, broadly 'aesthetic' in sensibility. Sharr explores possible implications of this contrast for his model of 'dwelling' and 'place'.

Drawing strongly on Heidegger's reading of how a site 'gathers' meaning,[55] Max Robinson follows Sharr's exposition of the specific character of the places Heidegger created for himself, with his essay 'Place-making: the notion of centre'. Robinson also requisitions both Norberg-Schulz's and Karsten Harries' readings of place to explore how the notion of 'centre' assists the definition of place and therefore of architecture.[56] Robinson also explores how architecture may recover a sense of place, suggesting that the notion of centre is key here. He seeks strongly to counter pluralism in which, characteristically, the divergence of outlooks has allowed 'centres' to comprise many different meanings for different peoples, and argues that, with the quest for universal objectivity (and the subsequent greater degree of abstraction) there is a disengagement and loss of meaning in its content. Robinson concludes that space should not be reduced to its objective basis, since this prevents

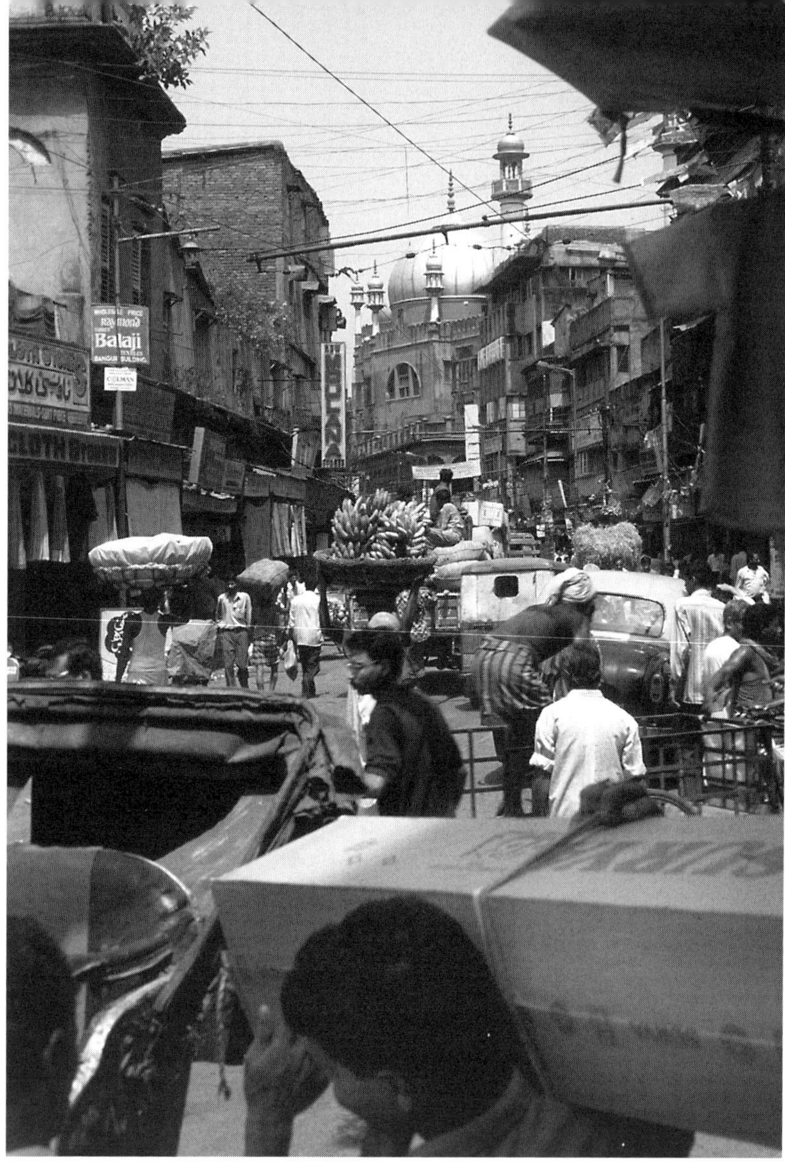

I.12
Rabindra Sarani. A street in Barabazaar, Kolkata, India

humankind really 'dwelling' in Heidegger's terms, which leads to a sense of 'homelessness'.

This is then followed by a detailed examination of an example of both cultural and historical layering of identities in India. The environment that Martin Beattie examines in 'Hybrid identities: "public" and "private" life in the courtyard houses of Barabazaar, Kolkata, India' offers a rich example of the meeting of different cultures, the creation of new building typologies, and an intriguing reading of the resultant urban milieu that cannot be adequately represented from within the binary oppositions of East versus West, 'them' versus 'us'. Underlying Beattie's essay is the notion of hybridity, which has become a key concept in the field of postcolonial studies. Taken from biological and botanical origins, the term has come to mean a cultural phenomenon which, as Homi K. Bhabha puts it, 'overcomes the given grounds of opposition and opens up a space of translation: a place of hybridity.'[57] The essay focuses on a past and present-day hybrid sense of place, found generally in the middle-class Bengali home in Kolkata, and the often heterodox and hybrid moves through which nineteenth-century Bengali modernity negotiated the distinction between 'private' and 'public' life, in a world shaped by colonialism (Fig. I.12). Beattie examines the changing and contradictory distinction between 'private' and 'public' life, and Bengali modernity that is still being negotiated today. Looked at obliquely, the continuing progress of modernity in Barabazaar from the nineteenth to the early twenty-first century is condensed into the three courthouses that Beattie analyses. In doing so he gives an example of the long-term evolution of place, and the complexities associated with group identity.

In '*Diagonal*: transversality and worldmaking', Andrew Ballantyne offers an analysis that sees 'place' as a construct of sensations and perceptions, as stimuli mediated by cultural appropriation. He takes the notion of the 'diagonal' to offer an image of multiple obliquities, but here particularly '*lire en diagonal*', which translates as 'skim reading'. In this way, Ballantyne suggests, we take some elements of experience as significant and formative, while others have little impact or simply pass us by. In effect we read the world *en diagonal*, developing ways of thinking that deal with the important things (neglecting the rest); and we do not do this alone, but are always implicated in society, networks, cultures and so on. Drawing on the concept of 'transversality' as found in Deleuze and Guattari's writings, Ballantyne explores how, when we see things in groups, something goes on between the members of the group that can produce effects not previously present in the constituent 'individuals', so that there is an emergent 'group identity'. Also requisitioning the idea that there is no isolation between phenomena (rather things are perceived in terms of flows and production, and in terms of processes) Ballantyne suggests that the 'individual' is produced in engagement with various groups, and an individual personality is just a particular case of group identity. Here he revisits the hybrid identities of protagonists or actors that Madanipour explicates. The 'self' is constructed in participation with others, and with inorganic things such as places and buildings, which can take on a role in the make-up of the group identity. Ballantyne argues that places are produced through the transversal interactions we make with their parts, settling his take on the term 'place' clearly in the Heideggerian conception.

The 'in-between' that is implicit in any discussion of relationship and interaction is explored by Stephen Kite in 'Modernity and the threshold: psychologizing the places in-between'. Kite exposes the 'in-between realms' as defined by the English art-writer Adrian Stokes, examining the consequences for place of the intermediary spaces between the 'carving' and 'modelling' modes of

artistic practice; practices that respectively define 'object-otherness' and 'object-envelopment'. In Stokes's post-1945 writings, his former privileging of 'carving' and the achievements of the depressive position – as explicated by the Freudian analyst Melanie Klein – transmutes to a more complex collection of views, as he gives a higher status to the 'modelling' process, and 'object-envelopment'. In the essay Kite explores these psychoanalytical abstractions in constructed places, for example Aldo Van Eyck's refuge, Hubertus House (Fig. I.13), in Amsterdam, 1976–8 (also addressed, later, by Coleman), where the architect sought to create 'in-between realms' to ease the 'psychic strain' of the occupants, allowing them to feel secure while negotiating routes out to the wider world. Kite also links this thinking to Appleton's theory of 'prospect and refuge' in the context of one of Stokes's favoured sites – the Ducal Palace of Urbino.

I.13
Children in the entrance of Hubertus Housing, Amsterdam
Aldo van Eyck Architects, 1982–7

The lack of refuge in the contemporary fascination with glass is explored in Kati Blom's essay 'Transparency and catatonia'. Blom explores how the retro-modernism fashion for extensive black glass boxes is resulting in a 'reduced' human environment, which she argues emphasizes the catatonic or static elements of construction (Fig. I.14). Requisitioning Julia Kristeva's post-structuralist theory of the human condition of communication, [58] the essay explores the static, dead core of glass architecture, and proposes an alternative revitalizing of modern architecture through the use of more dynamic or kinetic approaches to the built environment, giving examples of good practice in this sphere. Blom concludes that glass architecture has almost entirely used only transparency or reflection as a starting point, noting the consequent creation of environments where vertigo or claustrophobic reactions are normal, and where the spectators are driven into their inner fictional world. Shared reality is cut out, Blom argues, and there are few opportunities to enrich environmental experience, and the ability to give meaning to architecture. Therefore place is reduced and there is little accommodation of the creative self, little offering of an enticing encounter or an enriching relationship with the 'other' aspects of the environment. In this way part one closes with an examination of the world of deadening black boxes; one that is far removed from the rich phenomenological world conceived by Heidegger or expressed by Norberg-Schultz. Architecture that offers environmental anaesthesia rather than engaging enrichment does create place, but does not necessarily create an attractive place, and there are endless aesthetic, and perhaps more importantly, sociological and psychological consequences of such places.

I.14
'Lapakko' office block in Ruoholahti, Helsinki
Pekka Helin Architects, 2001

Matter

In the second part of the book architects (both practitioners and academics) examine the detailed character of place through examples of buildings and settings in the twentieth century. Many of them draw on ideas employed in the earlier part of the book. The essays are not only studies of buildings, but are also explorative analyses of less familiar examples of modern architecture, teasing out from the physical place, the creative intent (be it philosophical, psychological or artistic) of the architect, and the deep layers of character and meaning in the buildings.

This examination of the creation of material place in the last one hundred years is subdivided into two sections that study examples, first from late in the modernist period, and then from the late twentieth century. Indeed, there is a purposive focus on some lesser-known examples of constructed places by so-called 'modern masters', in order to draw out deeper, often ineffable agendas of these figures, such as Le Corbusier, Aalto and Saarinen, whose general approach has had, and continues to have, such a strong influence on the direction of contemporary architecture, yet whose more hidden agenda draws the attention of commentators less often. After examining the work of other twentieth-century architects, such as Utzon, whose approach explicates important aspects of conceptualizing and making place, the discussion then comes to rest, back nearer the present, in a series of studies of late twentieth-century examples of architectural place.

Modern mediation

The five essays in the 'Modern mediation' section explore the impact of place making in the early and mid-twentieth century. The collection of essays continues many of the preceding themes, looking at the specific manner in which certain architects placed their buildings in the setting, often creating or enhancing the setting itself. It also examines the way in which the buildings relate to the site, and what contributed to the architect's conception of place (built and natural) and, in many cases, their take on the metaphysical. The essays concern themselves with a cameo of a particular building, with the development of the work of an architect or designer in this sphere. Nathaniel Coleman's essay, 'Siting lives: postwar place-making' examines how buildings can invent a site through interpretation. Coleman explores how site and invention coincide through the examples of Le Corbusier's La Tourette on the striking slope of a hill outside Lyon, and van Eyck's Amsterdam Orphanage situated in an apparent non-place. These examples, designed and built between 1953 and 1960, exemplify a period when modernist architecture came under review for its limitations, including disregard for place (an apparent symptom of abstraction) and a neglect of broader and deeper concerns. Coleman suggests that the architects of these buildings viewed the site as generative, as a precedent condition that roots or grounds radical invention, and argues that both architects created a place that is modernist.

It is important to examine what is meant by a modernist place. For example, Le Corbusier is held by many to be the father of white modernist architecture, and yet, as Flora Samuel explores in '"Awakening" place: Le Corbusier at La Sainte Baume', his work was far from following any standard modernist agenda. Samuel examines Le Corbusier's extrapolation from his mystical and the mythical agenda into the creation of a very specific place on and in a hillside in Provence, and records his words that describe an awakening of the landscape, of the particular qualities latent in that place.[59] She explores how the scheme demonstrates the ways in which Le Corbusier utilized the landscape and legends of La Sainte Baume (Mary Magdalene), in his design for an underground basilica, museum and housing scheme on that site. Le Corbusier's deep interest in the Saint resulted in, among other things, the conception of the earth-built houses to be built in serried ranks across from her grotto as evocations of her cave – the intention being to encourage those that lived within them to emulate her life and aspirations. Here Samuel's essay revisits the theory posited by Kite, of Stokes's and Appleton's theories of enclosure and refuge. Through Le Corbusier's reinterpretation of the legend of Mary Magdalene, and his use of his system of proportion, the Modulor, the architect attempted to create at La Sainte Baume 'a radiant' community in harmony both with nature and with the traditions and 'spirit' of the place. The essay also offers an example of the non-rationalist character of modernism, akin to that which I explicate in my study of Aalto's Muuratsalo retreat. Although never built, the La Sainte Baume scheme provides an important part of the backdrop for a number of other schemes that Le Corbusier worked on during that period, most notably the chapel of Ronchamp and the Unité in Marseilles.

As Berleant suggested in the opening essay on environmental aesthetics, a core aspect of the relationship of the self to place is through a process of engagement. In my essay 'Retreating to dwell: playing and reality at Muuratsalo' I examine the relationship between place, self and creativity. In it I analyse Alvar Aalto's attitude to the nature and creation of place through a discussion of his approach to his own 'experimental' house – or, as he called it, 'playhouse' – on the island of Muuratsalo, and the manner in which Aalto's ideas about the psychology of play and his experience of nature impinge on the design of a place for himself. In particular the essay explores the correlation between Aalto's own psychology and that which he sought, with particular attention, to protect in others through his designs. Conscious of a break in the relationship of modern milieux to the natural environment, Aalto felt that this was key to the psychological alienation that was apparent in modern life. Here too there is a correlation with the ideas of psychologizing space – of envelopment and exposure, and of the place of the 'in-between' that Kite expounds –

and a sense of the need to reinforce contact with nature. The model of Aalto's house manifests his determination to assist modern architecture to recover 'place', yet it cannot be separated from his suggestion that all architecture must reflect the nature of human experience – above all, he believed, the 'psychological needs'.[60] Muuratsalo demonstrates that these two, natural place and human need, are isomorphic to Aalto, suggests through the manner of the intricacies and nuances inherent in the relationship between his architectural form and the natural environment.

Further reading of the creation of modern place is offered by Richard Weston's essay, 'From place to planet: Jørn Utzon's earthbound platforms and floating roofs', in which the genesis of Utzon's interest in stepped platforms is

I.15
Side of Alvar Aalto's own house, Helsinki, Finland (1934–6)

I.16
Fredensborg Housing
Jørn Utzon, 1963

illuminated. Weston explains how the experience of a visit, in 1949, to the Yucatan in Mexico to see the remains of the Mayan temple complexes deeply stimulated Utzon. Ascending the vast, stepped platforms to emerge above the claustrophobic jungle he discovered 'a completely independent thing floating in the air, separated from the earth ... from there you actually see nothing but the sky and the passing clouds, – a new planet'.[61] Weston elucidates how the experience was decisive, being manifest architecturally in all his later work. The essay further explores Utzon's fascination with the platform as a means of relating building to site through built and competition projects, and situated in the context of both the other traditional architectures which inspired him – in Greece, the Far East, and Islam – and of the transformation of traditional models by leading modernists of an older generation. Weston also refers back to Le Corbusier, through the 'fabricated terrain' of his monumental roof gardens ('wide horizons', which Le Corbusier believed 'confer dignity'),[62] which provide the springboard for Weston's speculative interpretation of Utzon's work as a continuation of the modern project through the extension of the discourse of place to a cross-cultural engagement with the entire planet (Fig. I.16).[63]

Immediately after the Second World War, architects were invited to design new places of work, research and living on an unprecedented scale. In Brian Carter's analysis of Eero Saarinen's General Motors' Technical Centre the discussion of the manner in which the modern architects were challenged to create new building types, and indeed often whole new contexts, changes from the broad steps of the iconic opera house on Sydney harbour to the vast flatlands outside Detroit. While in France Le Corbusier realized his Ville Radieuse, a form that was quickly developed elsewhere, and in Chicago Mies van der Rohe advanced the slick upward thrust of the universal towers for living and working, Eero Saarinen was commissioned to design what was the largest and most complex architectural commission of the time, thus representing (and celebrating) the new American icon, the car, with a new context, an auto-landscape. The General Motors scheme represents an emphatic statement about the nature of a place created specifically to research the design and construction of the car – the symbol of the machine age and arguably the most influential invention of the twentieth century.

Considerate intervention

Under the subheading 'Considerate intervention' the final four essays explore ideas of place-making, in architectural, landscape and urban planning terms through analysis of buildings that come after the modernist period, towards the end of the millennium (Fig. I.17).

The section opens with an argument for reviving the dimension of time and memory in Samia Rab's essay 'Rooted modernism: reconstructing memory in architecture'. Rab explores how the teaching of history in architecture tends to be conceived as an arena for imparting visual vocabulary of historical 'styles'. Rab demonstrates how, by inducing the ability to reconstruct history in architecture, students of the profession are enabled to create buildings that are rooted in place, time and society. She undertakes this through an analysis of three contemporary Australian buildings: the Education Centre, Riversdale by Murcutt, Lewin and Lark (Fig. I.18); the Ulura Kata-Tjuta Cultural Centre, near Alice Springs, by Gregory Burgess; and the new parliament building, Canberra by Mitchell, Giurgola and Thorp. Rab argues that these buildings can be demonstrated to be exactly rooted in place, time and society, due to their active reconstruction of history of an individual, a group and a nation.

This demonstration of consideration for the specificity of context is examined in Michael Linzey's essay 'Making our place: The Museum of New Zealand, Te Papa Tongarewa'. Linzey examines The Museum of New Zealand (Te Papa Tongarewa, 1998) as the form of a huge geological diagram, exploring how the building uses a geological diagram to pull together, and give meaning to the different spatial elements that house the visitor experience, arguing that the building raises questions about designing for bi-cultural difference in relation to modern semiology. Linzey explains the etymology of the name Te Papa Tongarewa, finding generative roots for it deep in Maori cultural identity generally,

I.17
Faith House, Holton Lee (respite care centre), Dorset
Tony Fretton Architects, 2002

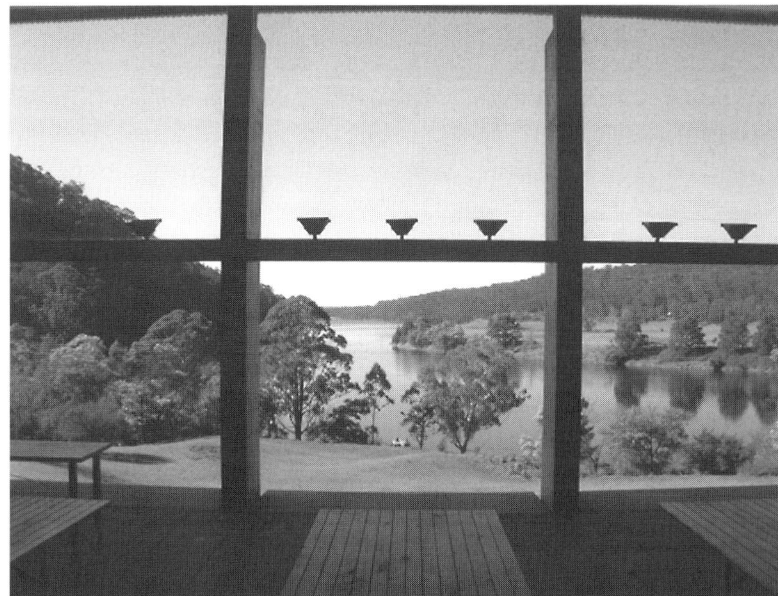

I.18
Connecting and framing the landscape. Arthur & Yvonne Boyd Art Education Centre, Riversdale, Australia

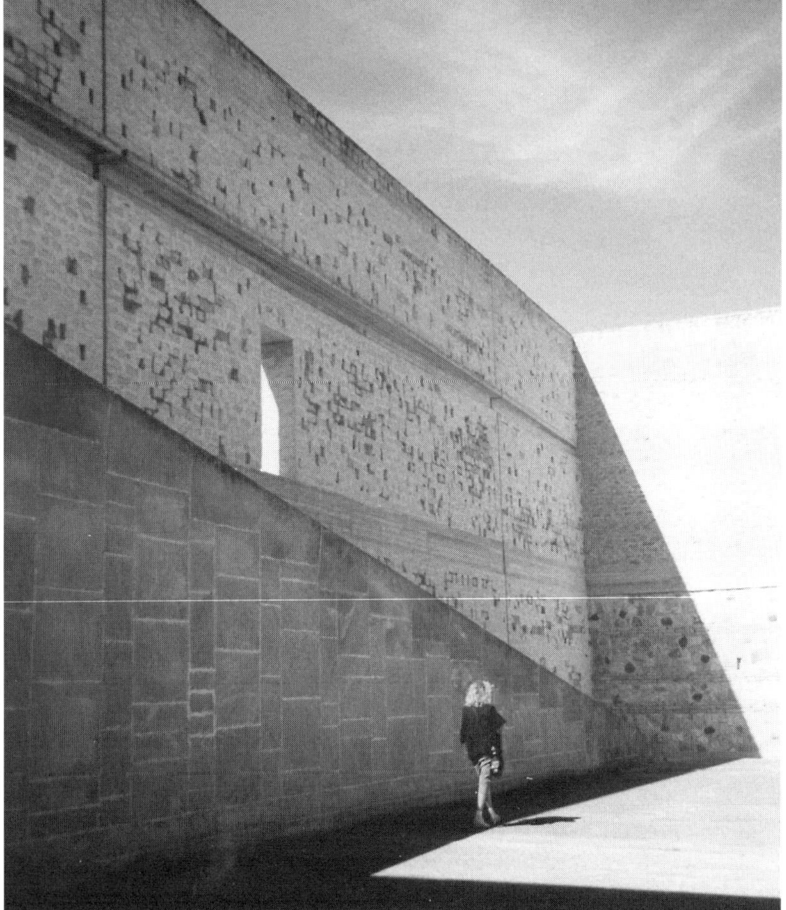

I.19
Interior/exterior courtyard of the Gibellina Museum showing the ramp – a spoliation of Malaparte's house, New Town of Gibellina, Sicily
Francesco Venezia, 1987

and in that culture's profound connectedness with the land (*whenua*). Demonstrating how particular architectural episodes in Maori meeting-houses simultaneously signify models of the modern cosmos that embraces all of these levels of meaning, he explains that the *taahu* (ridge-pole) of the meeting house 'points' to the openness of the *marae* (village or square) and closure at the rear. In a similar architectural gesture Te Papa also points to specific geography and the geological condition of the land, to Hawaiki and New Zealand, and to the shared immigrant condition of two cultures.

Here Linzey finds references back to what he suggests is Ballantyne's exposition of an implicit disjunction between Deleuze and Guattari in their supposedly empirical theory of transversality. Linzey argues that in their theory transversality is, at best, an illusion, whereas the sign that literally points (i.e. the *taahu* and the linear form of Te Papa) is not illusory (although Ballantyne would argue here that the 'pointing' is already an interpretation of what the timber is doing, and is therefore no less or more 'metaphysical' than transversality). Linzey demonstrates that a literal, multi-layered accumulation of meanings is 'pointed out' by the architecture of Te Papa Tongarewa, and it is therefore a significant work of bi-cultural architecture informed by the Maori architecture of the *marae*.

The gathering of cultural memory into a conception of new building is further examined by Annette Condello in 'Architectural spoils: Francesco Venezia and Sicily's *spogliatoia*'. Condello examines the term 'spoil' through an analysis of the work of the Italian architect Venezia, defining 'spoil' in this context as the improvisation of materials and ideas, through measuring or adjusting the specific image in question. Rather than pursuing the pilfering connotations of cultural fragments, Condello explores how spoils impact as a positive image of architecture on the construction of place (Fig. I.19). Examining how southern Italy's concern with the architecture of spoils started with its critical reconstruction of cultural fragments from the surplus of wars and natural catastrophes, Condello suggests that this practice is particularly significant in relation to the fragmentary projects built by Venezia from the 1970s onwards. Incorporating such fragments through the use of materials and ideas into new contexts, Venezia's work reveals literal or conceptual gestural spaces – what Condello defines as 'gestural spoils'. The application of this, she argues, produces forceful architectural variations in relation to the contingent placement of these forms with new meaning, and new 'wholes' that have agitated the cultural fabric of contemporary architecture, specifically those buildings located in the Belice Valley (Trapani) in Sicily. Explicating the use of the 'architecture of spoils' as the physical and conceptual contingent form, Condello demonstrates that the balance between past and present in this building strategy has formulated a valid practice of fusing spoils into gestural buildings, and thus creating a panoply of rich transformations.

This inter-creation of old and new forms and past and present functions underpins Suzanne Ewing's essay 'Horizon in the Hamar Museum: an instrument of architecture and a way of looking at site'. In it Ewing examines Sverre Fehn's mid-twentieth-century Archbishopric Museum at Hamar, Norway. Like Venezia's architecture, this museum is a site that has been consciously exposed and enriched. By studying the understanding, conception and use of 'horizon' as an instrument in this setting, a way of 'realising place',[64] Ewing pursues a deeper understanding of the way the site has been re-invented as museum spaces have been realized. She suggests that understanding the museum at Hamar as a consciously imagined and re-invented site reveals implicit aspects of Modernist conceptions of site and intervention

The arguments here return to the Heideggerian territory visited by Robinson and others earlier in the book. Citing Fehn's preoccupation with Heidegger's concepts of *horismos* and *raum*, Ewing examines how the 'realization of place' is manifest in the completion of the journey within the constructed boundaries of the site, with a sense of the whole – spaces above and below and the perceived site boundary – revealed at the highest point, the turn of the ramp above the external excavations. The interior spaces of the museum are realized in relation to the perceived and constructed 'horizon', further articulated by the display of the

I.20
Stonehenge

objects extracted from the ground and the narrative of recognized relation between intervention and setting that they thus embody. The essay concludes with reflection on the potential relevance of reviewing selected modernist attitudes to 'realising place' with regard to our current situation.[65] Part two closes in the rich context of Fehn's architecture, one that employs many layers of material and cultural fabric, which together prompt the recognition of rich layers of meaning.

Constructing place: mind and matter

The essays in the book variously examine the cooperative material relations that may exist between constructed buildings or landscapes and the environment. This symbiosis is identified by Hagan as a vital prerequisite in the socio-cultural manner in which we address the issues of environmental sustainability facing us all.[66] As Hagan has stated, there is a mistrust between contemporary architectural theorists and those active in environmental practice,[67] yet it is exactly this link between theory and practice that this book, and the conference it is based on, have sought to bridge. Hagan asks whether those in the camps of 'the environmental and the aesthetically experiential ... are mutually exclusive, matter and anti-matter, or whether they can inform each other'.[68] Indeed, the discourse which runs through this book comprises examinations of the hybrid reality in which both the mental and the material coincide and inform each other, the vagaries of human experience, and the rich and varied mix of different languages and cultures of thought and building practice that have developed throughout the world in the process and practice of constructing place. From this derives a picture of a hybrid reality that includes episodes of constructing place from quite different physical contexts, from the signification of recreational beach placings, to the manner in which the refugee creates a place with remnant cultural artefacts, and the harsh reality of creating shelter experienced by squatters with the scrounged detritus of building materials. This hybrid reality also encompasses the manner in which one modernist architect creates a refuge that addresses his deepest psychological vulnerability, while another conceives a womb-like basilica that speaks of the psycho-spiritual agenda of Orphic mysticism. In the sphere of contemporary architecture, hybrid reality embraces the psychological implications behind the fashion for expansive glass façades, the re-composition of architectural spoils in Sicily, and the situation in which architects in New Zealand and Australia construct new lines of identity founded in the tropes of Aboriginal *topophilia* and extrapolate these into the most contemporary of buildings.

Comprising explorations of the rich material nature and complex mental processes that imbue place with import, the book seeks to draw to the fore the relevance of the particularities of 'place' and their capacity to reflect, and in some cases enrich, human experience (Fig. I.20).

Notes

1 A. Rapoport, 'A critical look at the concept "place"', in R.P.B. Singh (ed.) *The Spirit and Power of Place*. Human Environment and Sacrality, Varanasi: Banaras Hindu University Press, 1994, pp. 31–45.

2 A. Rapoport, 'Cultural and the urban order', in J. Agnew, J. Mercer and D. Sopher (eds), *The City in Cultural Context*, London; Allen and Unwin, 1984, pp. 50–75.

3 Rapoport, 'A critical look', p. 32.

4 A. Rapoport, *House Form and Culture*, Foundations of Cultural Geography Series, Upper Saddle River: Prentice Hall, 1969, p. vii.

5 The place of perception and phenomenology in architecture is explored by Anne Stenros, who both accepts the import of place and offers examples of environmental analysis that might allay Rapoport's concerns: 'Orientation, identification, representation: space perception in architecture', in S. Aura, I. Alavalkama and H. Palmquist (eds), *Endoscopy as a Tool in Architecture*. Proceedings of the 1st European Architectural Endoscopy Association Conference, Tampere, August 25–28 1993, Tampere: Tampere University Press, 1993, p. 76.

6 Martin Heidegger, *Being and Time*, trans. J. Macquarrie and E. Robinson, New York: Harper, 1962, p. 137.

7 L. Irigaray, 'Place interval: a reading of Aristotle, *Physics IV*', in *An Ethics of Sexual Difference*, trans C. Burke and G.C. Gill, Ithaca: Cornell University Press, 1993, p. 59.

8 Although the remnant wooden huts create a sense of a barren waste of Auschwitz-Birkenau, the brick-built camp of Auschwitz itself has quite a different quality, as Pelt and Westfall examine. R. van Pelt & C.W. Westfall, *Architectural Principles in the Age of Historicism*, New Haven: Yale, 1991.

9 E.S. Casey, *Getting Back into Place*, Bloomington: Indiana University Press, 1993, p. x. See also A. Vidler, *The Architectural Uncanny*, Cambridge MA: MIT Press, 1994.
10 T.S. Eliot, 'Little Gidding', *Four Quartets*, London: Faber & Faber, 1986, p. 48.
11 D.W. Winnicott, 'Living creatively', in *Home is Where we Start From: Essays by a Psychoanalyst*, Harmondsworth: Penguin, 1986, pp. 42–3.
12 Winnicott, 'Living creatively', p. 42.
13 Winnicott, 'The concept of a healthy individual', in *Home is Where we Start From*, p. 36.
14 Ibid. In this Winnicott acknowledges he is close to Fred Plaut, who used the word 'trust' as key to the establishment of this area of healthy experience: in 'Reflections about not being able to imagine', *Journal of Analytical Psychology*, 1966, vol. 11.
15 I. Calvino, 'Cities and memory 4', in *Invisible Cities*, trans. Harcourt Brace Jovanovich Inc., London: Picador, 1979, p. 16.
16 A. Berleant, 'The aesthetics of art and nature', in S. Kemal and I. Gaskell (eds), *Landscape, Natural Beauty and the Arts*, Cambridge: Cambridge University Press, 1993, p. 230.
17 Plato, *Timaeus and Critias*, trans. H.D.P. Lee, Harmondsworth: Penguin, 1965, pp. 70–1.
18 Albert-Pérez-Gómez, 'The space of architecture: meaning as presence and representation', in *Questions of Phenomenology: Phenomenology in Architecture*, *A&U* July 1994, Special Issue, p. 13.
19 M. Merleau-Ponty, *Phenomenology of Perception*, London: Routledge, 1962.
20 'Daidala' was translated as 'cunningly crafted' and came to be applied often to textiles. See I.K. McEwan, *Socrates' Ancestor*, Cambridge MA: MIT Press, 1993, p. 53.
21 The phrase 'unrecorded reality' is taken from S.K. Langer, *Philosophy in a New Key*, Cambridge MA: Harvard University Press, 1993, p. 281.
22 S. Morris, *Daidalos and the Origins of Greek Art*, Princeton: Yale University Press, 1992, p. 14, and McEwan, *Socrates' Ancestor*, p. 58.
23 This is something that Casey addresses in depth in *The Fate of Place: A Philosophical History*, Berkeley: California University Press, 1998.
24 Irigaray, 'Place interval', p. 35.
25 Susannah Hagan examines this in *Taking Shape: A New Contract between Architecture and Nature*, Oxford: Architectural Press, 2001.
26 Martin Heidegger, *Being and Time*, p. 138.
27 John Brinckerhoff Jackson explores this in *A Sense of Place, a Sense of Time*, New Haven: Yale, 1994.
28 This view is drawing on Kleinian approach to psychoanalysis, and moves forward to Winnicott's work on the psyche's use of the 'environment' for normal mental growth.
29 Winnicott, who sought to shift the psychoanalytical movement of Freud and Klein from concentration on conflicts within the individual to understanding the experience and environment of the individual. Winnicott, *Home is Where we Start From*, p. 114.
30 D.W. Winnicott, 'Young children and other people', in *The Child, The Family and the Outside World*, Harmondsworth: Penguin, 1964.
31 Winnicott, 'Young children and other people', p. 109.
32 Winnicott, 'The concept of a healthy individual', p. 36.
33 Ibid., pp. 36–7.
34 Irigaray, 'Place Interval'.
35 Ibid., p. 35.
36 Ibid., p. 35.
37 Casey, *The Fate of Place*, p. 325.
38 L. Irigaray, 'Creating another space – outside any framework. The opening of openness', in *Elemental Passions*, trans. J. Collie and J. Still, New York: Routledge, 1992, p. 59.
39 J.H. Appleton, *The Experience of Landscape*, London: Wiley, 1996.

40 A. Stokes, 'Form in art', in M. Klein, P. Heinmann and R.E. Money-Kyrle (eds), *New Directions in Psycho-analysis. The Significance of Infant Conflict in the Pattern of Adult Behaviour*, London: Tavistock Publications, 1955, p. 406.
41 C. St John Wilson, 'The natural imagination: an essay on the experience of architecture', *The Architectural Review*, 1989, vol.185, no.1103, pp. 64–70, p. 66.
42 Casey, *The Fate of Place*, p. 336.
43 Ibid., p. 337.
44 Berleant opens his essay with a quotation from T. Coraghessan Boyle's short story 'Greasy Lake'.
45 Pauli Tapani Karjalainen, 'Real pace images', in A. Haapala (ed.) *The City as Cultural Metaphor*, Lahti, Finland: International Institute of Applied Aesthetics, 1998, pp. 95–101.
46 R.W. Hepburn, 'Restoring the sacred: sacred as a concept of aesthetics', in *The Reach of the Aesthetic*, Aldershot: Ashgate, 2001, pp. 124–5.
47 J.-L. Nancy, *The Inoperative Community*, trans P. Connor, Minneapolis: University of Minneapolis Press, 1991, p. 150.
48 Winnicott, 'Living creatively', pp. 40–1.
49 C. St John Wilson, 'Functionalism and the uncompleted project', in *Functionalism – Utopia or the Way Forward*, Jyväskylä: Alvar Aalto Symposium, 1992, p. 163.
50 Louis Kahn, in V. Scully, *Louis Kahn*, New York: Brazillier, 1962, pp. 114–21.
51 Hugo Häring used this phrase in 'Formulations towards a reorientation in applied arts', *Bauwelt*, 1927, vol.49, p. 1211.
52 Albert-Pérez-Gómez, adapting a sentence from Octavio Paz, *The Bow and the Lyre* (1914) p. 139, in 'The space of architecture', p. 8.
53 See Merleau-Ponty, *Phenomenology of Perception*.
54 A. Sharr and S. Unwin, 'Heidegger's Hut', *ARQ*, Spring 2001, vol.5, no.1, pp. 53–61.
55 M. Heidegger, *Poetry, Language and Thought*, trans. A. Hofstadter, New York: Harper and Row, 1971.
56 C. Norberg-Schulz, *Genius Loci*, New York: Rizzoli, 1979, and *Architecture: Meaning and Place*, New York: Electra/Rizzoli, 1986, and K. Harries, *The Ethical Function of Architecture*, Cambridge MA: MIT Press, 1997.
57 H.K. Bhabha, *The Location of Culture*, London: Routledge, 1994, p. 25.
58 J. Kristeva, 'Holbein's Dead Christ', in M. Feher, R.Naddaf and N. Tazi (eds), *Fragments for the History of the Human Body, Part One*, New York: Zone, 1989.
59 Le Corbusier, *Modulor 2*, London: Faber & Faber, 1955, p. 304. Originally published as Le Corbusier, *Le Modulor II*, Paris: Editions d'Architecture d'Aujourd'hui, 1955.
60 A. Aalto, 'The Reconstruction of Europe', 1941, reprinted in G. Schildt, *Alvar Aalto Own Words*, New York: Rizzoli, 1998, p. 154.
61 J. Utzon, 'Platforms and Plateaus', *Zodiac*, 1962, vol.10, pp. 113–41.
62 Le Corbusier, *Precisions. On the Present State of Architecture and City Planning*, trans. E.S. Aujame, Cambridge MA: MIT Press, 1991, p. 235.
63 Kenneth Frampton makes the basic analyses in *Studies in Tectonic Culture*, Cambridge MA: MIT Press, 1995.
64 Sverre Fehn, in C. Norberg-Schulz and G.Postiglione, *Sverre Fehn Works, Projects and Writing, 1949–1996*, New York: Monacelli, 1997, p. 243.
65 A. Khan, 'Overlooking: A look at how we look at site or … site a "discrete object" of desire', in D. McCorquodale, K. Reudi and S. Wigglesworth (eds), *Desiring Practices*, London: Black Dog, 1996, pp. 174–85.
66 Hagan, *Taking Shape*, p. xv.
67 Ibid., p. xvi.
68 Ibid., p. xvi.

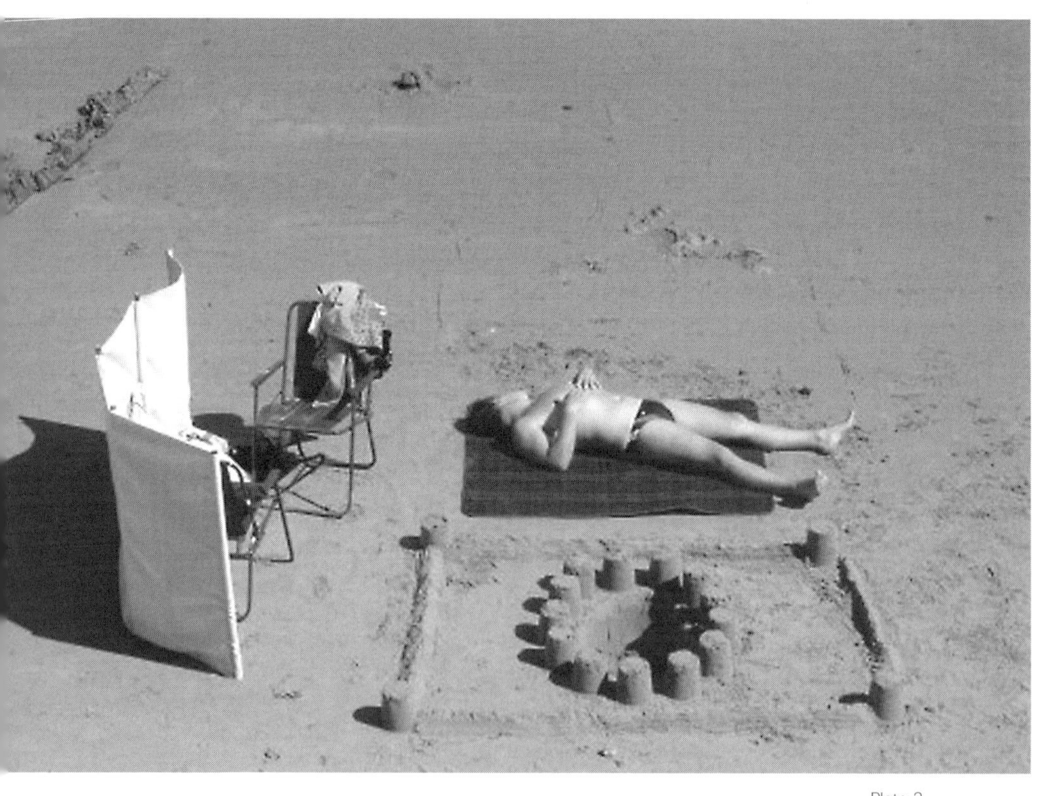

Plate 2
Beach claiming,
South Wales

Part 1

Mind

Plate 3
Bora ground showing the images carved with sticks that indicate the path
From Lindsey Black, *Bora Ground*, Sydney: Booth, 1940

Projecting a relationship

Chapter 1

The aesthetic in place

Arnold Berleant

Introduction

I want to begin with a quotation and then a question.

> At night we went up to Greasy Lake.
>
> Through the center of town, up the strip, past the housing developments and shopping malls, street lights giving way to the thin streaming illumination of the headlights, trees crowding the asphalt in a black unbroken wall: that was the way out to Greasy Lake. The Indians had called it Wakan, a reference to the clarity of its waters. Now it was fetid and murky, the mud banks glittering with broken glass and strewn with beer cans and the charred remains of bonfires. There was a single ravaged island a hundred yards from shore, so stripped of vegetation it looked as if the air force had strafed it. We went up to the lake because everyone went there, because we wanted to snuff the rich scent of possibility on the breeze, watch a girl take off her clothes and plunge into the festering murk, drink beer, smoke pot, howl at the stars, savor the incongruous full-throated roar of rock and roll against the primeval susurrus of frogs and crickets. This was nature.[1]

Now my question is, Is Greasy Lake a place? Perhaps by the time we come towards the end of this essay, we shall be able to answer it. And, if so, what kind of place? But if we cannot respond, can we dismiss the question?

'Place' has become an 'in' word. From the mass media to advertising, from the travel industry to the real estate industry, from sociology to geography, the fascination with place testifies, I suspect, not so much to the discovery of a hidden value as to a widespread if unconscious lament over its absence. Many of us, particularly in the industrial world, inhabit anonymous environments whose bland sterility is disguised by shiny plastic and glass surfaces. We live and work in industrialized landscapes of insular factories, strip malls and office towers, moving with clockwork regularity along highways that are self-propelled conveyor belts to faceless apartment buildings and generic suburbs. Yet we dream of some ideal place where we shall truly be at home. Besides creating an insatiable market for paradise in the form of idyllic vacations or escapes to exotic lands, the placelessness we suffer from reinforces – and perhaps epitomizes – a culture of dissatisfaction.

Yet what constitutes place? Many disciplines offer many answers, ranging from simple location to the intensely present, self-transcending experience of sacred space. Our understanding and respect for the importance of place have widened and deepened from the work undertaken over the past thirty years. But there is one dimension of place that is easily overlooked, a dimension that may be the most critical of all because it concerns experience of the most primary sort – aesthetic. Our understanding of place, multi-faceted though it be, can be enlarged still more from an increased awareness of its aesthetic dimension. To reveal this often hidden, often misunderstood dimension is what I want to undertake here. Further, I want to explore the possibility that, in grasping the aesthetic character of place, we are not merely identifying another aspect of this complex idea but rather are probing its very centre. Like Plotinus' sun, the aesthetic radiance of place illuminates its every appearance, even as its intensity decreases the further we go from its source, until place merges with the all-encompassing darkness of its negation.

Some determinants of place

In its most basic sense, place is the setting of the events of human living. It is the locus of action and intention, and present in all consciousness and perceptual experience. This human focus is what distinguishes place from the surrounding space or from simple location.[2] Humanistic geographers emphasize this anthropocentric meaning, a meaning that comes about through experience.[3] Place for them is the location of experience. It is realized as a set of 'environmental relations created in the process of human dwelling … internally connected with time and self … Place thus provides an organizing principle for … a person's engagement or immersion in the world around' him or her.[4] This most general condition is basic to an understanding of place, but by being basic and general it does not say enough about what is distinctive and memorable in this fundamental idea.

Some things can be said about place generally that few would contest. One of these is a special sense of physical *identity* that a location can convey. Certain qualities set it apart. It may be a physical unity conveyed through topographical features, such as being bounded by hills or mountains, or being partly or wholly surrounded by water. On the other hand, identity may be conferred by a central reference point rather than a boundary, such as a harbour, a mountain, or a monumental building, such as a church, temple or mosque. On a more modest scale, a centre may be a village common or square, a great or venerable tree, a monument, or a great pole.

Physical *coherence* is another trait that can convey a sense of place. A high degree of architectural similarity or compatibility may create the sense of a distinctive place. This is especially the case when it contrasts with other, nearby areas, as in a historic district, the old centre of a large city, or an architecturally distinguished new development. This last raises the issue of perceived value. A suburban development built to one or two conventional models has architectural coherence. But while this imparts identity to the neighbourhood, it is not likely to convey the feeling of enhanced presence that we associate with place. Coherence may also be conveyed by boundaries – as in an urban square, common or plaza – or a bounded interior space – such as the walls of a room or a house. We may realize place in a neighbourhood or town that possesses a high degree of coherence relative to its scale. This may be true, as well, of a region, such as a mountainous area or a coastline. Specific examples of all these may come easily to mind, but I hesitate to mention any here for fear of deflecting consideration of the validity of the idea by a dispute over particular cases.

Of course physical characteristics alone do not create place. Cultural geographers are right in joining the human factor to these features. Whether this connection comes about through actions, practices or institutions, or through the simple presence of a conscious, sensing person, it is in the interaction of human sensibility with an appropriate physical location that place acquires its distinctive *meaning*. One common form that this takes is when locations acquire historical or cultural associations. Sometimes these predominate in generating identity to a location not otherwise distinguished, as may occur with the site of a battlefield or a massacre, a building or site where an important document was signed, or the birthplace or home of a famous person. In such instances, place depends not so much on its physical characteristics as on the aura with which our knowledge about it invests the location. Personal memory may imbue an area with a similar distinction.

Such features, then, as distinguishing physical identity and coherence, together with the consciousness of significance, can contribute to the sense of a distinctive presence that we associate with the special character of place. These are important and they need to be carefully specified in each individual case. But there is, I think, something more to the special quality of place, a dimension that is not so much a physical characteristic or a cultural layer of meaning as something that underlies these more articulable features. This is its aesthetic dimension.

Let me develop this in two directions. One is to suggest a descriptive account of the aesthetic experience of place. Like any such description, aspects of it will be peculiar to the individual case and the personal experience, while other aspects will be characteristic of a cultural sensibility. Yet perhaps some features will possess a generality that may be theoretically useful. My second purpose is rather different. It is to draw out some of the implications of this description of experience for the design of place, or rather for designing the conditions in which a full experience of place can occur.

The aesthetic in place

We ordinarily think of aesthetics as referring to art, to the value that distinguishes the arts from other, more ordinary, objects and occasions. At times we readily ascribe this value beyond art to nature, as when we admire a landscape or delight in the intimate wonder of a spring flower or glorious sunset. But what can this aesthetic value have to do with place?

To deal with this question we need to focus not on the occasion or the object we call beautiful, but on the experience we have at such times and places, and on the qualities and characteristics of the situation of which that experience is a part. For what we value here lies, I think, not wholly in a work of art or a natural occurrence but in the conditions under which we encounter them and in what takes place. What, then, characterizes such an aesthetic situation?

To answer this, it is important to return to the etymological origins of the term itself.[5] The word 'aesthetic' comes from the Greek *aisthēsis*, literally perception by the senses. For Baumgarten, who in 1750 identified it as a distinct discipline, aesthetics is the science of sensory knowledge directed towards beauty, and art entails the perfection of sensory awareness.[6] This observation is not only historically important; it sets the scene for understanding the field of aesthetics squarely on the basis of sense perception. Moreover, there can be no perception, direct or imaginative, without the body and, as it is human experience we are concerned with, the conscious, active, human body. Given the development of the field of aesthetics into complex theoretical issues in the ensuing two and a half centuries, it is important to reaffirm this sensory connection. Aesthetic perception then becomes not a purely conscious act and not a merely subjective occurrence; rather it is grounded in the human body and the existential conditions of human life. These conditions are important to specify because they bear directly on our understanding of the aesthetics of place.

People are embedded in their world – their life-world, to use an important term from phenomenology. A constant exchange takes place between organism and environment, and these are so intimately bound up with each other that our conceptual discriminations serve only heuristic purposes and often mislead us. For instance, we readily speak of an interaction of person and object or person and place, but the term 'interaction' presupposes an initial division that is then bridged. Yet in the most basic sense of existence, there is no separation but rather a fusion of things usually thought of as discrete entities, such as body and consciousness, culture and organism, inner thought and an external world. Therefore we may understand the setting of human life as an integration of person and her or his environment.[7]

As humans we are inescapably embedded in a life-world that incorporates our physical bodies, our personal and communal histories, our social education and practices and, not least, our cultural ethos. Perception is integral to our experience of that world, and this means that the aesthetic is grounded in the very conditions of living. Perception, however, cannot be understood prejudicially as only or primarily visual. Particularly in environmental experience perception is synaesthetic, since all the senses are engaged in a homogeneous fashion. The usual discrimination of the senses into distance and contact receptors not only tends to denigrate our physical experience of the world but leads to the tendency to ignore the fundamental formative importance of the senses as closely bound up with the body. Environmental experience involves the contact senses; it is 'intimate sensing', as one geographer puts it.[8] These senses include the haptic sensory system, which includes not only touch but also the subcutaneous perception of surface texture, contour, pressure, temperature, humidity, pain, and visceral sensation. To this we must add the kinaesthetic sense, which includes muscular awareness and skeletal or joint sensation by means of which we perceive position and solidity through the degrees of resistance that surfaces have. And through the vestibular system we indirectly grasp body movement in climbing and descending, turning and twisting, moving freely or among obstructions. In such ways, environmental perception engages our full capacity for sensory perception in an interpenetration of body and context.[9]

To know a place is to experience that environment. What, then, is it to experience place? What is distinctive about the aesthetic experience of place?

One crucial feature is this, that by introducing the aesthetic dimension place becomes demarcated by the range of perception. This restricts its scope in any instance to the particular context of perceptual experience. Place in this sense, then, applies only to a complex field of perceptual experience involving person and setting, together with the range of historical and cultural influence, knowledge and meaning that invariably imbue that field. This is a critical point for our purposes, since it confines the aesthetics of place to contexts that embody direct experience, such as a room, home, building, street, square or neighbourhood, and only derivatively and by extension to a city, region or country. The same point applies in identifying places in a natural environment. This demarcation, moreover, is never sharp, for when the scope of an environment extends beyond perception that is immediate and direct, its vividness decreases as its scope increases from, say, a neighbourhood to an entire town, a province, or a country. Perhaps another way of recognizing this difference is to distinguish between place and environment. Environment is by far the wider concept. While it includes place, the range of its denotation can extend from the local to the cosmic.

The most general meaning of place as aesthetic, then, is a particular perceptual environment that joins a distinctive identity and coherence with a memorable character, and with which we actively engage in attention or action. An authentic sense of place, expressed in Heideggerian language, involves 'being inside and belonging to *your* place both as an individual and as a member of a community, and to know this without reflecting upon it.'[10]

Sacred space

A central concern in searching for the heart of place lies in identifying the human role. As with the concept of environment, place is usually understood as related to but distinct from the human participant. Karjalainen takes as basic the notion that 'places provide human beings with a framework for environmental involvement.' Both people and places make a contribution: 'Palpable landscapes and impalpable mindscapes continually intermingle and form internal relations with each other.'[11]

True as this characterization is, I do not believe that it entirely grasps what is exceptional about our most compelling experiences of place. This is where the idea of sacred space can serve as a guiding beacon. I should like to develop the idea of an aesthetics of place, then, not from the outside, carefully adding traits to the most general conditions of what constitutes place in order to arrive at a highly refined notion, but from inside the experience, as it were. And it is here that sacred space can be a powerful exemplar of the aesthetic in place. In sacred space, we find a touchstone from which to consider its other meanings and uses.[12]

Although I shall begin by citing some instances of sacred places, I am somewhat reluctant to do so because examples will inevitably suggest the idea that 'place' is a physical location. However, as I develop its aesthetic import it will become apparent that a sacred place is never a location only. As fully aesthetic, it becomes an environmental event that fuses participant and location in an aesthetic field. But, for the moment, it will be helpful to mention briefly the physical location of some of the most well-known sacred places. One is the Louvre, with its spreading magnificence of scale, structure, space. Another is the Guggenheim Museum, with its spiral exterior form and its ascending and descending spiralling interior space. The Piazza San Marco is probably the most famous of squares, with its articulated sides, active surfaces, and embracing but unconfining boundaries. The form of the Gothic cathedral is for many the physical embodiment of the religious sacred, joining the individual worshipper with the community and the transcendent order of things.[13]

Sacredness, however, lies not in the physical place alone but in the significance that people assign to it. 'Sacredness' is a human designation, and even here we find a range of meanings. In its most pallid sense, a sacred place may refer to land valued not for commercial reasons but because it is most beautiful, most healthy, most productive.[14] Generally, however, we concentrate considerably more normative significance on the idea than this. Let us explore it further.

The concept of the sacred can refer to a place, to an experience, or to something more complex: place experience. In associating the sacred with aesthetic experience, Hepburn identifies a strong perceptual focus, the recognition that things have more than utilitarian value but a condition 'where we can find … modes of being *other than our own*', together with respect, reverence and wonder. This last conveys a religious–metaphysical meaning that cannot be suppressed – the sense of humility and awe towards something that has intrinsic value.[15]

A place may be sacred because it is invested with great personal meaning, perhaps where an event of life-changing proportions occurred. Or, more modestly, it may be a place precious to us because it is where we can come in touch with our deepest layers. A sacred place may have irresistible force through its social or cultural significance. Yet the personal and social are themselves not clearly distinguishable, for our social experiences resonate deep in our most private thoughts, and the cultural process that shapes our language, speech, comportment and goals forms that person we call ourselves.

But whatever the primary source of its reverential significance, a place becomes sacred, I believe, by its power to assimilate a person, producing a synthesis of space, physical features, and the dynamic, conscious body. Often we recognize this occurrence by a feeling of wonder and perhaps even breathless awe. Part of this comes from the rarity of such a self-transcending event. Such an experience of place resembles our encounter with the noblest works of art, whose force overwhelms and engulfs those who engage with it. I call this experience of appreciative immersion 'aesthetic engagement', the perceptual experience of total absorption in the work at hand. Moreover, it serves equally well to describe the most compelling experiences of the so-called fine arts and of environment. A sacred place, then, offers the willing participant a high degree of aesthetic engagement and engenders an experience that is intensely positive. As we expand beyond our finite boundaries, we may be overcome by a pervasive benignity conjoined with a sense of humility at the power such a situation generates.

Our world has been gifted with many artists who, in their works, have created the conditions for experiencing the sacred. Such occasions occur in all the arts. Music is a particularly rich source of this, for it is an art whose auditory properties can convey the spatial and architectural characteristics we associate with place. Some works announce this quality at the very beginning, such as the Fauré *Requiem*, Beethoven's Ninth Symphony, and the Sibelius Violin Concerto, while others develop it cumulatively, as happens in Bach's *St Matthew Passion* and Handel's *Messiah*. Among the many instances from the arts of space and volume, my most overwhelming encounters of the aesthetic sacred have been with Brancusi's *Endless Column* and the Rothko Chapel. The last of these is a powerful illustration of a place explicitly designed to be sacred. Here, the force that the Chapel evokes is almost palpable as one approaches and enters it. These various examples I have cited, however, are only the *signs* of possible sacred occasions. They are reminders of what one may experience when engaging with those works. For such an experience to occur, a ready participant must join an evocative object in a compelling situation.

Sacred places offer a guide to what gives 'place' its special quality and force. Of course the world is mostly made up of less than sacred places. But their leading features – the full perceptual engagement of a perceiver with a location that possesses identity and coherence in a seamless unity of experience – lie at the centre of place. These occur with weaker intensity on less profound occasions. Yet however vivid it may be, the peculiar force of this experience of place lies in the fact that 'we do not grasp space only by our senses ... we live in it, we project our personality into it, we are tied to it by emotional bonds; space is not just perceived ... it is lived.'[16]

We can discover the aesthetic in the ordinary locations that bind us to them, and these place locations may occur on different scales. They may be a town common, a public building, a traditional path, or a room distinguished by strong emotional or use associations. Others may be a traditional beach, a hill or mountain, or a monument that stands as a focal point of local identity. A place may perhaps even be an empty lot in a city neighbourhood that exhibits little of the beauty of a landscaped garden but, for a local child, holds the wonder and charm of a realm of fantasy and adventure. Such locations as these can provide the circumstances to encourage something of the aesthetic engagement that sacred places have the capacity to evoke so forcefully. Wherever it be, the aesthetic experience of place is one of inhabitation, of 'dwelling,' to use Heidegger's term.

It is important to recall the dimension of meaning that contributes to this kind of experience. Place locations often possess a certain resonance as a repository of social, cultural, or personal significance. Traces of the past that are visible in a townscape form a kind of materialized memory. Walter Benjamin developed this idea in relation to Paris. He saw Paris and its arcades as the past materialized in space. They are the embodiment of a collective memory, and an historical index marks the date when these sights become legible. Place is thus not only a topographical–geographical designation but one that also embodies meaning: the city, one's body, and psychological space interpenetrate.[17] Memory may even confer an enhanced presence on a location that is otherwise undistinguished.[18] Material form, sensuous apprehension, and social or personal significance can together create the special perceptual experience of aesthetic engagement that distinguishes place from simple geographical location.

Some implications

Exploring the idea of place in this way leads to some curious questions and even more curious answers. For example, is 'place' a personal designation or a communal one? Surely we must acknowledge the public status of the location of many of our most striking experiences of place. On the other hand, if place is not simply a location but the *experience* of one, then it is necessary to think of place as something that is dependent on the presence and participation of people. It then identifies a particular sort of environmental encounter. So the question of whether place is personal or communal can be answered in the affirmative in both cases: place may be a communal designation for locations commonly experienced in the significant way I have tried to describe. But at the same time, place is ultimately an experiential event, and thus its referent is a contextual human situation centered in personal experience.

Another question is its locus. Does place require a physical location or can it be non-physical? Can the electronic space of the computer take on the attributes of place? Is there cyberplace in cyberspace?[19] How this is answered obviously depends on one's definition of place. If place requires a physical location, then clearly no place is possible in cyberspace. That would please many, since the view is common that the computer constructs a fictitious world in which nothing is real but only virtual. If, on the other hand, we define place as a location with which we become assimilated in aesthetic experience, then it may be that place does indeed exist in cyberspace. The same total absorption that people used to experience when they still read novels is now common with the computer.[20] The work being done in creating domains of virtual reality has great significance, for many of the same questions that can be asked about actual or, better yet, common-sense reality can also be posed here. The possibility of constructing cyberplace has applications in areas in addition to the virtual world of computer games, such as virtual archaeology.[21] But irrespective of where it is located, the human component is critical.

Questions about the locus of place do not appear only in relation to technology. Similar questions can be asked about dream space and imagined space. There is something to be gained in explanatory force with a definition of place that is not earthbound. It may be that some of our most vivid and compelling experiences of place occur in space that is imaginary or inhabits dreams. This may be taken as a comment on the spaces in which many of us live in industrialized environments, spaces at the least not memorable and that often provide what is perhaps our most common experience of location: placelessness. For there is an obverse side to the meaning of place found in built environments that are inauthentic, that have no distinctive identity, and that evoke experiences that are pallid or superficial. This leads us to ask whether a location that goes beyond the bland and becomes offensive or ugly can be experienced as a place: Is 'Greasy Lake' a sacred place?

Despite the repugnance with which we may hold the scene that Coraghessan Boyle described in his unusual story, it does, in fact, meet the criteria I developed in my discussion of place. The three youths in the story are sensitive to the compelling quality of Greasy Lake. They are caught up in its spirit, lose their sense of discrete selfhood, and engage in wild, impulsive, aggressive behaviour that exactly carries out meanings embodied in that place. But of course there is nothing edifying in the self-transcendence they experienced. Their response to the powerful force that the lake exercises on them is hardly positive. In fact, it is just the contrary. So, then, what kind of place is Greasy Lake?

One of the many confusions to which the term 'aesthetic' gives rise is the assumption that it denotes experiences that enrich and perhaps ennoble those who can engage in the special, highly valued perceptual situations we call aesthetic. I think this is a confusion because the very same qualities we praise as aesthetic – an intense sensory presence, directly felt, resonant meaning, and expanded awareness – can, on the other side of the scale, be offensive and possibly harmful. An aesthetic standard can be applied with equal effectiveness to failures of taste and to anaesthetized or oppressed sensibilities. Aesthetic perception is involved here, but it is frustrated, offended, even damaged. Rather than exclude such experiences from the realm of the aesthetic and therefore render them immune to critical aesthetic judgment, it seems far better to include them in an all-embracing aesthetic but to consider them to occupy the negative side of a scale of values. What is at work, then, is a negative aesthetic, one that shifts experience below the level of neutral ground and into 'the all-encompassing darkness' mentioned before, into the nether regions of negative value.[22] Negative place thus differs from placelessness. It is experience of the dark side of place and, in its own way, testifies to the power that place exercises on its inhabitants.

Greasy Lake appears, then, to be an 'anti-sacred' place, forcefully exhibiting the negation of many of the features of the sacred. But it may be too hasty to write it off as an aesthetic failure. Does Greasy Lake indeed possess a negative aesthetic? Our dismay at the events in the story, at their violence, sexuality, anger and fear, is indeed not so much an aesthetic concern as a moral one. Moreover, discomfort and even fear are also compatible with a positive aesthetic: witness the long fascination with the sublime. So perhaps our discomfiture with Greasy Lake raises ethical issues more than aesthetic ones. In its forceful presence and transcendent power, Greasy Lake may indeed be an aesthetic success.

Where, then, do negative places appear, if Greasy Lake is not one of them? While some places may be as forceful in their own way as Greasy Lake is in its, the aesthetic of most, whether positive or negative, does not quite achieve the power of the sacred and many fall well short of this. Yet that may, in fact, make negative places all the more insidious. Perhaps in its emptiness of all character, we may see placelessness as falling flat on the neutral centre of the scale. From this point on down the ladder of negativity we can find many familiar failures, from the depressing anonymity of suburban streets to the oppressive hyperstimulation of shopping malls, from the vulgarity of commercial strips to the raw devastation of strip mines. Interestingly, placeless or negative places may in time metamorphose into rewarding places through physical or conceptual changes. Levittown has changed from a development of anonymous regularity into an area of architectural variety and local pride.[23] Some regard the architectural design of Las Vegas not as a display of vulgar sensationalism but as a vibrant beacon of vitality.

Place, then, is not a physical location, nor is it a state of mind. Rather it is the engagement of the conscious body with the conditions of a specific location. This brings us to the further question of how this understanding of the aesthetics of place affects the making of place.

From what has been said here, we can infer that the goal of good place design is to create locations that convey a touch of the sacred. Such designs need not necessarily be profound but they must nonetheless have a significant presence. This is as much an artistic as a technological task; in fact, it engages science in the service of art. For no glib formula can achieve place, this being a sure prescription for the failures we find in such conventions as the mechanistic emulation of the international style, or the clichés of postmodern architectural design such as the Palladian window. Not only is there no convenient recipe for place-making, but the abstract visual techniques that are the stock-in-trade of architectural design, such as the plan, elevation, parti, model, and computer-generated simulations, are at best partial and more often misleading.

For place to be aesthetically successful, designers must develop their perceptual capacities, including kinaesthetic consciousness, somatic spatial awareness, the sensory recognition of volumes and textures, auditory acuteness, and the richly complex sensibility of synaesthetic perception. Each site, each project, each situation is different, and a sensitivity to the possibilities inherent in its unique features will help in designing distinctive and authentic places. It would be valuable, too, I think, for designers to acquire a phenomenological perspective – an intense awareness of the actual direct experience of sites and structures – and to learn to convert this into a sensitivity to the creative possibilities of specific locations. For it is in working through such experience that real places may emerge.[24] Like any art, place design combines technical mastery with aesthetic sensibility.

Place design may be compared with architectural design – in fact it can be considered to encompass it, for architecture is part of the larger endeavour to create human places. All these efforts demand the same combination of art and science and all possess the same vulnerability to prosaic formulas. Most importantly, they offer the same opportunity to create conditions in the world in which people can be at home. Like architecture, place design creates the conditions for dwelling.

Art, whatever more it may be, is at its etymological base the skill in making something. All the arts construct the conditions for intrinsic experience. If the design of place is to be an art, its goal must be that of all the arts, the shaping of experience. A poetics of place must put the aesthetic in place.

Notes

1 T. Coraghessan Boyle, "Greasy Lake," in *The Granta Book of American Short Story*, ed. Richard Ford (London: Granta Books, 1993), p.555.

2 See E. Relph, *Place and Placelessness*, London: Pion, 1976, pp.42–3.

3 Yi-Tu Tuan, 'Place: an experiential perspective', *The Geographical Review*, 1975, vol.65, no.2, 151.

4 P.T. Karjalainen, 'Place and intimate sensing', *Nordisk Samhällsgeografisk Tidskrift* [*The Nordic Journal of Social Geography*], 1998, vol.27, n.p.

5 Wolfgang Welch has emphasized the etymological sense of aesthetics (lit. *aisthēsis*, perception by the senses) in much of his work. See *Undoing Aesthetics*, London: Sage, 1997, pp.5–7. Also W. Welch, 'Aesthetics beyond aesthetics: toward a new form of the discipline,' *Literature and Aesthetics*, Oct. 1997, 17ff.

6 A.G. Baumgarten, *Aesthetica*, Vol. I, Frankfurt a. O., 1750.

7 'In this cultural environment, people are embedded in their world. We are implicated in a constant process of action and response from which it is not possible to stand apart. A physical interaction of body and setting, a psychological interconnection of consciousness and culture, a dynamic harmony of sensory awareness all make a person inseparable from his or her environmental situation. Traditional dualisms, such as those separating idea and object, self and others, inner consciousness and external world, dissolve in the integration of person and place. A new conception of the human being thus emerges. Humans are seen as organic, conscious, social organisms, experiential nodes that are both the product and the generator of environmental forces. These forces are not only physical objects and conditions, in the usual meaning of environment. As we have seen, they also include somatic, psychological, historical, and cultural conditions. Environment becomes the matrix of all such forces. As an integral part of an environmental field, we both shape and are formed by the multitude of forces that produce the experiential qualities of the universe we inhabit. These qualities constitute the perceptual domain in which we engage in aesthetic experience.' A. Berleant, 'The idea of a cultural aesthetic', in *The Great Book of Aesthetics: Proceedings of the XVT International Congress of Aesthetics*, Tokyo, Japan: forthcoming.

8 J.D. Porteous, 'Intimate sensing', *Area*, vol.18, 250–1. See also Karjalainen, 'Place and intimate sensing'.

9 See J. Gibson, *The Senses Considered as Perceptual Systems*, Boston: Houghton Mifflin, 1966. Also A. Berleant, 'Environmental aesthetics', in *Art and Environment*, Proceedings of Sanart III Symposium, Ankara, forthcoming.

10 Relph, *Place and Placelessness*, p.65.

11 P.T. Karjalainen, 'Real pace images', in A. Haapala (ed.), *The City as Cultural Metaphor*, Lahti, Finland: International Institute of Applied Aesthetics, 1998, pp.95, 101.

12 In the context of such a discussion of the sacred as this, it is common to speak of sacred space. However, I believe that space is both too abstract a term and too diaphanous to adequately denote the particularity and materiality of those locations where we experience the sacred. The discussion that follows, then, will centre on the notion of a place as sacred.

13 See A. Berleant, *The Aesthetics of Environment*, Philadelphia: Temple University Press, 1992, pp.74–5.

14 N. Perrin, 'Introduction' to D. Stock, *New England Memories*, Boston: Bullfinch Press, 1989.

15 R.W. Hepburn, 'Restoring the sacred: sacred as a concept of aesthetics,' in *The Reach of the Aesthetic*, Aldershot: Ashgate, 2001, pp.124–5, 127. Relph's characterization of existential space resembles this account of sacred space (*Place and Placelessness*).

16 G. Matoré, *L'Espace humain*, Paris: La Columbe, 1962, pp.22–3. Quoted in Relph, *Place and Placelessness*, p.10.

17 M. Laanemets, 'Places that remember', in K. Lehari and V. Sarapik (eds), *Koht ja Paik / Place and Location*, Estonian Academy of Arts, 2000, pp.73–5.

18 See F. Downing, *Remembrance and the Design of Place*, College Station: Texas A & M University Press, 2000.

19 William Gibson, who is considered to have coined the term 'cyberspace' in his novel *Neuromancer*, 'created a world in which information can be accessed via neurally wired maps that interconnect with the world-wide lattice of information flow, which registers the user's/immersant's location within the system': R.K. Merritt, 'From memory arts to the new code paradigm: the artist as engineer of virtual information space and virtual experience', *Leonardo*, 2001, vol.34, no.5, 405.

20 Software designers have made this explicit. There are about a dozen online computer role-playing games that establish virtual worlds. One of the most ambitious is Sony's game, EverQuest, whose half a million subscribers inhabit a virtual world called Norrath. The strong communities that develop around these games enter into commercial systems that use an internal currency. Yet these often spill out into the 'real' world through internet auction sites where digital goods are traded for cash. Sean Dodson, 'Playing for keeps in the cyberland of Norrath', *Guardian Weekly*, 28 March – 3 April 2002, 23.

21 A consortium of university researchers and private firms is developing life-size virtual reality applications, including haptic tools to enable one to feel draperies, clothing and structural surfaces. This is being applied to the virtual reconstruction of archeological sites, in particular the ninth century BCE palace of the Assyrian king Ashurnasirpal. See *UB Today*, Winter 2002. See also <http://www.learningsites.com/NWPalace/ NWPalhome.html> (accessed 3 March 2003).

22 This, of course, but mentions a large and important issue about which I have written elsewhere, but which would deflect us from our main purpose here if we were to pursue farther. See 'The human touch and the beauty of nature', in A. Berleant, *Living in the Landscape: Toward an Aesthetics of Environment*, Lawrence: University Press of Kansas, 1997.

23 Residents of Levittown have protested against raised ranches because they are seen as destroying the historic character of the area.

24 'You should never plan a road if you haven't visited the place many times. It is not enough to go there once ... You should go in different moods. You should go when you're drunk, and try the feeling of how it is to sing in the forest. You should go the following day when you have a hang-over. You should go when your heart is broken ... Then perhaps you know if you can build that road or not.' Risto Lotvonen, resident of Hyvinkää, quoted in P. von Bonsdorff (ed.), *Ymparistoestiikan Polkuja* (*Paths of Environmental Aesthetics*), International Institute of Applied Aesthetics Series, Vol. 2, Jyväskylä: Gummerus Kirjapaino Oy, 1966, p.130. Also mentioned by E. Brady, 'The aesthetics of the natural environment', in V. Pratt *et al.* (eds.), *Environment and Philosophy*, London: Routledge, 1999, p.159.

Chapter 2

The sacred environment

An investigation of the sacred and its implications for place-making

Fran Speed

Introduction

In our perception of environment(s) as sacred what provokes our veneration and what is its relevance for the place-making process? I begin with a quotation taken from James Swan's book *Sacred Places*.

> The more I have learned about sacred places, the more I have come to understand and respect the way that traditional cultures experience place and nature, which is very different from the way modern society teaches us to perceive. There is value in both ways of seeing and being, but, if people don't have *the sense of knowing that comes first from feeling*, then they have lost the root of being human, and application of the scientific method only tends to draw us further and further away from where we must go.[1] (My emphasis)

Throughout early history, and across cultures and religions, mountains, caves, rocks, trees and water have been revered as sacred. Chinese geomancy (the art of feng shui) is a belief system that responds to all such things in a reverential way. Trees often occupy a special place in the sacred. The belief in a sacred tree that serves as a world pole is common, as is the sanctioned status of sacred groves.[2] Water worship was an equally important and widespread practice in ancient religion. Evidence suggests that ancient wells and springs (indeed wherever water was released from the body of the earth) were considered sacred.[3] While the sacred nature of natural phenomenon remains an integral part of some traditional cultures and religious belief systems,[4] in our secular world such experience tends to be dismissed as irrational superstition. Yet for many people today the experience of environment(s) as sacred is no less real than it was for our ancient ancestors. This is not to imply that the modern-day experience is a consequence of either a kind of polytheism or pantheism, or necessarily influenced by any religious orthodoxy.

What constitutes the sacred has inspired many ideas and definitions. Amongst the most frequently voiced is the notion that the sacred has value that transcends human affairs, that its value is innate or intrinsic. Other definitions involve feelings of mystery and wonder. Sacredness is seen to relate to the magical, the inviolable, to the unique, and the inexplicable. In its various forms, although the sacred is most strikingly related to the unseeable and the unsayable, in experience it is clearly *felt*. So what is it about certain environments that gives rise to feelings that are beyond explanation?

This essay takes an aesthetic approach that is familiar to organizational theorists[5] but is at odds with the dominant conventional use of the word 'aesthetic'.[6] I use aesthetic to mean a function of perception, an emotional response to a perceived state.[7] Aesthetics, in this view, function as 'a way of knowing' or understanding that exposes the *emotive and empathic* nature of aesthetic experience for value judgement. The intention is to emphasize the role of emotion for perception and, as sacred implies, for moral perception. Importantly, an aesthetic approach reveals the relationship between emotion and *motivation* and its significance for moral responsibility. Because moral value is constituted by the experience of the perceiving subject within a specific context of experience, judgements about the 'correctness' or 'appropriateness' of perception are irrelevant. The approach is distinctly different from that of aesthetic 'appreciation'.[8]

The concept of sacred place-making or a community sacred structure, as one writer argues, is easy to accept in so-called primitive cultures.[9] It is more difficult to comprehend how we in secular societies may hold any place necessary to our daily lives as sacred. While it is obvious why we consider a church, a synagogue, a temple, a mosque, a shrine or a place of pilgrimage as sacred, is it useful or appropriate to consider environment in this way?

What is deemed 'sacred' in natural environments, says Ronald Hepburn, is to speak of what is 'irreplaceable', 'mysterious', or of 'reverence' or 'wonder'. Importantly it is to speak of what is above and beyond mere utilitarian value.[10] Hepburn, however, has reservations about the use of the term 'sacred' in our aesthetic appraisal of the environment. Because the sacred remains too 'impregnated' with its religious origins, he says, it demands as it were 'to be acknowledged as meaning more than its aesthetic application allows it to mean'.[11]

Arnold Berleant's view is that 'grasping the nature of sacred environments has some curious consequences, that such environments tell us something about what all environment is'.[12] Berleant provides a metaphorical example that has particular relevance to the comparison that I present here. In describing the Gothic cathedral as a man-made mountain, he illustrates that in its fullest development the sense of place is a sense of the sacred, to the extent, he adds, 'that it seems grotesquely incongruous to speak of urban places as sacred, to that degree has the city failed to become precious to its residents'.[13] The metaphor emphasizes the view that both the Gothic cathedral and the mountain 'refer not to kinds of places but rather to different settings of *experience*'.[14] The analysis that follows develops this view and explores what is common to the *environment as experience* that gives rise to its perception as sacred.

The analysis investigates a natural and an interventional environmental feature perceived as sacred. The first is a memorial to the war dead.[15] Commonly known as the 'Stone of Remembrance', the large stone monolith was designed by Edwin Lutyens for what is now known as the Commonwealth War Graves Commission (CWGC). The second is a large naturally formed granite rock situated by a lake in Northern America.[16] I have chosen these particular features for their geological orientation, the intention being to illustrate that, even though their ontological and formal qualities are comparable, the process that gives rise to the perception of the sacred in each is different. While both perceptions are guided by an understanding that emerges through the interpretative mechanisms of narrative, metaphor and symbol, in each experience their interpretative function operates in a different way. The distinction is intended to illustrate that regardless of the interpretative process involved, what is common to both experiences is the efficacy of imaginative interpretation for emotional engagement and hence that emotion is a necessary constituent for moral perception.

I submit that the significance of the sacred for environmental concern resides in opportunities for emotional investment. Such opportunities are those where 'meaning' is discovered through aesthetic experience that both induces and endorses a direct and personal relationship with place. In conclusion the paper briefly considers some pragmatic consequences of this proposition.

Sacred rocks

Lutyens' 'Stone of Remembrance' was designed to act as a common focal point in the design of war grave cemeteries of more than 1,000 graves. Described by

Lutyens, as 'a great fair stone',[17] the monolith weighing 10 tons (10.16 metric tonnes) and measuring 12 feet (3.6 metres) in length, lying raised upon three steps, bears the inscription, 'Their name liveth for evermore'.

While not wishing to imply that the CWGC set out intentionally to comment on the rights and wrongs of war, in the provision and maintenance of its cemeteries the organization deliberately decided to create an aesthetic that would mask an undesirable reality with a reality that achieved a desired emotional response. An aesthetic that, in the words of the CWGC, 'operates to provide a comforting sense of security and at the same time to defer action which may threaten the status quo'.[18] The designation of an ambience was very significant. The commission chose to achieve this objective by creating an aesthetic intended, 'to give a feeling of solace and peace and not of depression'.[19] The manner in which this was to be achieved, however, posed a dilemma.

The sheer scale of loss commemorated in these cemeteries was such that any attempt to lionize the dead and glorify war was considered both distasteful and inappropriate.[20] Nevertheless, a form of commemoration that paid honourable tribute to the manner of their deaths had to be found. Secondly, the tribute had to appeal to all creeds and none. It was decided to create a form of tribute that rejected placing stress on the heroism of the dead, rather emphasizing their common sacrifice. Although every element of the cemetery's design is consciously engineered to meet this objective, from the uniform quality of its grave stones to its setting in an 'English garden', I have chosen to focus on Lutyens' monolith because it achieves two things. Firstly, as in ancient Chinese place-making, it exemplifies the influence of the sacred on its surroundings, in the way that the monolith's 'sacred aura' is diffused over the neighbouring space and everything in it – from the trees and the horticultural features to the grave stones themselves, which are elevated by the association.[21] Secondly, its geological ontology and form provides a clearer analogy with my second example, that of the large, naturally formed, granite rock situated by a lake in Northern America.

An analysis of Lutyens' monolith reveals it to be a culturally construed symbol. The monolith's most striking formal reference is to that of an altar. Its symbolism allows for an ambiguous narrative interpretation and this meets the commission's objective in an effective way. While to many minds its formal and narrative connotations are unmistakably Christian, the stone's austere, simple form and its lack of Christian notation provides an interpretation of it as a *sacrificial* altar. The effect is to underscore not only the commission's intention to convey the idea of the Empire's honouring all creeds and none, but also the desired concept of common sacrifice. Sacrifice is an emotive concept. It prompts narratives that speak of courageous selfless offering in the relinquishment of life. Such imaginings may provoke feelings of pity, either because we feel sorrow for innocent lives that have been taken unjustly, or because it induces fear, in that what we fear for ourselves provokes our pity when it happens to others.

Further analysis of the monolith reveals a more subtle narrative, one that constitutes the basis for perception of the sacred in my next example, but which in this example also has an intentional aesthetic function. The stone has been described 'as durable as any work of man can be',[22] The significance of this perceptive observation deserves consideration, not least as it is one that I suspect Lutyens intended. Obvious formal qualities of the stone monolith are provided by its geological nature. While its appearance, its weight and mass reveal physical qualities that we associate with geological form, its perception 'as durable as any work of man can be' suggests further associations when disclosed in narrative terms. Mindful reflection gives rise to imaginings about the stone's ancient geological origins, revealing it as timeless and enduring to the degree that it comes to signify a sense of the eternal and thus both endorses its intended 'message' and reinforces the stone's inscription 'their name liveth for evermore'.

I now consider a naturally formed feature. The example is provided by Jim Cheney in a discussion about our ethical relations with rocks. Although the very idea that we might have ethical relationships with rocks is, as Cheney says, nearly unintelligible to the western mind (or proof of mental imbalance), traditional cultures have taken, and in some cases still do take rocks quite seriously, often regarding rock as the oldest and in some sense wisest of beings.[23] Cheney relates an experience while he was hiking near a high mountain lake in northern America. He came upon a huge granite rock that expressed the 'more-than-human' nature of the world in a particularly concentrated way, a way that he could only refer to – with a certain awe – as sacred. I shall describe the experience from Cheney's standpoint and largely in his words. A striking feature of the experience was that it was not apparent where this huge granite rock had come from. It appeared 'to have been from time out of mind in that place, by this wild and beautiful spangled lake'. It took on the character of 'a watchful, still, being, a still point of the turning world, an eternal serene and powerful presence in that place'.[24] The metaphor is of the granite rock as 'the oldest of beings'. As humans we might see the rock as a venerable old sage of quiet mindful stillness and mindful behaviour. Such a powerful and 'sagacious presence' in our midst might provoke a reciprocal sense of mindful behaviour.

Imaginative attentiveness allows things to disclose their stories to us. Rocks, perhaps more than any other natural phenomenon, disclose a narrative that allows us to glimpse a profound reality. In reflecting on the way that the rock arrived we might imagine it being swept to rest in this place on a glacial sea or as the sole survivor of the weathering and erosion that gave rise to this land, or it might provoke deeper imaginings about how it came to be born of great pressure and heat, or (if of a sedimentary type), of ancient seas and ancient life.

Considering the immense span of time that rock signifies we might come to understand it as embodying a singular experience about the way the world came to be, and thus in some deeper sense come to grasp the infinite, to glimpse the eternal. A synthesis of such imaginings may provoke a perception of the rock as a silent sentinel, a witness to and keeper of life's mysteries. As it discloses its story to us we can come to view it as a constant in our own lives, one that allows us to measure our own existence by comparison with its existence. Perhaps we come to see the relatively transitory nature of our own life in contrast to its enduring nature, perceiving how it has and will dwarf our lives many times. Thus the granite rock is understood as inviolable because of what it represents and embodies.

Emotion and the sacred

The significance of such narratives for perception, whether intentionally employed in the symbolism of Lutyens' monolith or through attentive reflection, as in the experience of the granite rock, is their emotive consequence. The sacred is first and foremost an emotional experience. Vine Deloria explains that emotional responses to sacred places are either *reflective* or *revelatory*; that a vast number of experiences are of the reflective kind, as I have illustrated. The revelatory, says Deloria, tells us things that we cannot possibly *know* in any other way. The distinction is that while reflectivity creates the awareness and sensitivity of people to the qualitative intensity of revelatory places, revelatory places are known only through prolonged occupation of an environment.[25]

Analysis serves to illustrate the efficacy of imaginative and empathic interpretation for emotional investment. [26] Narrative and metaphor engage us here in much the same way that poetry and stories reach us emotionally. It is argued that we gain moral knowledge from interaction with fictional narrative in the way that it allows us to 'test run' strategies that function as substitutes for real actions.[27] Metaphor as a form of interpretation allows us to view one element of experience in terms of another, and thus facilitates complex ideas, allowing us to 'reach insightfully into mystery'.[28]

In the experience of the granite rock, knowledge 'moves' by metaphor,[29] allowing us to access and process ideas that are felt. Meaning, as exemplified here, is not a consequence of cognitive rationality or scientific knowledge. Elementary knowledge of rocks would seem sufficient. It is the experiential nature of such things and their capacity to engage us emotionally that forges their perception as sacred and frequently leads to their function as symbol, as evidenced in Lutyens' monolith to which I shall now return.

While the Christian symbol of the cross clearly signifies Christian orthodoxy, the appeal of Lutyens' stone to all religions and none refutes the notion that there is any real or necessary correlation between its perception as sacred and religion per se, other than what the perceiving subject brings to the experience. Thus in the absence of any religious belief or orthodoxy the assertion worthy of emphasis here is that perception of the sacred is not morally determined in a religious sense. Further, the perception is clearly not merely a consequence of either its formal properties or its nature as a sculpture per se. Neither is it consequent on its geological nature in any scientific sense. Its function and geological nature, in artefactual terms, do not do justice to the complexity of its experience.

Rather its perception is the consequence of imaginative associations provoked by its symbolism. As a symbol the monolith provides the focus around which visitors can assemble both their individual and collective understanding, one that enables them to draw together diverse ideas that would otherwise not readily be associated. The stone's narrative symbolism and the ritualistic concepts that it evokes ensure a desired attitude by propagating fundamental ideas about sacrifice and perpetuating the promise of everlasting glory.

The relevance of Lutyens' monolith for my argument is that it exemplifies the efficacy of a *deliberate* aesthetic in eliciting a desired emotional response, particularly when we consider the profound reality that it masks, that of mass death in the horrific circumstances of war. Nevertheless, by its constant reinforcement, the denial of this horrific reality is encouraged in favour of its 'received wisdom'.[30] In endeavouring to 'shield' the reality it seeks to commemorate, the imposed aesthetic encourages visitors to look 'beyond the veil of death' and accept the implications of sacrifice. Its effect is to encourage visitors to experience the cemeteries as fields of remembrance rather than sites for burying the dead. Thus the perception of these landscapes as sacred is constituted by what is imagined and what is actual in experience.

An analysis of the sacred stresses that reality and invention in human experience are not rationally distinct, that what we value is not morally determined, that it stems not from cognitive rationality but is a consequence of emotional investment. Hence it stresses the significance of emotion for perception or, more accurately, for moral perception. In pragmatic terms it stresses the importance of opportunities for the kind of emotive experience to which the sacred alludes.

The sacred and place-making

The consequence of the sacred for the place-making process resides in the extent of an environment's emotional investment for the perceiving subject. It is the degree of our emotional investment in things and places that forms the basis for their moral significance. Although, as Karsten Harries says, 'meaning cannot finally be made or invented', only 'discovered',[31] the potential for discovery can be induced through artifice as evidenced in an analysis of Lutyens' monolith. In the place-making process, to achieve the kind of emotional investment to which the sacred alludes requires opportunities for direct and personal engagement, where the emergence of the formal settlement both induces and perpetuates personal meaning through its aesthetic experience. The management of land and resources proves no exception.

Pekka Virtanen demonstrates that sacredness is a powerful means of conservation, and describes how the sacredness of the forests in Mozambique has contributed substantially to their preservation, in terms of their relatively high biological diversity. Although these sacred sites have a spiritual dimension, 'their persistence cannot be assessed separately from the cultural institutions which make them meaningful and valuable for the local populations'.[32] The cultural anthropologist E.N. Anderson would appear to agree, when he argues that 'any management strategy that does not take human feelings into account simply will not work ... all too often strategies appeal either to a nebulous love of nature or to a narrowly practical economizing, expressed in tables of statistics or technical terms neither of these appeals works by itself.'[33] People work on an emotional economy that, he says, is not discussed in the ecology texts, 'but is actually the wellspring of all our actions'.[34]

Tim Ingold voices a similar view when he says that people operate with a *sentient ecology*,[35], i.e. based in *feeling*, 'consisting in the skills, sensitivities and orientations that have developed through long experience of conducting one's life in a particular environment'.[36] Ingold suggests that knowledge acquired through the sensitivity and responsiveness we term *intuition* constitutes a necessary foundation for ethics. Where logic 'leads to results that are counter-intuitive, we do not reject our intuitions but rather change the principles, so that they will generate results which conform more closely to what we *feel* is right' (original emphasis).[37] More recently Kay Milton has shown how emotion shapes the practice of nature protection in western societies. In what Milton terms an *ecology of emotion*, she demonstrates how nature protectionists in particular, and people in general, come to identify with nature and natural things, through a process where understanding and emotion are integral. The sacred, says Milton, describes what matters most to people, what they value above everything else.[38]

The sacred is an emotional construction. As a basis for place-making it can be promoted or prevented. It is argued that the most crucial agenda 'is to bring about the creation and extension of what is termed *moral space*, and to change those situations where it is diminished or extinguished'.[39] Anthony Weston suggests that the challenge is to create 'experiential space', where stronger environmental values can evolve. Weston terms this practical project as *enabling environmental practice*, and advocates the provision of intentional opportunities for the kind of encounter with nature and natural systems denied in modern urban living.[40] Weston's concept of experiential space, of reuniting the living world with humanity, remains an acknowledged tenet of ecological design.[41] 'Making nature *visible*' is considered a way of reacquainting us with natural systems, the object of which is to create 'a new kind of aesthetic for the built environment, one that explicitly *teaches* people about the potentially symbiotic relationship between culture, nature and design' (my emphasis).[42] However, while ecological design recognizes that direct and visual experience of natural systems is beneficial and to be encouraged, it tends to view such opportunities as essentially 'informative' and overlooks their significance for emotive experience.

The key, says Cheney, is not the sacred, but what he terms 'sacramental practice';[43] what is important is ritual. In order to affect desirable attitudes, environmental practices should serve to act as emotionally socialized 'ties' to the resources and place in question. Traditional societies that have succeeded in managing resources well over time have done this in part through religious or ritual representation of resource management . The key point 'is not religion per se, but the use of emotionally powerful cultural symbols to "sell" particular moral codes and management systems'.[44] Anthropological evidence suggests that experience and ritual are closely related. In orthodox religions 'symbolic knowledge' influences the emotional life of people and supports a pattern of attitudes considered favourable.[45] As Stephen Lansing has argued, 'religion does not so much create an ethical standard as supply the cultural and *emotional involvement that motivate* people to keep following an eminently pragmatic management system'(my emphasis).[46] Anderson's conclusion 'is not to imply that ecological practices must be "religious", but that any one interested in convincing people to manage the environment in a particular way would be well advised to embed it in a rich texture of emotion and experience'.[47]

The capacity for environmental concern in the context of place-making rests in the way that we, as individuals, come to experience the world around us: how we experience the world determines how we perceive it, and how we perceive it determines our attitudes and behaviour towards it. How we come to experience things and situations is of moral consequence. Hence, experiential opportunities for the kind of emotional investment alluded to as 'sacred' are to be encouraged.

Acknowledgements

I would like to thank Emily Brady-Haapala and Guy Herbert for their comments on draft versions of this paper.

Notes

1 J.A. Swan, *Sacred Places: How the Living Earth Seeks Our Friendship*, New York: Bear & Co, 1990, p.28. Current author's italics.

2 R. Cook, *The Tree of Life*, New York: Avon, 1974, cited in E.N. Anderson, *Ecologies of the Heart: Emotion, Belief and the Environment*, Oxford: Oxford University Press, 1996, pp.11–12.

3 J. Bord and C. Bord, *Sacred Waters: Holy Wells and Water Lore in Britain and Ireland*, London: Paladin Grafton, 1986.

4 J. Holm and J.Bowker, *Themes in Religious Studies: Sacred Place*, London: Continuum, 1994.

5 Aesthetics as a mode of epistemological inquiry is familiar in the field of organization studies. Antonio Strati's theoretical contribution to its development in this field is already considerable. See Antonio Strati, *Organisation and Aesthetics*, London: Sage, 1999.

6 By which I mean those uses of the term that refer to objective properties, i.e. that allude to the mere formal, material or visual properties of a thing or situation rather than the experiential process involved in formulating value judgement.

7 For further clarification of this distinction see P. Carter and N. Jackson, 'An-aesthetics', in S. Linstead and H. Hopfl (eds), *The Aesthetics of Organisation*, London: Sage, 2000, pp.180–3.

8 I find the term 'appreciation' problematic because of its association with the idea that appreciation can be developed by acquiring knowledge about a given thing, as is often the case in the evaluation of a work of art or an architectural form. The implication of this view leaves open the question raised by any personal experience of the given thing – for example, that of displeasure or revulsion – and thus ignores an important aspect of aesthetics as a mode of epistemological inquiry. The point intended is to raise a distinction between an educated or informed understanding, which can lead to an 'appreciation' of a given thing in an impersonal sense, and the kind of understanding acquired through personal and participatory experience. Thus, when I say that while I 'appreciate' jazz as a musical form, but don't enjoy listening to jazz, I distinguish between appreciation and personal judgement.

9 R.T. Hester, 'Sacred structures and everyday life: a return to Manteo, North Carolina', in D. Seamon (ed.), *Dwelling, Seeing and Designing: Toward a Phenomenological Ecology*, New York: State University of New York, 1993, p.279.

10 R. Hepburn, *The Reach of the Aesthetic: Collected Essays in Art and Nature*, London: Ashgate Publishing, 2001, pp.124–5.

11 Ibid., p.127

12 A. Berleant, *Living in the Landscape: Toward an Aesthetics of Environment*, Lawrence: University Press of Kansas, 1997, p.173. In Berleant's view such places make it clear that without a human presence they are neither sacred nor even environments.

13 A. Berleant, *The Aesthetics of Environment*,Philadelphia: Temple University Press Philadelphia, 1992, p.75.

14 Berleant, *Living in the Landscape*, p.171.

15 I am indebted to Pippa Carter and Norman Jackson, who provided the inspiration for this example in 'An-aesthetics', .

16 Jim Cheney provided the experience and discussion of the sacred here in 'The journey home', in A. Weston (ed.), *An Invitation to Environmental Philosophy*, Oxford: Oxford University Press, 1999, pp.141–67.

17 T.A.E. Gibson and G.K. Ward, *Courage Remembered*, London: HMSO, 1989, p.55, cited in Carter and Jackson, 'Un-Aesthetics', p.188.

18 Carter and Jackson, 'Un-Aesthetics', p.180.

19 Gibson and Ward, cited in Carter and Jackson, 'Un-Aesthetics', p.189.

20 D. Lloyd, *Battlefield Tourism: Pilgrimage and Commemoration of the Great War in Britain, Australia and Canada 1919–1939*, Oxford: Berg, 1998, p.312.

21 E.H. Schafer, 'The conservation of nature under the T'ang dynasty', *Journal of the Economic and Social History of the Orient*, 1962, vol.5, pp.280–1, cited in Yi-Fu Tuan, *Topophilia: A Study of Environmental Perception, Attitudes and Values*, New York: Columbia University Press, 1990, pp.145–8.

22 War Grave Matters: food for thought Campaigners for War Grave Commemorations, web site. Available online <http://www.cwgc.co.uk> (accessed 24 March 2003).

23 J. Cheney, 'The journey home', pp.144–147.

24 Ibid., p.146.

25 D. Vine Jr., 'Reflection and revelation: knowing land, places and ourselves', in J. Swan (ed.), *The Power of Place: Sacred Ground in Natural and Human Environments*, London: Gateway Books, 1993, pp. 28–40.

26 The role of imagination is outlined in R. Hepburn, 'Landscape and the metaphysical imagination', *Environmental Values*, 1996, vol.5, pp.191–204. See also E. Brady, 'Imagination and the aesthetic appreciation of nature', *Journal of Aesthetics and Art Criticism*, 1998, vol.56, no.2, pp.139–47, and *Aesthetics of the Natural Environment*, Edinburgh: Edinburgh University Press, 2003.

27 G. Currie, 'Realism of character and the value of fiction', in J. Levison (ed.), *Aesthetics and Ethics: Essays at the Intersection*, Cambridge: Cambridge University Press, 1998, pp.161–81.

28 J. Cheney, 'The journey home', p.145.

29 Ibid.

30 Carter and Jackson, 'Un-Aesthetics', p.193

31 K. Harries 'Thoughts on a nonarbitrary architecture', in Seamon (ed.), *Dwelling, Seeing and Designing*, p.47.

32 P. Virtanen 'The role of customary institutions in the conservation of biodiversity: sacred forests in Mozambique', *Environmental Values*, 2002, vol.11, no. 2, pp.227–41.

33 E.N. Anderson, *Ecologies of the Heart*, p.13.

34 Ibid.

35 The term 'sentient ecology' is credited to David Anderson, in *Identity and Ecology in Arctic Siberia*, Oxford: Oxford University Press, 2000, pp.116–17, cited in T. Ingold, *The Perception of the Environment: Essays in Livelihood, Dwelling and Skill*, London: Routledge, 2000, p.25.

36 Ibid.

37 Ibid.

38 K. Milton, *Loving Nature: Towards an Ecology of Emotion*, London: Routledge, 2002, p.104.

39 T. Kitwood, *Concern for Others*, London: Routledge, 1990, p.100, cited in A.J. Vetlesen, *Perception, Empathy and Judgement: An Inquiry into the Preconditions of Moral Performance*, Philadelphia: Pennsylvania State University Press, 1994, p.9.

40 A. Weston, 'Before environmental ethics', in A. Light and E. Katz (eds), *Environmental Pragmatism*, London: Routledge 1996, p.152.

41 Amongst those writers who address this view is the landscape architect R.L. Thayer, who coined the term visual ecology in *Gray World Green Heart: Technology, Nature, and the Sustainable Landscape*, Chichester: Wiley, 1994, p. 311.

42 S. Van Der Ryn and S.Conran, *Ecological Design*, Island Press, 1996, pp.164–5.

43 J. Cheney, 'The journey home', p.150.

44 E.N. Anderson, *Ecologies of the Heart*, p.166.

45 D. Sperber, *Rethinking Symbolism*, Cambridge: Cambridge University Press, 1975, cited by Douglas Davies, in 'Christianity: the sacred and ritual in theology and religious studies', in Holm and Bowker (eds), *Themes in Religious Studies*, p.52.

46 S.J. Lansing, 'Balinese water temples and the management of irrigation', *American Anthropologist*, 1987, vol. 89, pp.326–341, cited in Holm and Bowker (eds), *Themes in Religious Studies*, p.163.

47 Anderson, *Ecologies of the Heart*, p.167.

Chapter 3

What use is the *genius loci?*

Ian Thompson

In *Ecology, Community and Delight*,[1] I argued that contemporary landscape architecture is concerned with three overlapping fields of value – the aesthetic, the social and the environmental – and summarised this in a diagram (Fig. 3.1), at the centre of which was an area in which these overlapped, indicating the possibility of an approach to design which could create all three sorts of value, to which I attached the label 'trivalent design'. Although the book took a pluralist position towards values, trivalent design was held to be the richest sort of design, although not one often encountered in practice. Of the 26 landscape architects I interviewed for the book, a handful made passing mention of the Roman notion of *genius loci*, but I did not make much of it, because so few of my interviewees made much of it to me.[2] This now seems like an omission. *Genius loci* might be the keystone that can lock trivalent design together, a possibility that this paper will explore.

Ecology, Community and Delight took a catholic attitude towards the plurality of values found in practice. There seemed to be room for those who wished to practise as land-artists, those who saw themselves as applied ecologists and for those who were social workers manqué. However, this broad-church attitude did not slide into complete relativism, for it is possible to say that design which attempts to optimise social, ecological and aesthetic values is thereby richer than that which only attempts to maximise one sort of value. If the idea of the *genius loci* can help us to identify such design, and – better still, if it can help us to create it – it will justify our attention.

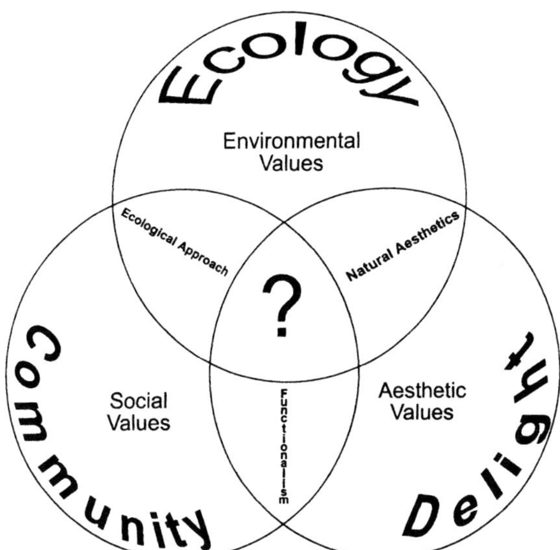

3.1
Aesthetic, social and environmental fields of value in landscape architecture

Genius loci is an ancient and persistent idea. The Romans believed that places, like people, had inner spirits that determined their essences. Just as they thought it was possible to read a person's character or spirit from observing the particularities of his or her face, so the genius of a place could be divined by paying attention to its individual features. This was a variety of animism, and similar ideas can be found in many cultures. Writing in 1979, Christian Norberg-Schulz made the *genius loci* into a cornerstone of his architectural phenomenology. He believes that the family of Greek gods symbolised the 'various roles and interactions of man on earth'.[3] The Greeks were also able to define particular kinds of places, and to relate these to human characteristics. Thus by dedicating a particular place to a particular god, the Greeks were actually making a threefold linkage between place, deity and some aspect of the human condition.

In the eighteenth century, the last time when landscape design was strongly driven by theory, the concept of *genius loci* was central to the guiding philosophy of the English Landscape School. Many passages might be quoted here, but the best known is from Alexander Pope's *Epistle to Lord Burlington* (1731), where the poet gives the following advice:

> To build, to plant, whatever you intend,
> To rear the Column or the Arch to bend,
> To swell the Terras or to sink the Grot;
> In all, let *Nature* never be forgot.
> Consult the *Genius of the Place* in all ...[4]

It is unsurprising that twentieth century landscape architects, so short of theory of their own, should place much reliance upon the ideas of their landscape gardening forebears. For example, in the introduction to his *Modern Gardens* (1953), the late Sir Peter Shepheard tells us that 'first, the landscape architect is concerned with the existing site; with its character and its *genius loci*... His first rule must be to let well alone: to preserve the natural features in which the character of the place resides.'[5] More recently Tom Turner has referred to Pope's injunction to 'Consult the Genius of the Place' as the 'Single Agreed Law of Landscape Architecture',[6] and although Turner is fond of irony, his tongue was not far into his cheek.

But the fact that an idea has a long pedigree does not make it true or useful, as can easily be seen from the persistence of astrology. The question is really whether the *genius loci* is just a poetic piece of animism or whether it can be given some more definite and useful sense.

The philosopher Isis Brook addresses this question in her paper 'Can "Spirit of Place" be a guide to ethical building?',[7] noting that *genius loci* is not a single notion but a nexus of ideas, and that the proliferation of interpretations given to it has done nothing to help the development of a robust idea. Unpicking this knot of meanings she finds many different strands. Alongside the ancient notion that certain places are the abodes of special beings, she also finds *genius loci* interpreted in terms of energy fields, authenticity, coherent narrative, local distinctiveness, essence, character, ecosystem, pantheism, panpsychism, health and special atmosphere.

Positivists might argue that this range of interpretations demonstrates that there is nothing to which *genius loci* genuinely refers, so the best policy would be to drop the expression altogether, but Brook identifies two other strategies. The first is to take an instrumental line. Talking about *genius loci* is useful if it helps us to defend places that are valued, culturally or ecologically, against damaging forms of development. *Genius loci* has practical value as a rhetorical device which will help us to argue for more sensitive approaches to planning, design and construction. Brook's preferred line, however, is to accept that there is something unambiguously real to which *genius loci* refers, and that this something would not be found amongst an inventory of the contents of a place or a description of our feelings about it.

We may baulk at the positivist position, which seems to involve the complete disenchantment of the landscape, but we might nevertheless agree that there are some senses of *genius loci* which cause difficulties for the modern mind and which should be avoided unless we are poets or mystics. There cannot be many design professionals who believe in nymphs, fairies or earth-spirits, so the ancient version of *genius loci* begins to look very unhelpful. There are similar difficulties with theistic or pantheistic views and also with occult ideas about energy fields or indwelling essences. Of Brook's possible interpretations of *genius loci*, the three that resonate most closely with the beliefs of contemporary landscape architects are those of character, local distinctiveness and ecosystem. Brook does not discuss the ecosystem view at length, but reassuringly has much to say that is positive about both local distinctiveness and character; indeed, she feels that the latter 'does seem a useful conceptual component of spirit of place and, clearly defined, could be a complete replacement'.[8]

Let us tentatively accept character as the central idea in *genius loci*. It can be regarded as an emergent property that in some way is related to the way in which places function socially, ecologically and aesthetically. There is an analogy between the character of a person and that of a place, but we need to keep in mind that these correspondences are metaphorical. However, just as human character is something which, in the absence of sudden trauma, develops slowly over time, yet admits fluctuating moods over shorter periods, so too does the character of a place develop slowly, yet admits fluctuations in mood or atmosphere following diurnal or seasonal cycles or patterns of use. Furthermore, if we consider that some spaces may have distinctive character, then the link to the value system associated with local distinctiveness is easily made. My purpose will be to see how this version of *genius loci* relates to the notion of trivalent design and its component value systems.

Aesthetics

We can trace a continuum in landscape architecture which has, at one pole, those works in which the primary purpose has been to blend seamlessly with nature or the vernacular landscape of cultivation, and, at the other, works in which the conscious imposition of cultural forms upon nature provided the *raison d'être* for the design. At the self-effacing end we find the works of the eighteenth-century English Landscape School, which were conceived as perfected versions of nature. At the other pole, where culture predominates, we find Le Nôtre, landscape design's greatest exponent of the grand gesture, who made nature subject to human reason. In the classical idiom the emphasis was upon symmetry and order, but there are also modernist gestures, such as Dan Kiley's grids, and postmodern ones too, like Bernard Tschumi's whirlwind of geometries at La Villette. Amongst contemporary British landscape architects there are those who believe that the hand of the landscape architect should never be seen, as well as those who believe that landscape architecture must regain its cultural significance through more assertive sorts of design.

Prima facie, the injunction to consult the *genius loci* would seem to favour the less obtrusive approach. Turner agrees; in *City as Landscape* he suggests that 'in areas of high landscape quality, whether urban or rural, [the *genius loci*] often prefers the conservation approach, which makes new development similar to its surroundings'.[9] If *genius loci* is taken to be a close synonym for character, then we all have some idea of what it is for something to be 'out of character'. Noting that the history of aesthetics has concentrated upon positive aesthetic categories, Arnold Berleant suggests some negative ones, amongst which we find the 'inappropriate'. Like a ball gown worn to an afternoon tea, he says, this arises when something is jarring in context, not in itself.[10] Perhaps we need something like an aesthetic precautionary principle which weighs against drastic change if the aesthetic consequences of a design intervention are difficult to gauge but potentially catastrophic.

Is the injunction to consult the *genius loci* therefore invariably conservative? Certainly it is weighted towards stability. Norberg-Schulz argues that places can change, sometimes rapidly, but that this does not necessarily mean that the *genius loci* changes or gets lost. The metaphors of consultation and dialogue, which are frequently found conjoined to references to the *genius loci*, do not suggest prohibitions or slavish determinism, but rather a reciprocity whereby the designer's intentions are shaped and modified by the site, but the site is ultimately altered by the designer.

Tom Turner has observed that there are logically only four possible relationships between any proposed development and its context: *identity*, *similarity*, *difference* and *coalition*.[11] He observes that if a gap appeared in a much-loved façade, most people would like it to be filled with a building which had a relationship of *identity* with its neighbours; whereas if a new reservoir were to be built in an Area of Outstanding Natural Beauty, the best design strategy would be one of *similarity* (Fig. 3.2).

The strategy of *difference* relies upon contrast. Interior design magazines often show images of contemporary furniture fitting successfully (in an aesthetic sense) into period or vernacular homes. This strategy has also worked where large-scale structures such as masts, radio antennae or power stations have had to be placed in the landscape. To attempt to camouflage or prettify them would be futile, but to accept them as forms of gigantic sculpture has often created a sort of man-made sublimity. 'In areas of low landscape quality', Turner suggests, the *genius loci* will favour 'an innovative approach, which creates a contrast between new development and its surroundings.'[12]

Turner's final possibility, *coalition*, is really a blend of the other three options. He gives the example of Geoffrey Jellicoe's work at Hope Cement Works, where a policy of *difference* was used for the huge factory buildings, *similarity* was used for the serpentine screening mounds and a principle of identity was used for the vegetation used to meld this composition into the surrounding countryside.

Respect for the *genius loci* points towards the strategies of *identity* and *similarity* but it does not close the door upon those of *difference* and *coalition*.

3.2
Development and context.
From T. Turner, *City as Landscape*, London: Spon, 1996.

Landscape architecture abounds with examples of the *genius loci* providing the springboard for imaginative yet appropriate design. In the USA, for example, George Hargreaves's design for Byxbee Park on a former landfill at Palo Alto on San Francisco Bay, California is influenced by the experimentation of Land Artists such as Michael Heizer and Walter de Maria, but also draws upon the context and history of the site. A grid of poles resembles beach groynes, but also echoes de Maria's iconic *Lightning Field*. The design is a *coalition* involving features similar to those that might have been found on site, but presented in ways that are novel. The sort of self-effacing design advocated by some landscape architects needs only *identity* or *similarity*, but any design that attempts to introduce new cultural meanings must include *difference*. Furthermore, we might hypothesise that a design that makes such an attempt while also seeking to respond to the *genius loci* will inevitably involve some form of *coalition*.

In England, a small cemetery on the edge of the Pennine moors designed by the Camlin Lonsdale practice eloquently demonstrates that it is possible to combine the most profound ideas with vernacular traditions. Its intersecting axes, Finite and Infinite, speak of mortality and the inexorable passage of time, yet the dominant elements in the design are belts of indigenous planting and drystone walls. It is intimate, familiar and comforting, yet at the same time deeply symbolic of the mysteries of life and death. The materials used are *identical* to those in the surrounding landscape, the walls and planting belts are *similar*, but the overall composition introduces a new pattern and it is this that carries the meaning (Fig. 3.3).

3.3
Saddleworth cemetery

If Hargreaves and Camlin Lonsdale have drawn upon preindustrial landscape characteristics, at Duisburg-Nord in Germany's Ruhr district, Peter Latz has shown that a designer can find and preserve value in a postindustrial landscape which might have been dismissed as degraded. Places, like people, can be traumatised, but like humans they can recover from their negative experiences, albeit with their characters altered. Latz has turned a former steel works into a landscape park. This place suffered the traumas of industrialisation and deindustrialisation, but in the process accrued new meanings and ecological values that a conventional reclamation scheme would have erased. Latz's intervention spared the site from this third upheaval by recognising its history and building upon its existing character, creating fern gardens in ore bunkers and making their mass concrete walls into facilities for rock climbers.

Ecology

Whether discussing people or landscapes, we recognise what is characteristic about them as belonging to a pattern. In a person it is a pattern of behaviour over time; in the case of a landscape it is the way in which details relate to wider regularities. The kinds of flora and fauna that a place will support are related to climate and geology, which together determine the conditions under which habitats can develop. The relatively recent discipline of landscape ecology focuses upon ecological processes at the scale of the landscape or region and provides a vocabulary for describing and discussing them. Landscape ecology deals with patterns and, since most of the world's landscapes have been altered by human activity, these patterns are cultural as much as natural. Some of them, the landscape ecologists inform us, promote biodiversity, whereas others do not. Dramstad, Olson and Forman have distilled current knowledge into a useful handbook for landscape planners and designers.[13] In general the sorts of landscapes that they advocate are those in which wildlife habitats are connected into networks; in more than one place in the book they illustrate this idea by showing aerial photographs of the English countryside where connectivity and circuitry are exemplified by the cultural landscape of hedgerows and small woodlands. It is not difficult to argue that developments damaging the *genius loci* of the evolved cultural landscape are also likely to cause fragmentation through loss or separation of habitats.

Any attitude towards a site which ignores whatever natural value has already accumulated, whether it be a thousand-year-old hedgerow or the first sprinkling of pioneer trees on a pit heap, is setting its face against the contemporary consensus. Conversely, consulting the genius of the place means paying close attention to underlying environmental factors. If our intention is to enhance existing character, for example through strengthening hedgerows, planting new woodlands or opening up a culverted river, the biological functioning of the landscape will be improved at the same time.

Similarly these basic environmental conditions place limits upon human activity, or at least they did so until they were transcended by technology. In clearing a field for agriculture, enough stone might be found to make the enclosing walls. If stone had to be quarried, it would be found locally, and this principle was as sound for the eighteenth-century country mansion as it was for the cottages in the village. At Belsay Hall in Northumberland the stone for the house was won from a quarry so close to the house that it was easy to turn the latter into a picturesque garden. However, a glance at a recent copy of the *External Works* catalogue shows that there are companies doing good business by importing sandstones from India, slate from Ireland, limestone pavings from Spain, and Ying stone from China for use in British architectural and landscape projects.

As Dunnett and Clayden observe, deciding upon the source of materials, both hard and soft, 'can be the most fundamental and straightforward way in which designers can influence landscape sustainability'.[14] Two of the principles they advocate for the selection of hard materials have bearing upon the *genius loci*. First they suggest that the efficient use of materials obliges us to seek ways of reusing or recycling materials that are found on site.[15] At Duisburg Nord, Peter Latz used the ground-down remnants of demolished buildings as path surfaces, aggregate and even as the basis for new soil. The second principle is that where new materials must be used it is generally better to find them locally, thus reducing the embodied energy cost of the material and the vehicular pollution that would be involved in bringing such materials from further afield.[16] The aesthetic benefit is that such materials are likely to be in character, to belong to the place in which they are used.

Turning to soft materials, Dunnett and Clayden note that traditional landscape planting has developed as a kind of global style, consisting of simple and static compositions such as trees in amenity grassland or single species blocks of shrub planting. These have low habitat value and require regular inputs of energy to keep them in their controlled and static condition.[17] The basis of sustainable planting, conversely, is to choose species that are suitable for the site.

Community

One need only to visit an amateur art show to be convinced that people can identify strongly with their local landscapes. In north-east England one would find countless iterations of the Tyne bridges and Durham Cathedral, together with newer icons such as Gateshead's Millennium Bridge and the Angel of the North. When the originals are so nearby, why should people want such images, if not to reinforce the positive feelings they already have towards such places?

As Berleant has pointed out,[18] aesthetic valuation is social. In the nineteenth century society's attitude changed towards the Lake District. From being seen as a gloomy and perilous place, it became an object of cultural tourism, a process accelerated by the influence of Wordsworth and his contemporaries. A similar revision of our attitudes towards wetlands is currently underway. Traditionally they were thought of as unproductive and unhealthy, and were filled in or drained wherever possible; now they are recognised as valuable and threatened habitats and this concern has brought with it a greater appreciation of their aesthetic characteristics.

This community identification with places is what gives such force to arguments for historic conservation. Perhaps the greatest success of the Heritage Lottery Fund, set up to disburse the proceeds of Britain's National Lottery, has been its Urban Parks Programme. David Jacques has surely identified the reasons for this when he writes that 'Memory is the unseen but guiding force determining most park users' responses... Visiting the place again is the trigger to remember and relive past events and pleasures. It becomes a dimension to one's self and society's self-image'.[19]

The homogenisation of landscape through the insidious processes of globalised capitalism is something that troubles many of the landscape architects I interviewed, and their disquiet is shared by the wider population. The charity Common Ground has promoted the notion of local distinctiveness as an antidote to this homogenisation.[20] It is a movement of gentle resistance that promotes local democracy and works for the empowerment of local people, often through artistic initiatives such as the New Milestones project, tree-dressing days or parish mapping. As we have seen, local distinctiveness was one of the possible synonyms for *genius loci* identified by Isis Brook, but it is very close in content to the notion of character. Just as to live with another human being is to recognise their physical and psychological uniqueness, so too is attachment to a landscape, and the sense of relationship and belonging this can bring, much easier to promote if that landscape has a recognisable character, full of the unique irregularities that add to distinction. Many commentators have observed that moves towards sustainable living must involve activities that foster social cohesion.[21] This suggests not only the need for a respectful attitude towards existing landscapes, but also the vision to create new places with which people can identify.

Genius loci and trivalent design

With Brook, I would argue that *genius loci* is something both real and useful. As it was rooted in ancient animism and has acquired other mysterious associations down the centuries, I do not think it is possible to eradicate such meanings by decree, nor indeed would it be desirable. Human beings need their mysteries, and we may take more care of an enchanted landscape than one that we value only in an instrumental way. Nevertheless, the notion of *genius loci* as *character*, together with the associated idea that this character might be *locally distinctive*, avoids the need to postulate mysterious spirits or essences and seems to be the most useful for the designer of landscapes. Paying attention to the existing character of a site offers a means to consider the aesthetic, ecological and social aspects of a place simultaneously. Such an approach is not incompatible with the somewhat discredited notion of Survey–Analysis–Design, and it is certainly compatible with phenomenological approaches to the understanding of landscape and with Tom Turner's recent advocacy of pattern-assisted design.[22] It is thus the lodestone that can guide the designer on to the path of trivalent design.

Notes

1 I.H. Thompson, *Ecology, Community and Delight: Sources of Values in Landscape Architecture*, London: Spon Press, 2000.
2 Ibid. One interviewee, bemoaning the loss of local distinctiveness in much contemporary landscape design, remarked that 'the genius loci will be away out of the window like it has for the architects', p.46.
3 C. Norberg-Schulz, *Genius Loci; Towards a Phenomenology of Architecture*, New York: Rizzoli, 1984, p.53.
4 See extract from A. Pope, 'An Epistle to Lord Burlington', in J.D. Hunt and P. Willis (eds.), *The Genius of the Place. The English Landscape Garden 1620-1820*, Cambridge MA: MIT Press, 1988, pp.211–14.
5 See P. Shepheard, 'Introduction to *Modern Gardens*', in J. Birksted (ed.), *Relating Landscape to Architecture*, London: Spon, 1999, pp.17–38.
6 T. Turner, *City as Landscape: A Post-Postmodern View of Design and Planning*, London: Spon, 1996, p.161.
7 I. Brook, 'Can "Spirit of Place" be a guide to ethical building?', in W. Fox (ed.), *Ethics and the Built Environment*, London: Routledge, 2000, pp.139–151.
8 Brook, 'Spirit of Place', p.146.
9 Turner, *City as Landscape*, p.172.
10 A. Berleant, *Living in the Landscape*, Kansas: University of Kansas Press, 1997, p.70.
11 Turner, *City as Landscape*, p.111.
12 Ibid., p.172.
13 W.E. Dramstad, J.D. Olson and R.T.T. Forman, *Landscape Ecology Principles in Landscape Architecture and Land-Use Planning*, Harvard: Island Press, 1996.
14 N. Dunnet and A. Clayden, 'Resources: the raw materials of landscape', in M.H. Roe and J.F. Benson (eds), *Landscape and Sustainability*, London: Spon Press, 2000, p.179.
15 Ibid., p.198.
16 Ibid., p.200.
17 Ibid., p.184.
18 Berleant, *Living in the Landscape*, p.13.
19 D. Jacques, 'Memory and value', in J. Woudstra and K. Fieldhouse (eds), *The Regeneration of Public Parks*, London: Spon, 2000, p.22.
20 The charity Common Ground was established in 1983. For information on the New Milestones Project see J. Moreland, *New Milestones, Sculpture, Community and the Land*, London: Common Ground, 1988.
21 See, for example, M.H. Roe, 'The social dimensions of landscape sustainability', and M.H. Roe and M. Rowe, 'The community and the landscape professional', both in Roe and Benson (eds), *Landscape and Sustainability*, pp. 52–77 and 235–64 respectively.
22 See, for example, T. Turner, 'Hyperlandscapes', *Landscape Design*, October 2001, vol.304, 28–32.

Chapter 4

Constructing place ... on the beach

Simon Unwin

Introduction

When we go the beach we put ourselves in a primitive relationship with the world. On the broad sweep of sand, and in the presence of the enormities of sea and sky, we remove some of our clothes, and present our selves to the sunshine, the wind, space, the sand, and the salty water. . . . Being on the beach stimulates all our five senses: in the bright light we see the colours and ceaseless motion of the sea and sky; we feel the warm sun on our bodies, the cool breeze brushing the hair on our skin, the soft sand between our toes, the cool water; we hear the surf, the gulls, the shouts of children; we smell and taste the air and sea.

The experience of being on the beach seems to intensify our perceptions in more subtle ways too: of being in space, held by gravity to the surface of the earth; of exposure to the forces of the sky, the sun and wind; of the size and scale of our bodies, the loci of movement of our arms and legs; of directions implicit in our bodies and in the landscape, and the possible relationships between them; of freedom from orthodox constraints; of detachment from the mundane and from other people; of being where our ancestors have been for millions of years. . . . In short, our awareness of existence is heightened.

With the mediating accoutrements of our daily lives stripped away, on the beach we engage more directly with the primal conditions of being.

The beach is the margin of land and sea, the zone where these opposites overlap. The beach seems eternal. It is a grandstand for the great and continually changing infinities of the ocean and space. It turns its back on the matrices of organized life and society on the land, and faces the uncontrollable and placeless sea and sky. The tides wash the sands clean twice a day. Timeless, the beach has no history; it is amnesiac, it remembers nothing for more than a few hours. It is poetic: on the beach we are face to face with eternity; ΘΑΛΑΣΣΑ ΚΛΥΖΕΙ ΠΑΝΤΑ ΤΑΝΘΡΩΠΩΝ ΚΑΚΑ – the sea washes away all humankind's effluent.

Situating ourselves is an a priori requisite of our existence in the world. Simply to be is to be in a place at a time. At all times we are placing ourselves: we have a sense of where we are, and of other places around us; we weigh up where we might put ourselves next... . We feel comfortable when we are settled in a place: in bed, in an armchair, at home... . We feel uncomfortable when we find ourselves in the 'wrong' place (at the 'wrong' time): in a field during a thunderstorm, embarrassingly exposed at some formal event, lost in an unfamiliar city... . In our lives we either establish places for ourselves, or have them established for us. We are constantly 'playing the game' of situating ourselves in relation to things, to people, to forces... . Whether simple or complex, places mediate between us and the world; they provide frames in which we exist and act. When they 'work', they make sense of the world for us; or we make sense of the world, in a physical and psychological sense, through them.

On the beach the need to construct place is more immediate than in the established settings of our everyday lives. At home, at work, in going about our daily activities of shopping, watching television, making meals... the places we use are generally ordained by specialists (architects, planners, urban designers, engineers, interior designers, builders...). We generally fit into the matrices of spatial and ceremonial organization these complexes of place suggest, maybe modifying them slightly by the arrangement of furniture, but generally accepting the form they give to our lives. On the beach we cannot do this – we must establish our places from scratch, for ourselves.

The majority of people who come to the beach for a day by the sea are unlikely ever to have thought consciously about the importance place plays in the structure of their lives. The ways in which they respond to the challenge of being on the beach, and of establishing places for themselves, are largely innate or self-acquired, unaffected by formal and conscious exposition (through theory and education for example). The places people make on the beach may be influenced by the formal patterns of the more permanent places they occupy

4.1
'Megaron'. People make 'temples' for themselves on the beach

and inhabit in their daily lives, and maybe by places they have seen other people (their parents perhaps) making on the beach, but even so the organizational patterns of the day-camps they make may be read as evidence of the ways in which people intuitively situate themselves in the world, the means they employ to modify a small part of the world to their own advantage, and the factors and relationships they take into account when doing so.

Four examples with commentary

These examples have been selected to illustrate some of the conceptual structures manifest in places people make on the beach. These examples are not fully representative of the range of places that one might find on a warm sunny day on a busy beach. They have been selected because of their clarity, and because of the ideas they appear to manifest. Rather than there being a typology of beach places, it seems more as if there is a repertoire of ideas, attitudes and concerns that people employ in their own ways.

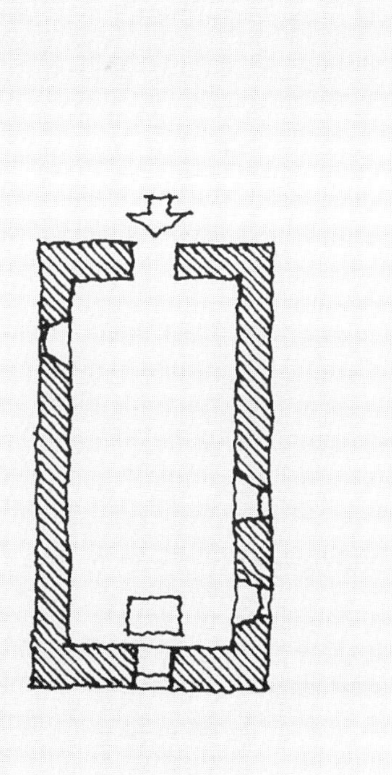

Example 1

Although the inhabitants of this place are absent (see Fig. 4.1), its formal organization clearly illustrates how it would be occupied. Much architecture on the beach makes use of a 'kit of elements', the first and perhaps most essential item in which is the towel or mat (other items will be seen in the other examples); most people bring a towel to the beach, to dry themselves after a swim, and to spread on the sand as a place to lie in the sun, i.e. to identify their place on the beach. Here the towel has been oriented, as seems often to be the case in beach places, with the 'feet' towards the sea, and 'head' to the land. The towel's rectangular shape (like a bed) accords with the cruciform symmetry of the human bodies that will lie on it (head, feet, arms to each side), and in this example its corners have been weighted with two pairs of shoes (apparently for reasons of emphasis rather than practical necessity – the shoes are like the bases of four columns of an imaginary aedicule framing the towel, and its inhabitants). The towel has been positioned, determinedly, with a rock of particular size and shape at its head. This rock 'anchors' the towel to a specific spot (rather than letting it 'float' in the open, undefined, expanse of the sands), and provides a 'table' on which objects may be placed to keep them off the damp and gritty sand. Finally, lines have been drawn in the sand, like four walls of an imaginary room, complete with a 'doorway', around the towel in the middle, with the rock at the 'focal' end, opposite the doorway. These 'walls' present no effective physical barrier to trespassers into this personal space; but they have the psychological effect of suggesting that 'strangers' should keep out. They are like a 'magic circle' (only rectangular) drawn in the sand; they separate out the place of the towel from everywhere else, making it special. They define a private area of ground over which the inhabitants have asserted their possession. They make the place into a 'chapel' or 'temple' (complete with 'altar') 'dedicated' to the inhabitants, framing their existence (even when they are not there). The form of this 'chapel' aligns the innate geometry of the inhabitants' bodies with that of the beach (eyes to the sea; back to the land; and arms each way along the sands), orienting the place towards the ocean, and establishing a link between the inhabitants and the ever-distant horizon.

Example 2

The makers and inhabitants of the place in Figure 4.2 have used a range of ready-made elements. There are mats, windbreaks, parasols, chairs and a small tent. As in the previous example the place is orthogonal, with its geometry oriented towards the sea. It has a basically symmetrical arrangement, in which

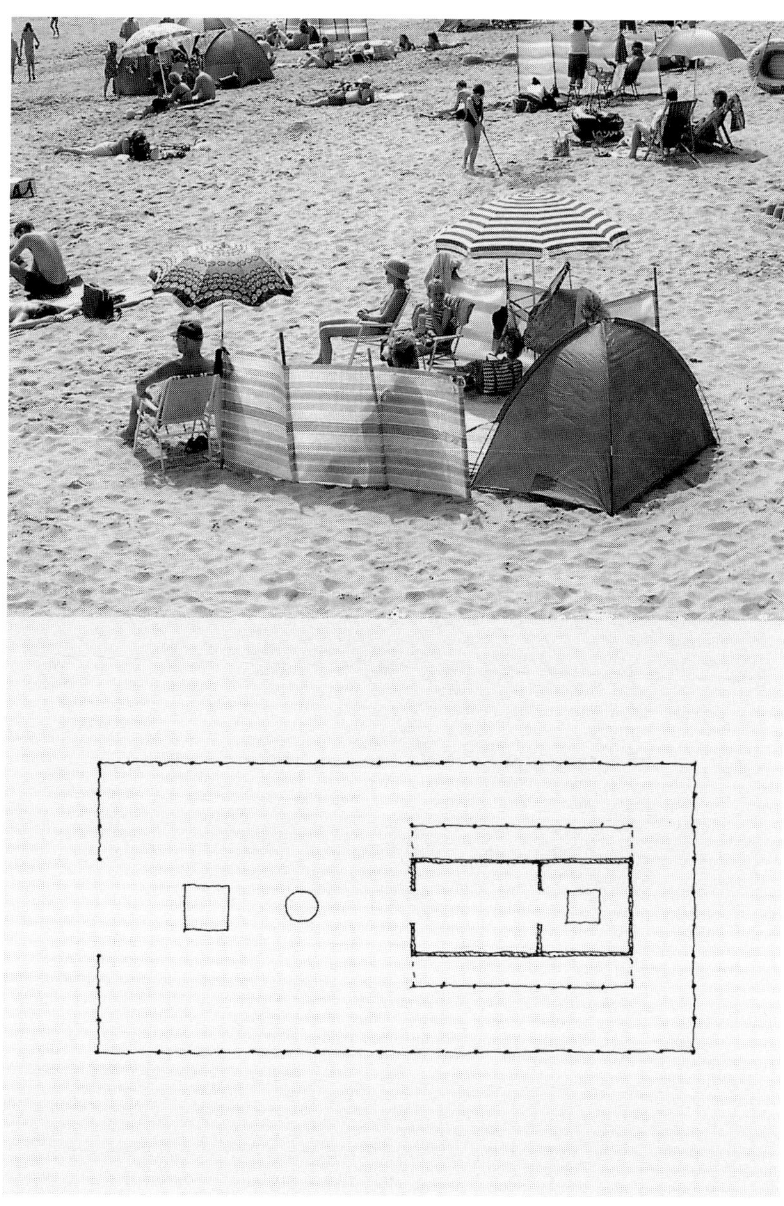

4.2
'Tabernacle'. Some encampments have sophisticated layouts, and ancient precedents

the line of axis runs perpendicular to the line of the beach, and projects out to the distant horizon. The two parallel windbreaks, which help to set up the axis of symmetry, also protect the flanks of the place – not just from the wind but psychologically too by providing some privacy – and the tent closes the rear. The one open direction, 'guarded' here by 'sentinels', is that facing the sea. The conceptual structure creates a hierarchy of privacy, between the open beach and the inside of the tent. It is that of an ancient Greek megaron or temple, with its *cella* and forecourt, or of the 'Tabernacle' constructed by Moses in the desert for the protection of the Ark of the Covenant. Just as in the Tabernacle the fabric walls enclose a compound, and inside the compound is a tent that forms its 'inner sanctum', its 'Holy of Holies'.

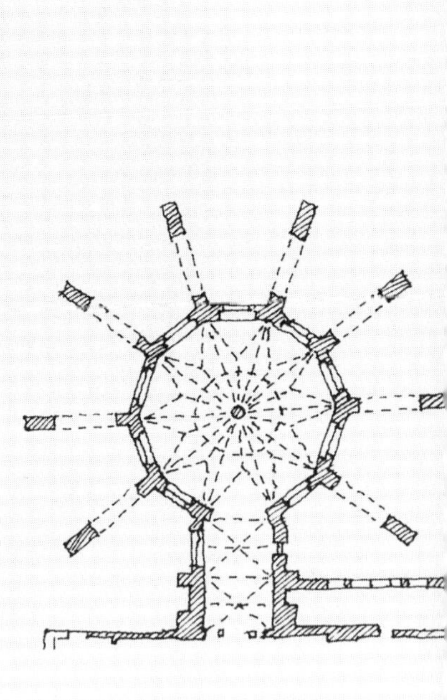

4.3
'Chapter house'. Social geometries evoke timeless place types: e.g. places for discussion

Example 3

These boys have arranged their deckchairs into a segment of a circle, a conceptual structure in harmony with their social relationship (Fig. 4.3). They seem to feel psychologically and physically comfortable in this arrangement. It allows each to see the faces of all the others equally, and it implies no hierarchy amongst them. They have provided themselves with a 'vaulted' roof of umbrellas to shade them from the sun, and screened their backs with a curved wall of windbreaks, forming a semicircular enclosure around them. Rather than relating to something outside of itself, this circle of friends seems enclosed and separate from the external world. Just as they are rapt in their conversation, so too are they wrapped in the place they have made for themselves. The arrangement is similar to that of a medieval chapter house, attached to a cathedral or monastery as a council chamber for monks to discuss the administration of their communal affairs. In both, the conceptual structure of the place derives from the instinctive way people position themselves in relation to each other when they sit in a group to talk.

4.4
'Village' layouts imply family relationships within a group

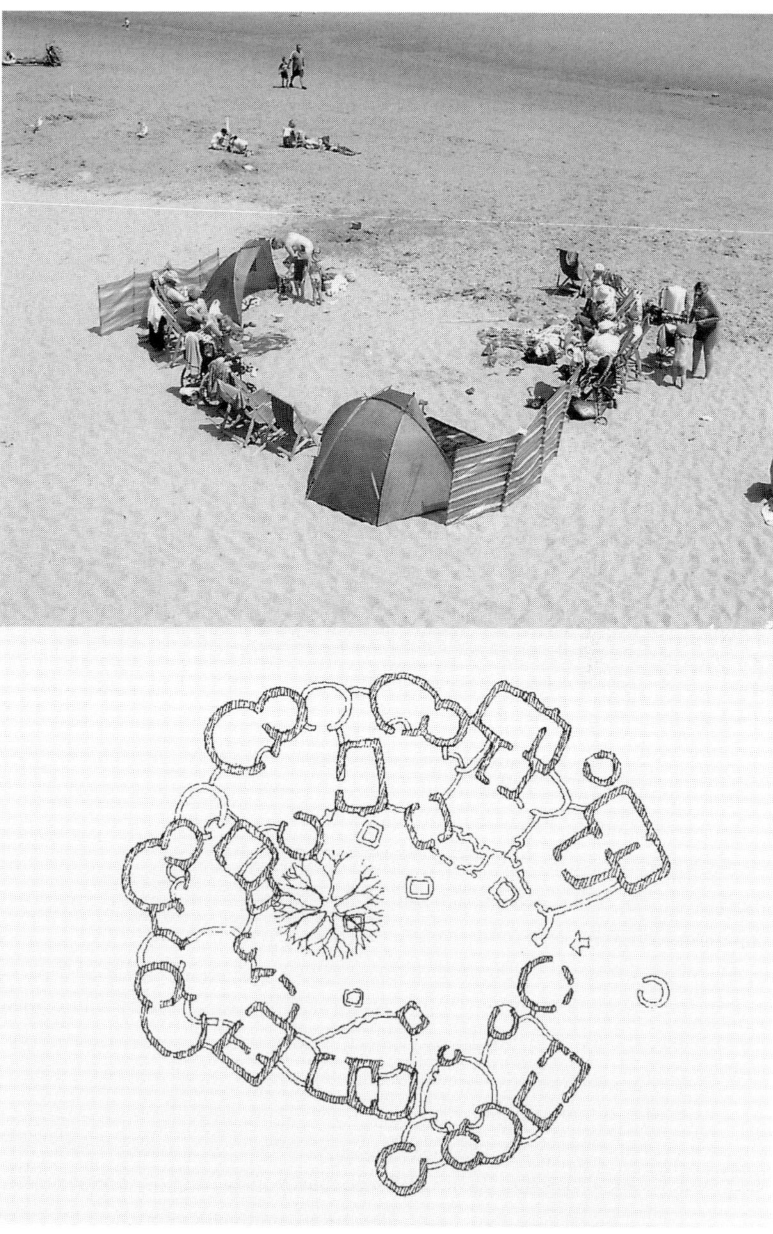

Example 4

The conceptual structures of places on the beach relate to the constitution of, and relationships within, the groups of people who construct and use them. Individuals and couples make simple places; families and groups of friends make more complex places, accommodating their internal relationships. In this example (Fig. 4.4), two or three families (possibly constituting one extended family) have come to the beach together, and constructed a place that includes 'home bases' (the tents) for each – rather like houses in a small village. The whole group is ranged around and defines a common area of ground, possessed by all. Although the composition is neither geometrically regular nor symmetrical, it has been laid out with an open face to the sea. It is related in its conceptual structure to that of a village, in which each family has its own house within a larger unified group arranged around a communal space.

Discussion

These few examples do not cover anywhere near the full range of places that people make for themselves on the beach, nor do they illustrate more than a small part of the rudimentary architectural 'language' they use. They are, however, particularly clear examples, which are sufficient to begin to identify and discuss some of the characteristics and components of that language.

Places on the beach depend on the people who make them not only for their conceptual organization, but also for their *raison d'être*. It is through places that people situate themselves in the landscape. Places mediate between their inhabitants and the world. The people who make them are their seed and their core. They make them to frame their lives, and to establish their existence. Even when they are not in them they manifest their presence.

People make places to assert possession of territory. They do this simply by laying out a towel, or by drawing a line in the sand; or maybe by digging a moat, or erecting windbreaks. They separate a place from everywhere else, and claim it as their own.

The places people identify become their 'homes' while they are on the beach. They become their datum. As they wander, or go for a swim, they relate themselves continually to their place as a reference point. It becomes part of their identity when they are there; they belong to their place, as it belongs to them.

The places people make accommodate and resonate with their physical human form. In the horizontal plane (with the ground beneath their feet, and the sky above their heads) people tend to organize the world in terms of their own four principal directions. The human face looks forward; the body has two sides and a back. Human beach places reflect this four-sided sense of the world, often protecting the body's sides and back whilst retaining one open face. In this way human places tend to establish a principal direction to which people can relate their own.

Some places are symmetrical, apparently structured to be in accord with the symmetry of the human body, rather than for abstract or aesthetic reasons. People seem to feel comfortable when the frame they have constructed for themselves has a symmetry in harmony with their own.

Directions and symmetry establish axes. Intuitively people orient their places towards the sea. They do this to watch the ocean, to face towards open sea stretching to the horizon. Sitting facing the sea their geometry is in harmony with the geometry of the beach.

People make places for their physical and psychological comfort. They lie on towels and sit on chairs, they screen their sides and backs with windbreaks and tents (even if they don't actually use them). People sit with their backs to the wall of a cliff. Some place themselves in an alcove between spurs of rocks. They use windbreaks to protect themselves from the breeze, and parasols for shade.

The conceptual structures of places reflect the social relationships of their inhabitants. People sit or lie next to their partners. They form small circular (or roughly circular) groups for conversation. They build small 'villages'. They set themselves apart from others they don't know, and build links with those they do.

The means people use to establish their places fall into three categories:

1. They use things that are already there. They position their places in relation to rocks, cliffs or pools, as if to anchor their places in the world.
2. They mould what they can to their own desires and needs. The sand on the beach can be dug, moulded, mounded. People build imaginary model castles from sand, but they also build castles for themselves by digging moats and mounding sand into walls.
3. They bring ready-made elements to the beach. They lay out towels and mats to create floors and beds. They erect windbreaks as walls. Tents provide ready-made rooms, into which they can withdraw from the agoraphobic openness of the beach and sea. They shelter from the sky under the canopies of umbrellas. They sit on collapsible and portable 'thrones', and lay out their food and possessions on small tables.

People do not do all these things in all cases. But then neither do they use all words, and all possible grammatical constructions when they use language. Just as language has many forms and ways of being used, so too does this common intuitive 'language' of architecture, evident in the places human beings make for themselves on the beach.

Conclusion

One might think of architecture as something artificial, distinct from the natural. One might think of architects as separated by their profession from 'ordinary' people. One might expect that the sorts of places 'ordinary' people make for themselves to be formless, without conceptual structure. One might think that architects are the providers of architecture, for people to receive, like customers, without understanding of its workings. One might think that student architects come into schools of architecture with none of the intellectual tools needed to become architects. The evidence of the places people make for themselves on the beach suggests these assumptions need rethinking.

Beach architecture is neither artificial nor natural, it just is. The two terms set up a dichotomy that is inappropriate: dividing the artificial (that which is ordained by the human mind) from the natural (that which occurs without reference to a human mind) is too simplisitic. Beach places illustrate an architecture that is concerned with situating people in the world. This is an architecture that mediates between people and the world, and through which they make sense of it for themselves. As such it is both natural and artificial, or neither.

Beach architecture illustrates that all people are, to some degree, architects. They are all involved in making places for themselves, and take into account a complex range of issues when they do it. They generate subtle and complex patterns of conceptual structure, taking into account relationships and geometries. The 'language' of architecture, at least at its rudimentary level, is shared by all.

This realization has consequences for how we understand the role of architecture in society, and how and to whom it should be taught. Architecture is as pervasive to our lives as language, yet it is rarely included in the curriculum of primary and secondary education. And if this intuitive 'language' of architecture exists, should it not be the foundation on which professional architectural education builds?

Chapter 5

Constructing informal places

Peter Kellett

Introduction

Throughout history the majority of the world's population have been responsible for creating their own places to live. Although traditional settlements have received considerable scholarly attention, most analysts have focused on environments designed and produced by specialist professionals for elite and relatively affluent populations. In contrast, the contemporary self-made environments produced in and around the rapidly expanding cities of the south have rarely been examined with the same analytical tools, even though such informal activities are responsible for producing such a high proportion of the urban built stock.

Although there is considerable diversity between settlements, most share three key characteristics. Firstly these environments are conceived and constructed by the occupants themselves independently of external controls or professional advice; secondly occupation and construction frequently take place simultaneously; and thirdly such places are usually in a process of dynamic change and demonstrate considerable ingenuity and creativity within limited resource constraints.

To explore these processes of informal place-making, and the resulting environments, this chapter will draw on data from a study of squatter settlements in northern Colombia.[1] Through analysis of the processes of making, both collectively and at household level, we will gain insights into the multiple influences on the decision-making processes involved. Far from the common image of inadequate, chaotically organized places, it will be argued that these environments respond to clear, culturally embedded ideas about how cities and dwellings should be configured. Given the relative transparency of the processes, the limited resources and the absence of intermediaries, informal settlements offer a particularly rich environment in which to explore the construction of meaning through the interlinkage between social and physical place.

Constructing home

In an essay celebrating the active role of 'ordinary' people it is fitting to begin with the words of the protagonists themselves. Here is a short extract from the testimony of Alba, a single mother of two in her early thirties who was previously living at her sister's house. She begins by describing the violence of the initial land invasion that marked the establishment of a new squatter settlement.

> I was in right at the beginning. We invaded here in the struggle to have a little piece of land, but the landowners retaliated and we were very badly treated by the police, and I was arrested. … The majority of us didn't have a house. Well we took a risk, without knowing if we were going to win or lose. … I made my first hut out of cardboard but they demolished it. Then I made another from wooden poles but we didn't have time to finish it before [the police] returned. … Later I made this little house from cardboard and poles. … All the time I am modernizing it, and I also decided to extend it, as I feel happy doing it. I get wood from the sawmill nearby: 100 pesos for each pole and the [roof] sheets were given to me by a friend. …
>
> My situation has improved because now I have what I didn't have before – a house of my own. [Although] the work situation has got worse, I must thank God that I've got enough to eat. I came here to have something of my own. I feel very content here in my little house. You can live well in a house of wooden boards especially if it's nicely kept, and I'm always doing something. I'm really so happy here: people ask me when am I going to rest from knocking in nails and things, but I am so delighted to be here: I've never had a house before!

Her optimism about the future is clear and she is relishing the independence and opportunity offered by having a home of her own. Despite the minimal physical attributes of her current home, she keeps it in pristine condition: it is a tangible symbol of her pride, self-esteem, independence and achievement.

Her account aptly illustrates one of the central components necessary to understanding informal housing. Although such phenonema are undoubtedly manifestations of injustice and poverty they are also, and perhaps more importantly, concerned with aspiration, with hope and with the future. We cannot interpret Alba's efforts as only attempts to resolve the shelter problems of herself and her children. Through the processes of occupation, construction and habitation she is actively re-constructing her place in the world.

As Leach paraphrases, Heidegger explained that 'one's capacity to live on this earth – to "dwell" in the phenomenological sense – is an essentially architectural experience. The very Being of being is linked to one's situatedness in the world.'[2] Similarly, John Turner has emphasized the existential dimension of self-made environments and believes that in home-building and local improvements a person can find 'the creative dialogue essential for self-discovery and growth. ... The man who would be free must build his own life. The existential value of the barriada is the product of three freedoms: the freedom of community self-selection; the freedom to budget one's own resources and the freedom to shape one's own environment.'[3] The absence of official control and regulation may facilitate the release of creative action and energy, which in other contexts can be severely inhibited, although it is vital not to over-romanticize nor to play down the issue of resource scarcity and constraint: most informal dwellers construct their homes through necessity not choice.[4] Despite such constraints, the resulting environments can be instructive for those concerned with understanding how places become meaningful. It is clear that even the humblest of dwellings can contain great depth of meaning, and the sense of purpose amongst many dweller builders is tangible. This is in sharp contrast to the despair and hopelessness frequently experienced by relatively disadvantaged groups in more affluent parts of the world.

Physical comfort, security and shelter cannot be taken for granted. Informal dwellers particularly appreciate these qualities as in many cases they have made sacrifices and confronted danger and hardship to achieve them. Alba's neighbour and friend Nancy has similar experiences, although she has the advantage of a stable relationship with her partner Julio and their two-year-old son. They were living in overcrowded conditions with Nancy's mother-in-law when they heard about a new land invasion. Julio was directly involved the first night, but had to be at work early the next morning at the petrol station, so Nancy played a key role:

> It was hard because I was six months pregnant at the time but it was me who had to guard the plot during the day. It was very violent and

> the police even hit some of the women, but when they saw that I was pregnant they said 'You, get off home!' … [But] if nobody had slept here we would have lost the plot. We made a small hut of poles and cardboard and five months later we started the foundations. Then we did more little by little, but it took a long time.

Twelve years later Nancy's house is a substantial four-room dwelling of concrete blocks with a cement-fibre roof. The tiny trees which they planted in the early weeks now tower over the street and house to provide much-welcome shade. They have dug a septic tank and through improvised connections have electricity and piped water. This is an impressive achievement.

Building the informal city

Alba and Nancy both live in the coastal city of Santa Marta (population *c.*240,000), where most people live in settlements that began as organized, illegal invasions of land, the first of which date from early in the twentieth century. After the invasion, land subdivision is carried out by the settlers with the aim of creating plots of equal dimensions within a conventional grid-iron layout. Through time most dwellers are able to change their temporary shelters into well-built, substantial houses: a change from small, single-room, unserviced dwellings towards multi-room, fully serviced houses that demonstrate a confident mastery of space and materials (see Figs I.10 and 5.1–5.4). Such changes occur at varying speeds with numerous factors impacting on the process, including cultural background and complex patterns of residential mobility, which mean that different households may occupy (and build) at different stages in the life of the dwelling.[5] It is clear that the majority continue to improve the dwelling well beyond the resolution of basic shelter needs. In addition to adding rooms, upgrading finishes and improving services, they introduce furniture, pictures, painting, trees and flowers. Such actions may be described as home-creating processes. Within the constraints of their context, people are each attempting to create dwelling environments that respond to their individual and collective understanding of the components, attributes and images which together give meaning to the idea of home.

Home has many attributes and levels of meaning, but at its centre is a 'highly complex system of ordered relations with place, an order that orientates us in space, in time, and in society'.[6] At one level it is concerned with the domestic spaces and activities of everyday life, and simultaneously it has broader dimensions, which relate to issues of identity, economic and social positions: in short, a person's place in society. There is a complex interrelationship between these two scales: the microcosm of the dwelling and the macrocosm of the world in which individuals and groups must define and make their place. We will explore some of these relations in order to demonstrate how home-creating processes are integrally linked to the position and place of informal dwellers within society.

Informal settlements

Informal settlements are now the dominant form of housing supply in most developing-world cities, and their manifestations vary greatly depending on the context. Of particular interest is the way that informal settlements have traditionally been defined in negative terms in relation to formal parts of the city. Effectively, informal settlements have achieved their identity through what they are not, or do not have, in comparison with the formal. In favourable circumstances such as this, the consolidation processes may be interpreted as a gradual movement away from what are regarded as informal characteristics towards increasing formality. Indeed, in the later stages of development many informal settlements are indistinguishable from formal ones. This of course is entirely intentional. The expressed aim of many settlers is precisely to produce places that are as close as possible to the dominant formal housing areas. They aspire to create conventional, legal, fully serviced housing areas.

Since colonial times urban areas in Latin America have been planned using orthogonal principles based on a grid-iron layout of standard blocks. Informal settlers begin with efforts to achieve a standard settlement layout, sometimes overriding the logic of topography. The most vital aspect of the grid layout is that it will be read as conventional, and have the potential to develop and become the same as other parts of the city. Similarly, but perhaps less forcefully, the design of the dwellings themselves echoes the same underlying values. Clearly established patterns of development are followed at different speeds, and the end products all fall well within a relatively narrow band of culturally prescribed characteristics. This echoes the conclusion of an early study of popular settlements in Barranquilla where the 'homogeneity of the house form and layout in these barrios ... can be explained in terms of an adherence by [the] builders to a common set of general principles and approved alternatives'.[7] Taken together, these principles mean that the dwellers are attempting within the constraints of their resources to create urban form and housing areas which are as close as possible to the dominant conventions. The informal dwellings and settlements can therefore be read as symbols of formal respectability and conventionality.

Place of memory

In conventional, formal housing systems the dweller will normally enter the process when the dwelling is completed and most key decisions about the physical form have been made. This means exclusion from much of the process of creation and construction. In contrast, informal settlers, especially those who endured the hardships and dangers of the invasion, inevitably have a different experience and relationship towards both the site and the dwelling. For many this is a long, slow process of construction and change, which is closely intertwined with other fundamental aspects of life (birth, death, household formation and separation), economic position (through income-generating activities in the dwelling), as well as apparently small details of everyday existence. The plot is not merely a demarcated piece of land, nor is the house only 'bricks and mortar': they are both full of memory and meaning. We can see this echoed in this extract of an account by Doña Carmen describing her plot in the early years, when the dwelling and her seven children were small and she was recently widowed:

> . . . all that area over there was open, we used to sit here, and there where the kitchen is now there used to be a large almond tree and we would rest below it. Just beyond the almond tree was the place for washing clothes. I used to wash there in peace and quiet. That was when the children were young.

In this example we can see how different parts of the dwelling are related to through memory to what was there before, and the activities which took place in particular places. However, rather than evoking affective responses of nostalgia, the recollection of deprivations and minimal living conditions in the past emphasizes present achievements as well as giving strength to hopes for the future. The focus is forwards, with little evidence of nostalgia for the past, either for earlier phases in the settlement or previous places of residence.

Imagined futures

A distinctive characteristic of informal settlements is that the dwellings are built by inhabitants at the same time as the space is inhabited. It is usually a long-term project of gradual improvement, which is highly responsive to changing domestic circumstances, budgets and opportunities. This emphasizes the idea of place making as fundamentally a process of change through time, a process in which the changing dwelling place can be seen as a symbolic vehicle of transformation along a route to different circumstances. This is an aspirational

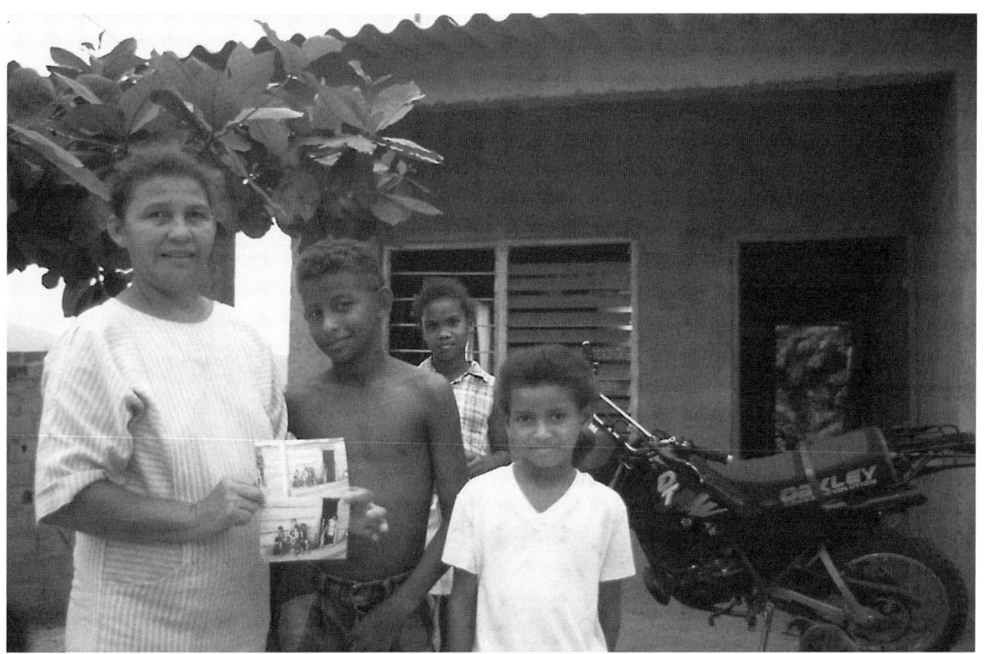

5.1
Olga and her children in 1996 holding a photograph of their improvised dwelling in 1991. Their home now has three rooms and is still being expanded and improved

journey from poverty towards prosperity, from the past towards the future, from exclusion towards inclusion and from the margins towards the centre.

In Figure 5.1 we can see the physical manifestation of these processes. Olga and her children are standing proudly outside their house in 1996. She is holding a photograph taken five years earlier of themselves outside their week-old temporary dwelling made of discarded planks from the timber yard. The construction of the new dwelling is a considerable acheivement, but they have also managed to consolidate their economic position and the children now go to school. Her neighbour, Rafael, and his family have also made a similar journey with the construction of their house:

> I did the building work myself with the help of my children, in fact I learnt how to build here in the barrio and now it's how I earn my money. I help my neighbours to build their houses and I sometimes also get work on construction jobs in town. The house now has three rooms with a kitchen at the back and it's certainly not finished … but I'm very proud of it. It will take many years before I get it like I want it to be.

The future dimension is crucial. The long-term nature of the process demonstrates that dwellers are not present-time focused, in contrast to the well-established myth of the poor as present-time oriented. They adopt forward-

5.2
A house in the process of consolidation. The symmetry of the dwelling is very apparent

looking strategies based on optimism and aspiration, and their dwellings embody future aspirations with little time for nostalgia or a rural past, rather a fascination with 'modern', urban, progressive images: a striving towards 'imagined futures'.[8]

Despite daily hardships and injustices, the world is seen as a place of opportunity and where effort and initiative can be rewarded. It is a world view in which change and modernity are welcomed. Such attitudes are reflected in the way people build. According to Lisa Peattie, 'the aesthetics of building [are] shaped ... by a view of the world as changing, as offering opportunities for individual progress, as being a place in which one looked beyond the neighbourhood in space and away from the past in time for models of success.'[9]

The settlers do not need to look far. The models of success are nearby in the low-density, middle-class areas of the city. Despite contrasting pedigrees and modes of production, these low-rise formal houses share numerous design features with the squatter dwellings: both have recessed, stepped entrances which are centrally positioned with verandas; both have rendered walls painted in pastel colours; both have front areas sharply demarcated with low walls with a distinctive semi-circular motif, sometimes with decorative security railings. The curved plastic forms sometimes link the walls with the façade, and both types of

5.3
A squatter dwelling that is fully consolidated. Internal and external walls are painted and the dwelling has electricity and water supply. This is the type of dwelling most informal dwellers aspire to

dwelling include trees and shrubs as integral parts of the front of the dwelling (see Figs 5.3 and 5.4). Shared aesthetic ideas may also be reinforced by proximity. All squatter builders will be familiar with their external appearance, and some will have more detailed involvement as domestic workers, gardeners or, in a few cases, as labourers in their construction.

There are significant differences in dwellings throughout the country, but in Santa Marta the similarity between well-consolidated, popular dwellings and middle-class houses suggests that local role models are

5.4
A middle-class dwelling in Santa Marta about one mile from the squatter settlements

significant in influencing the design vocabulary. Foster interprets the type of dwelling constructed by the poor as 'an economical copy of a more wealthy man's house'.[10] But it is much more than a simple copy. In a study from Brazil, Holston also identifies similar sources, but argues that low-income dwellers are not attempting to imitate, but rather to develop 'original copies', which display their origin as well as demonstrating sufficient uniqueness.[11] Through this complex translation process new hybrid forms are being produced that make reference to different sources of ideas and levels of meaning.

Some critics deny the architectural validity of such hybrid forms. In a study of spontaneous settlements in Medellin, Fernando Viviescas found 'considerable expressive potential', but argues that the

> circumstances under which these 'barrios' are established prohibits a reference to architecture. Rather, we are referring to the basic, immediate and desperate need for shelter. ... The spatial configuration of these barrios respond not so much to any authentic development initiating from within, but rather to an inevitable (given the material conditions) impoverished superimposition of ideological, aesthetic and environmental values originating in other more affluent parts of the city. ... The result tends inevitably towards a penurious kitsch.[12]

This echoes Bourdieu's assertion that the relatively disadvantaged in terms of power or resources are inarticulate in terms of taste, style or refinement, as they must concentrate instead on the most necessary and functional aspects of life.[13] However, evidence from this study does not bear out such reductionist claims. Indeed, a number of studies provide compelling evidence of lower-class residents participating with a rich palette of ideas and creativity to produce culturally authentic hybrid forms.[14]

What appear to be essentially physical changes can symbolize progress and achievement and more fundamental social and economic changes. The mass consumption of materials and consumer goods through the construction and furnishing of dwellings draws dwellers intimately into capitalist cycles of consumption, and parallel changes in social identity occur as people's role and position within society is redefined.

The social position of individuals in society plays a vital role in determining their actions. Squatters are highly conscious of their relatively low social status, which is reflected in their physical conditions. Therefore their construction efforts to transform their settlements can be partly interpreted as a striving for dignity and respect. From her personal experience of living in a squatter settlement in Venezuela, Lisa Peattie concluded that ' the construction characteristics and the service deficiencies ... have a common attribute; they represent attributes which are devalued and devaluing. People who live in this way are thought of as people to be looked down on. That is why the energy that goes into housing improvement … is as much a drive for respect as it is for comfort.'[15]

Such energy and values are manifest in the aesthetics of the built environment where

> the underclasses are constructing images and identities to counter those that subjugate. Not only are they transforming themselves as citizens but they are also changing the images of disrespect that bind them to a denigrated sense of their own persons. They are replacing these images with new ones of competence and knowledge in the production and consumption of what modern society considers important.'[16]

Informal settlement processes are now the dominant form of housing production in the rapidly expanding cities of Latin America. When viewed from a visual perspective such settlements may well appear disordered, chaotic and unplanned, especially in their early stages of development. But on closer analysis it is clear that far from being simple responses to shelter need they demonstrate clear, purposeful decisions and actions about how dwellings should be configured and how life should be ordered. The actions of informal dwellers go well beyond achieving the passive function of the house (the provision of shelter), to engage directly with its 'positive purpose: the creation of an environment best suited to the way of life of a people'.[17]

Such cities are the sum of the continuing actions of low-income households each attempting to construct in physical terms their vision of the life and values to which they aspire. As we have seen, such visions are ambitious and require the commitment of prodigious energy and creativity, leading in turn to a domestic architecture rich in meaning. Such informal place-making processes are powerful testimony to the extraordinary power and creative talent of those usually considered ordinary.

Notes

1 This study is based on fieldwork in Colombia where the author lived with a family in a squatter settlement for extended periods. The main method of data collection was the recording of oral testimonies to explore the residents' housing histories, their experiences and motivations for joining the land invasions and their aspirations for the future. Resource allocation, space configuration, and the use values and meanings associated with particular spaces and furnishings were examined. Forty households from two settlements were documented in detail over a six-year period (1986–91), with follow-up visits in 1996 and 1998. *See* P. Kellett, 'Voices from the Barrio: oral testimony and informal housing processes', *Third World Planning Review*, 2000, vol.22, no.2, 7–24. Some of the ideas in this essay have been expanded in P. Kellett, 'The construction of home in the informal city', *Journal of Romance Studies*, 2002, vol.2, no.3, 17–31.

2 N. Leach, 'The dark side of the Domus', in A. Ballantyne (ed.), *What is Architecture?*, London: Routledge, 2002, p.88.

3 J.F.C. Turner, 'The squatter settlement: an architecture that works', *Architectural Design*, 1968, vol.38, no.8, 355–60, p.357.

4 There is an increasing recognition by people in 'developed' parts of the world of the validity of such ideas, but for most the building of their own home would be considered a luxury. The paradox is that 'it is a luxury that almost all poor people in the so-called underdeveloped world enjoy'. Rybczynski quoted in L.R. Peattie, 'Aesthetic politics: shantytown architecture or new vernacular?', *Traditional Dwellings and Settlements Review*, 1992, vol.3, no.2, 23–32, p.29.

5 For more details about the processes involved see P. Kellett, 'Residential mobility and consolidation processes in spontaneous settlements: the case of Santa Marta, Colombia', *Third World Planning Review*, 1992, vol.14, no.4, 355–69; P. Kellett, 'Cultural values and housing behaviour in spontaneous settlements', *Journal of Architectural and Planning Research*, 1999, vol.16, no.3, 205–24.

6 K. Dovey, 'Home and homelessness', in I. Altman and C.M. Werner (eds), *Home Environments*, New York and London: Plenum Press, 1985, p.39.

7 D.W. Foster, 'Survival Strategies of Low-Income Households in a Colombian City', unpublished PhD dissertation, University of Illinois, 1975, p.180.

8 This is a term used by James Holston with reference to popular building in Brazil. J. Holston, 'Autoconstruction in working-class Brazil', *Cultural Anthropology*, 1991, vol.6, no.4, 447–65.

9 Peattie, 'Aesthetic politics', p.28.

10 Foster, 'Survival strategies of low-income households', p.180.

11 Holston, 'Autoconstruction in working-class Brazil', p.461.

12 F. Viviescas, 'Myth of self-build as popular architecture: the case of low-income housing in Colombian cities', *Open House International*, 1985, vol.4, 44–8. p.45. For further expansion of these ideas see: F. Viviescas, *Urbanización y ciudad en Colombia: Una cultura por construir en Colombia*, Bogotà: Foro Nacional por Colombia, 1989.

13 P. Bourdieu, *Distinction: A Social Critique of the Judgement of Taste*, London: Routledge, 1989.

14 See for example: R. Colloredo-Mansfeld, 'Architectural conspicuous consumption and economic change in the Andes', *American Anthropologist*, 1994, vol.96, no.4, 845–65; C. Klaufus, 'Dwelling as representation: values of architecture in an Ecuadorian squatter settlement', *Journal of Housing and the Built Environment*, 2000, vol.15, no.4, 341–65; E. Wiesenfeld, *La autoconstrucción: un estudio psicosocial del significado de la vivienda*, Caracas: Universidad Central de Venezuela, 2001.

15 Peattie, 'Aesthetic politics', p.29.

16 Holston, 'Autoconstruction in working-class Brazil', p.462.

17 A. Rapoport, *House Form and Culture*, Englewood Cliffs: Prentice-Hall, 1969, p.46.

Chapter 6

Migrant homes

Ethnicity, identity and domestic space culture

Didem Kılıçkıran

'Migrancy' appears to be the other of 'home', when confronted with conventional ways of understanding dwelling in Western thought. While migrancy signifies movement, change and being separated from an original place of belonging, Western conceptions of dwelling are based on notions of stability, permanency, belonging to and being rooted in a place. The opposition between migrancy and home has become more evident in a recent academic pessimism maintaining that it is impossible to conceive any notion of home in our times characterized by massive displacements of people around the globe and the resultant complexity of transnational/diasporic social relations. In such a condition, migrancy is seen to have become a metaphor for a supposedly universal feeling of alienation and homelessness.

In this essay, I will argue against both the conventional conceptions of dwelling in Western thought, and the reifications of migrancy as the paradigmatic feature of the contemporary situation, by focusing on the home-making practices of Kurdish refugee women from Turkey, who live in council housing in North London.[1] The central proposition to my argument will be that people who are physically separated from places they know as 'home' have a profound desire to re-create a home-place, and that the private world of domestic space plays a pivotal role in this. Drawing on interviews and participant observations, I will highlight Kurdish women's efforts in reconstructing a sense of stability and continuity in their dwellings which were allocated to them by the state. In this, I will mostly focus on the role of representations of ethnic and cultural identities, and of habitual, culturally informed ways of using space in re-creating a familiar environment. However, I will also emphasize aspects of change that materialize in Kurdish women's homes in various ways, and which Kurdish women relate to their experience of displacement and resettlement. I will conclude by questioning the validity of both conventional conceptions of home, and contemporary concerns about alienation and homelessness.

Migrancy and home

In wartime England in 1942, Simone Weil argued that 'to be rooted is perhaps the most important and least recognized need of the human soul'.[2] This spiritual need, for Weil, could only be satisfied by one's staying in one's national setting, as, Weil maintained 'Just as there are certain culture-beds for certain microscopic animals, certain types of soil for certain plants, so there is a certain part of the soul in every one and certain ways of thought and action communicated from one person to another which can only exist in a national setting'.[3] What is disclosed by Weil's use of the metaphor of 'roots' is a well-established belief in Western thought that there is a natural tie between peoples, identities, and particular geographical territories. This belief is also expressed by Heidegger, who, seeking for the truths of human existence, declares that 'We are plants which – whether we like to admit it to ourselves or not – must with our roots rise out of the earth in order to bloom in the ether and bear fruit'.[4] However, although it finds its best expression through the metaphor of 'roots' in the nationalistic tones of Weil's and Heidegger's discourses, the imagery of this invisible link between people and places is not only confined to the imagination of the *Heimat*; it also underlies a prevalent emphasis on stability, permanence and fixity in conventional conceptions of home, from the scale of the homeland to that of the house. This emphasis is mostly apparent in the way Heidegger associates 'Being' with 'dwelling', and 'dwelling' with the permanency of the act of 'building', the meaning of which, he underlines, is 'to remain, to stay in place'.[5] It is also central to Bachelard's phenomenological search for the essence of dwelling in a body of images that provide man (*sic*) with a knowledge of self via a representation of a sequence of fixations in the spaces of the being's stability,[6] or Relph's understanding of home as an 'existential insideness', maintaining that to be at home is to be *here* rather than there.[7]

This emphasis on stasis in conceptions of home is an outcome of what anthropologist Malkki calls a powerful ideology of 'sedentarism' in Western thought.[8] This ideology, which is 'deeply metaphysical', not only leads to a view of identity as rendered stable by the places we call home, but also to an understanding of home as a fixed place with an unchanging character. This circular logic is commonly held in conceptions of identity and place in humanist geography. For instance, Casey argues that the relationship between identity and place is far from a 'causal qualification', that place is one of the 'determining properties' of '[who] someone is',[9] while Birkerts, remembering the 'lost places' of his childhood, states that 'my best, truest … self is vitally connected to a few square miles of land'.[10] Such conceptions are also rooted in popular consciousness. As Tuan states, 'It is a current and popular belief that people do not know who they really are unless they can trace their roots'.[11]

What is more important is that this sedentarist ideology leads to an almost natural prioritization of stability and permanence in place over displacement and change, and hence to a vision of displacement as a loss of identity and as 'homelessness'.[12] Such a vision is particularly evident today in an academic pessimism maintaining that 'homelessness' has become a general condition of living in our times. It is argued that the massive displacements of people around the globe, and the resultant complexity of transnational/diasporic social relations, have made it impossible to conceive any notion of home as a place where identities are grounded.[13] Instead, many have recourse to notions such as 'migrancy', 'displacement' and 'exile' as metaphors that are believed to capture the increasing state of alienation caused by the rupture in people's attachments to places. Minh-ha, for instance, argues that our age is one of exile.[14] Casey, for his part, draws attention to an acute sense of nostalgia in Western societies – a grief for lost places that he associates with people who are displaced from their native lands.[15] Chambers, on the other hand, talks about 'migrancy' as a universal condition, to explain that any act of claiming an identity, and any process of 'home-coming' has become an impossibility.[16]

However, there is a paradox within the very idea of home, which withstands these two positions – i.e. a sedentarist notion of home that prioritizes stability and permanence in place over displacement, on the one hand, and a reified sense of displacement as the paradigmatic nature of the contemporary situation, on the other. This paradox is that 'it is perhaps only by way of … displacement that one achieves an ultimate sense of belonging'.[17] In other words, although they are almost naturally identified with contemporary concerns about rupture and alienation through metaphors such as 'migrancy' and 'displacement', it is probably the *real* displaced people – people who have been exiled, forced out of their homelands, and people, who, for a variety of reasons, have had to leave the places they knew as 'home' to continue their lives elsewhere – for whom home is most valuable. But is there a possible home-coming for those who are displaced? If so, how is a sense of home re-created after displacement? How do identities, displaced as they are, become re-inscribed in space for the construction of a new home-place? Does this construction, and the 'art of dwelling', necessarily depend on the recovery of roots as Heidegger proposes?[18] Or can there be a home in change, in Becoming?

In the following, I try to answer these questions through a study on the home-making practices of Kurdish refugee women from Turkey, living in council housing in North London. Drawing on some ethnographic vignettes, I discuss these practices ranging from the display of mementoes and some iconic objects representing ethnic and cultural identities, to the use of diasporic forms of mediation, and transformations of architectural space, in a way to reveal Kurdish women's efforts in searching for a sense of stability and continuity. However, I also underline aspects of change, which materialize particularly in decoration practices, and which Kurdish women relate to their experiences of displacement and resettlement.

Kurdish homes in North London

Kurds in Turkey have been subject to the assimilationist policies of the Turkish Republic ever since its founding in 1923. At its beginning, the Republic was based exclusively on Turkish culture and identity, and hence did not allow the Kurds to express their language and identity within its borders.[19] Since then, there has been a relentless repression of the Kurdish language: still to this day, no schooling in Kurdish is in operation, and neither radio nor television broadcasting in Kurdish is permitted. In addition, the prohibition on Kurdish has been strictly enforced during different periods, and speaking Kurdish in public was 'socially discouraged'.[20] The feeling of insecurity and alienation that Kurds have as a result of this repression has also been reinforced by the fact that the eastern and south-eastern regions of Turkey where the majority of the Kurds have been settled are socio-economically the poorest, least developed areas of the country. In such a context, a resistant ethno-nationalism has become a significant determinant of Kurdish ethnicity (and the so-called 'Kurdish problem' in Turkey), which materialized in the form of guerrilla movements among the Kurds, leading to armed conflicts between the Kurdish Workers' Party (PKK) and Turkish government forces between the mid-1980s and the late 1990s. As is well known today, this has resulted in the deaths of many on both sides, and the flight of a large number of Kurds from their homelands.

For subordinated peoples such as the Kurds, recovering their repressed histories and identities takes on a crucial importance after displacement. It seems that the private realm of the domestic space plays a significant role in this. In the case of Kurdish women, what is most striking is the display of some visual materials of representation related with Kurdish ethno-nationalism and identity. These take a variety of forms from posters, photographs and paintings depicting various political or religious

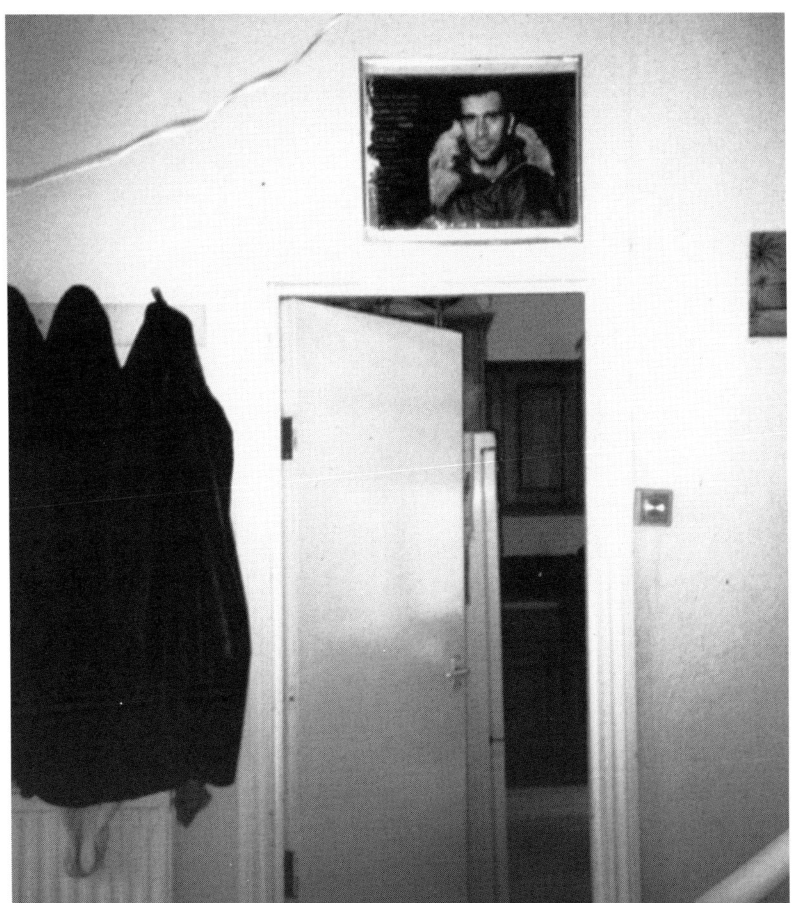

6.1
The photograph of Gezmis hung up above the entrance to Zeliha's kitchen

figures, to illustrated calendars featuring photographs of Kurdish soldiers fighting on the mountains of outh-east Turkey. For instance, the reproduction of a large portrait of the leader of the PKK – the ultimate symbol of the Kurdish ethno-nationalist resistance – takes its place on one of the walls of Basak's living room. Another portrait of the Kurdish leader, this time a photograph cut out of a newspaper, is attached to the cupboard in her five-year-old daughter's room, next to her paintings. For Basak, a 31-year-old woman from south-east Turkey, these are the symbols of the freedom of expression she has away from her homeland: 'In Turkey I did not have the freedom to express my own identity ... But I can say "I am Kurdish" here ... '.

Alevi[21] Kurdish women, on the other hand, reclaim their identities through some figures associated with leftist politics in Turkey.[22] For example, Zeliha, a 45-year-old *Alevi* woman, displays the photographs of Deniz Gezmis, the symbol of the radical leftist movement of the late 1960s, who was executed after the military coup of 1971. A reproduction of Gezmis's portrait, with a poem

6.2.
Postcard picturing Guney, next to others depicting the caliph Ali and his twelve disciples

on freedom written underneath, takes its place in Zeliha's living room next to a family photograph taken back in her home town; the same reproduction is also hung up above the threshold of the kitchen (Fig. 6.1). Apart from Gezmis, Yilmaz Guney, a famous actor and film director who became a political icon for the Kurdish population in Turkey after expressing the life conditions in Kurdish-populated areas of the country in his films, appears among the photographs of family members in the entrance hall of Zeliha's house. A small postcard picturing Guney is also displayed by Hayriye, another *Alevi* Kurdish woman, in her living room. This time, it is attached to the frame of a painting picturing a mountainous landscape, next to other similar paintings to which some postcards depicting the fourth caliph Ali and his twelve disciples, venerated by Turkey's *Alevi* community, are attached (Fig. 6.2). While these images, in Hayriye's terms, help her 'not to forget who [she is]', the paintings they are attached to remind her of landscapes of her home town – 'where [she comes] from'.

Apart from these visual emblems, a significant role is played by Med-TV in Kurdish women's recovery of their identity in their homes in London. A UK-based Kurdish television channel that broadcasts its programmes in Kurdish dialects and in Turkish, Med-TV has a target audience of Kurds living in Europe and the Kurdish areas of the Middle East. Although the Turkish government has brought pressure to bear on any country leasing airtime to Med-TV since it started regular broadcasting in 1995,[23] the channel continues to function to recreate the culture of an imaginary geography, the officially non-existent Kurdistan, in the domestic homes of those displaced from their geographical territories. This virtual home, named as 'Kurdistan in the Sky'[24] by the Kurdish diaspora population, has an enormous significance for Kurdish women in London. For Basak, for instance, Med-TV is another symbol of the freedom of expression she has in England: 'Here I can freely say "I am Kurdish", I am free to speak my language, and I am free to watch the Kurdish television ... ' Another young Kurdish woman, Hatice, mentions that thanks to Med-TV she can hear her mother tongue spoken away from home. For Hayriye, on the other hand, Med-TV is important because it brings distant but familiar images and sounds to her home in London: 'When they show Kurdish people and Kurdish villages, that's when I like watching it most ... Those images and sounds take me back to my home town.'

However, while they construct connections between their homes in London and their homelands via the diaspora television, the majority of these Kurdish women have little contact with the public sphere beyond their houses. For them, the reason is their lack of proficiency in English, recalling Adorno's argument that 'every language draws a circle around the people to which it belongs, a circle from which [one] can only escape in so far as one at the same time enters another one'.[25] Their homes are also the centre of their social life, which mainly consists of regular gatherings with their relatives and some Kurdish neighbours. During these gatherings, they cook their traditional food, listen to Kurdish and Turkish music, and perform folkloric dances if it is a special day. The small community of these gatherings provides them with a sense of continuity and familiarity they are unable to attain in the public sphere.

A sense of continuity can also be read between Kurdish women's home biographies and the ways they inhabit the spaces of their homes in London, in a way that explains what Bourdieu calls the 'habitus'[26] – a consistent amalgam of practices that links habits with dwelling. With their habitual practices, Kurdish women unconsciously transform architectural space to deal with the discrepancy between their own notions of a proper home and available state housing. Most striking is their use of spaces in a multi-functional way. For instance, many of them have their meals on cloths they spread on the floor in their living rooms, like they used to do back home. Although in some cases this is a necessity resulting from the lack of space in council houses and flats to place a dining table, they mention they enjoy having their meals in this way, and that sometimes this daily practice brings back the memories of their homes in Turkey. Likewise, other habitual practices such as preparing food or sleeping in living rooms, or entertaining friends in kitchens, transgress the strict functional separation of spaces in their council homes.

This ceases to be surprising, however, when the Kurdish women tell about their old houses, where in some cases core spaces brought together activities as diverse as cooking and sleeping. For instance, Zeliha comes from a south-east Turkish town where a core space in each house incorporated a variety of functions at different times of the day. Interestingly, this space was commonly named as *'ev'* (the house), differentiating it from the other domestic spaces. But what is more interesting is that Zeliha's family use the kitchen in their house in London in a similar way. The kitchen is the most public space of their house, where the family spend most of their time, and entertain their close friends and relatives. It is also the most embellished space, with flowers and ornamental objects on shelves, a photograph of Zeliha's village adorning the refrigerator, and a television and stereo set placed on the work surface. However, the transformations of domestic spaces that Kurdish women perform are not only limited with the introduction of their own ways of using space into their council dwellings. At times, these take the form of physical changes that are strictly forbidden by councils. Such is the case of Basak, who has transformed the front porch of her maisonette into a private outdoor space by closing it with a wooden fence (Fig. 6.3). Although this space cannot satisfy her longing for a garden like the one she had in Turkey, it still accommodates a variety of functions from leisure to drying clothes. On the other hand, it introduces Basak's own interpretation of the physical boundary between the private and the public, creating a threshold space between the entrance to her home and the public pathway serving the housing estate. In other Kurdish women's homes, this boundary is defined by taking shoes off before entering the house – a rule of the 'habitus', to use Bourdieu's terminology. Shoe cases or shoes aligned carefully on small rugs, sometimes in narrow entrance halls that were clearly not designed for such a practice, and sometimes outside the entrance door, welcome the visitors with a special texture that reminds them that they are at the threshold of a Muslim family's home-place.

Apart from these practices, which are literally translated from the old houses to the new ones, objects that are carried help in forming material and emotional links between these two sites, around which Kurdish women re-create a sense of home. These are mostly photographs of family members, and things that are products of their mothers' or sisters' hand-labour such as lace cloths, hand-woven objects like bags, small rugs and pillowcases, used to decorate the walls and sofas, and to create familiar sitting arrangements at the corners of living rooms, popularly called *'sark kosesi'* (eastern corners) (Fig. 6.4). Lace cloths are used on coffee tables, in display cabinets, and, interestingly, on televisions, videos and stereo sets, giving the impression that Kurdish women need to domesticate and personalize these things. Family photographs usually take their places in display cabinets among knick-knacks, or around television and stereo sets making them the crowning parts of living rooms. When asked about what else they would carry from their old houses if they could,

Kurdish women's answers are similar: things that are peculiar to the material culture of domesticity in their homelands, not only to keep a particular tradition alive, but also to remember and honour the people who produce them. In this sense, things that link their old and new homes also link their past and present, and help them to recover a sense of belonging to the social communities they left behind.

However, this does not mean that their homes are the settings of a continuing nostalgia that is commonly associated with displaced people. As Gillis argues, constructing links with the past is one of the ways one generates the hope and energy necessary to struggle for a better future.[27] For Kurdish women the past is not an end in itself – it is not 'mere nostalgia' for a 'home to return to', a nostalgia that 'closes one off from the living spontaneity of the present and denies the possibility of a future'.[28] Their attachment to their new homes in London, the investments they have made and continue to make in these spaces, is an evidence for this. Since the very first day they moved to their new dwellings, these Kurdish women have engaged in a project of creating better living conditions than they had in their homelands, a project where the past has been a constant source of reference. Hence it is possible to understand the sense of pride they communicate when they tell about the changes they have made in their homes – such as covering the floors with parquet flooring materials, changing wallpapers on a regular basis, or renewing pieces of furniture the councils had provided before they moved in. For instance, Nazli, who recently painted her living room a bright orange and bought two beige leather sofas and new curtains matching the overall colour scheme, believes that her new, 'modern' decoration is the evidence of the change she has gone through since she came to London. Such a 'modern' interior, which consists of

6.3
The front porch of Basak's maisonette

6.4
'Sark kosesi' in Hayriye's living room

'a comfortable atmosphere with matching colours' in Hatice's terms, is also what other young Kurdish women aspire for; however, financial difficulties mean it has to be a long-term project. Still, the partial changes they have made so far shows that now they prefer plain, less-ornamented surfaces, paintings on the walls rather than photographs of family members, and that artificial flowers will soon replace their plants. Nazli argues that these changes are both natural and necessary as part of a new life in London. Basak, on the other hand, comments with reference to the way she thinks of her identity:

> This is the house of a Kurdish family. Naturally, things that you see around tell you that a Kurdish family lives here. But this is not a typical Kurdish house ... Because it takes its identity from my identity, and I am, to be realistic, both Kurdish and Turkish at the same time – I come from a Kurdish family, but I grew up among Turkish people ... And I have been living here [in England] for a long time now ... There are things I have taken from all these cultures ... There are no limits to my identity, and probably this is somehow clear in this house ...

Migrant homes

Basak's remarks on the hybrid nature of her identity as reflected in her home-place in London show neither that identities can be territorialized within a particular geography, nor that homes are stable, fixed entities. As it is clear in the above analysis of Kurdish women's home-making practices, domestic space plays a crucial role in their struggle with displacement – in mending a broken link with their cultures, their pasts and their homelands. However, it is also clear that for them home is not only about recovering a sense of continuity and stability, and reviving their 'roots', but also about expressing the changes they have experienced through their displacement and resettlement. The 'art' in their dwelling practices is grounded in this simultaneous existence of a search for stability, and a desire for, and acknowledgement of, change; and in their ability to create a sense of home in the space that exists between loss and recuperation. It is in this sense that I choose to call Kurdish women's home-places as 'migrant homes' – a term that challenges not only conventional Western conceptions of home that prioritize stability and permanence over displacement and change, but also renders groundless recent conceptualizations of 'migrancy' as 'homelessness'. As for the contemporary concerns about a universal sense of homelessness and alienation, I suggest that they remain purely abstract when one finds ways to understand the practices of home-making in the ordinariness of everyday lives and spaces.

Notes

1 This study is part of my doctoral dissertation entitled *Migrant Homes: Identity and Cultures of Domestic Space among Kurdish and Turkish Women in North London*. The material that I present here is a partial outcome of the fieldwork I conducted between September 2000 and April 2002.

2 S. Weil, *The Need for Roots*, London: Routledge, 2002, p.43.

3 Ibid., p.157.

4 M. Heidegger, quoted in D. Harvey, *Justice, Nature and the Geography of Difference*, Oxford: Blackwell, 1996, p.301.

5 M. Heidegger, *Poetry, Language, Thought*, New York: Harper and Row, 1971, p.146.

6 G. Bachelard, *The Poetics of Space*, Boston: Beacon Press, 1994, p.8.

7 E. Relph, *Place and Placelessness*, London: Pion, 1976.

8 L. Malkki, 'National Geographic: the rooting of peoples and the territorialization of national identity among scholars and refugees', in A. Gupta and J. Ferguson (eds), *Culture, Power, Place*, Durham: Duke University Press, 1997, pp. 52–74, p.62.

9 E. Casey, *Getting Back into Place*, Bloomington: Indiana University Press, 1993, p.307.

10 S. Birkerts, quoted in ibid., p.37.

11 Y.F. Tuan, 'Rootedness versus sense of place', *Landscape*, 1980, no.25, 3–8, p.6.

12 Malkki, 'National Geographic', pp.61–2.

13 For a broader discussion on these arguments, see D. Massey, 'A place called home?', *New Formations*, 1992, vol.17, pp.3–15.

14 T. Minh-ha, 'Other than myself/my other self', in G. Robertson *et al.* (eds), *Travellers' Tales*, London: Routledge, 1994, pp.9–26.

15 Casey, *Getting Back into Place*, p.38.
16 I. Chambers, *Migrancy Culture Identity*, London: Routledge, 1994.
17 N. Rapport and A. Dawson, 'The topic and the book', in N. Rapport and A. Dawson (eds), *Migrants of Identity*, Oxford: Berg, 1998, pp.3–18, p.9.
18 Harvey, *Justice, Nature and the Geography of Difference*, p.301.
19 See A. Icduygu, D. Romano and I. Sirkeci, 'The ethnic question in an environment of insecurity: the Kurds in Turkey', *Ethnic and Racial Studies*, 1999, vol.22, no.6, 991–1010 for a broader discussion of the so-called 'Kurdish problem' in Turkey.
20 Ibid., p.1003.
21 The term *Alevi* stands for the Shia Muslim population in Turkey.
22 The majority of the *Alevi* community in Turkey support radical leftist politics.
23 P. Feuilherade, 'Med TV: "Kurdistan in the sky"', *World Media Watch* at www.bbc.co.uk, 23 March 1999.
24 Ibid.
25 T. Adorno quoted in D. Morley, *Home Territories*, London: Routledge, 2000.
26 See P. Bourdieu, *Outline of a Theory of Practice*, Cambridge: Cambridge University Press, 1977; and P. Bourdieu, *Distinction*, Cambridge MA: Harvard University Press, 1984.
27 J.R. Gillis, *A World of Their Own Making*, Oxford: Oxford University Press, 1997.
28 Ibid., p.5.

Chapter 7

Communities of dread

Simon Richards

Architecture and urbanism are more deeply involved in constructing selves than they are in constructing place, and it is imperative to scrutinize the intellectual heritage of the concepts of self that are implicit to them. In this essay I will explore this claim in two sections. First, I will introduce what I mean by 'concepts of self' and explain the reasoning behind this approach.[1] Secondly, I will apply it to community architecture.

Concepts of self

Throughout history, people have attempted to come to an understanding of what it is to be a human being. This has involved determining the qualities that must be present, or the processes that must be at work, for the individual to attain a meaningful sense of self-identity or self-knowledge. The debate has been vigorous and has occupied the attention of theologians, philosophers, sociologists, psychologists and others.

By 'concepts of self' I refer to the various positions in this immense body of thought. These positions differ radically and so does the terminology. The blanket-term 'self', however, has a broader history than certain other terms and is more widely applicable. These other terms, such as 'agent', 'identity', 'character' or 'subject', tend to be more firmly rooted in the historical and ideological circumstances from which they emerged.[2]

Two paradigms have dominated this body of thought.[3] The main ideas can be generalized as 'the self-sufficient self' and 'the self/other self'. Within the idea of *the self-sufficient self*, the self is a transcendental entity with a mental or spiritual nature that is capable of being perfected or brought under control. It should not allow itself to be affected by the events that occur around it in the external environment. Consequently the body and the information gathered through the senses are not constitutive of the self. Individual experience may be unimportant, even undesirable, with all selves tending towards an ideal uniformity. Alternatively, intense soul-searching may result in a violently unique sense of individuality. René Descartes and Plato are among the key figures in this category.

On the other hand, within the idea of *the self/other self*, the self is a fluid process upheld in a complex interchange of social, cultural and linguistic processes. It is embodied and therefore continually affected through the senses by the events that occur 'around' it. In fact, it is not considered possible to conceive the self separately from its external environment and the experiences it has there. Individual experience and community interaction may become fundamental, allowing for the formation of different identities. Alternatively, the environment may have a more controlling, coercive or destabilizing effect on the self. John Locke and David Hume are the seminal figures in this category, which has dominated opinion throughout the past two centuries.

The common denominator in all the countless positions is that the self is influenced by its 'environment'. Obviously we have to take the term 'environment' in the broadest sense, referring not only to its built fabric but also to its social dynamics. Most important for us, however, is that this 'equation' is reversible: architectural and urban theories are indebted to concepts of self and make assumptions about human being and behaviour accordingly. These theories always incline towards one or the other of the aforementioned paradigms.

How do these concepts manifest themselves? Most often they are unacknowledged and implicit, and can be glimpsed only vaguely. However, some designers admit that a particular concept of self holds a central role in their thinking, although this is rare. But a third manifestation is more alarming. In order to get a proposal accepted a powerful lever is required. It is therefore common practice for designers to remark upon how existing environmental conditions represent a 'human crisis'. The proposed intervention is forwarded as a way to bring these humans to a more desirable state. Invariably, the question of what human beings 'are' and what they 'need' is broached in a shallow manner for opportunistic ends.

The reason for trying to uncover these concepts is twofold: first, it allows us to gain a better understanding of some of the deepest motives of environmental design; second, it allows us to initiate a critique.[4] I will apply this now to aspects of the community architecture movement that has flourished since the middle of the twentieth century.

'Land of the Twee'

Demands for a community-oriented approach to the built environment came to the fore in the 1950s. It was felt that 'real' life was being destroyed by bureaucracy, consumerism, urban sprawl and high-rise. Attempts were made to involve people in the regeneration of their neighbourhoods and to create environmental forms that inspired and sustained this involvement. But the concept of 'community' is vague and no one is rushing to clarify it. This may be deliberate. As the political theorist Adrian Little observes, ' ... it is perhaps the lack of conceptual clarity around community that has made it such an attractive tool for politicians, theorists and policy makers'. Therefore we must ' ... ask its advocates to stop providing answers and to start recognising the questions'.[5]

When contemporary architects and urbanists use the term 'community' they seem to be indicating some ideal of living. But in order to get a clearer grasp of the issues at stake we need to reconstruct the intellectual milieu from which this movement emerged. We will look in detail at some of the dominant theories from the American scene and then summarize the points they hold in common.

The sociologist David Riesman explored 'social character' in *The Lonely Crowd* of 1950: '"Social character" is that part of "character" that is shared among significant social groups'.[6] It was also a 'mode of conformity', circumscribing the behaviour required by a particular society in order for it to function.[7] But Riesman was especially interested in the 'other-directed' type of social character: the sophisticates of modern urban America. These were the 'prodigals' committed to consuming the massive surpluses and leisure of a post-industrial society. But now, with the material necessities of life ensured, '*other people* are the problem'. Conformity to public opinion became paramount, and as this fluctuated rapidly the other-directed type exhibited 'an exceptional sensitivity to the actions and wishes of others'. They craved 'adjustment'. The 'peer-group and its mass-media organs' helped maintain good relations.[8]

Riesman's central concern, however, was for the development of 'a more autonomous type of social character'. But as the 'shadowy entanglements' of democratic society seemed so reasonable, the turn to autonomy 'is never an all-or-nothing affair'. Instead, it involved cultivating a 'heightened self-consciousness' within an ever-expanding middle class: 'The presence of the guiding and approving "others" is a vital element in his whole system of conformity and self-justification ... if the other-directed man is seeking autonomy, he cannot achieve it alone'. Nonetheless, Riesman objected to the peer-group of one's class, race or 'happenstance neighbourhood', which demanded unthinking conformity from the individual. Although sociability remained fundamental to the achievement of autonomy, then, we must resist the 'overpersonalized society'.[9]

But what did this have to do with housing and community? One of the major obstacles to his type of autonomy, Riesman maintained, were 'neotraditionalists' and city planners railing against 'urban anomie'. These people cultivated sophisticated tastes and travelled widely, yet decried the fact that ordinary people moved house every few years. They would prefer to 'freeze [them] into communities in which friendship will be based largely on propinquity … Here we find the classes attempting to force "roots" upon the masses'.[10] But some went further and maintained that 'enforced hardship' and 'catastrophe' were 'the only practicable source of group cohesion and individual strength of character'. This was a 'frontier' or 'war' mentality, which they sought to 'restore artificially'. But as Riesman brilliantly observed: 'The dispiriting sequel is familiar: the community, its major problems of sheer existence surmounted, became less interesting to live in, its cooperative store, built by so much energetic and ingenious effort, folded up.' When the threat was over, the community evaporated. The yearning for a fixed home was therefore pure nostalgia. Economic circumstances, together with the need to cultivate autonomy, 'means that no one can ever settle down assuredly for the rest of life'. Trailer parks and 'Buckminster Fuller-type houses' pointed the way forward.[11]

Another influential book was Vance Packard's *The Hidden Persuaders* of 1957, which explored the methods and ethics of 'Motivational Research'. Motivational Research was a branch of psychology developed in tandem with commercial firms and advertising agencies that sought to manipulate consumer need by appealing to subconscious desire. One of the most effective ways they did this was to give their products 'personalities' that sought out the prospective buyer by appealing to his or her narcissistic 'self-image'. The Marlboro Man was a brilliantly successful example. But also high on Packard's list of 'insidious' examples were the new model suburbs: 'A vast development of homes going up in Miramar, Florida, is being called the world's most perfect community by its backers.' Its advocates publicized this as an emerging 'trend to "packaged" homes in "packaged" communities', and celebrated the 'regimented recreation' of neighbours who pestered one to get involved in bridge clubs, literary teas and fish breeding.

Packard considered this a 'portentous' development, the 'ultimate' vindication of Riesman's thesis against 'other-mindedness' and 'group-living': 'Miramar … may also package your social life for you … friendship is being merchandised along with real estate, all in one glossy package'. The packaged community catered to the 'packaged soul': 'The most serious offence many of the depth manipulators commit … is that they try to invade the privacy of our minds'.[12]

Two other urban sociologists were more willing to endorse the benefits of 'community', but these endorsements were never unconditional.

In *The Urban Villagers* of 1962, Herbert Gans clarified the ways the 'peer-group' differed from the 'community'. Gans focused on an Italian-American neighbourhood in Boston's West End, taking it as representative of lower-class subcultures generally, and described the peer-group as a 'relatively unchanging' mix of family and close friends: 'Recruitment is not deliberate … self-conscious "mixing with people" is explicitly rejected.' The peer-group allowed for the exchange of gossip and reportage, which held the group together without the need for formal community networks and institutions. This also worked as a means of censure and control over the individuals within it, although the compatibility of 'background, interests, and attitudes' meant there was limited scope for deviancy or disagreement. In fact, 'contentious' or 'substantive' topics were consciously avoided: 'the subject is changed in order to maintain the relationship on an even keel'.

But the peer-group was not a 'cohesive and tightly-knit' entity, because its main purpose was 'to provide its members with an opportunity for displaying, expressing, and acting out their individuality'. It was acknowledged within the peer-group that everyone had the right to 'show themselves off' in this way, but even so it created a 'basic paradox': 'this group cannot work together'.[13] Also, the peer-group member 'personalized' all human relations with 'concepts based on individual motivation and morality'. Community institutions and administrative procedure were therefore judged self-seeking, corrupt and exploitative. This made it impossible for the peer-group to recognize larger community issues, 'even when it concerns the very survival of the group', such as in urban 'redevelopment and relocation'.[14]

Gans urged planners and policy-makers not to demolish these neighbourhoods as 'failed' communities, or to try to transform them into 'successful' communities, but instead to recognize them as fragile subcultures with their own 'values' and 'behaviour patterns'. Community, for Gans, was a 'social' rather than a 'spatial' phenomenon. It had little to do with 'an aggregate of people who occupy a common and bounded territory'. The exclusionary nature of the peer-group meant that 'propinquity' did not always breed closeness and cooperation, but 'also might reveal differences in background and behavior that preclude friendship'.[15]

Finally, we need to consider William H. Whyte's *The Organization Man* of 1956. Whyte investigated the new 'social ethic', 'that contemporary body of thought which makes morally legitimate the pressures of society against the individual'. This particular social ethic involved the application of science to achieve 'group-mindedness' and 'belonging'.

Whyte traced this to the 'human relations' school of industrial sociology, which was developed to achieve equilibrium in the workplace. The union and corporation had become the basis of our 'adaptive society', and conflict was now condemned as 'sickness' or the result of a 'breakdown in communication'. The central tenet was as follows: 'Man exists as a unit of society. Of himself, he is isolated, meaningless; only as he collaborates with others does he become worth while.'[16] But this compromised the 'autonomy' of the individual. Strife and discord should be 'respected' for 'the function they perform in the maintenance of individual freedom'. Whyte argued therefore for a movement away from group-mindedness, although not to the degree of 'nonconformity' or 'antagonism'. Instead, we must seek the 'elusive middle road' of 'individualism *within* organization life'. But there was a difficulty: group life seemed so 'beneficent' that the move towards individuality was 'excruciatingly difficult' to justify.[17]

Whyte was not entirely critical of the new social ethic, however: 'there is a real moral imperative behind it'. This was best exemplified by the 'new suburbia' and 'packaged villages', for although they were not 'typical communities' they did provide a 'new kind of rootedness' to counter the 'transiency' of organization life.[18]

The explanation was as follows: the need for a career forced people to leave their homes, and thus they were pitied 'as symptoms of malaise, psychological casualties'. But, increasingly, routine relocations would be considered a 'positive good' in creating the 'well-rounded' individual. In order to make this mobility as smooth as possible the built landscape of America would have to become more and more uniform and unremarkable. This was 'at once unsettling and encouraging'. The lives of these 'young suburbanites' were subject to considerable anxiety, but to root them in lovely places was no longer economically viable. It was better to encourage them to come to terms with uncertainty and change, for it 'bespeaks a considerable faith in the capacities of the individual'.[19]

Whyte maintained that people were initially attracted to the new suburban developments because they represented good value for money. In fact, they were repulsed by having so many near neighbours – 'so much propinquity'. It was only later that a special kind of community began to take shape, and later still before advertising men and architects seized on this and started selling 'belonging' and 'happiness' – homes rather than houses. Nonetheless, participation in the affairs of the community was real and disproportionately high, albeit odd: 'They hate it and they love it. Sometimes it seems as if they are drawn to the participation just for participation's sake ... Nor are meetings necessarily directed to any substantive purpose.' This participation replaced the old roots, a 'complex of geographical and family ties'. The 'new roots' of suburbia were shallow in order to facilitate easy 'transplanting', but 'even shallow roots, if there are enough of them, can give a great deal of support'. Whyte also noted, however, that the community evaporates when its crises have been resolved: 'Because the emergency pressures have vanished, the emergency spirit has too ... without the stimulus of necessity most people can take issues or leave them alone'.[20]

These summaries give us an indication of the richness of the debate about community at this time. Several key opinions emerged and persisted. First, there was scepticism about the way developers sought to package community along with suburbs as a value-added extra. Second, community was thought to coalesce only as a response to a particular crisis: once resolved, the community dispersed. Third, 'propinquity' was thought to breed as much contempt as neighbourly feeling. Fourth, there was an acknowledgment that mobility may be the inescapable condition for modern people. Fifth, issues of class were admitted as central: the 'peer group' was inimical with the 'community'. Sixth, too much community was believed to compromise the autonomy of the individual, but as the 'others' seemed so well-meaning it was difficult to break away.

Architects and urbanists began engaging with issues of community at around this time, but they turned for direction to Jane Jacobs' classic book of 1961, *The Death and Life of Great American Cities*. Although Jacobs was scathing about the suburbs, her proposals have been applied to the regeneration of city and suburb alike. But what made her arguments more attractive than those of Riesman, Packard, Gans and Whyte, which were very well known? Jacobs' approach to community was unproblematic and her proposals were easy to visualize. This stood in stark contrast to the circumspection and inconclusiveness of the other arguments.

Jacobs believed inner-city life to be a fragile ecosystem that could survive only the gentlest planning interventions, and proposed four 'generators of diversity' that would foment an interesting, safe and trusting street culture. The generators were as follows: mixed uses, short blocks, buildings of various ages, and a dense concentration of people. Ideally, these measures would root people into their neighbourhoods indefinitely.

Two benefits would emerge from this. First: informal political communities versatile enough to defend their interests not only against ordinary criminals, but also against a 'City Hall' committed to bulldozing their neighbourhoods. Cities may have 'difficulties in abundance', then, but they also 'have marvellous innate abilities for understanding, communicating, contriving, and inventing what is required to combat their difficulties'. The properly functioning city is a machine for resolving crises. The second benefit concerns 'human beings'. Life, for Jacobs, was made meaningful in this collective struggle for survival. Indeed, it was only through community relationships that people seemed to exist at all. 'Impersonal city streets make anonymous people', she said, whereas a street rich in 'tangible enterprises' gives them 'identity'. Also, 'real people' were not the 'statistical people' of the planning authorities: 'Real people are unique, they invest years of their lives in significant relationships with other unique people, and are not interchangeable in the least. Severed from their relationships, they are destroyed as effective social beings.'[21]

In short, Jacobs provided a clear programme whereas the others agonized over problems, but this meant she had to overlook most of the key issues.

The only one she addressed was that of the community evaporating once it had resolved its crisis: communities, she said, were in a state of *perpetual* crisis.[22] Her argument was not the expression of consensus. Nonetheless, many architects and urbanists use it as such to justify their faith in the benefits of community to individual well-being. And nowadays the rhetoric of crisis is indulged to such a degree that the 'Land of the Twee' is often saturated with dread.[23]

The most powerful advocates of community architecture in recent years have been the 'Congress for the New Urbanism'. Formed in America in 1993, the Congress has provided an exhaustive series of proposals on how best to overhaul the environment from 'corridor' to 'region'. This will improve 'quality of life', it will reconcile man with his 'deeper self' and 'most natural behaviour'. 'Community' is the guarantor of all this.[24] Not once are these concepts or their interrelations explained or justified. Nonetheless, they are demanded as a matter of emergency. The following are some typical examples of New Urbanist thought, and they reinforce the general pattern.

Peter Calthorpe and William Fulton begin their discussion of 'Communities of Place' by referring to the Osaka–Kobe earthquake in 1995. The 'mixed and ramshackle' Mano district had more survivors than high-rise districts. Even so, communities 'are essential to our well-being – not just in times of crisis, but also in our everyday lives'. To 'heal' the 'damage' and achieve participation, we need to provide the 'social capital' that 'broadens people's sense of self from "I" to "we"'. The 'everywhere community' of internet chat-rooms and mail-order is a 'threat', however, for it makes us believe that meaningful relationships can be created in ways 'completely divorced' from physical place.[25]

Vincent Scully proclaims the 'subversion of community' to be 'cataclysmic', for 'It is within that model that human beings live; they need it badly, and if it breaks down they may well become insane'. The suburbs are 'spawning'-grounds for 'neuroses' and 'madness', while community provides 'psychic protection'. But what is community? It is the 'brotherhood of mankind'. Scully illustrates this with the fourteenth-century frescoes of Ambrogio Lorenzetti in Siena, the 'Allegories of Good and Bad Government'. It seems that this most fractious and war-torn of city-states was the ideal community, and Scully compares it favourably with Seaside, the pre-eminent 'image of community' in modern times.[26]

Others focus on those who allegedly brought about the crisis, such as the car and tyre manufacturers, oil producers, and road construction companies. These manipulated the American government on to a pro-sprawl footing. 'Evil' geniuses such as Frank Lloyd Wright and Le Corbusier inspired the enterprise by disregarding 'the needs of humanity for human contact'. Both were 'Oblivious of the way [their proposals] would isolate occupants in anonymity'.[27] The human cost of this is welfare dependence, depression, obesity, child abuse, and the horrors of single-parent families and half-relations. But Disneyland's

'Main St USA' resonates with something profoundly human within every decent citizen: 'an individual belongs to something larger than the self'.[28]

The simple pattern pioneered by Jacobs remains intact: first, we are in crisis but community will save us; second, the creation of community is predominantly a spatial problem to be addressed by designers. A reluctance to engage the issues more deeply means that New Urbanism runs aground on tautology: the loss of community is bad because it represents the loss of community.[29]

How did this situation come about? In the 1950s the Modernists of CIAM were coming under attack for the social alienation caused by high-rise development.[30] The new generation needed an agenda to replace the old and some found it in 'community'. It is understandable that, in the rush to find a rallying call, omissions and simplifications would occur. But as a warning we should note Adrian Little's attempt to define 'community'. Although a broad historical sweep can be discerned there are countless positions and consensus is destroyed. Little argues, therefore, that the concept of community is 'under-theorised': it requires sustained analysis before it can be used in a meaningful and responsible way.[31]

With this in mind I would like to make two concluding points. First, contemporary architects and urbanists have achieved their consensus by neglecting many important sources: Riesman, Packard, Gans and Whyte are only the beginning. Although their terms are now somewhat anachronistic I believe they still warrant consideration. It is for this reason that I have reintroduced them. Second, contemporary architects and urbanists give force to their proposals by making claims about what human beings 'are' and 'need', exactly as the Modernists did before them. It is advisable to take stock of these claims before further consolidating yet another orthodoxy, for if there is a 'crisis' in community it may eventually develop here.

Notes

1 This forms the basis of a research project that I am conducting with Professor Jules Lubbock at the University of Essex: 'Concepts in Self in the Theory and Practice of Architecture and Town-Planning since 1945'. The Arts and Humanities Research Board (AHRB) is funding this research, which is scheduled for completion in 2005. For a further introduction to this approach, see D. Cuff and R. Ellis (eds), *Architects' People*, New York: Oxford University Press, 1989.

2 A. Elliott, *Concepts of the Self*, Cambridge: Polity Press, 2001, pp.2–4, 9.

3 For an introduction to the main positions, see R. Porter (ed.), *Rewriting the Self: Histories from the Renaissance to the Present*, London: Routledge, 1997; S. Gallagher and J. Shear (eds), *Models of the Self*, Thorverton: Imprint Academic, 1999; P. du Gay *et al.* (eds), *Identity: A Reader*, London: Sage, 2000.

4 These concerns are explored in depth in S. Richards, *Le Corbusier and the Concept of Self*, New Haven and London: Yale, 2003.

5 A. Little, *The Politics of Community: Theory and Practice*, Edinburgh: Edinburgh University Press, 2002, pp.1, 6.

6 D. Riesman *et al.*, *The Lonely Crowd: A Study of the Changing American Character* [1950], New Haven: Yale, 1963, pp.3–4.
7 Ibid., pp.5–7.
8 Ibid., pp.9–36, 66–82, 256.
9 Ibid., pp.239–77, 290–9, 304–7
10 Ibid., p.278.
11 Ibid., pp.67–8, 295–7.
12 V. Packard, *The Hidden Persuaders* [1957], London: Penguin, 1981, pp.27–37, 45–53 190–6, 207–16.
13 H. Gans, *The Urban Villagers: Group and Class in the Life of Italian-Americans* [1962], New York: Free Press, 1982, pp.xiii–xv, 74–89, 94, 104–10.
14 Ibid., pp.77–8, 88–97.
15 Ibid., pp.xiv, 76, 104–10, 295–310.
16 W.H. Whyte, *The Organization Man*, New York: Doubleday Anchor, 1956, pp.6–8, 16–66.
17 Ibid., pp.9–15, 33–4, 51, 64–6.
18 Ibid., pp.6, 10–11.
19 Ibid., pp.295–309.
20 Ibid., pp.310–29.
21 J. Jacobs, *The Death and Life of Great American Cities* [1961], London: Penguin, 1994, pp.13–84, 122–251, 442–62.
22 Jacobs refers to Gans' studies of the West-End in Boston and to Whyte's 'peripatetic junior executives of suburbia', but neglects their main arguments: Ibid., pp.286, 301, 146–7, and note.
23 D. Campbell, 'Land of the Twee', *The Guardian*, 8 July 2002, pp.12–14.
24 M. Leccese and K. McCormick (eds), *Charter of The New Urbanism*, New York: McGraw-Hill, 2000, passim.
25 P. Calthorpe and W. Fulton, *The Regional City*, Washington: Island Press, 2001, pp.31–40.
26 V. Scully, 'The Architecture of Community', in P. Katz, *The New Urbanism: Toward an Architecture of Community*, New York: McGraw-Hill, 1994, pp.221–30. See also pp.2–17 for an account of Seaside, one of the flagship New Urbanist communities.
27 The dominant criticism of Le Corbusier is that his proposed city-schemes would have killed the life of the city. They would do this by eliminating the traditional street and granting only limited space for cafés, community centres, theatres and suchlike. The social life of the city would unravel. Conclusion: Le Corbusier is guilty of a terrible oversight. But Le Corbusier's antisocial urbanism was intentional, the product of a concept of self that was attributable to the Enlightenment philosopher Blaise Pascal. (Richards, *Le Corbusier and the Concept of Self.*)
28 R. Moe and C. Wilkie, *Changing Places: Rebuilding Community in the Age of Sprawl*, New York: Henry Holt, 1997, passim., esp. pp.36–74, 260; J.H. Kunstler, *The Geography of Nowhere: The Rise and Decline of America's Man-Made Landscape*, New York: Touchstone, 1993, passim.
29 Architects and urbanists occasionally refer to other community theorists but this seldom clarifies the picture: a pro-establishment 'communitarian' might be cited next to an 'anarchist'. (A. Etzioni, *The Spirit of Community: Rights, Responsibilities and the Communitarian Agenda* [1993], London: Fontana, 1995; R. Sennett, *The Uses of Disorder: Personal Identity and City Life* [1970], London: Faber & Faber, 1996.)
30 For the most comprehensive account of CIAM (Congrès Internationaux d'Architecture Moderne), see E. Mumford, *The CIAM Discourse on Urbanism, 1928–1960*, Cambridge MA: MIT Press, 2000.
31 Little, *The Politics of Community*, pp.7–28.

Chapter 8

Design in the city

Actors and contexts

Ali Madanipour

Designers working in an urban context can suddenly become major actors posed with a challenge that can be both daunting and rewarding. The city is an agglomeration of living organisms and objects, come together in an historical process, creating a rich tapestry of meanings and possibilities. Any intervention in the city is an intervention in a multitude of layers of meaning, which can have the desired effect for some parties but can also have unintended consequences for them or undesirable effects for others. How do the designers approach this complex context? Do they leave this complexity as incomprehensible, irrelevant or beyond the scope of their work, focusing entirely on what can be done on a single site? Or do they try to take into account a broader context, with the complexity of meaning and significance that such breadth entails? Designers may feel confident about knowing their own actions, but how do they make sense of the city if they are to meet this serious challenge of intervention in what appears to be no more than a tangled web of complex issues?

This chapter seeks to make sense of this complexity by envisioning design in the city as an interaction between an actor and a number of frameworks that constitute the urban context. To do this, the chapter focuses on three separate but interrelated aspects of this interaction: actor, action and context. By exploring each of these aspects, the aim is to find a clearer understanding of the complexity of the design in the city.

The interaction between actors and contexts, or in other words between agencies and structures,[1] between habitus and field,[2] ultimately shapes the outcome of any such action in the city. This is, more generally, a relationship between individual and society, which is a key area of concern in social philosophy.[3] In all these interpretations, the debate is about the primacy of one or the other and about the tensions between the two. This is reflected in the paradigms at the heart of many academic disciplines. For example, philosophy, psychology and economics appear to emphasize the individual, while sociology and human geography rely more on the society as the basis of their understanding of the world. In arts, this is reflected in isolationism as distinctive from contextualism,[4] and in politics in the distinction between libertarians and communitarians.[5] In city design, this distinction is often reflected in the private and the public spheres, where freedom to exclude others is distinctive from being at the presence of strangers.[6] What needs to be emphasized, however, is the need to to see how an interaction is at work between the actor and the context in all these areas, rather than an unrealistic emphasis on one at the cost of disregarding the other.

Design as action

An interpretation of design as an action would require an analysis of its nature and dimensions. Some have regarded design as a subjective, irrational intervention. It is seen as a reflection of the subjectivity of a person and as such its qualities are mainly regarded as being personal. Others see design, especially city design, where many other actors are involved, as an objective rational intervention. Indeed design emerged after the medieval period as a rational activity, a careful use of designers' best efforts to predetermine the qualities of a product. With the rise of scientific rationalism, design was seen as a true reflection of order and reason, as famously announced by Descartes.[7] Some may see design, therefore, as an instrumental action, to mobilize the available resources to achieve a certain end. Yet it also is a meaningful action, through which expression and communication among people take place. It is a creative process, in which new ideas emerge as a result of interaction with a range of ideas, people and places.[8] Despite the parameters that define and limit the action, it is an expression of freedom for individuals, who can engage in making these connections and create new configurations.

The nature of action can also be characterized by its purpose, its place in the overall city building process, and its spatial scale. Is design in the city an exercise in visual transformation, in spatial (re)organization, in functional change, in social change, in economic gain, in seeking political legitimacy, or all of these purposes at the same time? Its purpose both defines its nature and sets a context for the designer to operate within. Where can design be placed in city building? Is it an isolated activity or is it an integral part of the development process, which also includes planning, development, management and use? Is design only able to focus on the small scale of a single site, or the spaces between buildings, or neighbourhoods and large parts of the city, or the entire urban region, or all the above? These defining features are other contextual frameworks in which action takes place.[9]

Design, therefore, is an action, or indeed an interaction, between the actor, whose subjectivity is formed by his/her place in social space,[10] and the urban environment, which is a material world of people, objects and events.

Designer as actor

The nature of actors can be studied at two levels: individual and institutional. Designer as actor can be seen as an individual engaged in free expression, in creative action, which is expected to be least disrupted and constrained by others. A designer may also work as a member of a team, and as such be engaged in a creative dialogue. Some designers see themselves as socially and environmentally concerned citizens, while others see their role as that of a professional hired by a client, unable to influence the course of events beyond a certain level. The place of the designer as an individual, therefore, becomes a framing context.

When they are part of organizations, which they are in many circumstances, the internal relations within the institution, its relations with other institutions, and its location in the development process become key issues. Here the institutional dynamics become a context for the actor.

The institutional actors that work within the urban context are complex, with changing natures, attitudes, and foci of action. One major change in the nature of actors is their changing relationship with the place in which they intervene. Designers and developers at one time were inevitably based in a locality. Local elites were acting as patrons of city building, not only for return on their investment but also for symbolic reasons, gaining prestige and inviting the respect of their fellow citizens. Architects and town planners were also based in the locality, developing regional styles or adapting national and international trends to the locality, using local building materials and labour. If there were a need to borrow money, the local bank would independently decide whether or not to fund the project.

All aspects of this relationship with place have now changed. Developers, construction companies, architects and town planners can be large-scale organizations based anywhere in the world, without the possibility of emotional or symbolic attachment to the place. Banks may be branches of national and international corporations and investors may be mere shareholders in an enterprise, not even knowing or caring where their money is being invested. All this creates actors with a cold detachment from the place and from the local people's needs and wishes.

As development companies have grown larger and have used new technologies, the size and nature of their developments have changed.[11] While the city was once developed site by site by different architects, builders and developers, now large parts of the city can be developed by one agency, as companies can assemble many sites and employ large amounts of money to acquire expertise, technology and labour. As the gap between exchange and use values increases, the development industry relies more and more on standardization of designs, using pattern books and/or open, flexible plans that can be used for various purposes.

As developers have access to massive productive capacities, they can build entire new towns in only a few years. New technologies, as tools of action, have worked alongside the changing organization and nature of actors in the city. The impacts of technology on urban form are well known: how trains helped create cities of the nineteenth century by making it easier for people to be freed from the countryside; how lifts made it possible to build high-rise buildings; how cars helped the growth of cities and suburbs; and how telecommunication technologies, from telegraph to the Internet, have helped change the spatial pattern of cities, spreading in all directions while agglomerating in new forms and places, such as at the nodes of new infrastructure networks. At the same time, the nature of expertise has changed. As professions, such as architecture, grew as autonomous territories, separated from laypersons by institutions and symbolic barriers, the tasks of city building became more and more professionalized, kept within the realm of technical experts. Specialization of professions has created subdivisions each associated with different scales of urban space, from landscape architects to town planners. But the unintended consequences of the experts' actions[12] have led to environmental crisis, as exemplified by inappropriate housing schemes and the disastrous, car-driven redevelopment of cities. There has emerged a crisis of confidence in the experts, who are expected to be more accountable to the public and to take social and environmental concerns into account in their work.

As a result of these changes in the nature of actors, the mode of intervention and the shape of the city have changed: from a fine grain of small-scale interventions, where the agencies were likely to be personally involved, to large-scale interventions by impersonal, distant professionals, creating larger-scale, more standardized environments that change at much faster cycles and whose unintended consequences of actions have caused much concern among citizens.

City as context

There is often a general distinction between social and physical, i.e. between people and objects. The agglomeration of people and their activities creates a social context, while the grouping of the objects creates a physical context in which design intervention takes place. The people who have come together to listen to a lecture, for example, constitute a social (albeit likely to be temporary) context. The room they gather in, with its walls, ceiling, doors, windows, lights, chairs, blackboard, etc. constitutes a physical (albeit small) context. The course of people's activities (in this case delivering and listening to the lecture) is directly influenced by the way these social and physical elements of a micro-context operate and relate to each other. We often do not separate the social and physical in our thinking about the world around us. Leon Battista Alberti, for example, in his discussion of the city kept the distinction between physical and social deliberately ambiguous, seeing them as closely intertwined.[13] The objects that constitute the built environment are, of course, ultimately made and interpreted by people. But for analytical clarity the two are often separated, as we treat them here.

The framework that appears to be most significant for designers is the aesthetic context of the city, how a new intervention treats the image and meaning of the city. But the complexity of the city goes beyond its aesthetic significance. Simultaneously, it is a vital node of economic activity, a meeting place catering for social needs, as well as an environment offering a variety of sensual and cultural experiences.

Design paradigms and how they change directly influence designers.[14] An architect is often responding to the aesthetic movements of the time, such as functionalism, neo-rationalism, etc. The response of designers working at the beginning, middle or end of an aesthetic movement, therefore, can be completely different from each other. But this is not the only framework for designers. The architect as the actor works within the framework of an urban fabric, which inspires, but also limits, what can or can't be done. Apart from aesthetic dimensions, this urban fabric works as a psychological framework of how we feel about a space and how multiple senses and bodily experiences react to a place.[15] It also has a spatial and functional framework of how a place is organized and used, a symbolic framework of how it has a meaning and value, and a temporal framework of how it has changed through historical time, and how it changes through the moments of day and year.

There are other frameworks too. The economic framework is first and foremost reflected in the relationship between the architect and client, which reflects the tense relationship between exchange value and use value; i.e. between how the market approaches the space of the city as a commodity and how people approach it as a meaningful, useful place. Wider economic contexts have a direct impact on how a city lives, such as the change from manufacturing industry to service economy and how the urban populations have increasingly become white-collar workers with different needs and expectations. Urban governance is another framework that is reflected in how and by whom decisions are made, and how public and private institutions try to shape the city by influencing the way it is developing.[16] The changing relationship between the public and private sphere, between the political and economic frameworks, suggests the need for constant awareness of shifting contexts and changing paradigms. Yet another framework is the constantly changing norms, behaviours, lifestyles and expectations of the different groups that make up the urban society. From the mass society of the industrial age to the individualized populations of the knowledge economy, the social context of the city has changed dramatically.[17]

The complexity of the city comes from the fact that these frameworks may all be at work at the same time in any one place and at any one moment. Furthermore, design is one stage in a series of actions which create the city, from planning and design to development, management and use, all involving a potentially large number of actors.

In the complex interplay of actors in the city, how can designers find their way? Is there only one correct expert view that should dominate? But we know that the experts may disagree and sometimes may not know all the possible outcomes. Is relativism the solution, then, accepting that everyone is right?[18] This cannot be the case, especially when the actors are in conflict. Can inter-subjective communication solve the problems? Here we may have the problem of imbalance of power, as different players in the process have different weights and influences. But it is ultimately from the interplay of the actors that the nature of action is determined.

Knowledge of the changing contexts and of the changing nature and role of actors is essential for the designers as one of the most important actors in the permanent process of creating cities. It is not possible for designer-as-citizen or designer-as-expert to be unaware of the contexts in which they work or the impact they potentially have on that context. Some may argue that knowing about this complexity is irrelevant to designers, who are engaged in a subjective, personal process of creativity, which might be stifled by too much attention to these unnecessary details, or that these frameworks are only conventions to be broken. While freedom of imagination is an absolute necessity for designers, a Quixotic approach may become counterproductive. Designers know that the design of the city is also a rational process, in which the means available are employed to achieve a certain, useful end, and to persuade others that this has been achieved successfully. Ignoring this and trying to mystify the design process does not take away its rational basis. Others may argue that the knowledge of these contexts may not be useful in practice, as designers are confined to their contractual obligations, which are often difficult to change. The limiting effect of contracts is of course felt in the design process, but designers, individually or collectively, can try to change its shape and contents, in the same way that they shape cities.

The frameworks and contexts do not determine the outcome of designers' efforts, as designers can be free to innovate and create new form. At the same time, designers are not entirely free to design in any way they wish, as they have to operate within complex sets of constraints, which range from the dominant aesthetic paradigm to the client's wishes and desires, from the value of land in the market to the changing nature of city management and changing lifestyles. It is from the interplay between these actions and contexts that the new forms are created and the city continues to evolve.

Notes

1 As Giddens might say. See A. Giddens, *The Constitution of Society: Outline of the Theory of Structuration*, Cambridge: Polity Press, 1984.

2 As Bourdieu might suggest. See P. Bourdieu, *Pascalian Meditations*, Cambridge: Polity Press, 2000.

3 N. Bobbio, *Liberalism and Democracy*, London: Verso, 1990.

4 This shows the tension between those who study the works of art in isolation with those who see it as a reflection of the environment in which the artist lives.

5 This is a tension between those who promote the expansion of individual freedoms as distinctive from those who see individuals as part of communities.

6 A. Madanipour, *Public and Private Spaces of the City*, London: Routledge, 2003.

7 See Descartes quoted, in E. Gellner, *Reason and Culture: The Historical Role of Rationality and Rationalism*, Oxford: Blackwell, 1992, or directly in his own *Discourse on Method and the Meditations*, London: Penguin, 1968, p.35.

8 See J. Habermas, *The Theory of Communicative Action*, London: Heinemann, 1984, for a broader analysis of communication and rationality.

9 For an extended analysis of the dimensions of city design see A. Madanipour, *Design of Urban Space*, Chichester: Wiley, 1996.

10 For a discussion on space in architecture see B. Tschumi, *Questions of Space*, London: Architectural Association, 1990; R. Scruton, *The Aesthetics of Architecture*, London: Methuen, 1979; or R. Krier, *Urban Space*, London: Academy Editions, 1975. For a discussion on social space see P. Bourdieu, *Pascalian Meditations*, Cambridge: Polity Press, 2000, and H. Lefebvre, *The Production of Space*, Oxford: Blackwell, 1991.

11 For an analysis of the changing nature of urban development and its impact on urban form, see J. Whitehand, *The Making of Urban Landscape*, Oxford: Blackwell, 1992.

12 A. Giddens, *The Consequences of Modernity*, Cambridge: Polity Press, 1990.

13 F. Borsi, *Leon Battista Alberti*, Phaidon, Oxford, 1977, p.13.

14 See A. Madanipour, *Design of Urban Space*, Chichester: Wiley, 1996.

15 See H. Lefebvre, *The Production of Space*, Oxford: Blackwell, 1991.

16 See A. Madanipour, A. Hull and P. Healey (eds), *The Governance of Place*, Aldershot: Ashgate, 2001.

17 See A. Madanipour, G. Cars and J. Allen (eds), *Social Exclusion in European Cities*, London: Jessica Kingsley/Routledge, 1998.

18 For a philosopher's argument against relativism, see J. Searle, *Mind, Language and Society: Philosophy in the Real World*, London: Weidenfeld & Nicolson, 1999.

Plate 4
Philosophy of place: *The Legend of the True Cross*; detail of the Annunciation. Piero della Francesca

Philosophy of place

Chapter 9

The professor's house

Martin Heidegger's house at Freiburg-im-Breisgau

Adam Sharr

The German thinker Martin Heidegger (1889–1976) remains a key figure in the philosophical history of 'place'.[1] His writing was influenced by a mountain hut built for his use in 1923 at Todtnauberg in the Black Forest. It was also related to another building made for the philosopher: a house 18 kilometres from the hut at Freiburg-im-Breisgau, the capital city of the Black Forest region. This paper describes and illustrates Heidegger's relationship with his city house, details of which have not been published before. It interprets Heidegger's relationship with the house in connection with his writings about 'dwelling' and 'place' and his engagement with the mountain hut. Heidegger sustained simultaneously quite different relationships with his house and hut – a disparity that contributes to an understanding of his philosophy and biography.

Heidegger's house still stands. The following account of the building is based upon the author's visit in May 1999 and an interview conducted on that occasion with the current occupant, Heidegger's granddaughter. Original architect's drawings were consulted in the preparation of the accompanying plans,[2] checked against photographs of the philosopher in residence.[3]

'Dwelling' and 'place'

Heidegger addressed issues of 'dwelling' and 'place' in a number of writings. Architects have found his work relevant to practice, among them Hans Scharoun, Christopher Alexander, Peter Zumthor and Steven Holl. Architectural critics such as Christian Norberg-Schulz, Kenneth Frampton and Hilde Heynen have addressed Heidegger's thought on 'place', as have many authors in this volume. The philosopher's work remains influential despite current debate over the extent of his early involvement with the Nazi regime in Germany.[4]

Heidegger's most explicit commentary on 'dwelling' and 'place' was given in 'Building Dwelling Thinking',[5] a paper first presented at a 1951 conference in Darmstadt attended by architects and engineers. He elaborated on this commentary in two contemporary papers, translated into English as 'The Thing' and '...poetically, Man dwells...'.[6] Heidegger favoured the notion of 'place' over that of 'space'. To him, 'place' described more accurately the situation of human existence. Particular 'places' remain bound with actions and routines of individuals who 'dwell' in them. For Heidegger, the physical structure of the world is understood as a matrix of 'places' configured by social and intellectual structures of their inhabitants. But this is also a reciprocal relationship. Human social and intellectual structures are determined by physical constraints of their specific situations. To Heidegger, 'place', known through the sensory engagement of a human mind with its situation, was more descriptively powerful than 'space', measured mathematically by dimension.

Finding authority in etymology, Heidegger suggested that 'building' and 'dwelling' remain one and the same. To him, they are the condition of an individual's existence in the world, rooted in 'places' of inhabitation. For Heidegger, eating was part of the same activity that sets places at a dining table, builds a room for the dining table and arranges the table in the room. This was not bookish philosophy but the demonstration of understanding configured physically through human experience. Heidegger suggested that 'places' are participants in rituals of everyday existence and human interrelationship. They report the presence of human life by accommodating and revealing necessities of subsistence, manifesting thoughtful experience. Heidegger felt that 'places' remain equal to words in their potential for philosophical expression.

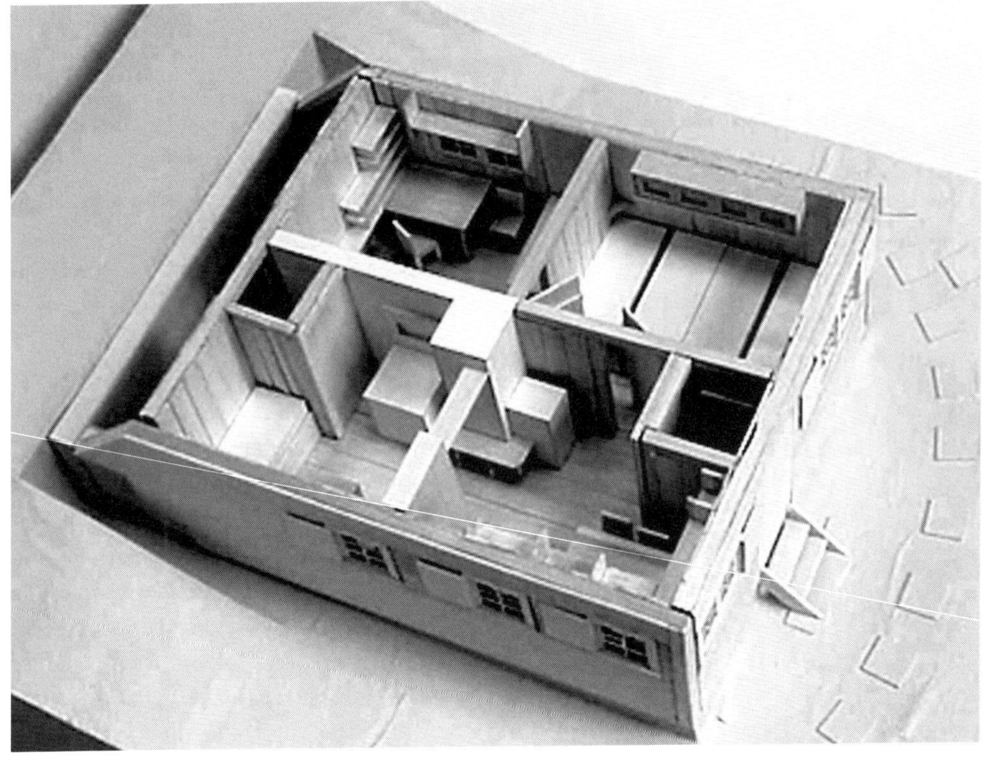

9.1
The author's model of Heidegger's Hut at Todtnauberg. The study is top left, bedroom top right and the *Vorraum* is below.

Heidegger's mountain hut

Heidegger's hut at Todtnauberg can be perceived as a physical manifestation of his writings about 'dwelling' and 'place'. The small timber-framed and clad structure was built in 1923 under the supervision of Elfride Heidegger, whom he married in 1917. It was intended as somewhere he could think and write. The intention appears to have been successful – he used the building many times during five subsequent decades.

The hut had three rooms: a bedroom, study, and *Vorraum* containing kitchen and dining areas (Fig. 9.1). It was built into a south-facing slope, surveying a distant view towards the Alps. The philosopher lived a routine of subsistence at the building, where he often stayed in solitude. There were few technological comforts and no mains services for many years.

In correspondence, Heidegger described life away from the hut as *unter* (literally, 'under' or 'down below'):

> I'm off to the cabin – and am looking forward a lot to the strong mountain air – this soft light stuff down here ruins one in the long run. Eight days lumbering – then again writing ... It's late night already – the storm is sweeping over the hill, the beams are creaking in the cabin, life lies pure, simple and great before the soul ... Sometimes I no longer understand that down there one can play such strange roles.[7]

Life at the hut was *über*: above, superior. Heidegger felt duty bound to respond to the mountains' challenge to philosophy there, writing in response to the reality of the terrain. He had an intense relationship with the building, the landscape and enveloping seasonal movements. His life there mixed concentrated philosophical work with walking, chopping logs, skiing, cooking, washing, eating, sleeping and – in younger days – occasionally assisting locals with forestry.

Heidegger's life at the hut was set out by activities of his routine in association with specific locations where they occurred. For example, meals were determined by the stoves and dining table; writing was configured by the desk in the study as related to the changing landscape beyond. Heidegger seems to have felt deeply an immediate relationship between life and such small 'places' for different purposes that it makes and occupies. In a number of writings, he acknowledged the debt that his work owed to particularities of the hut and its situation.[8]

The organization of Heidegger's hut appears significantly aligned with his philosophical writing.[9] Its basic comforts emphasized contact with the meteorological drama of the mountains, demanding immediate physical and intellectual contact with the world. Heidegger sensed his own transience there, considering his work to be one with the hut and its setting. Routines were rituals demarcating existence and experience, configuring his own 'building' and 'dwelling' in association with specifics of 'place' at a small scale. The hut set out physically Heidegger's relationship with the locality, the world and other people. It could be described as an acutely 'phenomenological' structure: offering opportunities for intellectual and emotional sustenance by framing the world around and prompting reflection.

Heidegger's city house and how it came to be built

As a professor of philosophy, Heidegger travelled to the mountains when time permitted but always maintained a residence in the city of his academy. From

1928 until 1971, that residence was a house at Zähringen on the edge of Freiburg-im-Breisgau.[10] The building was his formal residence for over four decades. Heidegger's life in Freiburg appears to have been rather different from that at Todtnauberg.

The building of the Freiburg house followed Heidegger's 1927 appointment to a chair in philosophy at his *alma mater*: Albert-Ludwig's University, Freiburg. This was a decisive year for the philosopher. His book *Being and Time* was published.[11] On the strength of that work, Edmund Husserl recommended Heidegger – then professor in Marburg – to the prestigious Freiburg chair upon his own retirement.[12] Hugo Ott describes Heidegger's return to Freiburg as almost triumphal, a reflection of his arrival in the first rank of German philosophers.[13] As a direct result of Heidegger's appointment, he and his family made arrangements to return to the Black Forest capital.

A building plot was found on the edge of Freiburg, alongside a country lane named Rötebuckweg that had been earmarked for suburban development. Heidegger's granddaughter reports that it was chosen for two reasons. First, it was comparatively cheap because it was then on the city perimeter. Second, it was close to open country whilst within a fifteen-minute walk of the nearest tram. Although the district is now a city suburb, cows grazed behind in 1928. Beyond was a view of a hilltop ruin, Zähringer Castle.

The Heidegger family's first step in procuring the house was to appoint an architect. Named Fetter, he also designed the cable-car station above Freiburg. He worked at that time as a *Regierungsbaurat* (city building inspector) simultaneously with private practice. Elfride Heidegger directed briefing. The philosopher made some design input, notably in placing his study and orientating rooms.[14] Construction lasted approximately six months. The family took up residence in autumn 1928.

The organization of the house

The constructional system of the house was not dissimilar to that of the hut (Fig. 9.2). A stone-filled timber frame was erected on a masonry plinth, following the tradition of farmhouses in the Black Forest.[15] The timber roof carcass was shingle-hung. Walls were clad externally with timber shingles and plastered or boarded internally. Several rooms in the house were organized around Biedermeier furniture inherited from Elfride Heidegger's family, which she was keen to show to good effect. The furniture of this period (approximately 1815–48) was inspired by an aesthetic view of the pastoral: heavy, simple and 'homely'.[16]

9.2
Heidegger's city house viewed from the gate. Timber shingle cladding and the masonry plinth of the structural timber frame are apparent.

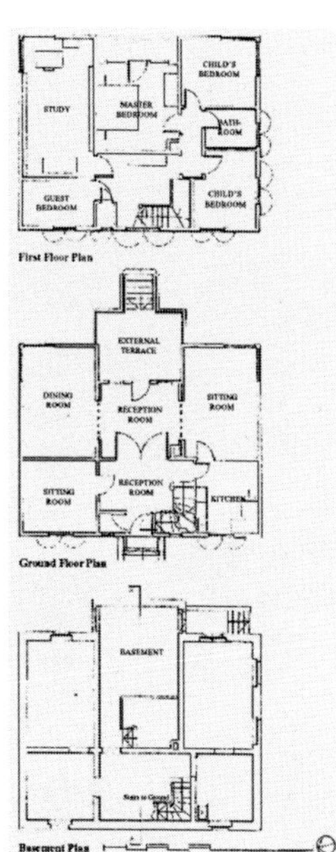

9.3
Plans of Heidegger's city house

The house has three stories, each broadly symmetrical in plan. A basement (Fig. 9.3) was used principally for storage. The front door at ground-floor level is located centrally on the street elevation, sheltered by a porch and reached by a brick path leading from a gate in a privet hedge. Painted on the lintel was a biblical inscription chosen by Heidegger, an opportune German rendering of Proverbs 4:23, which translates as: 'Shelter your heart with all vigilance; for from it flow the springs of life'.[17] The entrance floor had six principal rooms during Heidegger's residence: two reception rooms; two sitting rooms; a kitchen; and a dining room containing some of Elfride Heidegger's furniture (Fig. 9.4). One sitting room has since been opened to the kitchen. An external terrace, large enough for a table and chairs, addresses the garden.

The first floor is reached by a crafted timber stair that turns above the front door. The newel post of this stair bears the carved figure of a thinker given by Elfride Heidegger to her husband as a birthday present. This floor also has six principal rooms: two children's bedrooms; a master bedroom; a guest bedroom; a bathroom; and Heidegger's study, the largest room in the house (Fig. 9.5). The hallway and master bedroom were also organized around Biedermeier furniture. The board-lined study has been maintained as a memorial to the philosopher by his family. It has bookshelves on three walls. Dominant in the room is Heidegger's desk, facing the castle view through a corner window. To its left, next to the shelves, is a rack of pigeon-holes used for storing

9.4
Heidegger in the dining room of the house

9.5
Heidegger in his study

manuscripts in progress. To its right is a padded leather armchair. Here sat at various times 'a generation of visitors' including: Karl Jaspers, Jean-Paul Sartre, Jean Beaufret and Rudolf Bultmann.[18]

Impressions of the house

Heidegger wrote about many locations important to his life – especially the hut – and was later fond of autobiography. Yet, he did not write about the Freiburg house in any detail. There is, however, an enthusiastic account by Elfride Heidegger, which concerns the visit of a hypothetical student to the house:

> The young man walks across the straight garden path between the flower beds towards the door ... and climbs a couple of steps under a small roof designed for protection from the rain. However, before he rings the bell – beside which he reads on a little card 'Visits after 5 P.M.' – he is surprised. For above the wooden beam of the door, a proverb from the Bible is engraved ... Thus unexpectedly attuned to reflectiveness, he is confronted with another surprise on entering the house. The foyer is wide, separated by a floor-to-ceiling glass wall, and opens into a single, bright room in

> which there is a piano and an old armchair. Behind these is another large window, which reaches to the floor and opens onto a terrace half-covered by a protruding higher floor. The terrace provides a place for sitting and in summertime is the centre of life for the family. Wide steps lead from the terrace to a garden full of flowers. Thus upon entering the house, the visitor is enveloped by the whole radiating expanse of the meadows and the dark edge of the forest beyond. This is a house that 'seems to absorb the whole of nature' …
>
> A door is open on the side towards the dining room with a few beautiful pieces of furniture from the Biedermeier period. The waiting student, however, has no more time to look around, because he must now climb a well turned stairway – a craftsman's master-work – to the next floor, where beside a huge closet a clock, made in Hellerau, hangs on the wall – the pride of the family. Now things become serious: The professor is waiting.[19]

Elfride Heidegger structured her description of the house around its influence upon a stranger's impression. She seems to have been concerned with the house as a suitable expression of her husband's civic and academic role. This expression was given form by an impressive axial view from the front door, a procession to Heidegger's study and the calculated display of fine furniture. Elfride Heidegger seems to have had particular feelings about the building's status as a professor's house. Given her supervisorial involvement in construction, it seems likely that the house was contrived towards social aspiration around these architectural compositional devices.

An account survives by a student visitor like the one that Elfride Heidegger described. Reiner Schürmann visited Freiburg in 1969. Then a Dominican novitiate, he later became professor of philosophy at the New School in New York. He wrote:

> I have just returned from Heidegger's house. It was a real late-afternoon reception about the mystery of being … To begin with the folkloric aspect of the visit, I had my fill and more: a pious inscription above the door … ; a small man who looked like a peasant … let me in nearly without saying a word into a room that looked rather like a blockhouse; two glasses and a bottle on a small tray; and, especially, a two-hour long conversation which ended up, at least outwardly, in complete darkness. I knew that among things country he had a fondness for … the traditional: his writings speak of the pitcher of cool water, of the peasant's rough hands, of mud-caked clogs and

> such. I now know that he also likes discussions in the dark. However, the man is so shrewd, and … it felt like my meagre schoolboy questions were received by warm and reassuring hands.[20]

Schürmann appears to have interpreted the house as Elfride Heidegger hoped, somewhat in awe of her husband's intellectual stature. However, he also perceived the building through his reading of Heidegger's work. It became part of a personal mythology surrounding the philosopher's thought.

The professor's residence

The Heidegger household was organized according to traditional family roles. Plans of the house reflect this. The master bedroom, shared marital realm, was symbolically central to the upper floor. The children's realms had some removal from their parents by day, but were close to Martin and Elfride's supervisory bedroom by night. Heidegger had his own domain in the study. However, Elfride Heidegger's territory, the kitchen she ran as housewife, was less distinctly personal.

Although farmhouse construction techniques follow tradition for the hut in Todtnauberg, they are by no means typical of Freiburg. Nearly one thousand metres below the hut, building traditions in the city are different. Older buildings within the city perimeter were packed densely in long, thin plots with ornamental fronts, made in timber or masonry. The city also had a more recent tradition of suburban building by 1928. Houses of masonry construction employed newer building techniques: tighter construction affording more insulation; reinforced concrete lintels allowing bigger windows; and the provision of mains services – electric light, sanitation and water supply. Despite its timber frame and shingle cladding, Heidegger's house is closer to this tradition. It is effectively a suburban house in Black Forest clothing. It shares certain superficial characteristics with Black Forest farmhouses, but is otherwise built around statutory services with large extensively glazed rooms. Farmhouse constructional methods used in Todtnauberg followed local materials and experience – but such techniques used in Freiburg stand as affectation.

Affectation is also displayed in the intention to display Elfride Heidegger's Biedermeier furniture. The couple were aware that these pieces were loaded with the period's romanticized and aestheticized rustic values. The decision to contrive a setting for this furniture reports an aesthetic sympathy for which there is little evidence at the hut.

The house reinforces conventional patterns of family life more strongly than Todtnauberg. It indicates a suburban tension between aspirations towards a pastoral situation and the desire to build a family residence close to city and transportation. Issues of modern comfort appear to have been a driving issue in building the house, whereas there is little indication of such priority in the building of the hut. Moreover, the house was conceived with a sensibility for social and aesthetic appearances.

Heidegger's existence at the Freiburg house thus seems rather different to that he maintained in the mountains. It prioritized a number of social and intellectual issues seemingly absent in his hut life. Heidegger's lack of writing about the house suggests his ambivalence towards both the building and family life in comparison with his enthusiasm for solitary existence in the mountains and his perception of philosophical resonance there.

This may be considered partly a consequence of the house itself. Whilst any building has 'phenomenological' potential to frame its surroundings and prompt intellectual and emotional reflection, some buildings perhaps frame more sharply than others. The hut was smaller. It was less tightly sealed, involving its inhabitants with immediacies of seasonal and climatic movement. Its physical size intensified the interaction of individuals' 'dwelling' with 'places' of occupation. The lack of building services arguably made hut 'dwellers' more aware of demands of subsistence and required active participation with basic circumstances of existence. In contrast, the house was a stronger cocoon. It allowed greater detachment from subsistence and situation. Comfort was gained at the expense of 'phenomenological' resonance. This perhaps prompted Heidegger's apparent ambivalence towards the house.

Heidegger's house as a physical manifestation of philosophy

Arguably most important in Heidegger's writing on 'dwelling' and 'place' is his suggestion that physical manifestations of human minds' engagement with the world demonstrate philosophical thought. Heidegger's own hut and house are quite different but – interestingly – both seem to demonstrate the thinking behind their provenance and maintenance.

The philosophy manifested by Heidegger's hut is broadly that of his writing. It suggests a 'building' and 'dwelling' deeply involved with small 'places' and activities of life that they support. The hut stands for philosopher as engaged 'phenomenological' observer. It suggests attunement to the depth of the commonplace closely watched.

In contrast, the philosophy manifested by Heidegger's house is somewhat alien to Heidegger's writing. It is more 'aesthetic' than 'phenomenological', more attentive to the visual qualities of furniture and axial views than to emotion and experience. The house is rooted in suburban affectation and supportive of conventional social structures. It is also acceptant of technological comforts and their mediation of immediate experience of the world.

Respective roles of house and hut in the philosopher's life seem to hint at two sides to Heidegger's personality. One side, manifested physically in the house, was civic and somewhat affected. Here, Heidegger was professor, father and head of his family. He seems to have enjoyed this situation, at least insofar as it admitted a measure of hubris. This *milieu* was somehow necessary to support the other side, manifested in the hut. There, Heidegger's life was solitary by preference. He perceived it as simpler and more honest, attuned to emotion and experience. He favoured this second situation intellectually, finding it vital and sustaining. Importantly, though, Heidegger never followed one of these lives without the other.

The dichotomy apparent in Heidegger's relationship with his hut and house echoes two further tensions in his life and thought. First, one can perceive in his writings a tension between a desire to participate in the history of philosophical dialectic for example, his challenges to the notion of 'space' – and an impetus towards plain 'phenomenological' reporting of circumstance. Second, in the philosopher's life, one might perceive a tension between the Heidegger 'bewitched' by political ambition and the Heidegger content to retreat to the mountains and philosophize.[21] The philosophical content of Heidegger's house and hut manifested in 'place' is thus an original contribution to the philosopher's *oeuvre* and his intellectual biography – if not necessarily flattering or complimentary. His inhabitation of the house and hut demonstrates how 'places' can have potential for philosophical expression. It also demonstrates a complexity apparent in the man and his work.

Acknowledgements

The author is grateful to: Gertrud Heidegger for her assistance and permission to visit the house; Mark Giles for acting as translator on that occasion; and Herr Menzel of the City of Freiburg-im-Breisgau for providing drawings of the house. Simon Unwin and Jonathan Hale commented on aspects of this paper.

Note

The residents of the house ask potential visitors to note that the building is private property. They request that their privacy be respected.

Notes

1 E. Casey, *The Fate of Place: A Philosophical History*, London: University of California Press, 1997, pp. 243–84.

2 Accompanying drawings are based on the original architect's 'as built' drawings. Furniture indicated is as shown on the originals.

3 D. Meller Markovicz, *Martin Heidegger, Photos 23 September 1966 / 17+18 Juni 1968*, Frankfurt: Vittorio Klostermann, 1985.

4 There is a substantial body of material on Heidegger's involvement with fascism. A useful overview is: H. Ott, *Martin Heidegger: A Political Life*, trans. A. Blunden, London: Fontana, 1994.

5 M. Heidegger, 'Building Dwelling Thinking', in *Martin Heidegger: Basic Writings*, ed. D. Farrell Krell, London: Routledge, 1993, pp. 347–63. Heidegger deliberately omitted commas in the title.

6 M. Heidegger, 'The thing', in *Poetry, Language, Thought*, trans. A. Hofstadter, New York: Harper and Row, 1971, pp.163–86; '...poetically, Man dwells...', in *Poetry, Language, Thought*, pp. 211–29.

7 M. Heidegger and K. Jaspers, *Martin Heidegger & Karl Jaspers: Briefwechsel*, ed. W. Biemel & H. Saner, Frankfurt: Vittorio Klostermann, 1990, p.53. A translation of part of this correspondence appears in: R. Safranski, *Martin Heidegger: Between Good and Evil*, Cambridge MA: Harvard University Press, 1998, pp.142–3.

8 For example: M. Heidegger, 'Why do I stay in the provinces?', trans. T. Sheehan, in T. Sheehan (ed.), *Heidegger: The Man and the Thinker*, Chicago: Precedent, 1981, pp.27–8; M. Heidegger, 'The thinker as poet', in *Poetry, Language, Thought*, pp.1–14.

9 M. Heidegger, 'Why do I stay in the provinces?', p.28.

10 From 1923 to 1928, Heidegger's city home was a set of rented rooms in Marburg. From 1971 until 1976, it was a small retirement house built in the garden of the 1928 original. Although this house still stands, it has been substantially altered and divided in two. Neither Heidegger's family nor Freiburg City authorities have any record of the building's original condition.

11 M. Heidegger, *Being and Time*, trans. J. Stambaugh, Albany: State University of New York Press, 1996.

12 Husserl (1859–1938) taught philosophy at Göttingen and Freiburg, where he met Heidegger as a student. The relationship was initially distant, turning first to master and pupil and then friendship. Heidegger's subsequent breaking of the friendship with Jewish Husserl following his own success has been interpreted by some as anti-Semitism on the part of Heidegger. Refer to Ott, *Martin Heidegger: A Political Life*, pp. 172–86.

13 Hugo Ott writes: 'The great breakthrough predicted by Husserl had finally come ... Even before Heidegger had accepted the offer at Freiburg, the plot of land above Freiburg-Zähringen had been purchased, and the builders worked through the summer of 1928 to get the house ready for occupation by the winter. The exile had returned.' Ott, *Martin Heidegger: A Political Life*, p.129.

14 The author is grateful to Gertrud Heidegger for this information.

15 Heidegger wrote about such houses in 'Building Dwelling Thinking', pp.362–3.

16 The term 'Biedermeier' is equally applicable to literature and poetry: M.J. Norst, 'Biedermeier', in J.M. Ritchie (ed.) *Periods in German Literature*, London: Oswald Wolff, 1966, pp. 147–70.

17 Proverbs 4 concerns wisdom. Heidegger's translation is one of a number of possible renderings of the original Hebrew.

18 Safranski, *Martin Heidegger: Between Good and Evil*, p. 426.

19 A translation of this text appears in: H.-W. Petzet, *Encounters and Dialogues with Martin Heidegger*, London: University of Chicago Press, 1993, p.186.
20 R. Schürmann, 'Reiner Schürmann's report of his visit to Martin Heidegger', trans P. Adler, *Graduate Faculty Philosophy Journal*, 1997, vol.19, no.2 – vol.20, no.1, pp.67–8.
21 G. Steiner, 'An almost inebriate bewitchment: review of Young J., *Heidegger, Philosophy, Nazism*', *Times Literary Supplement*, 15 August 1997.

Chapter 10

Place-making: the notion of centre

A typological investigation of means and meanings

Max Robinson

Reflecting upon the nature of architecture, few aspects supplant its capacity for making places as an effective means to discern its essence. Consequently, place-making provokes many questions of substance and structure, a primary example being the relation between a built work and its locale. Every building resides upon a site positioned in a particular spot on the earth. Regardless of what may be erected – structure, shelter, land form or garden, it possesses a unique geographic location and an adjacent setting distinctive unto itself. The site, in turn, is as much a part of the ensemble as are the components of the object situated there. Every piece of architecture possesses the common denominator that ties the building to a specific situation – a set of circumstances in time and place that comprise its milieu. Obviously, every construction has a precise terrain upon which it is located, surroundings that constitute its physical environs and a context consisting of both material and immaterial features. These present a multitude of opportunities as each aspect is capable of shaping and shading a variety of experiences. So inevitably, this concern focuses upon the particular qualities of a place as it interacts with the things planned to occupy it.

As Christian Norberg-Schulz expounds repeatedly,[1] the comprehension of place is integral to an understanding of architecture. A building is more than a simple response to the requirements of the programme; it is also more than an artefact fashioned for a site like a jewel adorning the landscape. Conversely, the site is more than another conundrum in the genesis of a structure as it is capable of moulding experience. Besides being its physical foundation, the site serves a building as its metaphysical basis where intentions are accumulated and tangibly expressed. In Martin Heidegger's terms, it 'gathers' the meaning of a situation that poetically binds architecture and landscape into a cumulative and cultivated whole.[2] By fusing an edifice, its site and environs into a 'world' one inhabits, place-making establishes a phenomenological linkage that experientially combines them into an evolving organic entity.[3]

Therefore, a building transcends its purposeful criteria by conceptually commingling with its place. This interrelationship evolves beyond a simple programmatic resolution as site and surroundings stimulate thoughts underlying a solution's concept. The building uses the site to reinforce its *raison d'être*, and, conversely, the land receives meaning from the structure placed upon it. Place-making thus entails a metaphysical reciprocity as a site is affected by the piece designed for it.[4] A work of architecture does not encroach upon the landscape so much as it helps to reveal and explain it. It 'illuminates' or clarifies the nature of the place by amplifying its essential features and by making one more aware of its character.[5] It gives the setting meaning through what it communicates, and by exploiting this expressive potential it ascends to the level of art.

Place-making derives meaning from the qualities of a location and its surroundings as it envisions capitalizing upon the potential of their attributes. This is achieved when building and site successfully fuse with one another thereby contributing to their realization as a 'world' one inhabits. Norberg-Schulz has often stated that man's desire is to understand his existence as a meaningful thing and, therefore, the purpose of architecture is to create mean ingful places.[6] Meaning is given through comprehending our human condition as expressed by the drama of our actions performed upon the stage of these places. Successful architecture consequently necessitates places that mutually reinforce one's life experiences where happenings and settings interact as a totality. Only when such 'meaningful places' result, can architecture establish its significance and value, thereby becoming part of our cultural heritage.

If the making of such places is paramount, how then can they be realized? One way to substantiate their meaning is to utilize opportunities inherent within the notion of centre. Centre is integral to the idea of place as places are interpreted and understood as centres. This concept is intuitively ingrained in our collective consciousness as we use it to identify, describe and allude to the gravity of items in our everyday world. A multitude of designations employ the word to denote locations and attribute some degree of importance to them, while we infer other kinds of positional implications from synonymous and analogous terms . The linguistic definitions of centre as a position and a source also provide a basis for understanding place. Position distinguishes the middle or mid-point of a figure or system – a physical station that commutes with every other component of that grouping. Source denotes prime cause or reason and other terms indicating a place of origin. As derivations of position and source designate either explicit or implicit locations, the connective relevance of centre and place is further amplified.

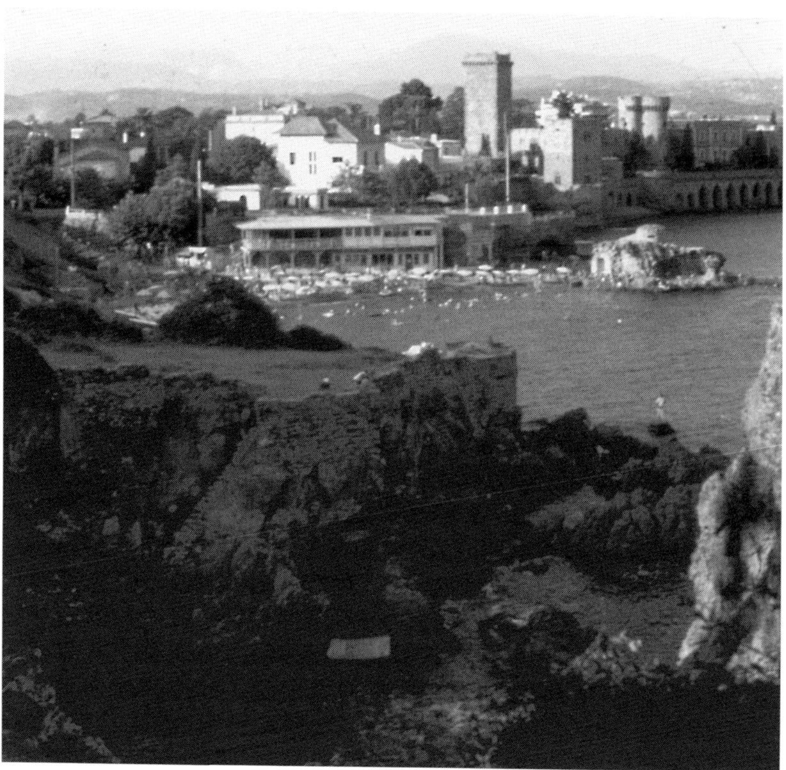

10.1
Built work, site, surroundings. The public beach facilities and the Henry Clews château on the Cote d'Azur at La Napoule, France.

Materializations of centres can be interpreted in three fashions: physically by their existence in real terms, functionally by how they are used, and symbolically by their meaning or how they represent more abstract ideas, things or events. In particular instances, one category may predominate; but most cases usually involve all in some fashion or another. Centre's manifestation can also be classified in terms of its abstract or concrete nature accounting for the tangible or intangible qualities of its presence. 'Centre is not a particular spot on the earth's surface; it is a concept in mythic thought'.[7] As a term, centre refers to places of particular significance associated with our living and thinking regardless of whether they exist physically in our real world or within our imagination. Abstractions based upon various cosmological, mythological or intellectual foundations are familiar: Heaven and Hell, the throne of God, the 'fiery furnace', habitats of evil spirits, Tolkien's 'Shire', or notions such as the New World and the American frontier. Each is associated with implications of centre. In actuality, centres may be classified as either natural or artificial, i.e. man-made in basis. They are realized as elements of the landscape or as architecture and urban settlements – the results of nature's evolution or products of man's construction.

Materializations of centre can also be categorized relative to levels of scale. One instance considers the concrete domains of the natural world in a

10.2
Meaningful place. Restaurant, dining terrace overlooking Gourdon, France.

geographic sense that ranges from the continental through the regional to the local level with many possible sub-categories. Another consists of representations of various social, political and economic constructs that exist in a multitude of forms too numerous to enumerate.[8] Additional consideration of a centre's realization includes the organizational qualities of its form. It can be interpreted as systems or elements relative to its compositional role. Systems denote assemblages of related components considered as a whole, while elements designate discrete entities as singularities unto themselves. Both can possess a natural or an artificial basis and can take the form of either landscape or architectural components.

The formal qualities of a centre's physical attributes enable the definition of a place as a specific and unique thing. They directly support its making in an architectonic sense and serve to interrelate building and landscape. First, centre can be categorized as either an object or a space. Kevin Lynch describes nodes as 'strategic foci into which the observer can enter ', i.e. spaces, and landmarks as 'point references … external to the observer', i.e. objects of some kind.[9] Norberg-Schulz also presumes that nodes are the concretization, i.e. the architecturally expressed counterpart, of place.[10] Fundamentally, they are entities of concentrated content and limited defined size. Although their precise configuration is variable, the inference is that centres are ideally circular or spherical. He quotes Karl Jaspers who postulated that, 'in itself, every existence appears round'.[11] Rudolf Arnheim also attributes a similar conclusion[12] to Gaston Bachelard who, while ruminating about the essence of interior space, contemplated that 'seen from the inside without exteriority, being can only be round'.[13] Norberg-Schulz further develops the proposition that the ideal geometry of a place is comprised of a middle and a periphery.[14] A round form possesses two elementary components: a mid-point establishing the convergence of the composition, and a perimeter prescribing its extent as well as distinguishing the whole of the arrangement as separate and distinct from other things. The centralized form is its main physical attribute, with the features of concentration, proximity and closure contributing to its realization.

Compositionally, centres may be either centroidal or linear types, for in either case a core is involved. This interior can focus upon a mid-point or extend longitudinally with other items organized to it. Another consequential property is its implied orientation; for visually, its directional impulse may be inwardly focused and concentrating or outwardly radiating and dispersing. Arnheim credits the qualities of concentricity and eccentricity as primary attributes of a centre's perceptible constitution. For him, the composition and resolution of visual forces either converging upon or diffusing from a nucleus is its main attainment.[15]

Centres can also be categorized as either occupied or occupiable. To be occupied incorporates an element integral to the composition within the middle of the arrangement, while being occupiable signifies that it is void or empty. An occupiable centre may be temporarily occupied by some person or thing, but since the thing is not essentially related to the composition this is not a permanent condition. It is also flexible in that it maintains the potential for accepting something. Therefore, centres can be typologically categorized as being either occupied or occupiable, determinate or indeterminate, as well as either object- or spatially oriented.

One of the most fundamental interpretations of 'centre' involves its egocentric nature, a matter based upon the 'self-centredness' of man's outlook where one's person is visualized as the focal point of the world one occupies and experiences. The hypothesis that one's world is essentially self-referential is supported by numerous studies of cognitive development, such as Jean Piaget's research into the learning processes employed by children. Things are reasoned and comprehended in relation to their interaction with self, thereby giving impetus to this supposition. Norberg-Schulz concludes that 'man's space is subjectively centered'[16] and others bolster that idea.[17] Being the focus of the world that one occupies also implies its domination which, in turn, affirms one's position and physically reinforces the significance of its meaning.

As a means of reference, centre employs its egocentric foundation where everything is measured in terms of the observer. Many sources postulate that our understanding of the earth's geography is based upon the intrinsic characteristics of the human body through the innate, four-square directional orientation of its form.[18] Man's body constitutes a portable reference system where everything orients with respect to itself as a central figure and thus assumes a particular significance. This matter of self acting as reference is exemplified by a comment from the title character in an otherwise undistinguished film as he said, 'No matter where you go, there you are.'[19]

Similarly, the egocentric implications of centre imply its use as a means of bearing. 'Centres are "externalised" (concretised) as points of reference in the environment.'[20] They function as markers enabling orientation, and accordingly provide both the physical and perceptual tools necessary to understand connections. If one's position is understood as occupying the middle, it is not problematic to comprehend relationships with other things. Man's sense of place develops out of his need to find a familiar position within the world that provides a refuge from the chaotic aspects of an irregular and unpredictable environment.[21] Centres provide the moorings to which man can mentally anchor, thereby mitigating the consequences of being set intellectually adrift in a disordered realm. Many of the effects attributable to a sense of place are generated by the function of orientation associated with the experience of occupying and engaging a particular locality. 'Man wants to order his experiences of the world; not surprisingly, the world so ordered revolves around him.'[22]

Centre constitutes a locus to which things organize referentially, and if this convergence is meaningful in content, its presence proclaims an important position where significant events of existence can be experienced.[23] Therefore, it acts as a goal – a location to which things aspire and are attracted. By consequentially providing man a means to orient, the structure of accompanying environmental phenomena can be understood. It also serves as a point of departure and return by providing an origin to which and from which things emanate. In doing so, it recalls the term's definition as a source. Origins can address either individual or collective needs by offering a location to which one relates either personally or publicly. Home and country, i.e. 'homeland', are two easily identifiable instances. The concept of 'home' embodies numerous implications that reinforce ideas about centre. Unfortunately, there are too many to consider within the limits of this inquiry, but the idea has many ramifications that contribute to the interpretation of the meanings of centre.

These considerations also can be extended from an individual to a collective application. Although originating in the self-focused position of an individual's viewpoint, the notion can be transposed by shifting level of scale and capacity of function to a larger body, one composed of many individuals joined by common agreement into a larger whole.[24] What is capable of being understood singularly and personally can be applied communally and collectively. As such, the notion of centre can artistically express a culture's interpretation of the structure of its world – its *imago mundi*. ' ... [Man creates] space to express the structure of his world as a real imago mundi'.[25] As a construction, it gives tangible presence to its representation and empowers communication of the thoughts it embodies. The symbolism of centre also explains other cosmological images and religious beliefs. 'Every construction or fabrication has the cosmogony as paradigmatic model. The creation of the world becomes the archetype of every creative human gesture.'[26]

The architectonic form of such constructions is often based upon the image of one primary archetype: the *axis mundi*. This schema – a horizontal plane pierced by a vertical axis – has been described as the simplest model of man's existential space.[27] As a construct, it proffers a clear conceptual framework for the notion and constitutes a cogent idealized figure to assist its realization. Regardless of its architectonic translation, this image is inextricably linked with its form. It structures both the physical and intellectual content of our environment into a complete, unified vision by providing the means to distinguish a particular location and empower it as a referential object. Arnheim reinforces this point by referencing Bachelard's idea that the image of a building (place) is vertical and centralized.[28] Consequently, a formal archetype upon which to base the physical reality of centre arises from these egocentric origins and engenders an opportunity to heighten human awareness. Experience is articulated through the creation of tangible places based upon a clear, common model. Yi-Fu Tuan notes that the cosmos logically has only one centre, but mythically it can have many – although one may dominate others.[29] As a result, world views emerge to express ideas, ones held individually as well as collectively, thereby giving reality and form to what is both consciously stated and emotionally felt.

With this background, consider two interpretations that effectively encapsulate centre's inherent meanings and relationships to ideas about place. In predicating his propositions about the basic schemata of spatial orientation, Norberg-Schulz identifies the components of place, path and domain. He then couples his ideas about place with its existential counterpart, centre. For him, centre belongs to a system of perceptual concepts enabling an understanding of the environment. It provides a representation founded upon generalizations drawn from the similarities of many phenomena, and it is realized as abstract diagrammatic images of elements that describe the physical nature of things. In so doing, centre permits place to be understood with reference to a relatively stable system of perceptual schemata.[30]

10.3
The accident of location. A chalet in the Swiss Alps.

Another interpretation of centre's meaning is contained within Mircea Eliade's analysis of religious experience. In examining the essence of sacred and profane space, he defines the realization of centre as a numinous encounter – a revelation of an aspect of divine power. It attains that quality by revealing itself as separate and different from the profane, the remaining space constituting the surrounding field. As such, this event is characterized as equivalent to the 'founding of a world', a primordial religious experience based upon the archetype of the act of creation. As a centre, it reveals an absolute fixed point that sets limits and establishes order. It also serves as reference for orientation. For Eliade, this constitutes a break in space between that which is sacred and that which is profane, thereby permitting connection and communication between the three cosmic levels of heavens, earth and underworld. He defines this as the universal pillar or cosmic axis positioned so that it is located in the middle or the hub of a world; hence, his depiction of centre as the 'navel of the earth', or, more appropriately, as an *axis mundi*.[31] This interpretation therefore entails a set of circumstances that rather profoundly amplifies the significance of centre as a place.

The concretizations of centre affirm its physical presence as an undeniably assertive thing. Places assume their significance by acting as referential and organizational devices where their dominance serves to materially reinforce the importance of their meaning. The ordering power of centre is therefore obvious, as it cannot exist without insinuating a clear hierarchical situation. Historically, though, the omnipresent nature of place engendered a domineering repercussion by circumscribing available opportunities. Mankind was subjected to what Karsten Harries terms the 'accident of location', a predestined condition of the sort where lives were essentially controlled by the context inherited from the particular circumstances of birth and residency.[32]

However, many technological advances – particularly in transportation and communication – have offered emancipation by allowing individuals to expand their association and participation with increasing numbers and subcultures. Limited by proximity and distance, place became less consequential and the lure of freedom challenged its binding power. An egalitarian, democratic ethos found expression in openness while freedom manifested itself in empty, vacant, unoccupied space, allowing many possibilities for movement. Unfortunately, freedom is accompanied by a lack of roots and a loss of community. The status of place with its fixation on location was subjected to reinterpretation and the notion of centre evolved.

New factors such as pluralism and relativism have contemporaneously devalued its singular, unalterable distinction. Humanity has fractured into many diverse cultures with dissimilar foundations and exclusive beliefs so that mankind's world views have acquired a multiplicity of directions and dimensions. This divergence of outlooks has allowed centres to simultaneously comprise different meanings for different people. In addition, the quest for universal objectivity results in a greater degree of abstraction, which coincides with a subsequent disengagement and loss of meaning in content.[33] Reducing space to its objective basis makes it impossible for man to discover his place in the world and leads to a sense of 'homelessness' that is characteristically modern. The environment is transformed and place is lamented as 'lost'.[34] As Hans Sedlmayr and others have variously noted: centre neither cannot, does not, nor will not hold.[35]

Although centre is capable of maintaining its architectonic supremacy, responses to changing circumstances contest its denotation of immediate and pervasive primacy making other means of interpretation necessary. Currently, centres need to be more flexible and formally adaptable. Non-hierarchical, repetitive spatial matrices are the main requisite features of such conditions. Both natural and man-made realms present numerous possibilities. Norberg-Schulz equates the American city subdivided with its grid of streets and parcels of property to the modern, open view of the world. The indeterminate occupiable pattern manifests a condition of opportunity and change by providing 'islands of meaning' where various elements can find their place.[36] Buildings based upon similar spatial qualities can also possess this capability.

10.4
The centre cannot hold. Backside of the harbour for the community of Ocracoke on Hatteras Island, North Carolina, USA.

If the purpose of architecture is to create meaningful places, then it should be concerned with transforming space into place so that one might 'dwell' in the sense that Heidegger truly meant.[37] 'The way we experience the world is inseparably tied to the activities in which we are engaged. Our experience of things is mediated by our body … and subject to the accident of its location in space and time'.[38] The world we live in remains egocentric in many ways and the notion of centre maintains its importance as the relativity of modern meanings needs a base of reference for their comprehension. As a result, it is important to recover a sense of place, and employment of the notion of centre offers a substantial mechanism to accomplish this process.

Notes

1 C. Norberg-Schulz, *Genius Loci*, New York: Rizzoli, 1979, passim; C. Norberg-Schulz, *The Concept of Dwelling*, New York: Electa/Rizzoli 1985, passim; C. Norberg-Schulz, *Architecture: Meaning and Place*, New York: Electa/Rizzoli, 1986, passim.

2 M. Heidegger, *Poetry, Language, Thought*, trans. A. Hofstadter, New York: Harper & Row, 1975, pp.152–4.
3 S. Holl, *Anchoring*, New York: Princeton Architectural Press, 1989, p.9.
4 Ibid., p.9.
5 Heidegger, *Poetry, Language, Thought*, pp.166–73.
6 Norberg-Schulz, *Genius Loci*, pp.160–70.
7 Y.-F. Tuan, *Space and Place*, Minneapolis: University of Minnesota Press, 1977, p.150.
8 C. Norberg-Schulz, *Existence, Space and Architecture*, New York: Praeger Publishers, 1971, pp.69–88.
9 K. Lynch,*The Image of the City*, Cambridge MA: MIT Press, 1960, pp.47–8.
10 Norberg-Schulz, *Existence, Space and Architecture*, pp.39–42.
11 Ibid, p.20.
12 R. Arnheim, *The Dynamics of Architectural Form*, Berkeley: University of California Press, 1977, p.94.
13 G. Bachelard, *The Poetics of Space*, trans. M. Jolas, Boston: Beacon Press, 1969, p.234.
14 Norberg-Schulz, *Existence, Space and Architecture*, p.20.
15 R. Arnheim, *The Power of Centre*, Berkeley: University of California Press, 1988, passim.
16 Norberg-Schulz, *Existence, Space and Architecture*, p.18.
17 Arnheim, *The Power of Centre*, passim; N. Crowe, *Nature and the Idea of a Man-Made World*, Cambridge MA: MIT, 1995, pp.49–58.
18 Crowe, *Nature and the Idea of a Man-Made World*, p.51.
19 E.M. Rauch, *The Adventures of Buckaroo Banzai across the Eight Dimension*, Century City: Twentieth Century Fox, 1984.
20 Norberg-Schulz, *Existence, Space and Architecture*, p.18.
21 Crowe, *Nature and the Idea of a Man-Made World*, p.71.
22 Tuan, *Space and Place*, p.93
23 Norberg-Schulz, *Existence, Space and Architecture*, p.19.
24 Norberg-Schulz, *The Concept of Dwelling*, p.71.
25 Norberg-Schulz, *Existence, Space and Architecture*, p.11.
26 M. Eliade, *The Sacred and the Profane*, trans. Willard R. Trask, New York: Harcourt Brace Jovanovich, 1959, p.45.
27 Arnheim, *The Dynamics of Architectural Form*, p.35; Crowe, *Nature and the Idea of a Man-Made World*, p.80; Norberg-Schulz, *Existence, Space and Architecture*, p.21.
28 Arnheim, *The Dynamics of Architectural Form*, p.36; Bachelard, *The Poetics of Space*, p.17.
29 Tuan, *Space and Place*, p.99.
30 Norberg-Schulz, *Existence, Space and Architecture*, pp.17–27.
31 Eliade, *The Sacred and the Profane*, pp.36–7.
32 K. Harries, *The Ethical Function of Architecture*, Cambridge MA: MIT Press, 1997, pp.168–9, 172.
33 Harries, *The Ethical Function of Architecture*, pp.173–4.
34 Norberg-Schulz, *Genius Loci*, pp.189–190; Norberg-Schulz, *The Concept of Dwelling*, pp.48–50, 69–70, 133–5; Norberg-Schulz, *Architecture: Meaning and Place*, pp.20–26, 181, 233–236.
35 Norberg-Schulz, *Existence, Space and Architecture*, pp.35–6.
36 C. Norberg-Schulz, *New World Architecture*, New York: The Architectural League of New York / Princeton Architectural Press, 1988, pp.27–41.
37 Heidegger, *Poetry, Language, Thought*, pp.160–1.
38 Harries, *The Ethical Function of Architecture*, p.173.

Chapter 11

Hybrid identities

'Public' and 'private' life in the courtyard houses of Barabazaar, Kolkata, India

Martin Beattie

Introduction: hybrid identities

The standard 'urban history of Kolkata' frequently cites public colonial buildings and monuments, such as the New Court House, Government House and the Town Hall, which have become markers on an imperial domain, illustrating the inevitable growth of Kolkata as a British colonial city.[1] Fuelled by interests within the British colonial enterprise, a vast body of textual and visual representations of India was produced during the last two centuries of colonial rule. This body of knowledge, constituting the bulwark of British Orientalism, primarily addressed a European audience, spoke for the Indian, and claimed to represent the authentic India.[2] This material supposedly uncovered an essential difference between the materialistic, rational, progressive West and a spiritual, irrational, and static India. The story rarely revealed contradictions and disruptions integral to the historical experience, and in so doing left out anything that did not fit; what Swati Chattopadhyay has called, the 'chaos-leads-to-order narrative'.[3] Reinforcing an essentializing colonial discourse, this account perpetuated the binary oppositions of 'self' versus 'other', 'us' versus 'them', 'colonizer' versus 'colonized', and 'core' versus 'periphery'.[4]

How is it possible to re-construct an urban history that avoids such binary thought? A potential antidote is hybridity theory. Although it has undergone some extensive reinterpretations, the theory has become a key concept within the field of postcolonial studies. The word 'hybrid' has developed from biological and botanical origins: in Latin it meant the offspring of a tame sow and a wild boar. According to Robert Young, 'in the nineteenth century [hybridity] was used to refer to a physiological phenomenon; in the twentieth century it has been reactivated to describe a cultural one'.[5] Within the context of India, the work of Homi K. Bhabha is routinely cited as authorizing hybrid identities. Bhabha in his seminal book *The Location of Culture* argues for a theoretical position which escapes the polarities of 'east' and 'west', 'self' and 'other', 'master' and 'slave', a position 'which overcomes the given grounds of opposition and opens up a space of translation: a place of hybridity'.[6]

Bhabha's concept of hybridity builds on Mikhail Bakhtin's notion of the 'intentional hybrid'.[7] In an astute move, Bhabha has shifted Bakhtin's ideas on the subversion of authority to the dialogical situation of colonialism, where it describes a process that 'reveals the ambivalence at the source of traditional discourses on authority'.[8] Hybridity is not just a mixing together, it is a dialogic dynamic in which certain elements of dominant cultures are appropriated by the colonized and re-articulated in subversive ways. Bhabha defines hybridity as'[a] problematic of colonial representation ... that reverses the effects of the colonial disavowal, so that other 'denied' knowledges enter upon the dominant discourse and estrange the basis of its authority.'[9]

Interaction between the two cultures proceeds with the illusion of transferable forms and transparent knowledge, but leads increasingly into resistant, opaque and dissonant exchanges. It is in this tension that a 'third space' emerges, which Bhabha believes can affect forms of political change that go beyond antagonistic binarisms between rulers and ruled.

Bhabha's idea of hybridity suggests an approach to reading place that understands the overlapping geographies, both indigenous and foreign, and mixed narratives of the past and present day that were, and are, constantly negotiated. Writing histories of such narratives must acknowledge other possibilities, including the contradictions and biases of the past and equally the present, not as an idealized linear narrative of progress, but rather as disjointed and discontinuous. The existence of competing images to describe the history of Kolkata has been presented by only a few scholars,[10] and it is within this framework of thought that I relate 'public' and 'private' life in the courtyard houses of Barabazaar.

Nineteenth-century Bengali culture

In 1793, Lord Cornwallis introduced a legislative instrument called 'Permanent Settlement', which attributed land ownership *de facto* to the landlords, or *zamindars*. It was this class of *zamindars* who, in the late eighteenth and early nineteenth centuries, began settling in the northern part of Kolkata and Barabazaar to work as agents, or *banians*, for the East India Company. It was the *zamindars* and *banians* who grew increasingly influential in the economy of the city, and at this time were dominated by the Deb family.

According to Chattopadhyay, Nabakrishna Deb, 'performed intelligent service for the Company during the military campaign against the Nawab of Bengal, supplied aid to the Company's army, and derived immense material benefits from the consequent dissolution of power in Murshidabad.'[11]

The Company was keen to foster ties with the indigenous elite, and after the change in political power in 1757 it was extremely important on the part of this elite that they were ranked highly in the social scale of the Company.[12] This they did through festive celebrations, charity, and by building large residences. The biggest public event in the Deb family was the annual *Durga Puja*, and was begun by Nabakrishna in 1757, when he entertained Colonel Robert Clive and other dignitaries after the battle of Plassey.[13]

Under the Mughals, displaying one's wealth through buildings was considered imprudent. However, as Dhriti Choudhoury points out, the British 'released a new urge to flaunt wealth, and set new norms for the standard of living'.[14] By the middle of the nineteenth century, a new hybrid house form had developed, consisting of the 'traditional' hall for the deity, or *thakur dalan*, with a new type of courtyard, which was required for public displays of wealth and pomp at festivals. Nowhere is this process of change better illustrated than at the complex of houses built by the Deb family in Shobhabazaar, and begun by Nabakrishna in 1757.

According to Choudhoury, the public courtyard and *thakur dalan*, which was the centrepiece of the northern complex, showed little European influence.[15] However, the lion gate at the main entrance of the Deb house was added at a later time to give the building a street façade. This interest in generating a 'front' was symptomatic of the new urge to display residences as symbols of wealth and status. Choudhoury goes on to contrast the developments in the public courtyard and *thakur dalan* in the newer house built by Nabakrishna Deb in 1789, across the street:

> Paired half-columns between the arches support an entablature of classical European origin. The moulding of the cushions is Vitruvian, the acanthus leaves crowning the whole common in Roman Corinthian entablature; but just below is a row of what looks uncommonly like the 'spear-head' design in Islamic architecture.[16]

The new house signified a transitional phase in Kolkata's architecture, when western influence was being gradually absorbed. However, the

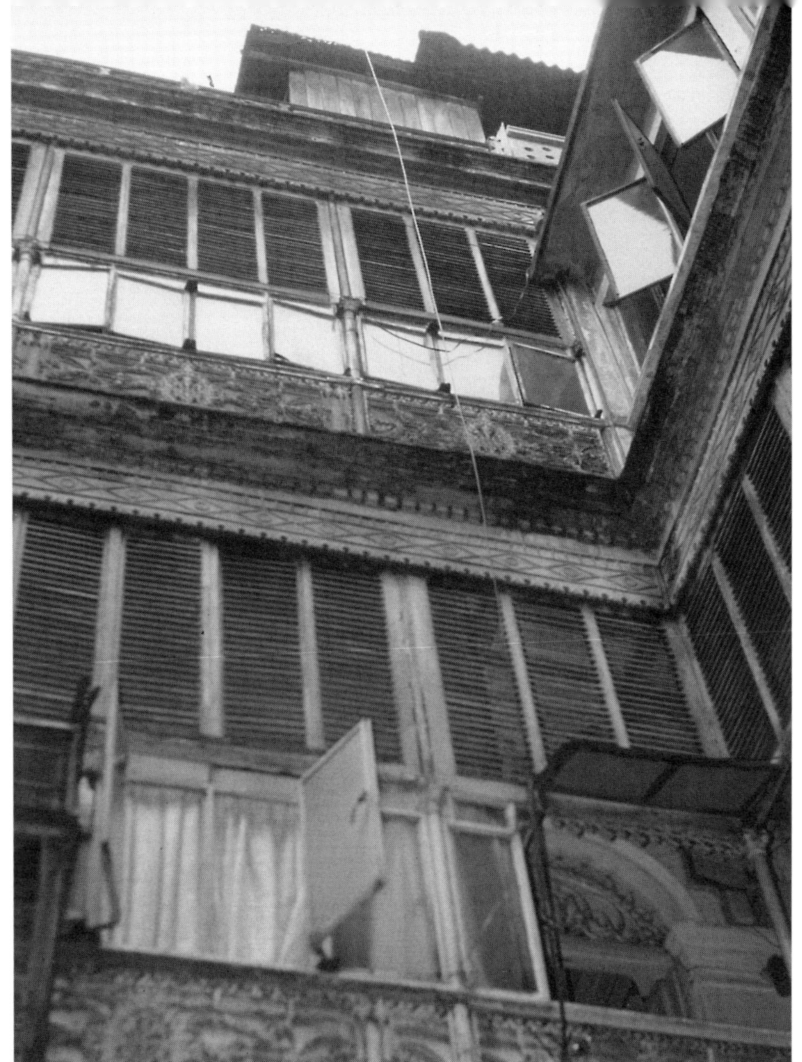

11.1
Rohatgi house. 'Public' courtyard, with family rooms at first and second floor. August 2000.

neo-classical style adopted was often full of architectural mistakes, and critics claimed that the Bengali elite lacked a 'true' understanding of the orders and were 'illiterate' in the grammar of the classical language.[17]

In addition to such criticism from the British colonial establishment, the Bengali elite began to be pilloried by Bengali thinkers, such as Bhabanicharan Banerji, who in *Kalikata Kamalalay* (1823) wrote 'they have simply grown rich by canvassing, commissioning, cheating and pimping'.[18] According to Sudipta Kaviraj, the Bengali middle-class home had 'become a theatre of serious conceptual conflicts since the start of British influence'.[19] Kaviraj explains how, at the beginning of the nineteenth century, British colonialism 'engaged in a powerful effort to persuade elite Indians of the truth of a celebratory narrative of European modernity',[20] of which the adoption of European architectural styles was a part. Of course, when Bengalis sought to enact a story of their own enlightenment, the British authorities obstructed that

11.2
Sett house. View from the street, August 2001.

process with the racist argument of the intellectual and cultural immaturity of Indians.[21]

At this point I wish to highlight the differing and often antithetical 'signs' under which the relationship between 'private' and 'public' life have been organized in the Bengali home in the past. Similarly, Bengalis had an ambivalent relationship with the modern colonial state and the narrative of European modernity that it represented, producing their own configuration of the modern. According to Bhabha, this is typical of 'the place of hybridity', which involves negotiation with 'antagonistic or contradictory elements'.[22] It is the distinction between 'private' living, and 'public' ritual/work space that is explored more fully in present-day case studies, after first briefly describing the social organization of the courtyard house.

Social organization of the courtyard house

Courtyard houses were constructed so as to provide pleasant spaces for different seasons and times of day. Through the doorway on the street there is often a passage that leads, sometimes via an offset, to a courtyard. In the more affluent houses of Barabazaar, with multiple courtyards, this would be the front 'public' courtyard and another passage would lead to the 'private' family courtyard(s) at the rear of the house. However, more often than not, in Barabazaar,

11.3
Daw house. *Thakur dalan* with *Durga* idol under construction. August 2002.

with its restriction on space (fig. I.12), the passage leads straight into the only courtyard. Houses are usually on more than one storey: the ground floor was, and sometimes still is, associated with 'public' religious ritual and work, and predominantly a male domain. Galleries run around the courtyard on upper levels opening to family rooms.

Typically, a veranda surrounds the open courtyard, beyond which is built a single row of rooms. The most formal contain the *thakur dalan* on the north or east side of the courtyard, and a range of public rooms. In Kolkata, with its prevailing southerly winds, typically, living accommodation was located on the south side of the house. Other rooms are used for kitchens, bathrooms and storage. The roof terrace may be used for drying food and clothes, and flying kites or pigeons.

'Private' living spaces

The three families surveyed in the case studies vary greatly in size. Mr Rohatgi lives with his wife in a 300-year-old house, owned by the family since the

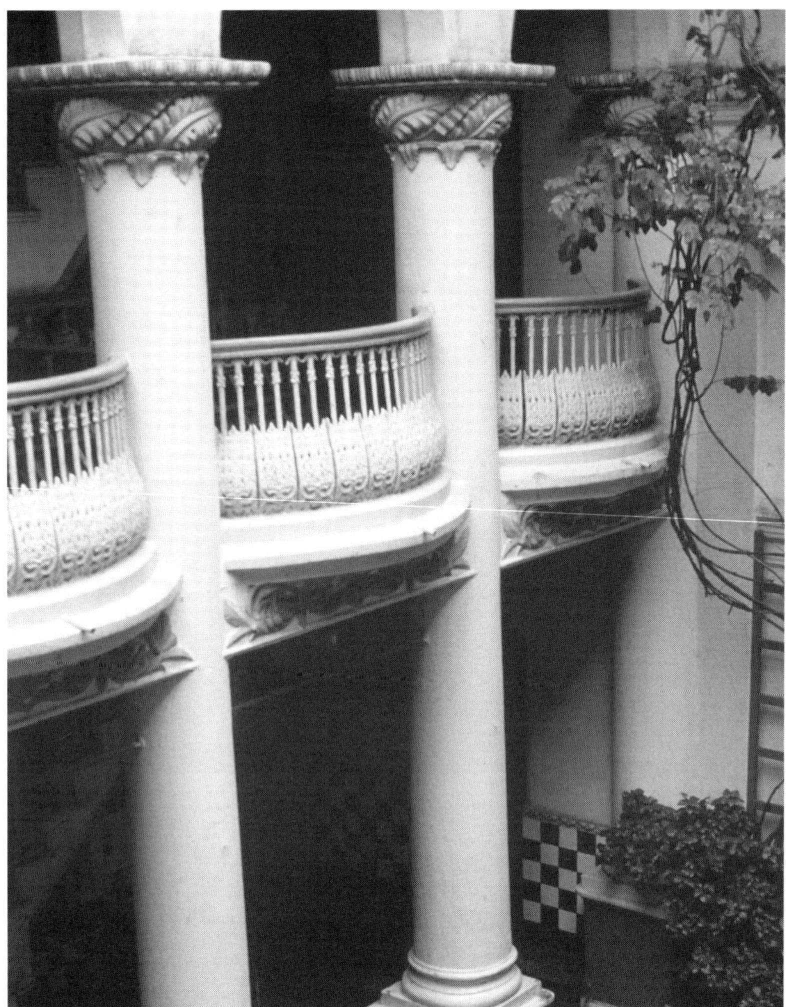

11.4
Daw house. 'Public' courtyard showing baroque style balconies. August 2002.

mid-eighteenth century (Fig. 11.1). Mr Sett lives with his mother and father, his wife, two children and with one of his brothers and his family in a house built mostly in the nineteenth century (Fig. 11.2). Mr Daw lives with his own family and his two brothers' families, and has about fifty other relatives living in the area around the two family houses, built mostly in the nineteenth century (Figs 11.3 and 11.4).

All three families live as extended families in different ways. The Rohatgi family was the smallest and most fragmented of those studied. The Rohatgis have one son, who has settled in Delhi, and one daughter, living in New York. The recent history of the family may illustrate how the size of the extended family appears to be shrinking. Mr Rohatgi is one of eleven children.

Now, his brothers and sisters are scattered all over India and have much smaller families; none has more than two children and some have none.

The Daw family, arguably the most conservative, lives fully as an extended family. The Sett family also lives fully as an extended family and, according to Mr Sett, 'we are living, staying, eating jointly'. Mr Sett was keen to stress what he saw as the 'positive' sides of the extended family. He pointed out that his business activities meant that 'we can really spend little time for our families'. For Mr Sett, one of the advantages of the extended family was stated as follows: 'well there is someone to talk to, my wife can talk to someone, it's not that she's alone'.[23]

When I pressed Mr Daw on whether he thought that the notion of the extended family was breaking up, he was fairly non-committal, simply saying, 'nuclear family will be started after my death'.[24] Mr Sett thought that 90 per cent of families in Kolkata lived as extended families. He modified this slightly when I asked him if he thought it was more common to live separately in the south of Kolkata, an area seen as more 'modern' than Barabazaar. His reply was, 'Yes, yes. In fact, the joint families stays in those old areas of [north] Kolkata, in Shyambazaar, in Bagbazaar.'[25]

'Public' ritual/work space

The two Daw houses use their 'public' courtyards for celebrating *Durga Puja*, following the 'tradition' set by Nabakrishna Deb, which has had a significant effect on the layout of the houses. The Sett family have their own temple, or *Thakur Bari*, dedicated to Radho Kanto (Lord Krishna), built in 1729, on the same block as their own house. Mr Daw summarized the present-day uses of the courtyard in his house:

> The courtyards are being used ... not as a playground, but for the airy purpose, the sun rays and that will be there ... Courtyards are generally used ... for the official purpose, that is the marriage occasion, and the *Durga Puja* ceremony, and other officials, say about some music conference, or any other conference for the courtyards are being used.[26]

Mr Rohatgi mentioned that when he was a boy the courtyard was often used as an overflow space; extended family members visiting on business for a day or two, from the family home in Patna, Bihar, would sleep there.[27]

Nowadays, with commercial pressures in Barabazaar, inevitably courtyards are being used more for businesses. Mr Sett described how the uses of the courtyard in his house had changed:

> [It] was actually used for playing, we used to play badminton in our child days, we used to play cricket over there … Now since it is become a business, commercial place, we are using it for business purpose, that is all.[28]

Whilst all the families surveyed originally situated themselves in Barabazaar because of their business dealings there, all of them now work largely outside the area, reflecting how 'public' work life has now moved away from the 'private' courtyard house. The Rohatgi family came to Kolkata from Patna, Bihar, and were employed by the East India Company as *banians*. More recently, Mr Rohatgi's father opened a factory making light bulbs and fluorescent light tubes.

Mr Daw's great-great-grandfather built the house so he could be close to what he called 'significant dignitaries'.[29] The family firm, established in 1835, now deals in antique weapons and modern sporting guns. The Daw family has owned a gun shop in central Kolkata for 100 years, as well as other shops throughout Eastern India. On one occasion, he seemed to suggest that those in the family who were receiving an education were going off to do their own thing.[30] Another time, Mr Daw seemed to contradict himself stating quite emphatically that 'Nobody is going to give the service to the other people, government employment, nothing. Their trading is arms and ammunition for time immemorial.'[31]

The Sett family have lived in Kolkata since the 1660s, 'merchants of the yarn and cloth market at Sutanuti'.[32] According to Deb, the Setts 'began to decline from the mid-eighteenth century – just as Calcutta began to grow into a substantial city'.[33] Mr Sett remarked that his father's generation was no longer in business: 'my father had three brothers, one of them was an attorney, and my father and my next uncle, they are both doctors'.[34] Nowadays, Mr Sett is a director of a firm of building contractors, which he started himself and now runs from offices in South Kolkata. One of his brothers is an eye surgeon, the other an accountant with a firm in London. There is also a joint family transportation business, which is run from the house in Barabazaar.

Concluding reflections on hybrid identities

Nowadays, courtyard houses built by the nineteenth-century Bengali elite and owned by one family are few and far between. Many have been subdivided and sold as extended family sizes have shrunk or become more scattered. Many families have moved to south Kolkata to avoid the noise and congestion of Barabazaar. Some houses have been converted to shops and offices and others demolished as new buildings commanding higher rents have been built. Both

Mr Sett and Mr Daw agreed that Barabazaar has become much more commercial. Mr Sett described the changes of building use in the area around his house:

> It's now almost 50 per cent commercial. It was previously totally for residential. The ground floor of most of the buildings have changed, in fact, in our building also, in the front part, the part which has been divided to my Uncle. The ground floor has been changed to shops. So that way building changes in the, mostly in the ground floor of the buildings, they have changed to commercial.[35]

Mr Sett linked the recent changes in social life with the influx into Barabazaar of migrants from various parts of India.[36] Bengalis dominated the city's indigenous economy until the mid-nineteenth century, when their decline in fortunes was matched by the arrival of the Rajasthani, or 'Marwari'. Mr Rohatgi talked of how in the past his family were seen as people of standing in the Bengali community. As he described it, they did not need to flaunt their wealth, like the 'new rich' do now; he stated, 'we do not need to go out in a new car, anything would do, my wife did not have to wear expensive jewellery'.[37] Undoubtedly, when Mr Rohatgi spoke of the 'new rich' he was referring to Marwaris, who have now come to dominate the economy and life of Barabazaar.

Mirroring changes in urban life, the collective form of privacy found in the extended family, and embodied in the architecture and social practices of the courtyard house, is slowly beginning to change as families live their 'private' lives more separately. The house that clearly illustrates this process is the Rohatgi house, and for Mr Rohatgi, the break-up and reduction in size of his own extended family was a favourite topic of conversation, and one clearly tinged with some disappointment. In many ways, the Rohatgis did not live in their house as it had originally been conceived, with living centred in the courtyard. Instead, they now had a self-contained flat on the first floor that opened on to one side of a neglected courtyard.

Inevitably, the place of religious ritual in the courtyard house is changing. Nowadays, as families have become more scattered and rarely live in the family courtyard house, a committee of local residents run most *Pujas*. As Chaliha and Gupta comment, 'community lunch on the Puja days restores the spirit of the joint family without its problems'.[38] Mr Gupta, a Barabazaar paper trader pointed out that weddings are now mostly held in hotels or in purpose-built centres, rather than the family courtyard house.[39]

This conclusion cannot offer a closure, far less a definitive explanation for a changing and contradictory distinction between 'private' and 'public' life, and for a Bengali modern that is still being negotiated in Barabazaar today. As

Bhabha notes, attention to place does not presuppose closure, for the representation of identity most often occurs precisely at the point when there has been displacement.[40] For Bhabha the hybrid is formed out of the dual process of displacement and correspondence in the act of translation. Meaning seldom translates with pristine integrity, and often requires a degree of improvisation. Hybrid identities, therefore, are formed not out of an excavation and transferral of foreigness into the familiar, but out of this awareness of the incomplete interpretation that lingers on. It is from this position of 'in-betweenness' that Bhabha suggests the most interrogative forms of culture are produced, situated as they are at the cleavages and fissures of class, race, gender, nation and location. Bhabha encourages us to perceive this irresolvable, borderline, interstitial culture, which is at once, 'the *time* of cultural displacement, and the *space* of the 'untranslatable''.[41] The case of hybridity is pressed because the process of translation is, in his view, one of the most compelling tasks for the cultural critic in the modern world today.

Acknowledgements

The initial research for this chapter was made possible by a grant from the Indian National Trust for Art and Cultural Heritage (INTACH UK Trust).

Notes

1 For an overview of the colonial history of Kolkata, see P.T. Nair, *Calcutta Tercentenary Bibliography*, vols 1 and 2, Calcutta: The Asiatic Society, 1993.

2 Edward Said's ideas presented in his seminal work, *Orientalism* (Harmondsworth: Penguin, 1985), have been developed in the Indian context by Mark Crinson, *Empire Building, Orientalism and Victorian Architecture*, London: Routledge, 1996; and Richard Cronin, *Imagining India*, London: Macmillan, 1989.

3 Ibid., p.xxii.

4 In Kolkata, these essential differences between East and West can be clearly seen in the city and are illustrated by the former racial division of the 'black' and 'white' towns.

5 R.J.C. Young, *Colonial Desire: Hybridity in Theory, Culture and Race*, London: Routledge, 1995, p.6.

6 H.K. Bhabha, *The Location of Culture*, London: Routledge, 1994, p.25.

7 M. Bakhtin, *The Dialogic Imagination*, ed. M. Holquist, trans. C. Emerson and M. Holquist, Austin: University of Texas Press, 1981.

8 Bhabha, *The Location of Culture*, p.114.

9 Bhabha, *The Location of Culture*, p.112.

10 See D. Chakrabarty, 'Of garbage, modernity and the citizen's gaze', *Economic and Political Weekly*, 7–14 March 1992, pp.541–7; 'Postcoloniality and the artifice of history: who speaks for 'Indian' pasts?', *Representations*, Winter 1992, vol.37, pp.1–26; and 'Modernity and ethnicity in India', in D. Bennett (ed.), *Multicultural States Rethinking Difference and Identity*, London and New York: Routledge, 1998; S. Chattopadhyay, *Depicting Calcutta*, PhD Thesis, University of California, 1997; S. Kaviraj, 'Filth and the public sphere: concepts and practices about space in Calcutta', *Public Culture*, 1997, vol.10, part 1, pp.83–113.

11 Chattopadhyay, *Depicting Calcutta*, p.254.

12 In 1757, Colonel Robert Clive following his victory at Plassey installed Mir Jafar as the Nawab of Bengal, and the position of the East India Company strengthened considerably.

13 *Durga Puja*, held in the Bengali month of *Ashwin* (September–October), commemorates the 'universal resurgence of the power of creation and destruction'. Traditionally, celebrations begin in the courtyards of the houses, where a straw and clay idol of *Durga* is constructed in the *thakur dalan*.

14 D.K.L. Choudhoury, 'Trends in Calcutta architecture 1690–1903', in S. Chaudhuri (ed.), *Calcutta The Living City, Volume I: The Past*, Oxford: Oxford University Press, 1990, pp.156–75, p.174.

15 Ibid.

16 Ibid.

17 G.H.R. Tillotson, *The Tradition of Indian Architecture: Continuity, Controversy and Change since 1850*, New Haven: Yale University Press, 1989, taken from Chattopadhyay, *Depicting Calcutta*, p.265.

18 C. Deb, 'The "great houses" of Old Calcutta', in S. Chaudhuri (ed.), *Calcutta The Living City*, pp.56–63, p.61.

19 Kaviraj, 'Filth and the public sphere', p.91.

20 Ibid., p.92.

21 According to Edward Said, John Westlake's *Chapters on the Principles of International Law* (1894) advised that the 'uncivilised' sections of the globe should be annexed and occupied by the 'civilised' and advanced powers: Said, *Orientalism*, p.207.

22 Bhabha, *The Location of Culture*, p.25.

23 Mr A. Sett, interview with the author, Kolkata, 1 August 2001.

24 Mr S. Daw, interview with the author, Kolkata, 23 July 2001.

25 Mr A. Sett, interview with the author, Kolkata, 1 August 2001.

26 Mr S. Daw, interview with the author, Kolkata, 23 July 2001.

27 Mr P. Rohatgi, interview with the author, Kolkata, 30 July 2000.

28 Mr A. Sett, interview with the author, Kolkata, 1 August 2001.

29 Mr S. Daw, interview with the author, Kolkata, 19 August 2000.

30 Ibid., 17 August 2000.

31 Ibid., 23 July 2001.

32 Deb, 'The "great houses" of Old Calcutta', p.56.

33 Deb, 'The "great houses" of Old Calcutta', p.56.

34 Mr A. Sett, interview with the author, Kolkata, 1 August 2001.

35 Ibid.

36 Ibid.

37 Mr P. Rohatgi, interview with the author, Kolkata, 13 August 2000.

38 J. Chaliha and B. Gupta, 'Durga Puja in Calcutta', in Chaudhuri (ed.), *Calcutta The Living City*, pp.331–6, p.335.

39 Mr R. Gupta, interview with the author, Kolkata, 24 July 2001.

40 Bhabha, *The Location of Culture*, p.185.

41 Bhabha, *The Location of Culture*, p.225.

Chapter 12

Diagonal
Transversality and worldmaking

Andrew Ballantyne

Jean-Luc Godard famously said that 'Photography is truth, and the cinema is the truth twenty-four times a second'. Photography can be a kind of truth, but it is never the whole truth, and it can often be very misleading; for example, the 'magic of Hollywood' is not any straightforward kind of truth. Cinema can make a soundstage in the suburbs of Sydney conjure up a vision of *fin-de-siècle* Paris (in *Moulin Rouge*) or Pinewood studios look like the Himalayas (in *Black Narcissus*).[1] These are highly artificial 'constructions of place', and involve using models of parts of buildings as well as painted backdrops, photographic back-projection and digital effects. The sheer artificiality of the traditional Hollywood film-making process is extraordinary. Even something that looks like a simple conversation when we watch it play on the screen might have been filmed over several days, with the voices dubbed on afterwards, to give proper continuity in the soundtrack.

Godard's films used more direct means, using real settings more often than specially made sets, though even here the 'constructed place' of the action – the place that the viewer construes – is a tendentious idea of 'truth'. In *Alphaville*, Godard presented a view of a bleak future-world, which was filmed entirely in and around Paris.[2] But it is not recognizable as Paris. The recent housing projects and motorways of the 1960s are cut together without any intervening historic city fabric, so that we witness events unfolding in a world that is both real in one way and highly fabricated in another. Part of the irony in the line 'Photography is truth, and the cinema is the truth twenty-four times a second' is that it was delivered by a fictional character, in Godard's film *Le Petit Soldat* of 1960.[3] It was voiced by the character Bruno Forestier, a photographer, played by an actor (Michel Subor) who in the scene was just pretending to take photographs. The delivery of the line is very neatly framed by camera clicks. He takes one picture, delivers the line, and then takes another picture. Godard's camera follows his movements, so there is no need for an edit in the film. Subor's camera did not click loudly enough to be recorded with the same microphone as the dialogue, so the camera clicks were dubbed in afterwards, along with the voiceover that accompanies the scene. From one camera click to the other there is a time lapse of ten seconds, so we have witnessed the scene 240 times. However when we see these 240 images, what we want to say is that we have seen one image, and that it moved. Furthermore, although we are all perfectly ready to admit to seeing this movement, it is not there in the images. The film can be stopped, frame by frame, and we can see one still image after another – the movement is not in the images. It is an effect of the persistence of vision, which is something to do with the way that our eyes and minds work, not something that is there in the pictures. The illusion of movement arises on account of the relations between the pictures, and on account of the relations between the pictures and us. It would not work if we jumbled the order of the images. They must be carefully organized, but the experience is not dependent solely on them. If we saw the same sequence of images without having any memory, then we would not have a sense of movement. The illusion depends on our reception of it as well as on the images that are set before us. Without memory we could have absolutely no intuition of time or movement, and it would not have entered our heads that these things might be in the world. We can measure time and movement with a high degree of precision and objectivity, but without memory no one would ever have wanted to say that they existed.

Transversality 1: identity fused from fragments

The process by which we fuse different impressions into an impression of something continuous has been given the name 'transversality'. It is the process by means of which we have an impression of travelling through the countryside when we look out of the window of a moving train, an impression formed from glimpses of different non-continuous parts of the scenery.[4] The philosopher Gilles Deleuze makes use of this idea (and this term) in his analysis of the author Marcel Proust (1871–1922) and the way in which his great narrative *A la recherche du temps perdu* works.[5] What Proust did in the narrative was to give apparently unconnected impressions of various people as they participate in events, and the reader is left to piece them together, as in fact we would have to in life, if we were to meet these characters in a variety of circumstances and form an impression of them as individuals with a range of aspects to their lives. We link our varied impressions of a person together, and tell ourselves that they are all impressions of one person, who continues between the impressions. In Proust's narrative, then, the impressions are not unconnected after all. Not only are they are all part of the same work, placed there by Proust, they are also connected together by the reader, who forms an impression of the characters.[6] Roland Barthes remarked that it was Proust's great good fortune that on each re-reading we skip different passages in the text, so it seems to remain alive, and to be a different experience each time it is revisited.[7]

In normal circumstances this fusion of impressions happens without our thinking about it. If the effect does not work for us spontaneously then we do not read very far. One of the astonishing things about film (and it is prefigured in literature) is how we find ourselves responding at a visceral and emotional level to sequences of words or moving images that are in many ways unlike the things that they depict. There are no edits in nature, but we instinctively know how to piece together a scene with complex editing, such as the famous shower scene in Alfred Hitchcock's *Psycho*.[8] It is not necessary for someone to explain how to read these images – we know, and we feel anxiety as we watch them.

This brings me to the 'diagonal' in the title. There is an idiomatic French expression, meaning to skim-read, which is '*lire en diagonal*' – to read on the diagonal. This of course is what we do when we experience the world. We do not give everything equal attention. Hence the connection with my other starting point: Nelson Goodman's argument in *Ways of Worldmaking* that in effect we live alongside others, but in different worlds, because different groups deal with the world using different sets of ideas, and therefore have different sets of experiences, even when they are going through apparently similar moves in similar places.[9] It is an idea developed from William James's 'pluralistic universe', and has an echo in the writing of Félix Guattari, when he mentions 'universes of value'.[10] We live on the diagonal, noticing some aspects of the world, neglecting others. What is of interest to me here is that there is a multiplicity of these diagonal readings that intersect in any individual thing, whether that thing is concrete, abstract, organic or inorganic. Each of these diagonals might be termed a 'vector' (which is Deleuze's term). If we turn the idea to bear on building, for example, there is a famous double-page spread in Le Corbusier's *Vers une architecture*, in which he shows us at the top of the page two images of Greek temples, both Doric temples.[11] The first is very early: one of the temples at Paestum. The second shows the Parthenon, the most refined and accomplished version of the Doric temple, dating from some 300 years later. A vector runs along this line of development. What Le Corbusier did was to suggest that we would see a comparable development in the motor car, and at the foot of the two pages he showed two models which to us look rather similar, but which would have had a different effect in their day – the first would have been seen as antiquated, the second as sophisticated and new. There is a clear geometry here: the vector that connects one car with the other runs in parallel with the vector that connects the two buildings.

Transversality 2: group identity

Up to this point, I have used the term 'transversality' in the way that Deleuze used it in his 'Proust' text. In fact Deleuze gave two sources for the word 'transversality'. One of them is Proust himself (and it is from him that Deleuze developed his more general idea set out above),[12] the second is from a paper by Guattari.[13] The expectation set up by this reference is that the term would be explained at greater length and in more detail in Guattari's essay, but in fact if we turn to it then what we find is utterly unlike anything in Proust, and the idea is not recognizable as the basis of the idea used by Deleuze. The paper is about group-identity phenomena in psychiatric institutions. The term derives from Freud's 'transference', whereby the patient being analysed 'bonds' with the analyst. Guattari tried to set up situations so that this type of relationship developed differently, without the investment of patriarchal authority in the analyst.[14]

Deleuze and Guattari have from the beginning of their collaborations taken the view that the personality (the subject) is always multiple. There are group phenomena where parts of the personalities in the group form significant interactions, which makes for the development of a group 'personality' or subject. Guattari developed the idea from reading the anthropologist Gregory Bateson. Guattari wrote:

> Gregory Bateson has clearly shown that what he calls the 'ecology of ideas' cannot be contained within the domain of the psychology of the individual, but organizes itself into systems or 'minds', the boundaries of which no longer coincide with the participant individuals.[15]

Even in institutions such as universities, where the 'individuals' usually pass as sane, the group dynamics can nevertheless lead to collective insanities. In a psychiatric hospital the group dynamics can influence a patient's chances of recovery, and are far from incidental to the institution's effectiveness. An individual building's identity is caught up with that of the group. For example, the Villa Savoye has various group identities. It is part of a series of villas designed in the 1920s by Le Corbusier, all of them having certain principles and elements in common. In this group, the villa is normative and conformist in character, at the heart of the group, which it is often chosen to exemplify. If we took a different grouping, however, such as the group of all houses built during the 1920s, then the villa would be so peripheral as almost to face exclusion from the group. The typical 1920s house was not remotely like this, and if the villa is noticed in this group then it would be seen as exceptional and innovative. Another way of looking at the house would be to examine the politics of the household, which are quite easily read in the plan. This aspect of the house is very conservative. There is living accommodation for several servants, and the service areas are clearly separated from the rooms to be occupied by the masters. In this respect the Villa Savoye is less forward-looking than were the most traditional houses of the peasant farmers in the neighbourhood, with their informal and egalitarian living arrangements. So, if we analyse the role that the Villa Savoye plays in each of the groups, we can see that in the first group it is seen as normative, in the second it is seen as revolutionary, and in the third it is seen as reactionary. Which is the 'real' Villa Savoye? The answer is that they are all real, and all of them coexist. What actually matters will depend on the context, which is to say: it will depend on relations of transversality in whatever grouping is constituted around it.

If we go back to Deleuze's world of lines and vectors, we could describe the various trajectories of the Corbusian *'objet-type'* villa, the general 1920s house and the domestic history of developing social relations, and see all of these lines intersecting in the single building. There is in each line an idea of group identity (in establishing the line) and then various ideas of politics, both in establishing the importance of incidents along the line, and in determining the relative importance of one line with respect to another.

Transversality 3: group politics

Politics are even more clearly at work in Guattari's paper on transversality. The traditional way to regulate matters is for the doctors to have total control of decision-making processes, while the patients have none, which makes for an apparently straightforward set of political relations. To follow Guattari's terminology: the doctors would form a group subject and would objectify the patients – turn them into objects, rather than include them in the group subject. In fact the way things work out is more complex than that, and there is a degree of influence in each direction – a degree of 'transversality', here using the word in a new sense, used only by Guattari.

Guattari worked at a clinic where he tried to induce a higher 'coefficient of transversality' by setting up a rota in which staff in the institution would perform a range of tasks, so that the doctors were no longer seen as remote figures with unquestioned authority.[16] There were problems, because although the doctors could be persuaded to work in the kitchens and to do cleaning, the kitchen staff could not be persuaded to look after patients. Meanwhile patients' clubs were set up, allowing the patients to set goals, raise money, and achieve those goals, independently of approval from the medical staff. This was all described as having a high level of transversality, which is here plainly a political term, and clearly value-laden – transversality is good, and the more of it the better. The system proved to be very effective. The patients remained psychotic and would have been unable to function in the wider community, but in their specialized environment they were capable of cooperative lively activity, in marked distinction from the lethargy that is usual in such groups.

Micropolitics and the ecology of ideas

My identity is always in part determined by the group that I am seen to be in, and by my role in that group. In the world of Deleuze and Guattari, the 'individual' is far from being indivisible, but is produced by these various identities and roles, which have 'political' relations with one another. The term that they coined for this 'politics-within-the-individual' is 'micropolitics'. In the Deleuze-and-Guattari world there is recognition of experience, but it is always associated with an application of strict logic that is never part of common sense. Where politics is concerned, it seems to be all the same whether we are dealing with nation states, minority groups, familial groups, individuals or molecules. The logic runs right through the different scales, regardless of the fact that we have different common-sense ways of thinking about these things, and a different range of names for the relations in different scales of operation. What is an illness at one scale is a war at another. This leads to a blurring of any definite distinction between the living and the inorganic. Living things are composed of inorganic elements.[17] Guattari cited Bateson: 'There is an ecology of bad ideas, just as there is an ecology of weeds',[18] and continued:

> Now more than ever, nature cannot be separated from culture; in order to comprehend the interactions between eco-systems, the mecanosphere and social and individual Universes of reference, we must learn to think 'transversally'. Just as monstrous and mutant algae invade the lagoon of Venice, so our television screens are populated, saturated, by 'degenerate' images and statements. In the field of social ecology, men like Donald Trump are permitted to proliferate freely, like another species of algae, taking over entire districts of New York and Atlantic City; he 'redevelops' by raising

> rents, thereby driving out tens of thousands of poor families, most of whom are condemned to homelessness, becoming the equivalent of the dead fish of environmental ecology.[19]

We must see the unit of survival, not as an individual organic species, but the species plus its habitat. However, there is a style of speaking at work in his texts, which fuses the inorganic parts of a habitat as part of the living 'unit of survival' (species plus habitat). So buildings are certainly included in the equation, and Guattari also mentioned 'incorporeal species such as music, the arts, cinema',[20] in the company of which the gestural art of architecture certainly belongs. In this sort of ecology a *genius loci* can clearly flourish. The 'spirit of the place' cannot live as an independent entity and, as it has no body, if we try to separate it from its habitat it not only dies but vanishes altogether. It is a product of transversality, and does not inhere in the parts of the place, individually or collectively, but is produced when those material elements come into contact with a suitably prepared observer. In one manner of speaking it is an illusion, and does not exist. But if we continue to speak in that manner then we have to allow that there is not movement in the cinema, only twenty-four stillnesses a second. And we have to allow that our disparate fragmentary identities do not really cohere into a unified 'self'.

The crack-up

Something like this idea has been around since the eighteenth century, when David Hume found that if he started to think about the idea of the self, it became difficult to pin down as a distinct persona that persisted through everything he did and said.[21] In this aspect of his thinking Hume can be seen as a proto-poststructuralist.[22] Deleuze and Guattari were to take up the idea of the divided or dispersed mind in their collaborative works, especially the two volumes that carry the title *Capitalism and Schizophrenia*.[23] They were not being eccentric in taking this view. 'The test of a first-rate intelligence', said F. Scott Fitzgerald, 'is the ability to hold two opposed ideas in the mind at the same time, and still retain the ability to function'.[24] This is the most observable kind of example, when the mental conflict is conscious. However, most of what goes on in the mind is unconscious, and many such conflicts are resolved without coming to the surface. We follow habit, rather than calling every repetition of a comparable situation for a fresh judgement. In fact Deleuze and Guattari do not characterize the mind as being composed of two parts, but of crowds, swarms or tribes. It has a parallel in Marvin Minsky's work on artifical intelligence, which he sought to explain to a non-specialist audience in his book *The Society of Mind*.[25] He sets out a way in which we can imagine how the mind, being made of non-thinking parts, can nevertheless think. The key here, as in Hume's thought, is the multiplicity of connections between the multifarious parts. The subject can be dispersed.

One key concept in *Anti-Oedipus* is the machine – composed of a minimum of two parts, it produces something. The things that are brought together might be different parts of the mind, or they might involve something external, such as someone else's mind, in which case the thinking and the production could be said to go on between the two. In the Guattari-world, there are machines everywhere, swarms of them, and they produce not only the things that would ordinarily be expected, but also emotional states – especially desire (which is produced when machines break down).

If this is one's view of 'the subject', then there is no very clear threshold that marks its limits, and in Deleuze and Guattari's world there is no discomfort in allowing a computer or an information flow from a television programme to be part of the range of elements that constitutes the subject.[26] Buildings have a role to play here. Caves and labyrinths, spires and towers, haunt imaginations and connect with our desires. They play a role in the way we think, and in the formation of the subject. Therefore they are part of the subject. 'They are in us as much as we are in them', as Bachelard put it.[27] The building is part of the unit of survival.

Dispersal

The direction of Guattari's use of the term 'transversality' is to make an accommodation to the various parts of the subject-properly-conceived, so that we do not find all the power concentrated in a single part, which would result in micro-fascisms and objectification. So, for example, if we see the architect as the sole originator of form in the building process, then this sort of architect will see it as necessary to bend everything else to his or her will without modification or compromise. This is the 'Fountainhead' view of architecture – I refer to Ayn Rand's novel, where the triumph of the architect's will is presented in absolutely heroic terms.[28] It serves well as an example of a view of the unified will, which clearly has fascist overtones. It could not be further removed from Guattari's conception of the architecture-world, with its de-centered subjects in transversalized working relationships. The practical effects and attitudes of his vision seem to be reminiscent of William Morris's idealized medievalism, but Guattari's language is full of references to 'machines' in a way that Morris's never was, and the conception of inter-personal relations is utterly different. In Guattari's analysis, the conditions of subjectivity have irrevocably changed, and there is no point in cultivating a nostalgia for the works of another age, even though we cannot hold ourselves back from aestheticizing them and thinking that we have some appreciation of them as 'works of art', even though they were produced long before there was such a category to put them in.[29] The productions of other cultures may look to us irresistibly like works of art, and for us that is the way they work. But in a culture that has not developed this category, its role would be utterly different. The particular object is taken up in different worlds, and the cultural value in one world is incommensurable with its cultural value in the other.

The subject

If we are to follow Guattari's model of the dispersed personality that becomes insparable from its environment and its ecology, then not only would we start to think of ourselves as having a strong rapport with our surroundings, but we would start to think of them as part of ourselves. Not only is the architect displaced from the position of the individualistic tyrant with a will to form, but other voices come to be heard. Again, this means not only other human voices (empowered members of a 'design team') but the view of the subject is such that the building's materials would be conceived as part of the living subject that is producing the architecture, and they should therefore have a transversal relation with the other parts of that subject, and have a voice in the form-making. The material is conceived as an active agent, as part of the schizoanalytic subject, and one would try to avoid objectifying it, in a way that would turn it into a passive 'patient'. In Louis Kahn's famous conversation with a brick, the brick says 'I like an arch',[30] which sound like a concern for traditional craft values to inform the production of modern buildings. Guattari's voice is very different, the appeal being made for the sake of the mental health of the subject. If Lake Erie can go mad, then so can architecture, especially if we see it in connection with the systems of commercial development. There is a political dimension to the thinking, and an awareness that the aesthetic is caught up in this thinking, but no attempt to define or promote a particular artistic style.

Conclusion

What we have here is a heady mix of politics, ecology and psychoanalysis, which works by way of a rather exotic set of concepts to a conclusion that sounds rather like a romantic investment in feeling caught up in the spiritual being of a place. A romantic such as Wordsworth could call the earth 'the soul of all my moral being',[31] which certainly involves a complex process of transversality. (In Guattari's language it would be described as making use of the earth as an instrument of subjectification). In fact in Deleuze and Guattari's hands the conclusion is utterly unlike the romantic attachment to place, because it is linked in their writings with ideas of nomadism, constant reformulation and re-subjectification.[32] Their concern is never to recapture the original primary sensibility of the noble savage, but to go forward in an experimental frame of mind, to produce new ways of living, new ways of becoming. Deleuze and Guattari enjoined us to reinvent ourselves – an enterprise that can look inefficient or insane – the preserve of a leisured elite or of the terminally disadvantaged, such as the patients at the La Borde clinic. Personalities are produced from the micropolitics of the unconscious, interacting in connection with others and the habitat. Places are produced through the transversal interactions that we make with their parts, noticed in a fragmentary way, on the diagonal.

Notes

1 Baz Luhrmann, *Moulin Rouge* (2001); Michael Powell and Emeric Pressburger, *Black Narcissus*, (1947)
2 Jean-Luc Godard, *Alphaville* (1965).
3 Jean-Luc Godard, *Le Petit Soldat*, 1960. The screenplay was translated by Nicholas Garnham as *Le Petit Soldat: A Film by Jean-Luc Godard*, New York: Simon and Schuster, 1967, p.39.
4 G. Deleuze, *Proust et les signes*, Paris: Presses Universitaires de France, 1972; trans. R. Howard, *Proust and Signs*, London: Athlone, 2000 p.168.
5 M. Proust, *A la recherche du temps perdu*, 12 vols, Paris: Gallimard, 1969; trans. S. Moncrieff, A. Mayor and T. Kilmartin, rev. D.J. Enright, *In Search of Lost Time*, 6 vols, London: Chatto & Windus, 1992.
6 Deleuze, *Proust*, pp.168–9.
7 R. Barthes, *Le Plaisir du texte*, Paris: Editions du Seuil, 1973; trans. R. Miller, *The Pleasure of the Text*, New York: Farrar, Straus and Giroux, 1975, p.11.
8 Alfred Hitchcock, *Psycho* (1960).
9 N. Goodman, *Ways of Worldmaking*, Indianapolis: Hackett, 1978.
10 W. James, *A Pluralistic Universe*, New York: Longmans, Green and Co., 1909; cited by Goodman, *Worldmaking*, p.2. F. Guattari, *Les trois écologies*, Paris: Galilée, 1989; trans. I. Pindar and P. Sutton *The Three Ecologies*, London: Athlone, 2000, p.45.
11 Le Corbusier, *Vers une architecture*, Paris: Crès, 1923; trans. by F. Etchells, *Towards a New Architecture*, London: Architectural Press, 1987, pp.134–5.
12 Proust, *Recherche*, III, p.1029.
13 F. Guattari, 'Psychanalyse et transversalité', a report presented to the first International Psycho-Drama Congress, Paris, 1964, published in the *Revue de psychothérapie institutionelle*, no. 1; trans. R. Sheed, 'Transversality', in *Molecular Revolution*, Harmondsworth: Penguin, 1984; cited by Deleuze, *Proust*, p.188.
14 The idea's history has been helpfully traced by Gary Genosko, who confirms that Deleuze and Guattari did not reach a consensus on the word's meaning. G. Genosko, 'The acceleration of transversality in the middle', in M. Toy (ed.), *Hypersurface Architecture*, London: Wiley, 1998, pp.32–7; G. Genosko, 'The life and work of Félix Guattari: from transversality to ecosophy', in Guattari, *Three Ecologies*, pp.106–59; G. Genosko, 'Transversality', in *Félix Guattari: an Abberant Introduction*, London: Continuum, 2002, pp.66–121.

15 Guattari, *Three Ecologies*, p.54; see also Genosko, 'From transversality to ecosophy', p.93, note 56. G. Bateson, *Steps to an Ecology of Mind*, New York: Chandler, 1972, p.339.

16 Guattari, *Three Ecologies*, p.111.

17 Quoted J. Marks, *Deleuze*, London: Pluto, 1998, p.29. G. Deleuze, *Pourparlers 1972–1990*, Paris: Minuit, 1990; trans. M. Joughin, *Negotiations*, New York: Columbia University Press, 1997, p.143.

18 Guattari, *Three Ecologies*, p.27. G. Bateson, 'Pathologies of Epistemology', in *Steps to an Ecology of Mind*, pp.454–63; p.460; cited in Guattari, *Three Ecologies*, p.71.

19 Guattari, *Three Ecologies*, p.43.

20 Félix Guattari, *Chaosmose*, Paris: Galilée, 1992; trans. by P. Bains and J. Pefanis, *Chaosmosis: An Ethico-Aesthetic Paradigm*, Sydney: Power, 1995, p.120.

21 D. Hume, *A Treatise of Human Nature* [1739], eds L.A. Selby-Bigge and P.H. Nidditch, Oxford: Clarendon, 1978, p.218; and see Book I, part IV, section VI, 'Of personal identity', pp.251–63.

22 G. Deleuze, *Empirisme et subjectivité: essai sur la nature humaine selon Hume*, Paris: Presses Universitaires de France, 1953; trans. C.V. Boundas, *Empiricism and Subjectivity: An Essay on Hume's Theory of Human Nature*, New York: Columbia University Press, 1991.

23 G. Deleuze and F. Guattari, *L'Anti-Oedipe; Capitalisme et schizophrénie t. 1*, Paris: Minuit, 1972; trans. H.R. Lane, R. Hurley and M. Seem, *Anti-Oedipus; Capitalism and Schizophrenia volume 1*, New York: Viking, 1977. G. Deleuze and F. Guattari, *Mille plateaux; Capitalisme et schizophrénie t. 2*, Paris: Minuit, 1980; trans. B. Massumi, *A Thousand Plateaus; Capitalism and Schizophrenia volume 2*, London: Athlone, 1987.

24 F. Scott Fitzgerald, 'The Crack-up' (1936), in *The Crack-up with other Pieces and Stories*, Harmondsworth: Penguin, 1965, p.39. The piece is discussed in Deleuze and Guattari, *Thousand Plateaus*, pp.198–200.

25 M. Minsky, *The Society of Mind*, London: Heinemann, 1987.

26 Guattari, *Chaosmosis*, p.4.

27 G. Bachelard, *La Poétique de l'espace*, Paris: Presses Universitaires de France, 1958; trans. M. Jolas, *The Poetics of Space*, Boston: Beacon Press, 1969, p.xxxiii.

28 A. Rand, *The Fountainhead*, New York: Bobbs Merrill, 1943.

29 Guattari, *Chaosmosis*, p.99.

30 L.I. Kahn, *Writings, Lectures, Interviews*, ed. A. Latour, New York: Rizzoli, 1991, pp.293, 296.

31 W. Wordsworth, 'Lines written a few miles above Tintern Abbey' (1798), lines 111–12.

32 The romantic attachment to place was of course explored very significantly by Heidegger. See A. Ballantyne, *What is Architecture?*, London: Routledge, 2002, pp.15–25 and the references therein.

Chapter 13

Modernity and the threshold

Psychologizing the places in-between

Stephen Kite

In James Tiptree's science fiction short story 'The psychologist who wouldn't do awful things to rats', the researcher Lipsitz sketches the edge behaviour of the common rat (Fig. 13.1), and explains:

> There's an enormous difference between the way Rattus and Cricetus – [rats and hamsters] – behave in the open field, and they're both *rodents*. Even as simple a thing as edge behaviour – ... Edges. I mean the way the animal responds to edges and the shape of the environment ... it's basic to living and nobody seems to have explored it.[1]

I shall argue here that in the sphere of human behaviour the notion of edges has not only been explored in modernism, but is central to modernity's construction of place. Even in this spoof image of *rattus rattus* we readily recognize edge behaviours that pertain to the psychology of the human condition like 'edge-peering' and 'edge-tracking'; and most would confess to 'rim-teetering', 'cill-perching', 'wall-clinging' and so on.

The twentieth-century Dutch architect and thinker Aldo van Eyck, for instance, attracted by the spatial ambiguities projected by modernist designers such as Duiker and Rietveld, maintained that humanity's 'home realm is the in-between realm – the realm architecture sets out to articulate'.[2] In exploring this 'in-between realm' my argument will centre on the psychoanalytical aesthetics

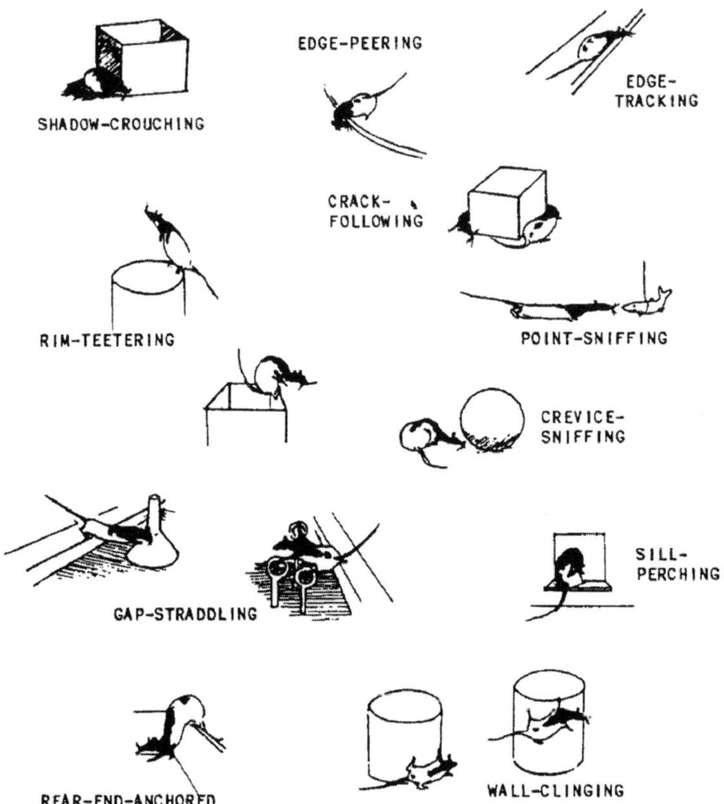

13.1
The edge behaviour of *Rattus Rattus*. (From J.R. Tiptree, in D. Hartwell and K. Cramer, (eds), *The Ascent of Wonder The Evolution of Hard SF*, London: Orbit, 1994, Fig.18.)

of the significant modernist English art-writer, painter and poet, Adrian Stokes (1902–72). Stokes stresses the 'otherness' of the artwork in a theory of art that reifies the role of limestone and marble, and the fantasies connected with these materials, in European civilization. In his *Form in Art* of 1955, Stokes stresses this lapidary standpoint: 'The work of art, then, because it is expressively self-subsistent, should invoke in us some such idea as one of "entity." It is as if the various emotions had been rounded like a stone.'[3] Yet Stokes's own paintings draw us into more complex and nuanced spaces that mediate between the otherness of the artwork and a more enveloping condition. In fact in the same paper, *Form in Art*, together with his longstanding assertion of the pebble-like apartness of the artwork, Stokes entertains the role that fusion might play in the making and appreciation of art, *together* with object-otherness. Here his postwar (Second World War) writing is enriched by his own research into artists of a more plastic approach to form, predominantly Michelangelo, and shifts within the aesthetic thinking of English object-relations psychoanalysis that gave increasing recognition to the role of 'oceanic feeling' – in Freud's adopted phrase – in the creation and experience of art and architecture.

My concern here is to examine these theories in the actual constructed places of embodied experience. For example, when Aldo van Eyck built the Hubertus House in Amsterdam between 1976 and 1978 as a refuge for single mothers and their children, he sought to create a nesting of 'in-between places' that mitigated the 'psychic strain' of the occupants, allowing them to feel secure while negotiating routes back to the outer world.[4] The building's rich spatiality demonstrates van Eyck's success in finding a counterform to these complex psychological ambitions; it is simultaneously open and protective (Fig. 1.13).

At this point it is important to outline those aspects of Adrian Stokes's theory and biography relevant to this essay. One of his most seminal experiences was the discovery of Italy; on New Year's Eve 1921–2, while still an undergraduate at Oxford, he travelled to Rapallo on the 'Italian Riviera', experiencing the passage through the Alps and the Mont Cenis tunnel into Italy as a revelatory discovery of place and space. Throughout the 1920s he travelled widely in Italy, discovering Venice, Rimini and Urbino. These sites of Renaissance culture became the revered centres of his aesthetic. At Urbino he was overwhelmed by Luciano Laurana's fifteenth-century courtyard in the Ducal Palace, and the affinities between this architecture and the artist invariably associated with the Urbino court, Piero della Francesca. Laurana's 'columns are brothers'[5] he writes, and describes Piero della Francesca's forms as 'brothers and sisters at ease within the ancestral hall of space'.[6] In a Piero painting such as *The Annunciation* (Plate 4), the spaces between forms and figures are as significant and measured as the forms themselves; a cognate sensibility pervades the arcades of Luciano Laurana's Palace courtyard.

Equal to the Italian sisterhood of form in space is the southern materiality – the 'love of stone' – particularly the compacted sea-life that is limestone. In an organicist strategy of interpretation Stokes employs the phrase 'stone-blossom' to describe how in certain *quattrocento* artworks – notably Agostino di Duccio's reliefs in the Tempio Malatestiano at Rimini – artists made the stone to 'bloom' by realizing, on the surface of the marble, fantasies read in the depths of the medium. In *Stones of Rimini* (1934), Stokes focuses these organicist notions by relating them to the psychologies of artistic process, to articulate one of his most central themes: the dyad of 'carving–modelling':

> A figure carved in stone is fine carving when one feels that not the figure, but the stone through the medium of the figure, has come to life. Plastic conception, [modelling] on the other hand, is uppermost when the material … from which, a figure has been made appears no more than as so much suitable stuff for this creation.[7]

The 'carver' does not approach the medium aggressively; but is an attentive lover who woos the stone; as the 'cultivator works the surface of the

Mother Earth, so the sculptor rubs his stone to elicit the shapes that his eye has sown in the matrix.'[8] *Stones of Rimini* is a prolonged reflection on the encounter with Agostino di Duccio's low-relief sculptures in Alberti's Tempio Malatestiano at Rimini, first seen by Stokes in July 1925.[9] Crucial to the issues of constructing place explored here is Stokes's mapping of the carving–modelling theories of artistic process on to the object-relations theories of that strand of Freudian psychoanalysis developed by the analyst Melanie Klein in her work on infantile development. From 1930 Stokes underwent seven years of analysis with Klein; her ideas, and the terminology of psychoanalysis, become increasingly evident in his postwar texts. Klein concentrates on the early years of child development, maintaining that in the early stage of life – defined as the 'paranoid-schizoid' position – the infant is in a state of oneness with the mother. At this stage the child relates only to part-objects, such as the mother's breast, which may be 'good' or 'bad', satisfying or frustrating. Gradually, in the first few weeks of life, the 'paranoid-schizoid' position matures to the 'depressive' stage of the ego where the child now recognizes both its own identity and the mother, as a whole other person, and concurrently suffers guilt at the pain and aggression previously inflicted on the mother. Klein assumes an in-born flux of love and destructive feeling wherein maturity entails coming to terms with this inherent polarity of drives. In Stokes's theory, architecture and art plays a fundamental role in this on-going process of maturation. Paintings, buildings or sculptures are acts of repair the artist makes in the outer world that correspond to processes of integration within the psyche. Stokes contends that the cardinal role of art is to ensure 'a milieu for adults, for true adults, for heroes of a well-integrated inner world to live in'.[10]

The most significant development in Stokes's later books is to map the dyad of the artistic processes of 'carving–modelling' on to the two states identified by Klein in child development. So, 'carving' – reflecting the depressive position – represents a more mature stage of ego-development in regard to art-making, than the 'modelling' aspects of the first, 'paranoid-schizoid' position. At the same time, however, Stokes increasingly recognizes that 'carving–modelling' and the two psychoanalytical positions are inter-compensatory, both in the experience of and the creation of art. The viewpoint that had previously privileged carving and the achievements of the depressive Kleinian position transmutes to a more complex position; greater credence is now given to the modelling process and the role that fusion plays in the creation and appreciation of the art object, together with object-otherness.

Stokes now posits a new position – 'the aesthetic position' – that, he maintains, 'deserves a category of its own', a position that exists in reciprocity between the two fundamental Kleinian positions, encompassing 'homogeneity or fusion combined, in differing proportions, with the sense of object-otherness'.[11]

Commentators have noted the parallels between Stokes's 'aesthetic position' and Winnicott's notion of 'potential space', the 'hypothetical area that exists ... between the baby and the object (mother or part of mother) during the phase of the repudiation of the object as not-me, that is, at the end of being merged in with the object.'[12] Winnicott argues that it is in this space that the first objects are created out of the child's imagination; the 'transitional object' – the 'special woollen square, or the mother's handkerchief'. According to Winnicott these found objects represent 'the beginning of the infant's creation of the world, ... we have to admit that in the case of every infant the world has to be created anew. The world as it presents itself is of no meaning to the newly-developing human being unless it is created as well as discovered.'[13] It is with these vital transitional spaces and objects that we construct at the 'beginning of our personal worlds' with which this essay is concerned.

Envelopment and exposure

Terms such as 'homogeneity', 'object-otherness' or the 'aesthetic position' – difficult to grasp in the contemplation of painting and sculpture – can be readily recognized in constructed places as factors of common experience; the pole positions of envelopment and exposure. In an important essay 'The natural imagination, an essay on the experience of architecture', published in *The Architectural Review* of January 1989, Colin St John Wilson aimed to explicate the riches of Adrian Stokes's psychologized spatial theories to a wider audience.

Envelopment (relating to the Kleinian oceanic paranoid-schizoid position), states Wilson, finds its architectural analogue in 'the architectural experience of interior space that is modelled in rhythmic forms of flowing and merging continuity'.[14] Hans Scharoun's Philarmonic Hall, for the Berlin Philharmonic (1956–63), epitomizes these womb-like spaces; the concert audience is gathered on to interlocking terraces within the great enfolding tent-like roof of the hall. In the contrary position of exposure – relating to the Kleinian depressive position of the child's later development – the detached awareness of object-otherness is demonstrated by the architectural experience 'of open space and the external confrontation with a building's wholeness and self-sufficiency, the carved and massive frontality of its stance over-against you'.[15] Wilson illustrates this 'position' with the frontality of Le Corbusier's Villa Stein at Garches (1927). With reference to those texts in which Stokes develops his intermediary 'aesthetic position', Wilson stresses the originality of Stokes's argument that it is 'uniquely the role of the masterpiece to make possible the *simultaneous* experience of these two polar modes [identified by Melanie Klein] enjoyment at the same time of intense sensations of being inside and outside, of envelopment and detachment, of oneness and separateness.' Stokes alone, he contends, 'perceives the secret to lie in [the] *fusion* [of these two polar modes] and upon this rests the originality and significance of his vision'.[16] Stokes's later texts multiply instances of those architectural elements that conflate the two experiences; 'the great work of art', he writes, 'is surrounded by silence. It remains palpably 'out there', yet none the less enwraps us; we do not so much absorb as become ourselves absorbed'.[17]

In an article that draws on Stokes's memories of *Living in Ticino, 1947–50*, Stokes evokes the immense sense of security that these in-between physical realms of portico, arcade and loggia can offer:

> As I walk under the arcade of Locarno's main square, I see in a clear and liquid shade a café table with a light-blue cloth that touches a stone pier. I think I would be entirely safe there: leaning against the pillar I would be able to partake utterly of every thought: I would be immobile, provided for, as in the womb yet out-of-doors: existence within and existence without would be thinly divided: in the blue tablecloth I would clutch the sky.[18]

Wilson takes the head of Schinkel's staircase in the Altes Museum, Berlin (1822–30) as a masterly demonstration of the fusion of elation and calm evoked by these mediating aedicular spaces. Observers feel suspended in the grove of Ionic columns of the great portico of the Museum as they gaze through and beyond them to the open spaces of the Lustgarten.

Prospect – refuge

Interesting confirmation of these psychoanalytically derived theories can be found in later research into the psychology of landscape and environmental behaviour, in particular the theory of 'prospect and refuge' advanced by the English geographer Jay Appleton in his *The Experience of Landscape* of 1975.[19] Appleton arrives at his theory of prospect and refuge from the angle of evolutionary behaviourism, yet his conclusions strikingly parallel Stokes. While Appleton is clearly aware of the sexually charged and anthropomorphic responses to, and interpretations of, landscape that precede and post-date Freud – notions that the relationship of humanity to the habitat is that of 'the child to the "Earth-Mother"' – he stresses that the imperative need of primitive man-the-hunter – transmitted to his modern descendants – is the 'desire to see without being seen'.[20] Humanity, like most creatures, has two key requirements of the habitat: a 'foraging-ground' to provide food and other requirements and a 'nesting-place' related to the foraging ground in which to shelter and raise the young. In these twin concepts, argues Appleton, will be found 'the basis of that interaction between a creature and its habitat on which the survival of the species ultimately depends'.[21] There is only one short paper in which Appleton extends prospect-refuge theory into the territory of architectural spaces, his *Landscape and Architecture* of 1993. Here the conclusions he draws again echo Stokes:

> Among environmental scientists there is an increasing recognition that we are attached to both of these contrasting elements [foraging-ground and nesting-place] by deep bonds of association involving attraction, anxiety, repulsion and other feelings.... To everyone the terms 'indoors' and 'outdoors' suggest a pair of complementary concepts whose importance can be easily understood in everyday environmental experience.... [The] many problems of architectural aesthetics hinge on the interaction between these two conditions.[22]

Like Stokes at Ticino he enumerates those architectural elements that offer a 'potential place of refuge from the "great outdoors"', namely: 'arcades, porticoes, verandas, balconies, overhanging eaves, exterior staircases, and recesses of all kinds' elements that 'render the separation of indoors and outdoors to some degree less absolute'.[23] Here Appleton refers to Grant Hildebrand's work on Frank Lloyd Wright, his *The Wright Space. Pattern and Meaning in Frank Lloyd Wright's Houses*, which, in applying prospect-refuge theory to the interpretation of Wright's domestic architecture, seems to explain the telluric power of these dwellings. Unlike Appleton, Hildebrand shows some awareness of Stokes's theories. For example, in his analysis of one of the earliest of Wright's Prairie Houses, the Cheney House of 1904, he quotes Wilson's paraphrase of Stokes that the masterpiece allows 'the *simultaneous* experience of [the] two polar modes; enjoyment at the same time of intense sensations of being inside and outside, of envelopment and detachment, of oneness and separateness'.[24] The Cheney house is an early demonstration of the Wrightian spatial archetype of an anchoring refuge hearth burning at the core of the house, related to prospect vistas through extended bands of glazing, subtly managed in plan and section to allow the occupant to see without being seen; to command the beyond, while feeling deeply rooted and secure. In a note to his study, Hildebrand suggests that Stokes's 'envelopment and exposure' is a 'close cousin' to Appleton's 'refuge and prospect'.[25] A further spatial pattern that Hildebrand identifies in the Cheney House is its 'edge of the wood' character; the refuge womb-like hearth parts of the house are enfolded in the grove, 'the primordial refuge of nature', while the prospect parts reach forward from these refuge places, projecting the gaze into the furthest reaches of the prospect-space.

Urbino – envelopment and exposure

At the end of this chapter we return to Stokes's aesthetic starting point – the Palace of Urbino – an epitome of constructed place – to address the positions of envelopment and exposure as evidenced in its architecture. Federico da Montefeltro's new palace was constructed from the mid-fifteenth century onwards and reflects the new Renaissance sense of homology between the city as entity and the constructed landscape of vine and terrace; the 'experience of being in the urban fabric is defined and clarified by the viewer's simultaneous perception of its opposite the countryside'.[26]

The 'aesthetic position' – 'the simultaneous perception of opposites' – that the palace organizes at the city–countryside level, is reflected in the experience of moving through the palace complex; a sequence of subtle displacements, mediated enclosures and prospect opportunities that concludes in Duke Federigo's personal suite of *studiolo*, chapel and loggia (Fig. 13.2) This suite is a simulacrum of the city–region organization instituted by the palace as a whole that allows, in a few strides, progression from the complete womb-like envelopment of the *studiolo* to the exhilarating release of the loggia. There is not space here to analyse the palace as a whole; in the context of the threshold I shall focus on the shared refuge space – hidden to the outside world and the semi-

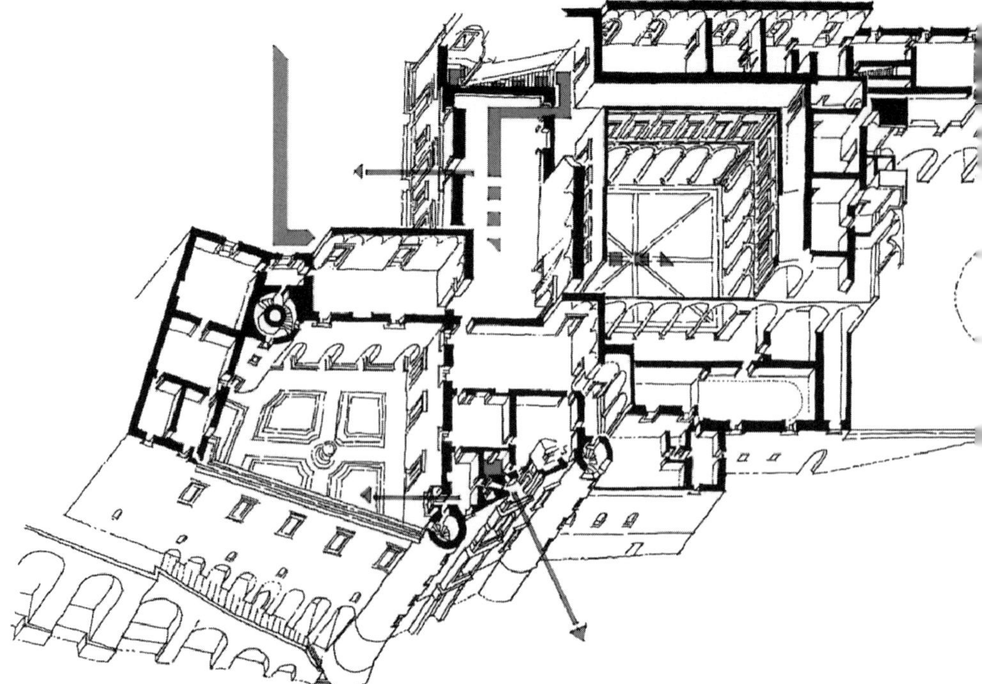

13.3
Detail of defining wall to the 'hanging garden' in the Palace of Urbino.

public parts of the palace – of the secret garden around which the personal apartments of the Duke and Duchess are arranged. This hanging garden – the *giardino pensile* – is a deeply poetic example of the subtleties with which envelopment-prospect conditions are configured throughout the palace complex. The garden parterres and fountain occupy the trapezium-shaped space formed between the angled wing of the Duchess's quarters and the ducal block with the *torricini* frontispiece. Within the shelter of these wings, the garden could simply have been designed to command an unbroken prospect over the landscape to the west, similar to the elevated panoramas found in many hill towns, such as the Piazza della Signoria in Gubbio, where the Dukes of Montefeltro also built a Palazzo Ducale modelled on that of Urbino.

13.2
Envelopment and otherness in the Palace of Urbino. Progression through the Palace showing route via courtyard and staircase to the Throne Room on the *piano nobile*, and prospect views from the sanctum of the Duke's *studiolo*. The 'hanging garden' is the semi-enclosed court with the fountain and four parterres. (After P. Rotondi, *The Ducal Palace of Urbino. Its Architecture and Decoration*, London: Alec Tiranti, 1969, Fig.54.)

Instead, Francesco di Giorgio defined a far more nuanced relationship of 'hereness' and 'thereness'; he reinforced the sanctum-like enclosure of the garden with a wall that, at the same time, allows framed views of the hillside beyond through five *quattrocento* apertures (Fig. 13.3). These openings rhyme with those of the palace wings, confirming the parterre as an outdoor room.

Similar openings on to the landscape figure in the paintings of the period; in those of Francesco di Giorgio himself, in Vecchietta, Mantegna and so on. In *The Experience of Landscape*, Appleton discusses how paintings of this period hold prospect and refuge in balance, avoiding either prospect and refuge dominance, through the 'device of a marginal vista flanking a central refuge'. Among the examples he chooses to illustrate this is Lorenzo di Credi's (1458–1537) *Virgin and Child* in London's National Gallery (Fig. 13.4). The sense of

13.4
The Virgin and Child, Lorenzo di Credi (*c.*1458–1537). Oil and egg tempera on wood, 71.1 × 49.5 cm.

refuge induced by the Virgin cradling and breast-feeding the infant Jesus is balanced by the arched openings on either side of the mother's head that disclose miniature landscapes of hills, trees and water. In this connection, Appleton uses the stagecraft term 'coulisse' to describe the refuge device of framing wings that intensify the sense of recession of a prospect while, on a behavioural level, allowing opportunities of concealment; a condition evident in the person who peeps through a window, down into the street, masked by the shelter and security of the flanking walls. Stokes – also an enthusiastic writer on ballet – was well aware of such devices and often alludes to the architecture of the stage. Returning this account of the hanging garden to the object-relations theory of psychoanalysis, we have noted Stokes's increasing recognition of the role that part-object relationships play in the creation and appreciation of art. In *The Invitation in Art*, Stokes asks: 'Why does aesthetic contemplation demand closeness as well as detachment of the viewer?'[27] The answer he gives is that in contemplating a work of art, we read aspects of our inner states 'in the sense of varied attachment to objects both internal and external'. 'In many works of visual art', he suggests, 'we clamour to enter in the pursuit of a part-object relationship, while at the same time we are standing back in full acceptance of self-sufficient figures or – to take the case particularly of some landscape – in an acceptance of the work considered for its entirety'.[28]

Part of the moving power of this garden, and of other similar places throughout the palace, is the ability to enjoy, in the fully physical world, something of what the Lorenzo di Credi *Virgin and Child* offers; a complete sense of protective enclosure, with a concurrent apprehension of the entire ideal landscapes that the openings fetch for us from the outer world.

The still epicentre of the Palace is the suite of the Duke's *studiolo*, chapel and loggia. In the intarsia work of the study – an almost windowless space of total envelopment less than four metres square – near and distant are brought together. Stokes writes of how 'in the landscape pieces, distance is brought near along the bright wood'.[29] Nearness could border on claustrophobia in this panelled cave, without the imaginative release of the landscape panoramas realized in the wood, or the recognition that the *studiolo*'s intense enclosure must be understood in the context of the nexus it forms with the adjoining chapel and loggia; Rotondi stresses 'the spiritual significance of these loggias [that establish] a direct contact with nature … nature itself is called upon to take a direct part in exalting the universal values promoted by the architecture of the palace: humanity, religion and poetry'.[30] In the few steps from the absolute enclosure of the *studiolo*, through the nodal vestibule, to the prospect-dominant loggia, the play of simultaneity between the opposed 'positions' of envelopment and exposure can be experienced at its maximum dynamic. I therefore conclude this essay and the analysis of the psychologizing of threshold standing in the supreme aedicular space of this loggia. It is probably this loggia, and the linking of *studiolo* 'sanctum' to the 'thunderous day' of the Marche landscape, that Stokes has in mind when he writes in *Smooth and Rough*:

> A loggia of fine proportion may enchant us, particularly when built aloft, when light strikes up from the floor to reveal over every inch the recesses of coffered ceiling or of vault. The quality of sanctum, of privacy, joins the thunderous day. A loggia eases the bitterness of birth: it secures the interior to the exterior: affirms that in adopting a wider existence, we activate the pristine peace.[31]

Notes

1 J. Tiptree, Jr,'The psychologist who wouldn't do awful things to rats', in D. Hartwell and K. Cramer (eds), *The Ascent of Wonder. The Evolution of Hard SF*, London: Orbit, 1994, p.676.

2 H. Hertzberger, A. van Roijen-Wortmann and F. Strauven, *Aldo van Eyck, Hubertus House*, Amsterdam: Stichting Wonen, 1982, p.44.
3 A. Stokes, 'Form in art', in M. Klein, P. Heimann and R.E. Money-Kyrle (eds), *New Directions in Psycho-analysis. The Significance of Infant Conflict in the Pattern of Adult Behaviour*, London: Tavistock Publications, 1955, p.406.
4 Hertzberger *et al.*, *Aldo van Eyck, Hubertus House*, p.45.
5 A. Stokes *The Critical Writings of Adrian Stokes. Vol. 1 1930–1937*; *Vol. II 1937–1958*; *Vol. III 1955–1967*, ed. L. Gowing, London: Thames and Hudson, 1978. *Vol. I, The Quattro Cento*, p.134. Subsequent references in the form: *CW, I, The Quattro Cento*, p.134.
6 Stokes, *CW, II, Art and Science*, p.195.
7 Stokes, *CW, I, Stones of Rimini*, p.230.
8 Ibid..
9 See S. Kite, Introduction to *Stones of Rimini*, in A. Stokes, *The Quattro Cento and Stones of Rimini*, Pennsylvania, The Pennsylvania State University Press, 2002.
10 Stokes, *CW, III, The Invitation in Art*, p.266.
11 Stokes, 'Form in art', p.407.
12 Quoted in T. Pinkney, *Women in the Poetry of T. S. Eliot. A Psychological Approach*, London: Macmillan, 1984, p.14.
13 D.W. Winnicott, *The Child and the Family. First Relationships*, London: Tavistock Publications, 1957, p.133.
14 C. St John Wilson, 'The natural imagination. An essay on the experience of architecture', *The Architectural Review*, 1989, vol.185, no.1103, 64–70, p.66.
15 Ibid., p.66.
16 Ibid.
17 Stokes, *CW, III, Three Essays on the Painting of our Time*, p.158.
18 R. Wollheim (ed.), *The Image in Form: Selected Writings of Adrian Stokes*, Harmondsworth: Penguin Books, 1972, p.316.
19 See J. Appleton, *The Experience of Landscape* (rev. ed.), Chichester: John Wiley & Sons, 1996. For Appleton's own reflections on the theory and its later commentators and critics see J. Appleton, 'Prospects and refuges re-visited', *Landscape Journal*, 1984, vol.3, no.2, pp.91–103. Appleton only extended his theory into architectural space in one short paper: J. Appleton, 'Landscape and architecture', in B. Farmer and H. Louw (eds), *Companion to Contemporary Architectural Thought*, London and New York: Routledge, 1993, pp.74–7.
20 Appleton, *The Experience of Landscape*, p.76.
21 Appleton, 'Landscape and architecture', p.74.
22 Ibid.
23 Ibid.
24 Quoted in G. Hildebrand, *The Wright Space. Pattern and Meaning in Frank Lloyd Wright's Houses*, Seattle: University of Washington Press, 1991, p.44.
25 Ibid., p.184.
26 C. Smith, *Architecture in the Culture of Early Humanism. Ethics, Aesthetics and Eloquence 1400–1470*, Oxford: Oxford University Press, 1992, p.125.
27 Stokes, *CW, III, The Invitation in Art*, p.290.
28 Ibid., p.294.
29 Stokes, *CW, I, The Quattro Cento*, p.163.
30 P. Rotondi, *Il Palazzo Ducale di Urbino. La sua architettura e la sua decorazione*, London: Alec Tiranti, 1969, p.79.
31 Stokes, *CW, II, Smooth and Rough*, p.240.

Chapter 14

Transparency and catatonia

Kati Blom

Introduction

In current architectural trends the most significant element is the nature of architects' fascination with glass. Glass is used as a cladding material, not only in the 1950s manner of curtain walls, but also as an independent planar cover. A sophisticated example of this is Peter Zumthor's Bergenz Museum (1997). The use of glass is often inconsistent, and assessment of its role in the architecture is not easy to grasp as such because of the positive connotations given to it in our society. The environmental effect of black glass boxes is resulting in what can be called a reduced human environment; one that I shall argue emphasizes the catatonic or static elements of construction. Mannerist use of glass can be seen in new clusters of commercial or office building that utilize curtain walls in green glass.

This essay discusses the static, dead core of glass architecture, and proposes the enlivenment of modern architecture by the use of more dynamic (or kinetic) approaches to the built environment. I refer to the ideas of Julia Kristeva and Sigmund Freud, and look at ways to implement some findings in environmental aesthetics to cure one-dimensional architecture.

Modes of communication in Julia Kristeva

In her post-structural theory, Julia Kristeva has circumscribed the human condition of communication. Kristeva traces three different levels of communication covering the entire spectrum of possible modes of speech, 'parole'.[1] Kristeva identifies 'pre-semiotic', 'semiotic' and 'symbolic' qualities in communication, and characterizes each of them. 'Pre-semiotic' and 'semiotic' are distinguished from each other by the amount of choice given to the style of speech. 'Pre-semiotic' refers to digital, mineral and stiff communication; I describe this here as 'catatonic', and suggest that in architecture this 'pre-semiotic' quality implies huge, overwhelming mega-structures, with minimal and precise articulation of details. Kristeva characterizes 'semiotic' as repetitive, organic and analogical, which I suggest translates in to architecture as implying organic and/or repetitive forms and informalities. This may be characterized further in the built environment as expressionistic, generative features in which the totality of expressions given us offers a choice of signs or gestures to interpret in the gestures of the building's form and fabric. This generative manner of expression gives us a broader spectrum of optional gestures to choose from.

Catatonic

The etymology of 'catatonic' needs to be explained in further detail. In Greek, '*kata*' means down. Words with a prefix 'cata-' suggest a motionless stage; i.e. to go down, driven down by emotions of fear. For instance, the word 'cataplectic' refers to amazement, the word 'cataplexy' refers to a condition of immobility induced by emotion – in animals a state of shamming death. The word 'catabolic' describes a disruptive processes of chemical change in organisms, or a process of striving apart – a destructive metabolism, opposed to anabolism. The latter part of the word 'catatonia' comes from '*tenos*', meaning stretching or straining. 'Catatonia' thus describes a type of schizophrenia characterized by periodic states of stupor or immobility. It also alludes to rigor mortis. All of these refer to a dead state – a stiff, paralysed posture caused by fearful emotions or the actual closeness to death. We are paralysed, for instance, when we unexpectedly meet something horrifying; but also, when something is in a stiff posture, we, as biological creatures, read the state as a dead form.[2]

Catatonia is present in architecture through what might be called 'dead', trendy coffins, such as the tyre shop in Zürich by Camenzind and Gräfensteiner (2001) or Tschumi's Glass Video Gallery in Groningen (1990).

Coffins are usually used for enclosing something dead or something that we want to be concealed in a vacuum, or in their purist form in protecting something valuable from the evils of time – such as that in which Snow White's body is held. Here I argue for the recognition of 'catatonia' in crystalline structures, some of which might appear appealingly, terrifyingly beautiful, but may, nonetheless, be dead. I am suggesting an association between fashionable glass buildings and coffins – indeed the proposition that current architecture is producing glass coffins. Often these are used in association with listed buildings, art, sculptures, when we want to interfere as little as possible with the structure of an existing historically valuable building. One example from The Netherlands is a music hall implanted, by Zaanen and Eekhout (1990), into Berlage's Stock Exchange in Amsterdam. It keeps the existing valuable space as untouched as possible. However, the darker side of such crystalline, catatonic edifices is, I suggest, related to the mega-structures first generated in the United States by Mies van der Rohe. The hypnotizing effect caused by the ephemeral and mystical associations of glass disable us to perceive the negative qualities of mega-structures.

Glass is used for practical reasons, but at the same time it is loaded with expectation and symbolism, part of which is hidden. Transparency has genuinely positive connotations. Yet the use of transparent, 'light' glass panels has produced heavy modular-based buildings that are somehow abstract. I argue that these structures speak the language of destruction, although at the same time the glass suggests a language of openness, freedom, imagination and even of the sacred. Do we really think that these business palaces or power institutions, where glass is so widely used, are more sacred than human settlements and children's playgrounds? The glorification of power structures takes place through an intense use of socially loaded signs, just like the 'sign' of 'transparency' in the use of glass. This indicates something of how powerful hidden signs are, and how the given content of a sign can persuade us to believe something different from the message we get in our bodies in that context.

As biological animals we recognize death in this living sphere of ours, but as rational, socially bound entities we do not want to address death. We do not want to receive the messages from our environments that are pregnant with hostile or threatening elements. Although we produce death through wars, conflicts and pollution, we do not want to discuss it. We do not recognize that we as a society produce dead, static structures because destruction is such a prominent part of our culture. The result is an ambivalent and unsatisfactory psychological state, where we can't fully use our capacities to orientate or be active in our environment.

Das Unheimliche

Kristeva requisitions Sigmund Freud's ideas and approaches when she defines the mineral as digital ('pre-semiotic') or the biological as analogical ('semiotic').[3] Here it is interesting to recognize the connection between catatonic features and death, the 'other', or the indescribable, unrepresentational transcendence. In technical terms, this is the sublime. Freud's contribution to the theory of the sublime is the notion of *das Unheimliche*, the uncanny.[4] When something unnoticed becomes notable, the beginning of the process is distinguished by the emotion aroused by horrifying elements. This process can lead to relief when we notice that we are not actually threatened by this horrifying element, but that it is purely fictional. Freud describes this moment by saying that it arises when something unexpected suddenly appears in the perceiver's consciousness, when something forgotten comes into one's mind.

The uncanny is always closely connected to fear, especially the fear of death. In his essay, 'The "uncanny"', Freud makes a remark that the fear of death, especially our own death, becomes apparent with a slightest provocation.

> Since most of us still think as savages do on this topic, it is no matter for surprise that primitive fear of the dead is still so strong within us and is always ready to come to the surface on any provocation.[5]

The emotion of horror or fear is aroused by some 'outer' (i.e. real) features in the environment, but it can also be caused by something accidental; something that has some personal connotations. Freud lists a large variety of these objects of the uncanny – automata, dolls, doubles, repetition, female flesh, reflection, etc., and including some real phenomena, such as the vertigo effect caused by high places or by mirrors.

Here there is a clear correlation between those things that can trigger such emotions of fear and common motifs in contemporary architecture. Glazed stairs and glazed floors are frequent design features, in spite of the fact that they cause dizziness or vertigo. Equally, many find totally glazed stairs or balconies in high empty places such as atriums so disturbing that they are paralysed by claustrophobic attacks. Something which was 'designed' to be light, transparent and liberating turns out to be horrifying, and therefore rejecting. Here something in the building materializes a cataplexy state; something is pulling and pushing at the same time.

The 'uncanny' is something we are part of as emotional and social creatures, and something in our communication, *parole*, can lead to experience of horror. In *The Architectural Uncanny* Anthony Vidler states that architecture in itself can never be *'unheimlich'*, although society may sometimes invest in

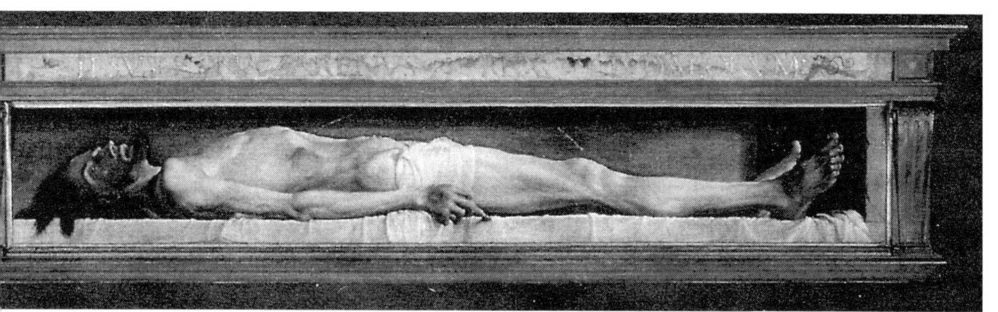

14.1
Hans Holbein the younger: *The Body of the Dead Christ in the Tomb* (1521–22).

architectural elements that may be described as uncanny, which is 'in its aesthetic dimension, a representation of a mental state of projection that precisely elides the boundaries of the real and the unreal in order to provoke a disturbing ambiguity, a slippage between waking and dreaming'.[6]

Vehicles of *das Unheimliche*, minimal gestures

The link between the horrifying or the uncanny (*das Unheimliche*) in our inner mind, and the factual, outer reality is intensified by specific elements. I shall look at these elements more closely, referring to them as the items, the objects or vehicles of the uncanny.

Here I return to Kristeva, who concentrates almost entirely on speech and literature in her theory. Although she rarely discusses visual arts, there is one fortunate exception, namely Hans Holbein's painting *The Body of the Dead Christ in the Tomb* (1521 or 1522, Fig. 14.1), which she addresses in detail in one chapter in her book *Black Sun: Depression and Melancholia*.[7] In this essay Kristeva posits Holbein's particular minimalism as something essential to the painting; something that denotes death.

> Like Pascal's invisible tomb, death cannot be represented in Freud's unconscious. It is imprinted there, however, as noted earlier, by spacing, blanks, discontinuities or the destruction of representation. Consequently, death reveals itself as such to imaginative ability of the self in the isolation of signs or their banalization up to the point of disappearing: such is Holbein's minimalism.[8]

Here there is a direct link from the minimal style of the painting to the appealing strategy architects use in order to minimize their structures in glass buildings. Architects have insisted on creating glass walls without a hint of the structure, despite the fact that two-dimensional glass needs a support. The engineers'

solution has been to create structural glass, which has resulted in glass architecture consisting of gigantic modular creations. Huge glass walls in Vilette and I.M. Pei's Louvre pyramid (construction design by Rice, Francis, Ritchie) or the Grande Arche de La Défense in Paris are good examples of this (Fig. 14.2).

The obsession with glass seems to be enmeshed in a dream of socially acceptable expressions. Nevertheless, these expressions also allude to other, more marginal, references that society does not discuss, and may even deny. Already in the development of curtain walling, from Gropius' early factory designs onwards, there was a tendency to glorify the use of steel–glass structures as one form of social progress, openness and development of welfare. The sociological value given to glass buildings dismisses the actual contrasting effect of them. Architects have been, and clearly are still, bewitched by the ephemeral qualities and associations of glass.

Interestingly, Leatherbarrow and Mostafi have suggested that the master and original parent of modern glass buildings, Mies van der Rohe, had a predilection for structure on top of skin.[9] The transparency he preferred in his early buildings was used because he saw the raw sublime structure as the core

14.2
La Grande Arche, Paris, France (Johann Otto von Spreckelsen, 1982–90).

14.3
Sanomatalo, Helsinki, Finland (Antti-Matti Siikala, 1999).

of architecture, something repeated in the Sanomatalo building in Helsinki (1999), designed by Antti-Matti Siikala (Fig. 14.3).

Minimal and the sublime

Kristeva's statement about minimalism as an intentional style of Holbein's in this particular painting links closely with the idea of the sublime. Jean-François Lyotard, too, connects minimalism with the sublime as one manner in which the rhetoric of classicism can be broken (i.e. challenged),[10] but does so not through Freud's constructs, but through those of aesthetics. This statement by Lyotard is associated with the negative sublime. Grotesqueness and disgust belong to the same category of negative sublime aesthetic responses. The disgust aroused by fleshy, formless ambiguity is close to the fear of being overwhelmed by (the mother's) body, the fear of disappearing into something infinite and limitless. Here Kristeva's term 'abject' (i.e. that which refers to the pre-symbolic period of infancy) reveals even more of the essence of this response. Similarly, in disgust, *das Ding* in its ambiguity is present.[11] Interestingly, here there is a connection between disgust and fear.

In his discussion of the architectural uncanny Vidler addresses transparency.[12] As a result of architects' tendency to veer towards the minimal in design, glass architecture has tended to overemphasize only limited qualities of glass, such as its transparency or reflection, as the starting points in design. This has created environments where vertigo or claustrophobic reactions are normal, and where the spectator is driven to her or his inner fictional world. By studying the so-called mirror effect, Vidler describes how the factuality of the real world is thus cut out.[13] In aesthetic terms there are few possibilities to enrich one's experiences of the environment, and this results in neglect of one's ability to give meaning to architecture.

Why is the notion of transparency so important in connection with the minimal or the sublime? It has been one of the main notions in creating an improved modern world. Yet the use of transparent designs has also had unintentional, negative effects on the environment. One such detrimental effect is the overwhelming power of transparency. Such associations with power are rooted in the ancient dream of a crystalline palace; but since the development of the steel and glass industries in the modern world we can actually materialize the dream. For example, the fascination of fragile, sensitive, ethereal glass is clearly seen in the Barcelona Pavilion by Mies van der Rohe from 1927. The building has been praised for its fluidity, and for the collapse of the notions of outer and inner spaces achieved through the juxtaposition of plain solid stone and glass walls. The time–space dimension is part of its dynamics, but there are many who now oppose this view. Jose Quetglas has stated that the whole setting can be seen as a stage, where movement is paralysed, and any possibility of experiencing the space in all its sensuous qualities is stopped.[14] Again the contraplexity of the message is clear, comprising both seduction and rejection; the seemingly easy access in contrast with the actual cessation of movement. This state of things is causing immobility, or cataplexy.

This has a clear link to the aesthetical experience of the mega-structures of transparent office blocks that are now found all over the world. Something in the core of modern perception of space results in undesired architectural effects that may paralyse movement and one's perception of space. Clear, pure images and the sharp detailing that lack any opaque surfaces does reduce the space solely into a sight orientation, to the exclusion of all other sensuous information of the space. As a result, in an extreme case, visually impaired or partially blind people cannot use glass entrances, since they cannot perceive the whole entity of the building. Yet also more generally the body is encapsulated and confused. It has less and less relevant sensory information about the environment, and is unable to invoice all of its capacities. Arguably reality is lost and the realm of the unreal entered. This is what I refer to as a reduced environment.

Theory of architecture

Architectural theory has tackled the problem of transparency since the 1960s. In their article 'Literal and phenomenal transparency', Colin Rowe and Robert Slutzky suggest that so-called 'phenomenal transparency' is the desirable core of modern architecture, instead of the more simple 'literal transparency' in material terms.[15] It has been argued that the legacy of this foundational essay in the study of transparency has led the discussion towards a theory based on solely visual perception. Referring back to Rowe and Slutzky, Detlef Mertins points out that even this notion of 'phenomenal transparency' has an element of static viewing.[16] Mertins argues that the preference for the abstract formation of space in the mind of the perceiver (i.e. 'phenomenal transparency') can exclude the experience of the actual space. If the closeness of the interior is frightening, everything must be done in order to delay or avoid direct contact with this threatening materiality of space.[17]

In architectural theory there is much speculation about the reflective qualities of glass. Quetglas has noted that the reflective qualities of the walls in Mies' Pavilion discussed above does not reveal anything of the core of the building,[18] and the glass mirrors the reflection of our surrounding and our selves instead. Vidler has noted that transparency achieved with reflective surfaces flattens buildings, and excludes any hint of location or place, and thus the message is given to move from the idea of individuality towards the personal identification of the abstract notion of state.[19] Here, both Quetglas and Vidler recognize that the unreal is present in the reflection in glass.

Surface vs. form – transparency vs. structure

Terence Riley has suggested that the current trend towards the surface (as opposed to form) and materiality of glass boxes (as opposed to the abstract, geometrical view) is more complex and interesting than the old idea of 'phenomenal transparency'.[20] He declines to discuss the three-dimensional structures supporting these opaque, ambiguous planes, but rather revisits the fallacies of Rowe and Slutzky by stressing the abstract quality of the surface instead of seeing the reality of space in all its qualities, i.e. dismissing its haptic and kinetic sides. The tendency to emphasize the abstract core of any idea, such as 'phenomenal transparency', looms behind architectural theory, making it difficult to tackle the problems of literal transparency and its companions, or to understand the glazed environment's actual impact on human experience. For instance Rowe and Slutzky claim there is a level of difficulty in understanding the idea of transparency, and thus they seem to block the comprehension of it for their readers, positing it as a virtually impenetrable concept. I argue that the discussion of transparency is more accessible through the aesthetic realm than through Rowe and Slutzky's realm.

> For, while painting can only imply the third dimension, architecture cannot suppress it. Provided with the reality rather than the counterfeit of three dimensions, in architecture, literal transparency can become a physical fact; but phenomenal transparency will be more difficult to achieve – and is, indeed, so difficult to discuss that generally critics have been entirely willing to associate transparency in architecture exclusively with a transparency of materials.[21]

In recent architecture there are symptoms that hint that we understand transparency and its ambiguous consequences in a more coherent way. The way opaque planes are used in Peter Zumthor's gallery in Bergenz (1997) is promising, as it takes advantage fully of the different appearance of the opaque planes in daylight and at night. Nevertheless, it remains the case in the current architectural milieu that heavy glass panels must still be lifted up and kept in place, usually by mega-structures. The more sober way to deal with frame skeleton structures is to make a conceptual leap from conceiving architecture as a form, to a level of understanding in which human beings are at the centre of the design – at this level phobias (such as vertigo) that are associated with the

14.4
Scottish Widows Building, 30 Finsbury Square, London EC2, U.K (Eric Parry Architects, 2002).

experience of transparent architecture would be seen as unacceptable. The result of this reorientation may be less reduced, and therefore more lively, built environments.

Remedies – body and transparency

One remedy open to architects is to emphasize the fragility of buildings and environments by choosing the way of incompleteness. Instead of complete, often impenetrable, design, schemes may be conceived with choice and diversity in mind. For example there could be choices of architectural space, both functional and sensory, that are equivalent to the choice that is present in a mode of speech identified by Kristeva as 'semiotic'.[22] Place may again become dynamic by addressing all the senses, starting perhaps with the kinetic sense, and also by avoiding reflective surfaces in areas where people are entering buildings.

An example of such richness can be found in Eric Parry's design for an office building in Finsbury Square, London (Fig. 14.4). With a sensuous and complex façade construction the elevation is like a huge filter of light and sound, ready to absorb the motions and forces of the city. The design reflects the

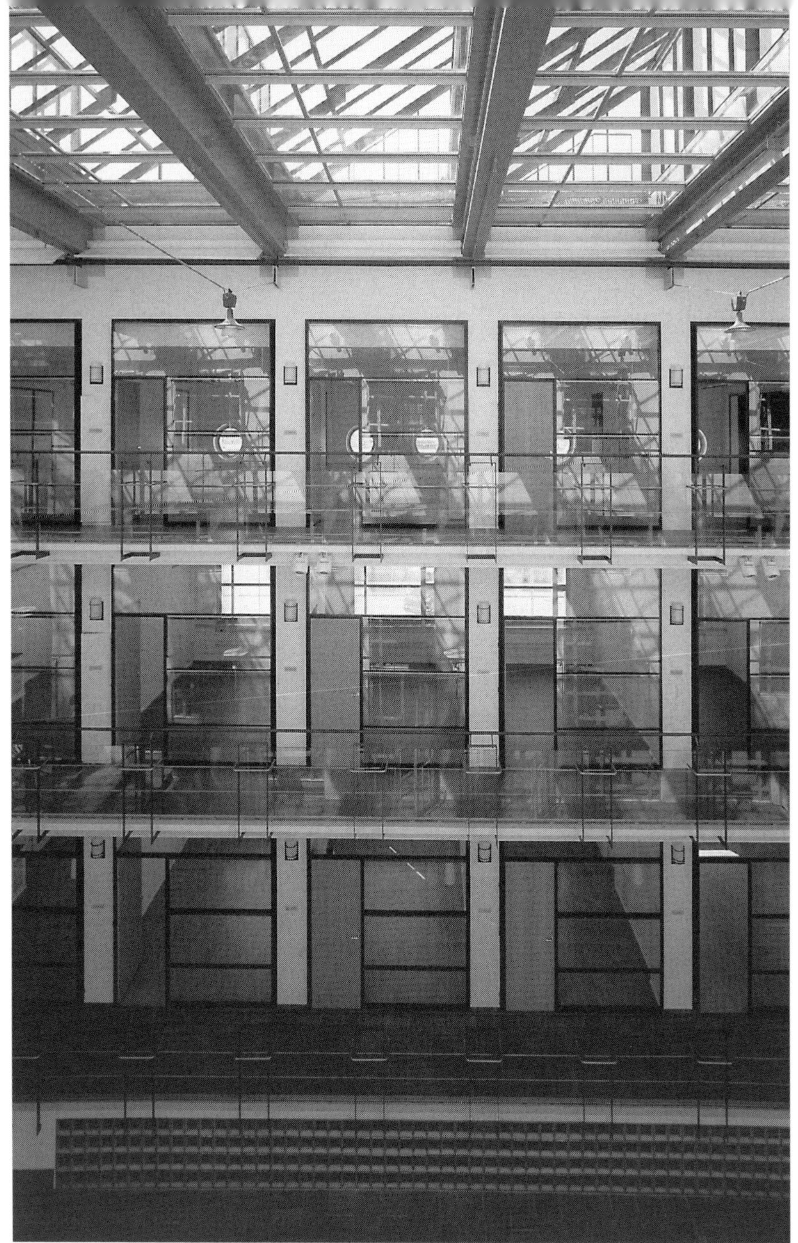

14.5
Foreign Ministry building, Helsinki, Finland (Olli-Pekka Jokela, 1994).

environment of a traditional London square in a complex way. Thus, by using opaque or filtered walls together with transparent elements, architects can seek to guide people in their enriched built environment. Spaces can be graded to make a clear distinction between important and less important, the linear and the static. These techniques would increase the sense of freedom in form and the choices of movement that people experience in our environment. Yet part of this, again, is the need for architects to reorient their conceptions about the nature of the built environment, making critical enquiry into the nature of constructing place – i.e. the goals of their designs.

It is also important to encourage students of architecture to be aware of their design goals, and to be critical of a purely formal fascination with materials and its associated tendency to ignore or disguise hidden signs and associations. The moral of a design can, of course, be a starting point in itself.[23] The discipline of environmental aesthetics can give hints to enliven the sensuous elements in design, all of which may prevent the creation of what might be called unintentionally autistic environments. The true values and aspirations of a human society may be the starting point for our designs, so that the use of any form is given a broader and deeper meaning than the merely formal.

The spatial complexity and affordability of environment gives enough real places to rest, meditate or monitor the environment without having to experience the horror or disgust described above. In Lille, Jean-Marc Ibos and Myrto Vitart use glass in an inspirational way, using all its qualities to emphasize an existing old museum's dignity (Museum of Art in Lille, 1997). In Finland, in the Foreign Ministry building, Olli-Pekka Jokela avoids the use of glass in the southern filtered wall, so that the only fully transparent wall is facing Alvar Aalto's Enso-Gutzeit building in a perfect shadow. The transparency of the west wall connects the atrium and outer yard in a manner that emphasizes the importance of the existing terrace (Fig. 14.5). The whole design is transparent towards the old mint and Aalto's design, and combines outer and inner spaces in an interesting way.

Discussion

The notion of transparency is often used in architecture as an excuse to use fashionable double-glazed or planar-glazed façades, but it is used without thinking of the environmental effect. The requisite huge structure that supports this transparency often causes a certain stiffness in architectural form. The glass façade as such is not uncanny in itself, nor one-dimensional in its aesthetic impact, but it is often perceived as uncanny in connection to the spatial or contextual solution as a whole. If the solution is formal, without sensitiveness towards the surroundings or the user's psychology, it may arouse *das Unheimliche* in the mind, with accompanying feelings of horror that bring the perceiver closer to her or his fictional world.

Notes

1 J. Kristeva, *Black Sun: Depression and Melancholia*, trans. L.S. Roudiez, New York: Colombia, 1992; orig. pub. *Soleil noir, dépression et mélancolie*, Paris: Editions Gallimard, 1987; and in Finnish as *Musta aurinko, masennus ja melankolia*, Finnish trans. M. Siimes and P. Sivenius, Helsinki: Nemo, 1999.

2 *Chambers English Dictionary*, Cambridge: Chambers, 1989.

3 Kristeva, *Musta aurinko, masennus ja melankolia*, pp.54–5, 25.

4 S. Freud, 'The "uncanny"', in J. Strachey and A. Freud (eds), *The Standard Edition of the Complete Psychological works of Sigmund Freud*, vol. XVII, London: The Hogarth Press and the Institute of Psychoanalysis, 1955, pp.218–56.

5 Freud, 'The "uncanny"', p.242.

6 A. Vidler, *The Architectural Uncanny*, Cambridge MA: MIT Press, 1996, p.11.

7 J. Kristeva, 'Holbein's Dead Christ', from *Black Sun: Depression and Melancholia*; reprinted in M. Feher, R.Naddaf and N. Tazi (eds), *Fragments for the History of the Human Body*, Part one, New York: Zone, 1989.

8 Kristeva, 'Holbein's Dead Christ', p.265.

9 D. Leatherbarrow and M. Mostafi, 'Opacity', *AA files*, autumn 1996, no.32, p.59.

10 J.-F. Lyotard, 'Ylevä ja avantgarde' ('Sublime et avant garde' [1984]), in J. Kotkavirta and E. Sironen (eds), *Moderni / Postmoderni*, Helsinki: Tutkijaliitto, 1986, pp.137–80, p.165.

11 Kristeva, *Musta aurinko, masennus ja melankolia*, pp.290–1.

12 Vidler, *The Architectural Uncanny*, pp.217–25.

13 Ibid., pp.222–5.

14 J. Quetglas, 'Loss of synthesis: Mies's pavilion', in K.M. Hays (ed.), *Architecture, Theory since 1968*, A Columbia book of architecture, Cambridge MA and London: MIT Press, 1998, pp.358–91.

15 C. Rowe and R. Slutzky, 'Transparency: literal and phenomenal', *Perspecta*, 1963, vol.8, pp. 45–54.

16 D. Mertins, 'Transparency, autonomy and relationality', *AA files*, 1996, vol.32, 3–11.

17 Ibid., p.9.

18 J. Quetglas, 'Loss of synthetis', p.391.

19 Vidler, *The Architectural Uncanny*, p.220.

20 T. Riley, *Light Construction*, New York: Museum of Modern Art, 1995.

21 Rowe and Slutzky, 'Transparency: literal and phenomenal', pp.45–54.

22 Therein the joy of speech in its pre-linguistic level – with its repetitive, rythmical and musical elements – is dominant. Kristeva, *Musta aurinko, masennus ja melankolia*, p.299.

23 This was the case in the work of Rural studio with Sam Mockbee in the United States. C. Slessor, 'Rural mission', *Architectural Review*, March 2001, vol.209, no.1249, 54–61.

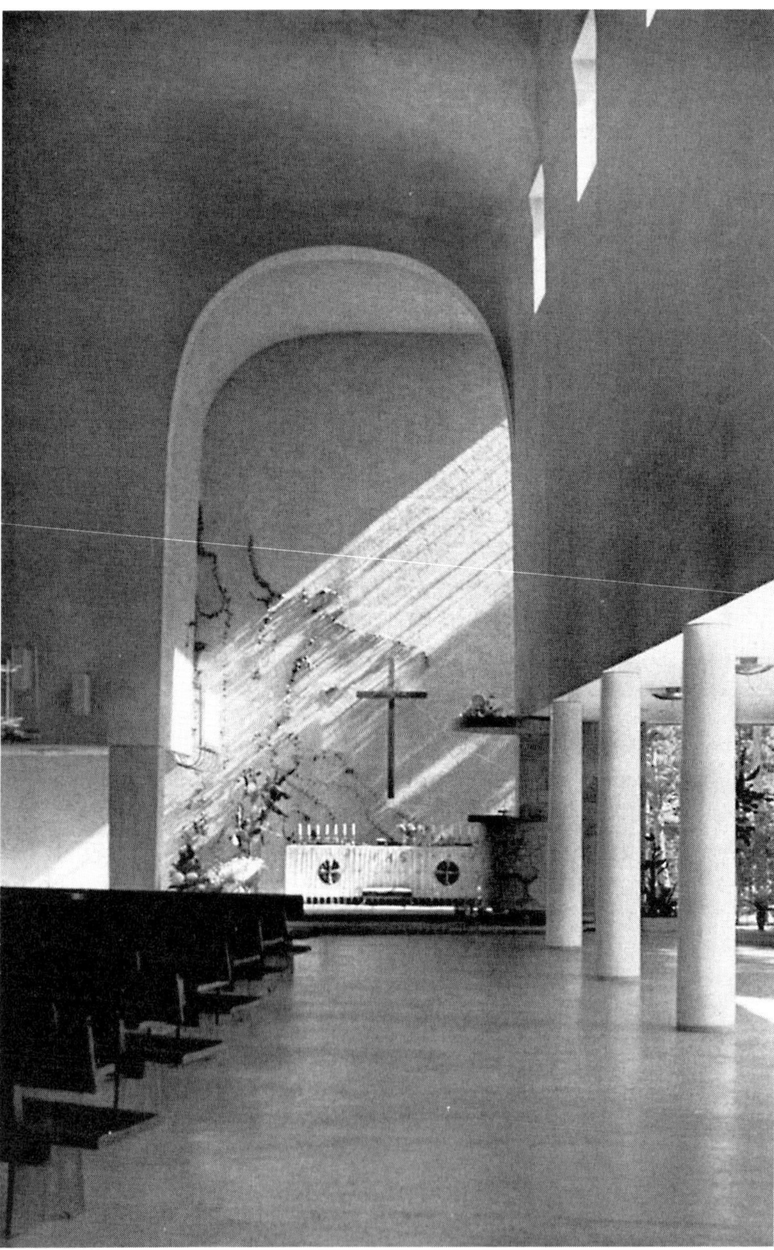

Plate 5
Resurrection Chapel, Turku, Finland
Erik Bryggman, 1939–41

Part 2

Matter

Plate 6
Child in the Orphanage, Amsterdam
Aldo van Eyck, 1955–60

Modern mediation

Chapter 15

Siting lives

Postwar place-making

Nathaniel Coleman

Introduction

Modern architecture is characterized by its harshest critics as being 'judgmental', 'intolerant', and in the business of 'altering' the existing environment rather than *enhancing* it. Such are the complaints Robert Venturi, Denise Scott Brown and Steven Izenour advanced in *Learning From Las Vegas*. The modern architecture they criticize is 'orthodox Modern architecture'.[1] Earlier, in *Complexity and Contradiction in Architecture*, Le Corbusier is praised for rejecting simplicity in his works, which Venturi argues embody both complexity and contradiction.[2] If Le Corbusier does not represent orthodox modern architecture, then followers of Mies van der Rohe's reductive paradox that *less is more* must. Indeed, Venturi's text supports this reading.[3]

Venturi *et al.* take issue not with modern architecture per se but with reductive orthodox modern architecture that changes the environment rather than enhancing it. Such architecture is unsympathetic and disregards location and inhabitation. Conversely, non-orthodox modern architecture – of which Le Corbusier's work is an exemplar – is humble and responsive to the environment, while enhancing it. Such an architecture would also be sympathetic and specific to both location and inhabitation. In the introduction to *Modern Architecture, A*

Critical History, Kenneth Frampton establishes just such a dialectic, made up of a synthesis of orthodox and non-orthodox modern architecture, which, although apparently opposed, are the only options available to contemporary architecture assuring a significant outcome. Conventional modern architecture is wholly consistent with current techniques of construction and habits of consumption, whereas unconventional modern architecture resists the status quo. The first, according to Frampton, follows Mies van der Rohe's ideal of

> 'almost nothing' [and is concerned with] optimising production [while reducing] the building task to the status of industrial design on an enormous scale. [Accordingly, such architecture] has little or no interest in the city [and] projects a well-serviced, well-packaged, non-rhetorical functionalism whose glazed 'invisibility' reduces form to silence.[4]

An architecture of 'almost nothing' is the orthodox modern architecture criticized in *Complexity and Contradiction in Architecture* and in *Learning From Las Vegas*.

The other side of Frampton's dialectic is an architecture resistant to the reductive limitations of modernist orthodoxy. This architecture is 'patently "visible" and often takes the form of a masonry enclosure that establishes within its limited "monastic" domain a reasonably open but nonetheless concrete set of relationships linking man to man and man to nature'. Frampton goes on to say that the 'introverted' character of such enclaves is 'an attempt to escape, however partially, from the conditioning perspectives of the Enlightenment'.[5]

Although the two courses observed by Frampton oppose one another, both have difficulty with broader conceptions of place identification: the first with the city, the second with the continuum into which it is placed. For the former, this difficulty is a sign of indifference; for the second, it is a sign of resistance. According to Frampton, 'the sole hope for a significant discourse in the immediate future lies ... in a creative contact between these two extreme points of view'.[6] Work elaborating this synthesis would be coherent with prevailing modes of production (if not necessarily consumption) and well-serviced, as it extends reductive functionalism by being patently visible, thus rhetorical. The both/and condition of a reasonably open enclosure could establish comprehensible relationships between individuals and communities, and between those communities and the world beyond, whether nature or city. Coexistence of specificity and ambiguity, without a loss of comprehensibility, renders such work defiant. Its partial enclosure might be an escape, but not escapism.

The forms of resistance described by Frampton could appear as rejections of place. Actually, partial inwardness calls attention to, while responding to, the difficulties of sustaining urban culture in the face of the vulgarizing effects of speculative over-development. Each defiant structure establishes an independent city-like condition, which makes a piecemeal contribution to sustaining urban culture by providing vital settings for it. In *Modern Architecture, A Critical History*, Alvar Aalto (especially at the Säynätsalo Town Hall, 1952), emerges as an exemplar of the synthesis for which Frampton argues.[7]

Here, though, I elaborate on my understanding of the synthesis Frampton envisions, and place identification, by appealing to other examples: Le Corbusier's La Tourette, Eveux-sur-l'Abresle, France (1953–60) and Aldo van Eyck's Orphanage, Amstelveenseweg, Amsterdam (1955–60). Both architects viewed site as generative, embracing the land where a building goes – in a city, at its edge, or beyond its boundaries – as a precedent condition that grounds radical invention; both structures demonstrate how building can invent a site through interpretation without disregarding or obliterating it. The two complexes were also constructed when modern architecture was beginning to be challenged for its limitations, especially its abstractness, disregard for place, and neglect of human desire. Accordingly, my examples are notable because they are places made at a time when modern architecture seemed incapable of doing so.

La Tourette: constructing place in the present

> I had to try to give them what men most need today: silence and peace. The Dominicans fill this silence with God. This monastery of rough concrete is a work of love. It does not talk all by itself. Its life comes from inside. It is inside that the essential takes place.[8]

La Tourette occupies an impressive sloping site near Lyon overlooking a small town in the valley below, which affords unobstructed views far into the distance. The land where the building rests is expansive enough to have permitted easier locations for building; even so, Le Corbusier chose the most difficult area of the site. Such a selection – especially because grading the hill was neither desired nor economically feasible – determined much about the structure to come. As a result, La Tourette reaffirms the place receiving it, and by so doing makes that place remarkably present (Fig. 15.1).

Approaching La Tourette reveals the striking compromise the convent makes between nature and building. The complex is further situated by sharing a number of characteristics with structures in nearby Lyon, especially bold presentation of clear geometry and large unrelieved areas of wall. It also shares these qualities with La Thoronet, the twelfth-century Cistercian Abbey in Provence that Le Corbusier visited before designing La Tourette.

As one comes closer, the partial openness of the complex, including the structures collected in its cloister, emphasize it as a city on a hill while

15.1
City on a hill. View towards south facing façade of La Tourette, near Lyon (Le Corbusier, 1957–60).

referring to unique characteristics of the Dominican order, including the prior location of their houses in cities until Church and State split in France during the nineteenth century. Because Dominicans are preachers and not monks, though they live in community, La Tourette is a convent, not a monastery.

By being a limited monastic enclosure, made using contemporary methods of construction, La Tourette demonstrates the synthesis Frampton argues for. Social relationships are clearly defined within and around the building, including the occupants' relation to nature, demonstrated by the structure's interpretation of its hilltop location; the site moves on to, under, and through it. La Tourette is a realistic product of the age: craft is gone, architecture has been standardized, and stone is rarely used to make buildings. Concrete is presented as an analogue of stone but it is a *new* stone, cheaper to use and easier to manipulate. Here the realities of construction since the Second World War are simultaneously embraced and questioned. The concrete is rough; indeed the entire complex is rough – inside and out – presenting itself as a virtue of poverty, in opposition to the slickness and affluence of conventional postwar industrialized building (Fig. 15.2).

La Tourette defers to the forces of nature, which act forcefully upon it; it exists in time and shows its vulnerability as it begins to crumble. The structure is overrun by nature in places, including the overgrown court, the roof-walk, and the roofs of the various structures in the court. Eventually the earth will subsume La Tourette, already deeply rooted in the ground. The Convent is also outward

15.2
Partial enclosure. View into court towards south facing wall the chapel at La Tourette (Le Corbusier, 1957–60).

looking; directing attention away from itself towards the land, the horizon, the village in the valley, the mountains, and the world beyond them, for which the way of life contained, as much as the container, might be a model of possibility.

La Tourette demonstrates Le Corbusier's conviction that problems of a social dimension require an appropriate setting. He imagined that the forms he invented were the content of solutions to social problems made manifest. Such an architecture is comprehensible through reference to bodily experience rather than as representation; as such La Tourette attempts, by force of will, to invent a location that challenges what is (alienation) with what could be (wholeness), modelled by a setting that struggles to collapse the divide separating form from content. Le Corbusier confirms this in his conviction that reconciliation of individual and collective requires a setting that models this condition:

> But in the resolution of this problem another equally decisive lesson was to be learned: that to solve a large proportion of human problems you need locations and accommodation. And that means architecture and town planning. The Ema charterhouse was a location, and the accommodation was arranged in the finest architectural biology.[9]

Much has been, and can be, made of the influence of Ema (a Carthusian monastery near Florence) on La Tourette.[10] More importantly, Le Corbusier confirms that Ema became a golden model he drew upon for reform of architecture in the present:

> The beginning of these studies [for dwellings of a human scale], for me, goes back to my visit to the Carthusian monastery of Ema near Florence, in 1907. In the musical landscape of Tuscany I saw a *modern city* crowning a hill. ... I thought I had never seen such a happy interpretation of dwelling. ... This 'modern city' dates from the fifteenth century. Its radiant vision has always stayed with me.[11]

At Ema, Le Corbusier found the solution to a particularly modern dilemma: 'here the equation which it is the task of human wit to solve, the "reconciliation of individual" on the one hand and "collectivity" on the other, lay resolved.'[12] The monastery inspired him to invent a modern setting at La Tourette. Consequently, La Tourette shares many features with Ema: its crowning location on a hill; framed views from each cell – which open on to a common passage; and emphasis on communal spaces, including passageways. Both have cloisters, but at La Tourette an enclosed hall separates the cells from the cloister 3–5 levels below. At Ema, the cells are arranged in a U closed at the end by the church and other common areas; at La Tourette, the church is linked to the rest of the convent – by passages that cut through the cloister – and is physically separated from it – by being pulled away from the cells and other functions, which face off against its massive block.

The life within

What La Tourette shares with Ema and La Thoronet, and its departures from both, responds to the peculiarities of Dominicans, especially the cloister, which is as open as it is closed to both nature and the world. Le Corbusier understood that Dominicans[13] and Carthusians[14] are different. Both organize their lives in community, but Dominicans sleep and study in a simple cell, whereas Carthusians sleep, eat and work in independent houses. Dominicans eat in community; Carthusians in solitude. Dominicans are preachers; Carthusians hardly ever speak.

The setting envisioned by Le Corbusier and Father Couturier (the Dominican priest who secured the commission for La Tourette for Le Corbusier) referred to the total enclosure of monastic life while diverging from it. Couturier encouraged Le Corbusier to visit La Thoronet and gave him sketches of its organization; the abbey was a radical model of an ideal community Le Corbusier interpreted for Dominican practice at La Tourette.[15] The medieval roughness of La Thoronet, its enclosed organization and clear geometries, inspired Le Corbusier to interpret Ema on his own terms, especially by introducing an openness appropriate to a Dominican Convent absent from both monasteries. In its partial enclosure, La Tourette analogizes Dominicans' struggle to discover a middle passage between the certainty of monastic clarity and the confusing uncertainty of worldly experience.[16]

Religious and social changes during the 1960s encouraged French Dominicans to return to cities. They sold off many of their rural holdings but kept La Tourette because it was a focus of international interest. Retention of the complex included expansion of its original mission (as a Dominican college) to include forums of open inquiry, secular as well as sacred. Despite its rural location, the Convent has been urbanized. It is now a cosmopolitan city on a hill.

Because La Tourette is *elastic* enough to allow imaginative reinvention of its purpose, its occupants can continuously perfect their inhabitation of the complex. Happily, this could occur without requiring total abandonment of its original programme, a transformation analogous to the Dominicans' perpetual search for self-perfection through experiment rather than violent change. That Le Corbusier's building encourages such investment is a testament to the architect's vision for modern life. Had La Tourette been an indifferent building, the Dominican Order would have sold it off.

La Tourette is a particularly persuasive example of place-making because it persists as a viable pattern for occupation flexible enough to permit re-invention and re-use without being indeterminate generic space or requiring radical alteration. Ultimately, the lesson of La Tourette is its specificity at every level subsumed within a general conception of community, attuned to the particular community occupying it at a unique location. It is a building that even after many changes continues to give form to the desires of the Dominicans who occupy it. In this way, La Tourette remains a model of the possible though it already exists. By being responsive to the contradictions of time and necessity, it is a container ever ready to be filled anew by life.

Configuring non-places

> A city, however, is a very complex artefact and, like all artefacts, fits no pseudobiological analogy. It is a man-made aggregate subject to continual metamorphosis to which it either manages or fails to respond. Accordingly, it is either transfigured or disfigured. Our experience is founded on the latter, our hopes on the former – that is the plight we are in now.[17]

Urban settings at the edges of city centres do not lend themselves to the kind of place identification possible at La Tourette. The non-places of decomposed urban culture challenge an architect's place-making abilities, which makes Aldo van Eyck's Amsterdam Orphanage a remarkable achievement (Plate 6). In this instance, a non-place, at the outer edge of the historic centre of Amsterdam, becomes a forum for exploring a full range of architectural elements capable of analogizing persistent human desire to be somewhere – to set aside a unique location from apparently infinite expanses of space.

Ever since Paxton's Crystal Palace (1851), contemporary building has become ever more determined by the advantages of modularized and industrialized techniques of construction. But these advantages are conditioned by economy and efficiency, which tends to frustrate desire for a built environment as a *counterform* to emotion. Failure of industrialized building technique turns on the meagreness of first instances of repetitive units, whose qualitative vitality (associative potential) cannot survive beyond even the first instance of a particular unit. Consequently, repetition calls attention to the emptiness of meagre elements.

For van Eyck, meaning at 'vast scale' is a problem of how 'significant content' could at every stage of multiplication be 'transposed through structural and configurative invention into architecture'.[18] He envisioned 'a new reality', as he called it, in which social places emerge to analogize individual and collective relations without dictating the life they house. Van Eyck's places encourage social relations by accounting for emotion and existence as an in-between condition. Configured places articulate a realm for human beings by situating in-betweens as a focus of human habitats, rather than eradicating them – common to an architecture of excessive rationality. Ultimately, extreme rationalization requires a splitting mentality antithetical to psychic tension, reciprocal relations, and ambivalence.

As an embodiment of van Eyck's method for elaborating an enriched built realm, the Orphanage is a building with far-reaching implications for constructing place in the present. His social, psychological, and spatial aims are so effectively articulated at the Orphanage that even emptied of its intended use it remains a model of enriched practice for architecture and urbanism. Not surprisingly, both client and architect envisioned the Orphanage as an ideal city to house an institution with an enlightened social programme.

Constructing place: a configurative discipline

The Orphanage is configured out of a basic constructive spatial unit: four columns arranged equidistant from one another joined by architraves with a void cut into them. It is an assembly that forms a house-room with a primal quality, both referential and structural. Comprehensibility, or legibility, is attained (and maintained) throughout by clearly articulating each element in the interior and exterior of the building. Restatement of the basic spatial unit occurs at roof level where 336 precast concrete domes cover 336 house-room units. There are also eight units composed of nine combined house-room units capped by larger domes, four of which are two-storeys in height. These larger units previously housed the children's living quarters, originally organized according to age, and by gender for older children, who resided in the two-storey units. Precast concrete panels, with openings as required, enclose second-level sections of the building throughout.

The Orphanage includes two main wings that slide past each other. The complex is organized around a central court, formerly the building's social and emotional, rather than geometric, centre. Entry was made through this main court by passing under an elevated section – originally filled with staff functions – which links the two wings of the Orphanage. Although more than four hundred house-units extend outward from the main court toward the cardinal points forming an irregular grid, the result is anything but *foursquare*; rather it is remarkably diverse and dynamic. The dynamism results in part from the *imperfect* and opposed arrangement of each wing as a stepped triangle in plan. A meandering interior street, really articulated as a street, links the various sections of the Orphanage. Subtle shifts of level further articulated the interior within the predominantly single-storey structure.

By stepping the two triangles in plan, van Eyck was able to include a wide variety of open-air places either fully enclosed by the exterior building walls or partially protected by them. The main court and others created by the assemblage of multiples gives the Orphanage its unique village-like character. Overall, the effect of such careful articulation – material, spatial and psychological – is a building of exceptional social legibility (Fig. 15.3).

A remarkable feature of van Eyck's configurative method is the nearly infinite figurative potential drawn from a surprisingly limited number of elements. Even though the basic units and the whole are all of the same *stuff*, openings established by repetition of two columns and an architrave allowed

15.3
Part/whole. View from south into court on north-west side of the orphanage, Amsterdam (Aldo van Eyck, 1955–60).

for almost limitless possibilities of infill, which related to interior occupation, and explained what surrounds the building, including how it configures its abstract environs through its presence. Inside and out, doorways (and windows) are direct expressions of *inbetweens* that reconcile *twin phenomena*: a door, according to the logic of dualistic thinking, separates inside from outside, this room from that one, here from there, and so on. Here, though, doors are thresholds – direct presentations of liminality; less boundary than link, articulated by delaying entry (not confusing it) through careful definition so that it goes beyond functional necessity alone.[19] In this way, open and closed are woven together qualitatively.

The Orphanage is assembled from quantitatively similar parts 'extended in a qualitative dimension' through 'configurative multiplication'.[20] As a result, a persuasive basic unit gains in richness. Dynamism rather than monotony is established. And legibility is assured throughout because parts are organized to emphasize reciprocal relations among them, thus rendering the whole comprehensible. By investigating repetition of 'essentially similar' parts as a means for establishing difference through repetition, van Eyck took account of the realities of contemporary industrialized construction without being defeated by the tendency towards banality demanded by it. At the Orphanage the result is near-infinite combinative and reciprocal possibility in a constructed realm both simple and complex, established through a combination of initial units that is fugal rather than Cartesian.

15.4
Village in the trees. View from the south toward two-storey units of the orphanage, Amsterdam (Aldo van Eyck, 1955–60).

As a dynamic ideal city, limited in scale and geometrically complex, the Orphanage demonstrates that modern architecture need be neither totalizing nor static. By elaborating 'the inbetween realm', which van Eyck argued architecture 'sets out to articulate', he established settings that provide for the fundamental human condition of residing in places and occasions between birth and death.[21] Streets, spaces between buildings, corridors, hallways, stairways, entry halls, windows, doors, and so on are attuned to this condition by defining it.[22]

Van Eyck's achievement at the Orphanage was to construct a realm where wholeness could be understood in terms of the inbetween, equilibrium in terms of the dynamic, and the permanent in terms of relativity. More remarkably, it was occupied for a while in just such ways, and even in its present condition it continues to tell the *story of another idea*, which architects and clients can return to as a *model* for imagining and constructing places (Fig. 15.4).

Notes

1 R.Venturi, D. Scott Brown and S. Izenour, *Learning From Las Vegas*, Cambridge MA: MIT Press, 1977, p.3.
2 R.Venturi, *Complexity and Contradiction in Architecture*, New York: Museum of Modern Art, 1977, p.18.
3 Ibid. pp.16–17.
4 K. Frampton, *Modern Architecture: A Critical History*, New York: Thames & Hudson, 1992, p.10.
5 Ibid.
6 Ibid.
7 Ibid. pp.200, 343.
8 Le Corbusier, quoted, *Couvent Sainte Marie de la Tourette built by Le Corbusier*, Photocopied Pamphlet, L'Arbresle: Dominican Convent of La Tourette, *c.*1999), p.1.
9 Le Corbusier, quoted in J. Petit, *Le Corbusier lui-même*, Geneva: Rousseau, 1970, p.44; trans,, cited and reprinted in A. Sutcliffe, 'A vision of Utopia', in R. Walden (ed.), *The Open Hand: Essays on Le Corbusier*, Cambridge MA: MIT Press, 1977, pp.218–19.
10 For example, P. Serenyi, 'Le Corbusier, Fourier, and the Monastery of Ema,' *Art Bulletin*, 1967, vol. 49, pp.277–86.
11 Le Corbusier, *Precisions: On the Present State of Architecture and City Planning* [1930], trans. E. Schreiber Aujame, Cambridge MA: MIT Press, 1991, p.91.
12 Le Cobusier, quoted in Petit, *Le Corbusier lui-même*, p.44; reprinted Sutcliffe, 'A Vision of Utopia,'p.218.
13 Much of what follows, in addition to conversations with a Dominican Friar at La Tourette (July 1999), as regards Dominicans, is drawn from P. Mandonnet 'Order of preachers', *The Catholic Encyclopedia*. Online. Available HTTP: <http://www.newadvent.org/cathen/12354c.htm> (accessed 13 February 2000). J.B. O'Conner 'Saint Dominic', *The Catholic Encyclopedia*. Online. Available HTTP: <http://www.newadvent.org/cathen/05106a.htm≥ (accessed 13 February 2000).
14 Much of what follows, as regards Carthusians, is drawn from R. Webster 'The Carthusian Order', *The Catholic Encyclopedia*. Online. Available HTTP: <http://www.newadvent.org/cathen/03388a.htm> (accessed 31 March 2000). A. Mougel 'Saint Bruno', *The Catholic Encyclopedia*. Online. Available HTTP: <http://www.newadvent.org/cathen/03014b.htm> (accessed 31 March 2000).
15 M. Purdy, 'Le Corbusier and the theological program,' in Walden (ed.), *The Open Hand*, pp.292, 302, 303, 305.
16 C. Rowe, 'La Tourette' [1961], *Mathematics of the Ideal Villa and Other Essays*, Cambridge MA: MIT Press, 1976, pp.185–203.
17 A. van Eyck, 'Towards a configurative discipline', *Forum*, 3 August 1962, pp. 81–93; reprinted in J. Ockman, *Architecture Culture: 1943–1968*, New York: Rizzoli, 1993, p.354.
18 Ibid. pp.350–1.
19 Ibid. p.348.
20 Ibid. p.349.
21 A. van Eyck, 'The medicine of reciprocity tentatively illustrated', *Architects Yearbook*, 1962, no.10, pp. 173–8; reprinted in van Eyck, *Aldo van Eyck Works*, ed. V. Ligtelijin, Basel: Birkhäuser, 1999, p.89.
22 van Eyck, 'Towards a configurative discipline,' p.349.

Chapter 16

'Awakening' place

Le Corbusier at La Sainte Baume

Flora Samuel

> We are at La Sainte Baume in Provence, the sacred plateau, the high place dedicated to Saint Mary Magdalene. Centuries of faith. Then of oblivion. Then a possible awakening in this age of every conceivable ferocity: tumult, disorder, revolutionary inventions. One would like to think, collect oneself, meditate. For years, Trouin and I had prepared a major awakening – architectural and iconographical – for La Sainte Baume; underground basilica, mystery and twilight...and outside, living people, living in genuine simplicity to the scale of the landscape, the scale of their gestures and their hearts. It was beautiful.[1]

Le Corbusier wrote of his scheme for La Sainte Baume in Provence in terms of an awakening of the landscape, of the particular qualities latent in that place. In his opinion La Sainte Baume formed part of a 'a brilliant landscape, an architectural site, a place of meditation for meetings, capable of allowing you to enjoy its real value, the spirit which reigns over the area', that of Mary Magdalene.[2] In this essay I will focus upon the ways in which he and his client Edouard Trouin tried to awaken her spirit through their designs for the site. Work on this 'marvellous undertaking' continued from 1945 into the early 1960s. Although never built, it provides an important part of the backdrop for a number of other schemes that Le Corbusier worked on during that period, most notably the Chapel of Ronchamp and the Unité in Marseilles.

Most of the material contained in this paper is unpublished, largely extracted from documentary sources in the Fondation Le Corbusier. Very little has ever been published on La Sainte Baume, almost nothing in English. Where interpretations are made of certain aspects of Le Corbusier's work ideas are taken from the writings of his contemporaries, in an (admittedly flawed, but still instructive) attempt to try to gain as accurate a picture as possible of what Le Corbusier himself might have been thinking at that time. [3]

I will dwell upon the spiritual aspects of Le Corbusier's work, but this is not to deny the importance of his interest in technology and his wish to create efficient buildings. Le Corbusier's faith in nature, his belief in evolution was clearly allied to his faith in science, and his desire to believe in an overall pattern governing all things.

Le Corbusier's paintings, like his architecture, have a complex symbolic programme. Early in his life the architect wrote of his 'obsession' with symbolism, describing it as 'a yearning for a language limited to only a few words'.[4] This fascination, learnt it seems during his studies of ancient art and architecture, was to remain with Le Corbusier for the rest of his life.

Having briefly described the background to the project and the characteristics of the site, I shall describe the aspects of the legend of Mary Magdalene that were of particular interest to the two men. I shall then discuss the ways in which they tried to evoke these aspects of her life through the different parts of the scheme.

Background

Trouin, the owner of much of the land at La Sainte Baume was, according to Le Corbusier, a 'geometer',[5] that is to say a surveyor, an interesting occupation in Le Corbusier's terms because of its connections to geometry.[6] Trouin came to Paris to find an architect for his project in 1946. An opportunist, he quickly infiltrated the intellectual circles in which Le Corbusier moved. Auguste Perret produced a scheme for the project, but it was evidently Le Corbusier who felt a real affinity for it, as can be seen by his relaxed attitude to fees.

Le Corbusier wrote admiringly in the *Oeuvre Complète* of the way in which Trouin covered the walls and even the ceiling of his garret room with images of Mary Magdalene (Fig. 16.1).[7] Together with Father Couturier, the editor of the influential journal *L'Art sacré*, they developed a scheme for an underground Basilica, housing for both permanent and transitory members of the community and a museum dedicated to the subject of Mary Magdalene. Le Corbusier was to become a close friend of Trouin and was to work on the scheme for the next fifteen years. The duration of his involvement with the scheme and

16.1
Mary Magdalene. A detail of the Isenheim Altarpiece (1513), by Mathias Grünewald. Cropped by Le Corbusier and included in Le Corbusier, *Oeuvre Complète, Volume V*, p.27.

the warmth of his letters to Trouin suggest the degree of his emotional investment in the project.

La Sainte Baume

La Sainte Baume is situated in Provence in the south of France 40 kilometres to the east of Marseilles. It is widely recognized that Le Corbusier had a special affinity for this part of the world, reflected through his admiration of the Mediterranean and its culture, notably that of ancient Greece.

The La Sainte Baume Massif is the highest of the Provençal mountain ranges, reaching 1,148 metres above sea level at its highest point. It extends twelve miles from east to west. The grotto of Mary Magdalene, a popular site of pilgrimage, is itself set into a limestone ridge to the north side of the ridge 700 metres above sea level. The massif contains many caves, like that of the grotto at La Sainte Baume below which the northern face of the ridge is shrouded in forest, consisting largely of beech, lime and maple trees. Because of its altitude La Sainte Baume is also markedly different in climate from other areas in the Midi; in contrast with its hot and dusty surroundings it is almost Scandinavian in character.

Mary Magdalene

The first two pages of the section in Le Corbusier's *Oeuvre Complète* devoted to La Sainte Baume are dominated by images from Trouin's collection of

Magdalenic iconography (Fig. 16.1).[8] Le Corbusier noted in a letter to Trouin that he had taken great care with the design of these pages.[9]

Versions of her story

Mary Magdalene is usually associated with the sinful woman who washed Jesus' feet with her hair as a sign of her humility and repentance. Although there are only a few brief and inconsistent references to the Magdalene in the New Testament, there is some consensus on certain important issues. Firstly, the apostles agree that Mary Magdalene was indeed one of Christ's female followers and that she was present at his crucifixion. Secondly, they agree that she was a witness to his resurrection and that she was the first to receive his message and the first to spread his word to the people. There are a number of different versions of the Provençal legend of the Magdalene, the best known being that she travelled to France by boat in the company of Saint Maximin.[10]

The master carpenter Antoine Moles, an acquaintance of Le Corbusier's,[11] gave a further version of the story of the Magdalene in his book on the cathedral builders of the Middle Ages, the birth of the guilds and of Masonry, *Histoire des Charpentiers*, within which he dedicated an entire chapter to La Sainte Baume.[12] Le Corbusier owned a copy of this book. According to Moles, Mary Magdalene arrived in Provence in the company of the first 'campagnons bâtisseurs', the companion builders, who came from the plateaux of Asia. The suggestion is that together they brought with them to Europe the knowledge of geometry developed by the ancient Greeks and Egyptians. Mary Magdalene was in some way seen as the protectress of their knowledge. It was for this reason that she was held in great respect by the 'Compagnons du Tour de France', a guild of master craftsmen who were to be involved in the development of the Basilica scheme.[13]

Le Corbusier's version of her story, reasons for his interest in the Magdalene

In this section I will identify the attributes of the Magdalene that were of particular interest to Le Corbusier and Trouin, attributes that they then tried to emphasize through the design for the scheme in order to reawaken her spirit at La Sainte Baume.

Next to the images of the Magdalene in the *Oeuvre Complète* (Fig. 16.1) Le Corbusier gave his version of her legend.

> Half-way up this massive vertical rock face is the black hole of a cave: here lived Mary Magdalene, the friend of Jesus, who came from Palestine in a small boat, with the other Marys. Every morning angels came to the cave and carried her 200 metres up to the summit of the mountain called 'Le Pilon', where she used to pray. From there the mountain falls away as far as Toulon and the Mediterranean. The legend has made La Sainte Baume a divine place, which today is guarded by the Dominicans. On the plain at the foot of the hills is The Basilica of St Maximin, where the beautiful head (skeleton) of Mary Magdalene is kept in a golden casket.[14]

It is significant that Le Corbusier referred to the other Marys, fully aware of the blurring of boundaries between the various saints of that name and indeed the Virgin herself.

Jacobus de Voragine described in his *Legenda Aurea* (1275) how every day 'at the seven canonical hours she [Mary Magdalene] was carried aloft by angels and with her bodily ears heard the glorious chants of the celestial hosts'.[15] It seems likely that Le Corbusier was drawing from his account of her legend in his version of the story.[16]

According to Voragine Mary Magdalene could be symbolized through light.[17] Like the figure of Icône in Le Corbusier's paintings, the Magdalene was the bringer of illumination. Her presence could therefore be implied through the careful manipulation of light. This will be seen in the Basilica scheme.

Le Corbusier and Trouin placed emphasis upon the Magdalene's role as hermit and penitent. Le Corbusier himself had long been fascinated by the possibilities of an ascetic existence.[18] For Trouin she was a 'perfect symbol',[19] a woman who, with her hair, wiped the perfumed oil from the feet of 'a God' to whom she gave her own life. Trouin wrote 'Renan wrote that the vision of this woman in love gave the world a resurrected god and that the church called him the "APOSTLE of APOSTLES". Not at all bad for an ex-prostitute.'[20] Trouin was referring to Ernest Renan's description of the Resurrection in which the Magdalene, crazed by love, had a vision of Christ, a vision that had then became the foundation of the Christian religion. From the number of annotations made by Le Corbusier in Renan's *La Vie de Jésus* it is evident that this work occupied an important position in his own collection of books.

It is apparent from a close reading of *The Radiant City* that Le Corbusier saw the cosmos in terms of a balance between male and female elements; he believed this to be a natural law. It seems that he was particularly fascinated with the idea of Mary (she has a prominent role in his *Poem of the Right Angle*), whether Virgin or Magdalene, because he saw her presence within Catholicism as a remnant of ancient earth-goddess worship. To promulgate her position in religion was to redress the balance of the sexes within the Church. (It should be noted that Mary's precise role was at that time under review in the Church).[21]

As a prostitute saint, the Magdalene encompassed those oppositions that were a continuing fascination for the architect. Susan Haskins has written that the Magdalene has been used as a standard vehicle by artists to express ideas about sexuality; indeed, it is very possible that Le Corbusier would have been interested in the figure for this reason.[22]

16.2
Le Corbusier's design for the Basilica.
Le Corbusier, *Oeuvre Complète Volume V*, p.30.

Le Corbusier, who was fascinated by the ascetic life of a monk, was evidently impressed by the tale of her hermitage in the cave and her religious ecstasy that carried her to the top of the mountain, defying the usual limitations of space. (It should be noted that Le Corbusier thought of religious ecstasy in terms of the experience of ineffable space.)

Linked to the history of Freemasonry, Mary Magdalene also had a role in protection of a Masonic knowledge, that of geometry, again a fascination for Le Corbusier. Also, and this cannot be stressed too much, she was a specifically Provençal saint. (There was after World War Two a revival in interest in Provençal culture and its links to the classical tradition).[23] She had a very particular role in bringing the Christian religion of the East to France.

The basilica

I will now examine the ways in which these attributes of the Magdalene (light, paradox, geometry, pagan religion, asceticism, balance, the Mediterranean) were developed in the scheme for La Sainte Baume in an attempt to reawaken her spirit.

The design for the Basilica at La Sainte Baume evolved over the years 1946 to 1948, at which point it was rejected as a proposition by the Church, much to Le Corbusier's disgust. The first design, largely conceived by Trouin, was influenced heavily by St Teresa's book *The Interior Castle* (a fascinating exploration of mystical space and cabalistic knowledge). [24] I am going to focus on the version designed by Le Corbusier (Fig. 16.2) that seems to have been based upon one of his favourite symbols, that of the sign for the 24-hour day (Fig. 16.3), used, for example on the entrance stone of the Unité apartment block. He wrote that 'If, in the course of the mutation of the machine civilization, I have been able to contribute something, as a person with some rationality and intelligence, as technician, as a thoughtful man, it will be this sign'.[25] For Le Corbusier it provided the means to discover again the 'Lost Paradise'.[26] The life of Mary Magdalene, the paradoxical prostitute saint, could be expressed by such a sign.

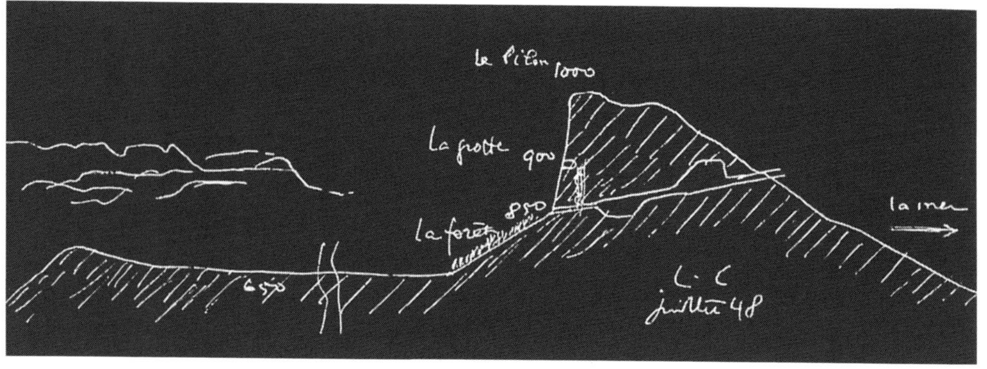

The visitor to the Basilica would climb the wooded foothills of the mountain and enter it through the grotto of Mary Magdalene herself. In a sense the pilgrim would re-enact her story. He or she would then travel down into a lower dark chamber (evocative of the Magdalene's life of bodily excess) before moving on to an upper chamber (evocative of the sun coming up and indeed the presence of Jesus in the life of the Magdalene). It should be mentioned that Le Corbusier felt it vital to engage with the body in order to achieve spiritual enlightenment. The whole complex would be proportioned in accordance with the Modulor, Le Corbusier's system of proportion, based on the geometrical laws of nature. Light, sound, colour, rhythm and space would be used to introduce the body to a sense of geometric harmony resulting in a state of spiritual transformation. At the end of this disorienting trip, likened to an initiation, the neophyte would re-enact her journey to the top of the mountain, emerging on the plateau above where he or she would be greeted by a sparkling view of the Mediterranean and the sun to the south, climax of the spiritual quest.[27]

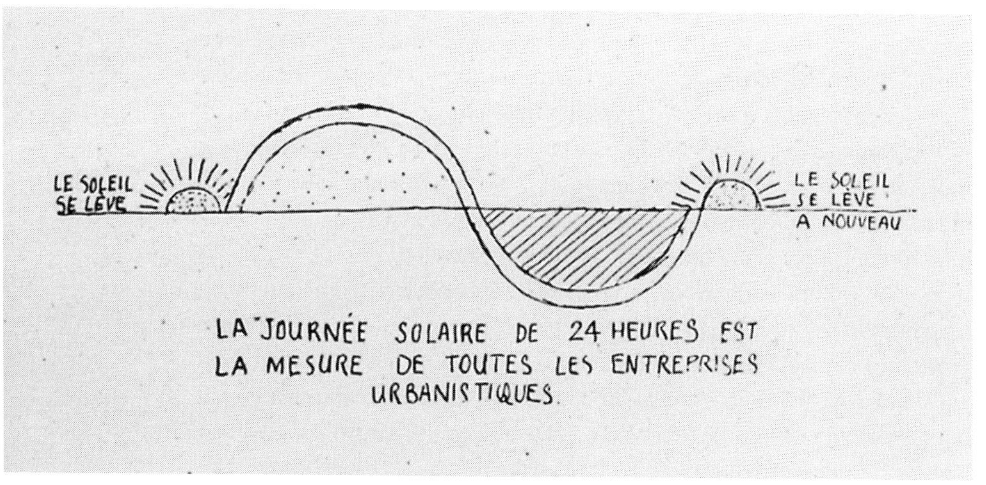

LE SOLEIL
SE LÈVE
LE SOLEIL
SE LÈVE
A NOUVEAU
LA JOURNÉE SOLAIRE DE 24 HEURES EST
LA MESURE DE TOUTES LES ENTREPRISES
URBANISTIQUES.

16.3
Sign of the 24-hour day.
From Le Corbusier, *When the Cathedrals were White: A Journey to the Country of the Timid People*, New York: Reynal and Hitchcock, 1947, p.xviii.

Permanent City

Le Corbusier also tried to evoke the life of the Magdalene through the design of what was known as the permanent city. This part of the project began ambitiously, but was then whittled down in size to just a few dwellings owing, largely, to difficulties with planners. Here would live a 'radiant' community of people who wanted to live in the sprit of the Magdalene.[28] This small housing development was to be built on the other side of the plateau of La Sainte Baume with direct views across the valley floor to the grotto itself (Fig. 16.4). The scheme, based on the idea of a North African casbah would, like the Magdalene herself, embody the melding of orient with occident.

Built of rammed earth, the vaulted houses would be cavelike, dark and cool within. Roofed with grass they would be evocative of a tomb or a cave like that of the Magdalene beyond. It was Le Corbusier's belief that materials and detail could influence the lives of those that lived within his buildings.[29] So by building in earth he may have been trying to encourage those that lived within to live simply within nature like the Magdalene herself.

The materials of houses would be from the site itself, literally of the land, to encourage this sense of connection with all that it meant. Built to Modulor proportions the houses would be in harmony with nature, just as Mary Magdalene was thought, via her connection to the ancient master craftsmen, to have a special connection to the realm of geometry.

16.4
Perspective along a street of the Permanent City.
FLC 17786

The museum

The plan of the development seems to have been based on one of a Roman town included by Le Corbusier in *The Radiant City*.[30] Within what Le Corbusier and Trouin wrote of as the forum of La Sainte Baume would be the museum of Mary Magdalene, occupying the position more usually given to the temple. Indeed it seems that for the two men the museum, allied to a chapel, would have a religious role. It was in their eyes a sacred space. Trouin wrote of the museum as a 'museon', literally the house of the Muses, more usually associated with ancient Greek temples. Here the life of the Magdalene, muse of Jesus, guardian of harmony and geometry, would be celebrated.

The museum would house Trouin's collection of images of the Magdalene, the aim being to show how this paradoxical figure had been interpreted in a number of different ways over the years, it was to be situated in an old sheep-fold, the simple rubble building being left as plain and cave-like as possible again to evoke the existence of the Magdalene. Within it would be a table, a raw block of stone. Glass tiles within the roof would allow beams of life

to penetrate into the space as if from a crevice in a roof of rock. By reusing the old sheep-fold the two men would exploit existing elements of the landscape to further their purpose of evoking the spirit of the place.

The park

Together, through a series of letters and drawings, Le Corbusier and Trouin developed ideas about the reforestation of the site and the planning of the park on the site.[31] Through its design the two men would be able to extend the message implicit within the architecture of the city out into the countryside.

From a reading of Trouin's letters it becomes evident that both he and Le Corbusier enjoyed making analogies between the landscape of La Sainte Baume and the contours of the human body. For Trouin the landscape was 'vocal'; it could speak to those who came there.[32] In ancient Greece, the Muses were honoured in grottos and in what Marie Luise Gothein referred to as 'philosopher's gardens'.[33] These would contain a particular message for the initiated. It is apparent that Le Corbusier and Trouin may have had a similar idea in mind for the park at La Sainte Baume.

It is important to remember that many visitors to La Sainte Baume climb the pleasant path that leads through the oak forest up past a number of small shrines to the grotto and thence to the peak of St Pilon above. From this high viewpoint the valley floor can be seen almost like a flat canvas below, an open area, interspersed with small trees. It may have been for this reason that Le Corbusier chose to approach the design of the landscape below almost as he would a painting. Here the contours of the plateau would be translated quite literally into the form of the Magdalene's body. Trouin wrote of Le Corbusier's plan:

> As for Saint Magdalene, she remains from you with the first ring for her head, for wings, the two great leafy plateaux, for her lap the cedar plateau and for her stellar tail the most South-Easterly cedars.
>
> And a second figure of Magdalene superimposes itself on the first and has for its head the second ring, for chest, the central leafy plateau and for buttock and suggestion of thigh the Eastern plateau. [34]

Le Corbusier wanted to create, within the park, two figures of the Magdalene, one overlapping the other. Given that Trouin wrote of her as the prostitute saint, it would seem likely that Le Corbusier would associate one Magdalene with the spirit and one with the body, further evidence for this supposition being provided by the fact that one of the figures would have wings. It seems very likely that he would have seen Mary Magdalene as a figure who continued within her aspects of a more ancient deity. By interpreting the contours of her body in terms of the landscape of La Sainte Baume, Le Corbusier would make links between the Magdalene and the most ancient primal deities.

Conclusion

Le Corbusier and Trouin wrote of reawakening the spirit of La Sainte Baume embodied in the figure of Mary Magdalene. Le Corbusier and Trouin tried to reawaken her spirit in a number of ways through creating a route of initiate through her mountain along which the visitor would re-enact her story; through the use of geometry; through the use of simple materials to create spaces evocative of her cave; and by drawing attention to the rich symbolism of her story within the museum. Lastly, as if the connection between the Magdalene and the landscape was not already clear enough, they would design a park in the form of her body. To enter the grotto would thus be to enter the very body of the Magdalene, an experience simultaneously spiritual and wildly sexual. In this way the pilgrims to the site would feel the sense of her presence in a very tangible way.

Notes

1 Le Corbusier, *Modulor 2*, London: Faber & Faber, 1955, p.304.
2 Le Corbusier, *Oeuvre Complète Volume 5, 1946–1952*, Zurich: Les Editions d'Architecture, 1995, p.24.
3 See S. Menin and F. Samuel, *Nature and Space: Aalto and Le Corbusier*, London: Routledge, 2003, for a more detailed analysis of Le Corbusier's attitude to nature in particular.
4 Le Corbusier, *Journey to the East*, Cambridge MA: MIT Press, 1987, p.62.
5 Le Corbusier, *Oeuvre Complète 5*, p.24.
6 Le Corbusier, *Le Modulor*, Zurich: Les Editions de l'Architecture, 1950, p.223.
7 Le Corbusier, *Oeuvre Complète 5*, p.27.
8 Ibid., pp.26–7.
9 Letter Le Corbusier to Trouin, 14 September 1953, Fondation Le Corbusier (hereafter referred to as FLC) 13 01 77.
10 L. Réau, *Iconographie de l'art chrétien*, Volume 3.2, Paris: Presses Universitaires de France, 1957, pp.854–5.
11 Letter Trouin to Le Corbusier, 8 February 1955, FLC 13 01 301.
12 A. Moles, *Histoire des charpentiers*, Paris: Librairie Gründ, 1949, in FLC.
13 Moles, *Histoire*, p.114, in FLC.
14 Le Corbusier, *Oeuvre Complète 5*, p.27.
15 J. de Voragine, *The Golden Legend*, Volume 1, Princeton: Princeton University Press, 1993, p.380.
16 Emile Mâle – who was, according to Trouin, iconographical consultant for the Basilica scheme – wrote of the 'special value' of Voragine's book. E. Mâle, *The Gothic Image* [1910], New York, Harper & Row, 1972, p.273.
17 Voragine, *The Golden Legend*, p.375.
18 Le Corbusier, *Precisions*, Cambridge MA: MIT Press, 1991, p.91.
19 Trouin, 'Plan D'Aups ou Plan-Plan D'Aups', n.d., FLC 13 01 366.
20 Letter Trouin to Picasso, 23 February 1956, FLC P5 02 37.
21 F. Samuel, 'A profane annunciation; the representation of sexuality in the architecture of Ronchamp', *Journal of Architectural Education*, 1999, vol.53, no.2, 74–90.
22 S. Haskins, *Mary Magdalene*, London: Harper Collins, 1994, p.365.
23 A.V. Roche, *Provençal Regionalism*, Illinois: Northwestern University Studies, 1954, pp.76–7.
24 F. Samuel, 'The philosophical city of Rabelais and St Teresa', *Literature and Theology*, 1999, vol.13, no.2, 111–26.
25 Le Corbusier, *When the Cathedrals were White: A Journey to the Country of the Timid People*, New York: Reynal and Hitchcock, 1947. p.xviii.
26 Ibid., p.xvii.
27 F. Samuel, 'Le Corbusier, Rabelais and oracle of the holy bottle', *Word and Image*, 2001, vol.17, no.4, 325–38.
28 Letter Trouin to Le Corbusier, 29 January 1958, FLC 13 01 143.
29 Le Corbusier, *Oeuvre Complète 5*, p.190.
30 Le Corbusier, *The Radiant City*, London: Faber, 1967, p.186. Originally published 1935.
31 Letter Trouin to Le Corbusier, 27 November 1950, FLC 13 01 51. See FLC drawings 17748 and 17749.
32 Letter Trouin to Le Corbusier, 2 April 1945, FLC 13 01 03.
33 M.L. Gothein, *A History of Garden Art*, Volume 1, London: Dent, 1928, p.88.
34 Letter Trouin to Le Corbusier, 11 November 1950, FLC 13 01 45.

Chapter 17

Retreating to dwell

Playing and reality at Muuratsalo

Sarah Menin

The correlation of habitation and place, indeed the concept of inhabiting place, is central to Aalto's notion of architecture. This correlation of the notion of creating place and creating dwelling will be examined through analysis of his summer-house on the island of Muuratsalo, in Central Finland, from 1953, and two of Aalto's articles, 'From doorstep to living room' from 1926, and 'The reconstruction of Europe' from 1941.

The house

Set back from the shore of an isolated island, high upon the smooth granite rock Aalto conceived his Experimental Summer-house (Fig. 17.1). It has a basically square footprint, central to which is a paved courtyard, and around which the living accommodation seems to spiral (Fig. 17.2).

One side of the L-shaped plan comprises the main room that denotes something of the vernacular multi-purpose 'tupa' living space, here too with an open fire. There is also the addition of a small studio loft space nestling beneath the apex of the roof. A cloister-like corridor leads from a small kitchen to the modest bedrooms. Although facing the courtyard this is, by seasons, either pierced by the sun or shuttered tight against the cold.

17.1
View of Aalto's Summer House, Muuratsalo, Central Finland.
Alvar Aalto, 1953.

This living accommodation forms two sides of a brick-paved courtyard, enclosed on the third side by a tall, yet punctured, brick wall. The fourth side is largely open, although the walls return to suggest a degree of enclosure and protection. These high external wall planes envelope the outside living space, but do not restrict it, allowing the space to extend beyond the bounds of the cultured courtyard, across the granite boulders, down to the water, where tiny jetties assist access to and from the lake.

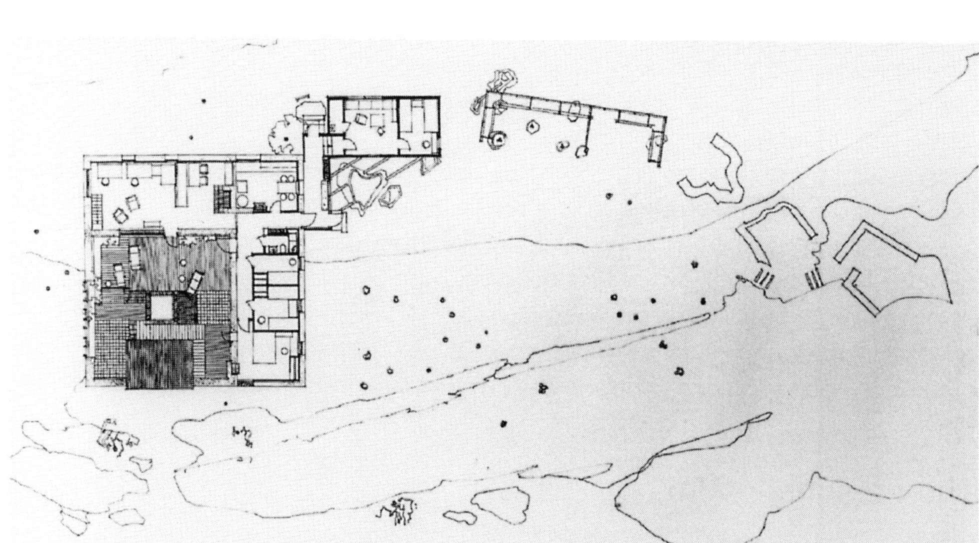

17.2
Plan of Summer House and outbuildings, *c.*1953.

17.3
View of Summer House from elevated position on the rock.

A door leads from the kitchen area at the back of the building into the guest accommodation, beyond which is a free-standing woodshed. There is a great contrast between the form and fabric of the courtyard dwelling and the timber 'tail', which bleeds in to the floor of the forest, as it drapes its way up the contours of the granite hill (Fig. 17.3).

The house has both a modest structure and form, built (in part) from the bricks rejected from the Säynätsalo Town Hall project. From without the complex projects a cool, dramatic image, while from within the fabric has the warmth of an 'old tweed coat'[1] or a worn tapestry, as the dossier of some fifty experimental-brick panels age.

In addition to experimenting with brick types and configurations, Aalto also tried using an ancient granite-boulder foundation system, and even sought to heat the house in the winter with a heat pump using solar energy from the lake. When describing the scheme in 1953 he noted that 'Proximity to nature can give fresh inspiration both in terms of form and construction'.[2] The intriguing little sauna building also demonstrates an experiment with an inverted vernacular accent, as the simple turf-covered mono-pitch is formed by piling naturally tapering logs upon each other.

The personal realm

Although the significance of the building cannot be divorced from the foregoing character of its experimentation and technology, it is possible to say that Aalto invested his personal retreat at Muuratsalo with a distillation of his attitude not only to life and dwelling, but to nature, mysticism and the environment.

In Aalto's mind it was not just preferable, but rather essential to be able to access at least aspects of the natural environment, as the development of his ideas about the necessity for direct access to nature from dwellings demonstrates. For him personally, contact with the natural environment may be said to have been therapeutic, even medicinal.

Of course, the notions of dwelling, embrace and sustenance have often been related, not least by philosophers such a Heideggar and Bachelard.[3] The psychological realm of dwelling is closely related to Self, which undoubtedly comprises dangling threads of unrecorded reality. Childhood experiences,[4] often preverbal (if not primal) may generate these threads.

Here I argue that, just as in any creative process, Aalto's psyche was a crucial ingredient in understanding his agenda for his architecture generally, and human dwelling in particular. For instance, the nature of his innumerable affairs may in part be further evidence of his fear of being alone.[5] But such contact may also be seen to revisit the close physical warmth and intimacy he reported having enjoyed with his mother before her sudden death from meningitis when he was just eight.[6]

Although the extent of the adult psychopathology of this man is difficult to determine with precision, there is sufficient evidence to suggest that he exhibited episodes of great drive, verging on manic behaviour. Indeed, his friend and biographer Göran Schildt reports that Aalto was so 'obsessed with his need or desire to create that anything that might hinder his work aroused distaste'.[7] Coupled with recollections of this, Schildt and others record bouts of great psychological and physical depression.[8]

The nature of the psyche's dwelling

In common with others, in *The Ecology of Imagination in Childhood*, Edith Cobb has identified a process of symbolically reforming aspects of oneself through creative endeavour, and engagement with nature.[9]

One aspect of Aalto's troubled psyche was the undoubted fear of being alone that expressed itself beneath his ebullient extroverted character. Indeed, as psychiatrist Anthony Storr indicates, 'The capacity to be alone thus becomes linked with self-discovery and self-realisation; with becoming aware of one's deepest needs, feelings and impulses.'[10] Clinging behaviour, which Aalto exhibited throughout life, is indicative of insecurity and the roots of dependency, and can be seen to be intertwined with manic-depressive disorders. This assists in the generation of a clearer understanding about Aalto's attitude to both dwelling and nature – and his own need to draw sustenance from the presence of something 'Other'.

Isolation triggered a downward cycle of depression for Aalto, and solitude had to be filled with activity, the company of others, hard mind-occupying work, and more commonly drink.[11] He wrote to his wife Aino in 1932, 'Always when I thought of you in my loneliness, it was as if I had begged you to help me . . . I missed you terribly and at the same time there was something painful about it'.[12]

Thus, despite the bravado, Aalto appears to have been a deeply insecure individual. I demonstrate elsewhere that such insecurity may very well have been the grounding, so to speak, on which he built his creative process.[13] This was a process, it seems, of self-maintenance that involved instigating episodes where symbolically charged, disparate forms could find relationship in architecture. Once inhabited by the users, these episodes demonstrate part of Aalto's deep agenda of facilitating human interaction.

Yet, the complete achievement depended upon the successful outworking of his drive to expunge human alienation from nature wherever he found it, and orient his architectural detail to express a sense of this connectedness whereever possible, a connectedness that is particularly relevant to the problem of dwelling.

Aalto's insecurity may, thus, have been the grounding, so to speak, on which Aalto built his creative process, a process, it seems, of self-maintenance that involved designing episodes of 'relating' forms or facilitating the interaction of people and place.[14] Hence his psyche is a crucial ingredient in understanding his agenda for human dwelling. Whilst working upon the scheme for his retreat at Muuratsalo, having been so recently triggered by death, it may be argued that Aalto was simultaneously working and re-working malformed structures of his Self. Such structures, psychiatrists argue, are formed (or deformed) in childhood, depending on the power exerted by impingements and deprivations in the child's environment.[15]

Indeed, a glance at his personal circumstances and architectural preoccupations leading up to 1952 when he conceived the building indicates a time of upheaval that is telling, drawing to the fore aspects of his personality and motivation.

The outbreak of war in 1939 had ruptured Aalto's mind. After being found cowering in psychosis having run away to a Stockholm hotel at the outbreak of hostilities with Russia, 'unable to admit his trauma',[16] Aalto spent years running from the reality of war. His compulsion to create was impeded by both circumstances and his own traumatized psyche, as his memories of his mother's death resurfaced, triggered by his brother's suicide when he was called to the Front. I suggest that it is no accident that during his psychologically vulnerable war years Aalto channelled much of his creativity into the problem of housing, and in particular the notion of relationship, in this case dwelling and place, central to which was the search for facilitation of contact with nature.

In a wartime lecture given in the safe environs of Switzerland, in 1941, Aalto explored how the 'psychological slums'[17] of the modern milieu, and its lack of harmony, could be addressed through contact with nature – suggesting that '[at] the root of this disharmony is a break with the individual's genuine psychological needs'.[18] For this reason he believed that the 'psychological pressure' of living in 'stereotyped, unnatural communities', as he put it, could be rectified if standardization were inspired by nature's 'biological diversity', and if the building took something of its character from the site, thereby becoming 'an instrument that collects all the positive influences in nature for man's benefit, while also sheltering him from all the unfavourable influences that appear in nature'. He went on, 'Architecture should always have a means to solve the problems of a building's organic connection with nature (including people and human life as the most important consideration)'.[19]

Therein Aalto argued that nature, in both broad and specific ways, held an answer to the problem of dwelling, and an answer to a degree of psychological alienation in society generally, and I suggest for him personally.

Busying himself with fantastical schemes through the war years, Aalto arranged trips to Switzerland, Germany, and the United States of America. Aalto had used his contacts in the USA to secure a visiting Professorship at MIT during the war. He returned thereafter and designed the undulating mass of Baker House Dormitory from 1946 onwards, visiting occasionally, but otherwise steering the project from Helsinki. He fled home immediately when his wife Aino's cancer was diagnosed in late 1948. The shock of her death a few months later, early in 1949, speaks volumes about his dependency on her.

Aalto was unable to be creatively effective for a long time after her death, filling life with restless travelling and with drink. A friend reports that 'He was totally disorientated, lost his customary ebullience and drank until his friends despaired of his future'.[20] Gone was Aino's motherly encouragement and anchoring, and her constant forgiveness. She had been a level-headed, protective figure who could critically share his vision, but bring his fantasies down to earth.

Muuratsalo and the mediation of memory: playing and reality

Only in 1952 did Aalto manage to rouse himself from his creative paralysis to concentrate lovingly on Säynätsalo Town Hall, and thereafter to confront the potent mingling of life and death in the air and conceive his summer-house. It is interesting to ask why this drew him from his catastrophic breakdown.

Säynätsalo is close to Jyväskylä in Central Finland, where Aalto had lived from a young age, and where his mother died. It was the natural environment in which, as a child, he had traipsed, endlessly following his surveyor father. It was also where he first set up practice and met and married Aino.

Aalto's attitude to nature generally, and this natural environment in particular, had been influenced by his father and, particularly, his grandfather, who had been a forester. As he learnt about the science of nature he had also become aware of the 'mystical' realm of the natural environment, as he was later to call it.[21] In his bereaved childhood state the forest may have offered a refuge for the gaping psyche of a child, and unencumbered by the demands that he should be 'Top dog', as his father repeatedly put it.[22] This could be the roots of what might be called his nature-dependency.

It is not surprising then that this particular environment roused him. Yet it was also during the design of the Säynätsalo project that Aalto had begun the relationship with a young assistant Elissa Mäkiniemi – someone who could become a new tutelary goddess, another mother figure who would guide and sustain him, and around whom he would fly creatively. Aalto and Elissa discovered an unusually attractive unspoilt shore site on the large granite island of Muuratsalo, close to Säynätsalo.

I suggest that the relationship, the natural environment and the architecture together manifest a new 'holding environment', as Winnicott put it.[23]

Cohabitation

The Muuratsalo scheme demonstrates many of the principles that Aalto set out in a 1926 article 'From doorstep to living room'.[24] Therein he called for a 'trinity of the human being, room and garden' – suggesting, in essence, that human interaction with nature should be at the heart of the creation of place – something we heard repeated in the war-time article of 1941 – and something he found in Fra Angelico's 'Annunciation'.

Here, early in his career, Aalto had promoted a reinvigoration of human contact with nature and the natural environment. At Muuratsalo the courtyard enclosure plan is an enactment of this call, offering a palimpsest of both the Roman villa type and the Finnish vernacular forms and configurations, such as Niemilä Farmstead – the deeply indigenous logic of which Aalto knew and loved, and integrated into his modern dwellings.[25]

At the same time Aalto was a thoroughly forward-looking, technology-loving Finn, who in 1926 had sought to emulate Le Corbusier's 'brilliant example' in *L'Esprit Nouveau Pavilion*, what he saw as 'the affinity of the home interior and garden'. Aalto asked, 'Is it a hall, beautifully open to the exterior and

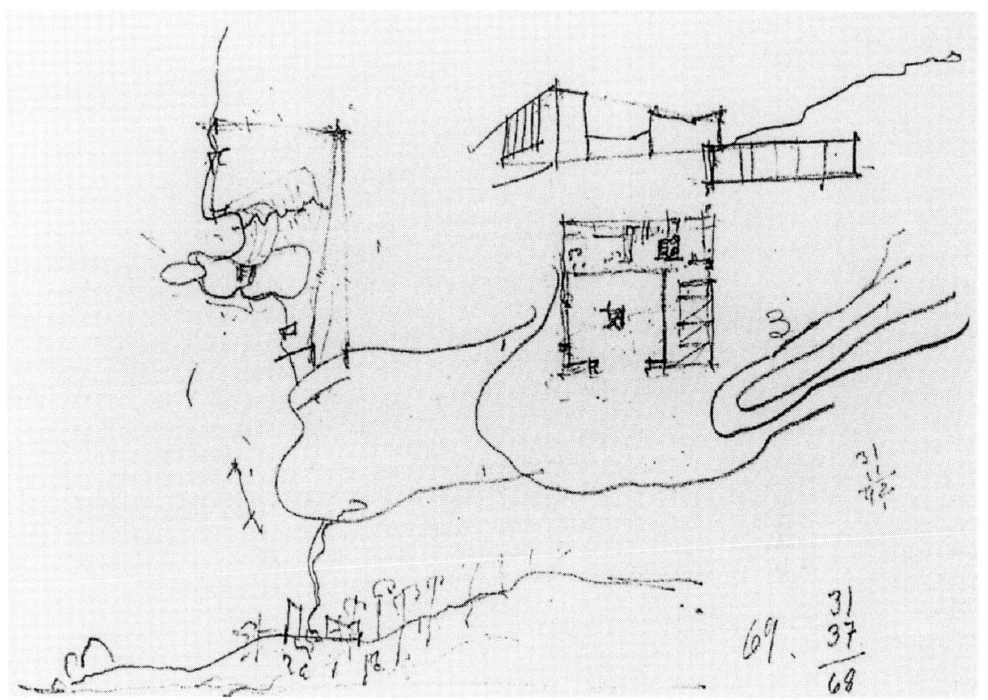

17.4
Design sketch of Summer House, *c.*1953.

taking its dominating character from the trees, or is it a garden built in to the house, a garden room?'[26]

The reconciliation of these simultaneous gestures towards the forest and the forum of architectural history is typical of Aalto's divergent thinking,[27] – a tendency to relate the disparate, but with a strong controlling hand.

In summer the Muuratsalo courtyard is a fully utilized outside room, satisfying the Finnish need for what he saw as an 'aesthetically direct contact with the world outside', as he put it in 1926. He went on to propose the conception that 'the garden wall' was the 'external wall of the house' and, therein, the courtyard is brought, metaphorically, into the volume of the dwelling, as part of the home (Fig. 17.4).[28]

The summer-house also offers a 'winter face', which 'turns inward and is seen in the interior design' emphasizing the 'warmth of our inner rooms' – a call for an interior landscape, which later became so common in Aalto's work.

In this scheme he uses the physical sky, rather than creating its metaphysical kin that he conceived in Viipuri and elsewhere. As a seasonally limited room, inhabited visually and symbolically when it is too cold to inhabit physically, the courtyard acts as a sensitive screen between inside warmth and outside cold.

It is thus a place of transition, a defensible space, like a Niemilä stockyard, enclosed by huts and fences.

17.5
Aalto tending a fire in the courtyard.

Here Aalto facilitates the cohabitation of the metaphysical with domestic reality in part through the degrees of physical inhabitation – degrees of what might be called dwelling enclosure and natural exclosure – a term meaning exactly this vernacular stockyard from which harmful natural forces are excluded, that so inspired Aalto. Here again there is a tantalizing and subtle drawing out of the user, to 'engage' beyond the 'bounds' and an invitation for nature to infiltrate those 'bounds' that is crucial.

This concerns Aalto's capacity to draw nature in and humankind out of confined space that is both clearly defined and partially connoted. It is as if here he is appealing to the sense and the psyche, enticing the body out of what he perceived as a stultifying modern (but not necessarily modernist) habit of offering tight spatial enclosure, into a more loosely defined realm. And the creeping vegetation is part of this. Yet, put another way, the place offers an example of intermingling of the boundaries of space – drawing out questions, for instance, of what is contained and what container, what is central and what edge. Each of these questions has clear psychological corollaries.

Perhaps for Aalto freedom came, in part, from the creation of a partially controlled domain – a limited world – cut off, literally, from the mainland of problems associated with professional, adult interaction with the world, and one in which nature and creativity are rampantly uncontrolled.

Elemental relationships

The scheme is thus, according to season, both introverted and extroverted. Its relationship with nature is seasonally mediated by the courtyard, at the heart of which is a sunken fire pit, signifying the oldest actions of humankind in relation to nature. Of it, Aalto wrote:

> The whole complex of buildings is dominated by the fire that burns at the centre of the patio and that, from the point of view of practicality and comfort, serves the same purpose as the campfire, where the glow from the fire and its reflections from the surrounding snow-banks create a pleasant, almost mystical feeling of warmth.[29] (Fig. 17.5)

The west wall of the courtyard is, in part, the outside wall of the living space, but goes on to be a sacral element, as it becomes a white timber screen through which sky light filters, as it does through the trees beyond. It denotes birch trees, sacred in Finnish folk-culture, and abundant on the site, becoming a symbolic interface between the simultaneous realities of the home-enclosure and the forest-exclosure, and between the physical and the metaphysical realms.

It may even offer something of a palimpsest of pagan ritual worship. The screen wall then comprises both 'decayed' brick (the void) and 'growing' wood (the trellis). The wall returns to form the fourth side of the courtyard, where the majority of wall is missing, leaving nature beyond to complete or challenge the enclosure.

Growth or dereliction of form

Here is an aura of immanence, of engagement with something in the process of happening.

Being integrated with nature and by gesturing towards both the vernacular and classical precedents Aalto tenders something of the precariousness of nature's flux. Indeed, in 1925 he had described such an imposition, 'placed in the landscape in a natural way, in harmony with the general contours',[30] going on to suggest that 'pure, original nature, with all its magic power, cannot surpass the sight of a landscape to which a human touch has added a harmonious, enhancing factor'.[31] Architectural intervention, he suggests, may considerately improve an otherwise uninhabited realm of nature.

The transition between the court-like house and the increasingly shed-like outbuildings seems also to represent a trope of nature/culture opposition. Yet this episode also challenges the very notion of the divide between civilization and nature by rooting the buildings physically to the forest and metaphorically to its culture. Here the memory of dwelling bleeds back in to the ragged floor of the forest, again in some state of flux. Indeed, not all his planned sheds were completed.

I suggest Aalto refers to both the glories and decay of civilization; the fact that man will affect the natural environment, and create great cultures, but that ultimately nature will engulf the proposition. At Muuratsalo he boldly adds a surging white form as a clarion amidst the wilderness, alluding perhaps to Mediterranean monasteries. He seems to declare the dominance of civilized man over nature, while simultaneously subverting this reading by creating a pantheistic call to prayer of the vulnerable amidst the power of nature.

Gesturing simultaneously towards dereliction of civilization and natural re-colonization, in 1926 Aalto had articulated the idea of providing elements that are 'deliberately presented as ruin',[32] such as the overgrown timber steps behind the main part of the house, pushing back the earth to gain a foothold in an archetypal way and gesturing towards remnants of a classical amphitheatre. Coupled to Demitri Porphyrios's excavations of the Picturesque cult of the ruin in his work,[33] here we can also read Aalto's symbolic use of the notion of 'ruin' and 'decay' as being rooted in his own experience of the forest ecology in which growth and decay are a continuum – a fact of which he needed to reassure himself continuously, particularly at this time, given his profound terror of death.[34]

The confrontation of culture and nature is speeded by Aalto's determination to prefigure this future moment of reconciliation in the present; as if to prove to himself reconciliation of severed realities may be made actual, rather than being merely a philosophical belief or psychological theory.

The scheme may therefore be read as a poem on the idea of *Sterben und Werden*, death and becoming – the creation of a formal, visual dialogue between depleted historic references and the forces of nature that over millennia would have caused such dereliction. This may signify a sort of harmony between the natural and man-made environment, but (at least) connotes dialogue of these realms.

This is crucial, because composed with death still in the air, and its aura re-manifest in the ineffable sense of constructed decay that pervades some of the details, the place Aalto creates at Muurtasalo is nonetheless the realization of a new beginning.

This new beginning is imbued with something of the child's sense of play and capacity to move one, and to invigorate any situation with a lightness of being which is both immediate, and deeply symbolic in its playfulness. It is the process of playing with reality, which Winnicott has famously explored, as a means to digest life's less palatable nature.[35]

Indeed, Aalto articulated his concern to create an environment in which creative play had dominion, and actually called the house a 'playhouse'. He described how play was 'of decisive importance when we build communities for people – large children',[36]demonstrating his intuitive understanding of the inner child, and suggesting that he was fully aware of requisitioning this part of himself in his creativity – facilitating the creative intervention of the building and its content in nature in a way that, as he put it, 'can not be measured'.[37]

Elsewhere he had noted that '[a]fterall, nature is a symbol of freedom. Sometimes it is actually the source of the concept of freedom, and its maintainer.'[38] Importantly, Aalto wrote this phrase a matter of days after Aino's death in 1949.

It is something of a testimony to the key place nature held in his mental balance at this time. Nature, with all its flux, is here a reassuring constant for Aalto.

Conclusion

In his retreat playhouse Aalto made manifest his determination to assist modern architecture to recover 'place', but this cannot be separated from his suggestion that all architecture must reflect the nature of human experience, above all, he believed, the 'psychological needs'.[39]

Nature and psychology were somehow isomorphic in Aalto's mind, and were key to his conception of dwelling.

Notes

1 Aalto made this reference to the desired effect for the façade of Baker House, MIT, in 1947 to architect Robert Dean, of Perry Shaw and Hepburn. Repeated in conversation with Sarah Menin, Boston, 15July 1985.

2 Aalto, *Experimental House*, Muuratsalo 1953. Reprinted in Aalto, *Experimental House*, Jyväskylä: Alvar Aalto Museum, 1985, unpaginated.

3 M. Heidegger, 'Building Dwelling Thinking', in M. Heidegger, *Martin Heidegger: Basic Writings*, ed. D. Farrell Krell, London: Routledge, 1993.

4 The phrase 'threads of unrecorded reality' is borrowed from Suzanne K. Langer, *Philosophy in a New Key*, Cambridge MA: Harvard University Press, 1993, p.281.

5 Schildt reports the memories of Viola Markelius, wife of his architect friend Sven Markelius, who recalled her affair with Aalto, stating that 'She stands in this biography for the many women Aalto had met during his long life, with whom he shared his zest for life'. G. Schildt, *Alvar Aalto: The Decisive Years*, New York: Rizzoli, 1986, p.52.

6 Aalto often talked about his mother's underwear. Schildt, *Decisive Years*, p.136.

7 G. Schildt, *Alvar Aalto: The Mature Years*, New York: Rizzoli, 1992, p.301.

8 For example Schildt, *Mature Years*, pp.14, 130 and 147.

9 E. Cobb, *The Ecology of Imagination in Childhood*, Dallas: Spring Pub., 1993, p.94.

10 A. Storr, *The School of Genius*, London: André Deutsch, 1988, p.21. Storr also refers to Winnicott's 'The capacity to be alone' in which he demonstrated how experience of being alone in the company of another (particularly the mother) is vital for development and security. D.W. Winnicott, 'The capacity to be alone', in *Maturational Processes and the Facilitating Environment*, London: The Hogarth Press, 1965, p.34.
11 This is analysed in depth in S. Menin, Relating the Past, Sibelius, Aalto and the Profound Logos, PhD thesis, University of Newcastle upon Tyne, 1997.
12 Aalto, in letter to Aino, undated, in Schildt, *The Mature Years*, p.130.
13 Menin, 'Relating the past'. The thesis is summarized in S. Menin, 'Relating the Past: the Creativity of Sibelius and Aalto', *Ptah* (Alvar Aalto Foundation), 1, 2001, pp.32–44.
14 S. Menin, 'Relating the past'.
15 Winnicott analyses such growth of the Self in his *Collected Papers: Through Paediatrics to Psychanalysis*, London: Tavistock, 1958.
16 Schildt, *Mature Years*, p.14.
17 Aalto, 'The reconstruction of Europe' [1941]; reprinted in G. Schildt, *Alvar Aalto Own Words*, New York: Rizzoli, 1998, p.154.
18 Ibid.
19 Ibid.
20 J.M. Richards, *Memories of an Unjust Fella*, London: Weidenfeld & Nicholson, 1980, p.203.
21 Aalto, *Experimental House*, unpaginated.
22 Schildt, *The Decisive Years*, p.117.
23 D.W. Winnicott, *The Child, the Family and the Outside World*, Harmondsworth: Penguin, 1964, pp.17–18.
24 Aalto, 'From doorstep to living room' [1926], reprinted in Schildt, *Own Words*, p.49.
25 Aalto was praised for having designed a 'modern Niemilä Farmstead' in his own house and studio in 1934. Schildt, *The Decisive Years*, p.130.
26 S. Menin and F. Samuel, *Nature and Space: Aalto and Le Corbusier*, London: Routledge, 2003.
27 J.P. Guilford, *The Nature of Human Intelligence*, New York: McGaw Hill, 1967.
28 Menin and Samuel, *Nature and Space*.
29 Aalto, *Experimental House*, 1953.
30 Aalto, 'Architecture in the Landscape of Central Finland', 1925, in Schildt, *Own Words*, pp.21–22.
31 Aalto, 'Architecture in the Landscape of Central Finland', p.21.
32 Aalto, 'From Doorstep to Living Room', 1926.
33 D. Porphyrios, *Sources of Modern Eclecticism: Studies on Alvar Aalto*, London: Academy, 1982, p.59–82.
34 Aalto, 'Interview for Television', July 1972 in Schildt, *Own Words*, p.274.
35 D.W. Winnicott, *Playing and Reality*, Harmondsworth: Penguin, 1972.
36 Aalto, *Experimental House, 1953.*
37 Aalto, *Experimental House, 1953.*
38 Aalto, 'National Planning and the Goals of Culture', 1949. Reprinted in Schildt, *Own Words*.
39 Aalto, 'Rationalism and Man', 1935, in Schildt, *Own Words*, pp.89–93.

Chapter 18

From place to planet

Jørn Utzon's earthbound platforms and floating roofs

Richard Weston

It is difficult to think of a more striking way to sum up the range of 'modern mediation' than by juxtaposing Le Corbusier's Villa Savoye with Can Lis, the house Jørn Utzon built for himself and his family on Majorca in 1973. Abstract, cubic and poised confidently above, more than 'on', its site, Madame Savoye's house is an ideal dwelling in the tradition of Palladio's Villa Rotonda. Can Lis, by contrast, is resolutely concrete, made of the stone on which it stands, fragmented rather than pure, rooted in the earth. If the Villa is the paradigmatic modern house, designed to land anywhere on the planet,[1] Can Lis might be mistaken for something built on Crete in the time of King Minos, inseparable from the Mediterranean environment and culture of stone from which it grows (Fig. 18.1).

The Villa Savoye greets the visitor frontally, with a self-conscious play on symmetry and a planar elevation that hints at the dominant long axis through the composition. Utzon's house, on the other hand, might almost be a huddle of old buildings, with low walls sheltering hidden patios and disclosing little about the splendours lurking out of sight. If the Villa is the quintessential house-as-object detached from the particularities of place, Can Lis suggests a cliff-top settlement: in place of an articulated field of space, we are offered – to borrow a phrase from Aldo van Eyck – a 'bunch of places'.[2]

To demonstrate the liberties of the *plan libre*, Le Corbusier favours continuity between spaces and floors, inside and outside; Utzon creates a succession of discrete rooms, some internal, some external. In the Villa Savoye

18.1
Can Lis, Utzon's own house designed on Majorca in 1973.

sunlight is an abstract, universal medium to reveal the 'magnificent play of masses brought together in light';[3] in Can Lis, the Mediterranean light is celebrated by allowing a Kahnian 'slice of the sun' to enter the living room for a few minutes, and then retreat, leaving only an orange glow in the tiny opening cut – after the room was built – for this purpose.

These differences can be summed up by adopting van Eyck's distinction between pre- and post-war modern architecture as the contrast between the celebration of 'space and time' and that of 'place and occasion'.[4] Yet, for all that, one might almost equally well stress how much they share. Both are emphatically *modern* and both skilfully *mediate* between site and dwelling. The terms are different, but not as different as they might at first appear. One only has to look at, say, the house on Lac Leman Le Corbusier built for his mother in the mid-1920s, or the house for Madame de Mandrot which was being designed as the Villa was completed, to see that a 'place-making' approach to architecture was latent, if not always dominant, throughout his work.[5] The Villa Savoye may be the definitive expression of the major tropes of the so-called Machine Style, but it is also a supremely memorable place, as anyone can attest who has sat on the first-floor terrace or enjoyed a packed lunch within the embrace of the screen walls of the roof-top solarium.

Describing the genesis of Can Lis, Utzon has said that he thought of the plan as being 'like an ideal rectangle descending onto the site, fragmenting and then adjusting to the horizon'.[6] The result recalls the contrast between the ideal square and the site adjusted 'tail' of Alvar Aalto's Muuratsalo house, and at first sight could hardly be more different to the compact Villa Savoye. Yet in both we see shared, Classical, preoccupations. In Utzon these are manifested in a sequence of artful plays on symmetry and asymmetry in the articulation of space and form, and in the manipulation of a seemingly rudimentary language of columns and beams to evoke archetypal forms.

Utzon's description of his house's genesis brings to mind Rex Martienssen's suggestion that 'the creation of a level plane … has wider significance than that of its purely "useful" aspect. … A horizontal plane or series of horizontal planes is the first essential in any system of formal arrangement intended to embrace the activities of organized life'.[7]

Martienssen had in mind not only the platforms and stylobates of Greek acropolises and temples, but also their reinterpretation and transformation in the work of leading European modernists. Greek prototypes are not difficult to detect in the plinth of Mies van der Rohe's Barcelona Pavilion, and they surely also haunt Le Corbusier's 'The Five Points of a New Architecture', with their implication that an entire building can be conceptualized as a giant podium to support the ultimate 'free space' of the roof garden. At Can Lis, a square, stoa-like enclosure forms the 'head' of the composition, and the overall planning has more to do with the layouts of Classical Greek sites and engagement with the distant horizon, than with the purely local adjustments to rocks and trees of the 'tail' of Aalto's summer-house.

Utzon's decisive architectural experience did not, however, come in Greece, but in Mexico, which he visited in 1949 after paying court to Mies van der Rohe and Frank Lloyd Wright – whose debts to Mesoamerican architecture have, of course, been much discussed.[8] For Utzon, the power of the Mayan complexes lay in their ability to transform the experience of the landscape. By placing their temples on vast platforms as high as the surrounding jungle, a radically new relationship to the surroundings was established: the claustrophobia of the dense jungle, with its almost complete occlusion of open space, gave way to seemingly unlimited horizons as the tree-tops became a green ocean. At Monte Albán, where the mountain-top was first levelled and then framed by a perimeter of buildings and steps to eliminate immediate contact with even the tree-tops, this newly created world seemed, as Utzon later wrote in a revealing essay entitled 'Platforms and Plateaus' (*sic*), 'a completely independent thing floating in the air, separated from the earth … from there you actually see nothing but the sky and the passing clouds, – a new planet.'[9]

On his return to Denmark Utzon sketched an idea for a 'canyon house'. Conceived as a series of stepped platforms roofed by a cluster of leaf-like forms, he described it as follows:

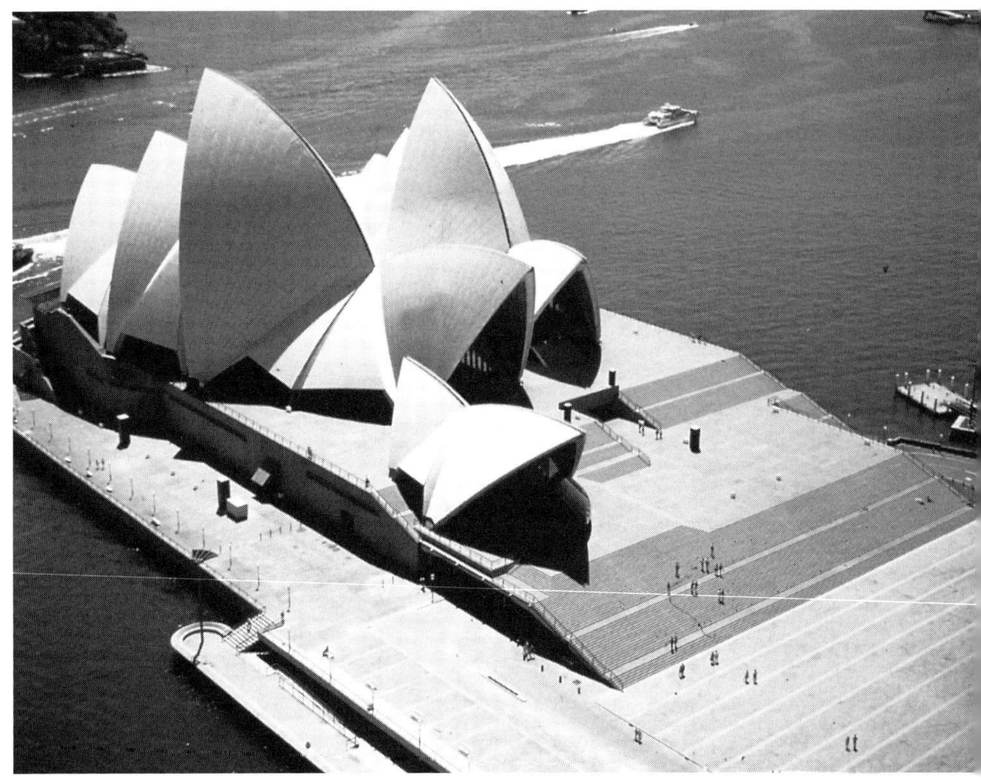

> The roof can be hanging above, it can be spanning across or jumping over you in one big leap or in many small ones. The problem is to master the waterproofing, the structural requirements and the heat insulation in one mass-produced element, which in combination with itself can give various roof forms, a nice problem to be solved.[10]

18.2
Sydney Opera House.
Jørn Utzon, 1957–65, completed 1973.

The terms of his future explorations – the earth-bound platform allied to a floating superstructure that exploits industrial means of production yet whose forms are of organic inspiration – had been established. They achieved definitive and monumental expression less than a decade later with the design of Sydney Opera House.

'Sydney', with its unforgettable image of vast 'sails' floating above one of the world's great harbours, has become so familiar on everything from travel advertising to wine labels that it is increasingly difficult to approach it as architecture (Fig. 18.2). From the outset of the competition Utzon realized that the building's situation at the end of a peninsula beneath the Harbour Bridge demanded forms that would present an ever-changing sculptural experience as they unfolded from all angles, and also a roof that could become an engaging 'fifth façade' when seen from above.

Utzon had discovered the surface vitality he wanted in the mosques of Isfahan, but it took some three years to develop the tiles he needed. Typically, the analogies he used to describe what he was after were drawn from nature. The finish, he said, should combine the contrasting textures of flesh seen directly and through a finger nail, or be like the juxtaposition of the perfect, matt surface of newly fallen snow with an uneven, frozen layer below exposed by wind. A more direct precedent was found in Japanese half-glazed ceramics, and the final solution combined fully glazed tiles – in which tiny pieces of previously fired clay were incorporated in the aggregate to give the necessary unevenness – with perfectly smooth, unglazed matt tiles. The matt tiles could be cut without their edges breaking up, whereas the glazed ones were always to be used whole; laying the tiles at 45 degrees generated feathered edges which subtly highlighted the underlying pattern of the precast 'tile-lids'.

The resulting surfaces are amongst the most visually alive in architecture. They have no inherent colour and so, like the white or metallic surfaces of a minimalist installation, are free to respond to each other and to the surroundings, above all to the ever-changing play of light. As passing clouds, the sun or the observer move by, the shells glow, gleam or flash with light. As you get closer, waves of tiles scintillate like diamonds or tiny stars. Move closer still and focus on a single tile, and miniature constellations appear and disappear below the minutely undulating surface, suggesting an inner life, like blood beneath skin. Walking down the narrow 'street' between the halls, you move between mountains of glistening ice and blue shade, which in places glows mysteriously with pools of light reflected from a sunny neighbour.

Compelling though the building is as a visual spectacle, it is, I would argue, as one of the twentieth-century's greatest built places that Sydney should ultimately be valued. In this respect, it is the vast platform that is vital – and it is this, not the eye-catching shells, about which Utzon was certain from early in the design. The inspiration may have been Mayan, but whilst preparing the competition project he consulted aerial photographs of Greek sites, and in the competition report likened the journey from the city out along the peninsula to the procession to a Greek theatre sited just outside the city, in the landscape. What he designed, in effect, was a low acropolis, an artificial landform which *became* the site and out of which the auditoria appear to be carved – emphasized by the way they were rendered in the plan, which was by far the most impressive of the famously incomplete competition drawings.

A key inspiration in Sydney was the image of a traditional Islamic city as a uniform and apparently continuous fabric surmounted by exotic domes and minarets. It was to prove one of the most potent in all Utzon's work. Just as the city is made of bricks baked of the earth from which it rises, so Utzon's platform is clad with reconstructed stone panels which echo the red sandstone bedrock of Sydney. For all its undoubted debts to the ancient, the use to which Utzon put his ideas is, however, unmistakably modern. Like a grand-scale version of Louis Kahn's servant and served spaces, the building is abstracted to the interplay between two elements: the built ground of the platform, containing all the non-public 'servant' spaces; and the spherical roofs that, despite their actual weight, seem to spring weightless from its surface. Utzon may, as Kenneth Frampton has suggested, be a major exponent of 'tectonic culture',[11] but seen from outside the feeling in Sydney is of the defiance of, not obedience to, gravity.

Radically modern too is the abstraction of the platform's surfaces, some 90 metres wide and almost unarticulated save for the changes of level achieved by vast banks of steps. Water drains through the gaps between the precast slabs, eliminating the need for any deviation from the ideal of an absolutely level, horizontal plane. Abstraction on such a grand scale is rare, and brings to mind what Sigfried Giedion called 'the relentless planes of the Cheops pyramid'.[12] In Egypt the sublime power of smooth, dazzling planes was designed to repel the touch of mortals and there were, inevitably, countless gainsayers who deemed Utzon's proposals 'inhuman' – too vast, too unarticulated, to become a human place.

Life, it hardly needs saying, has proved Utzon right, and his horizontal planes have been – to borrow Martienssen's terms – both embraced by public life and acted as a catalyst for a rich variety of informal activities. The Opera House platform is now the pre-eminent public space not only in Sydney, but arguably in Australia as a whole, the setting for outdoor concerts, political rallies and protests, as well as a place to wander, meet friends, jog or simply sit and watch or enjoy the views. Characteristically, Utzon's confidence in its success was based on his direct observation of people and of nature:

> I have seen how beautifully and naturally people move through the landscape. I have seen the way they sit, on a midsummer night along the rocky coast of Sweden, facing the water, watching a sailing race. They sit just like birds on the rocks. I have noticed how beautiful they are when in groups without being controlled.[13]

Sydney's success clearly owes something to the magnificent setting, with exhilarating views in all directions, but equally clearly the character of the architecture is also vital. Although a supreme work of artifice, the Opera House exemplifies what Michael Benedikt has called 'the "emptiness of intention" we attribute to nature',[14] offering opportunities for inhabitation without

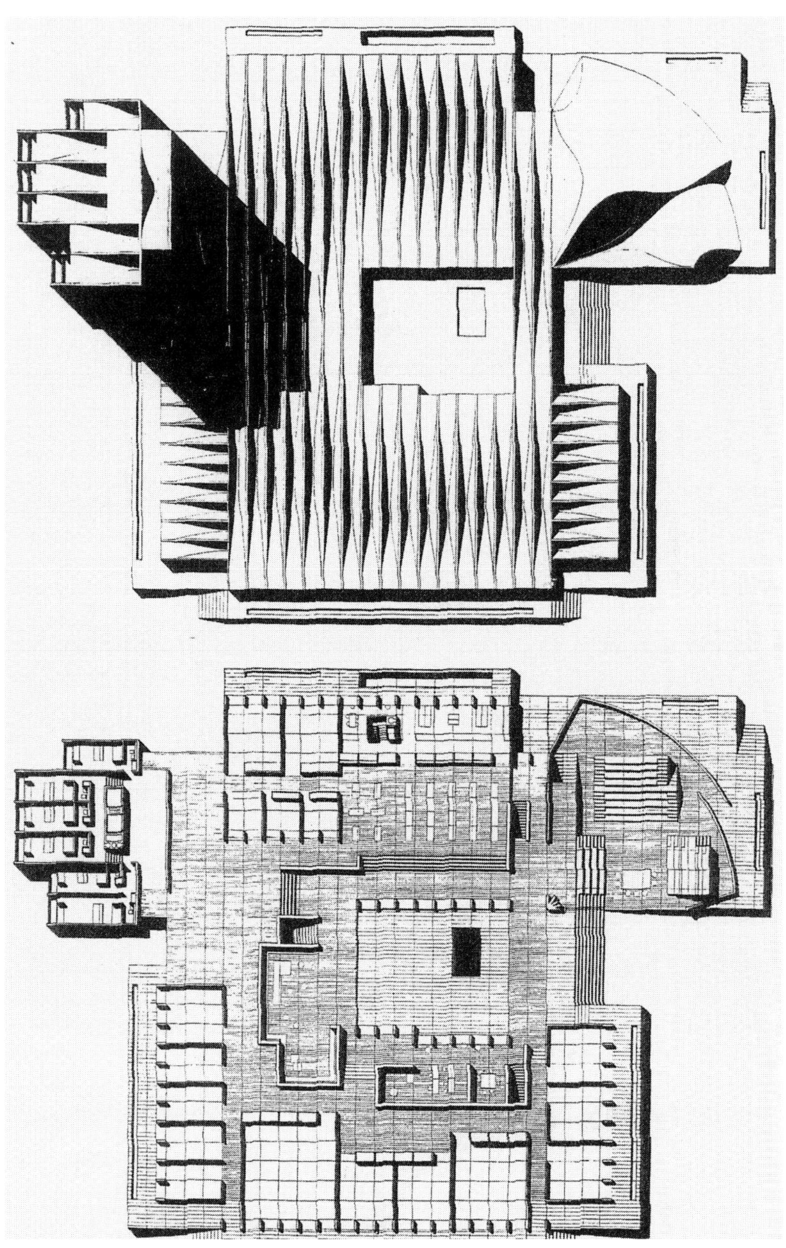

18.3
Technical High School, Højstrup.
Jørn Utzon, 1958.

being in any way ingratiating (unlike, sadly, so many unduly self-conscious works in the 'place-making' tradition typified by Aldo van Eyck and Herman Hertzberger). Like Kahn's sublimely empty plaza at the Salk Institute, Utzon's platform seems to gather land, water and sky into a new unity: it does not need our presence, but it feels unfinished without us.

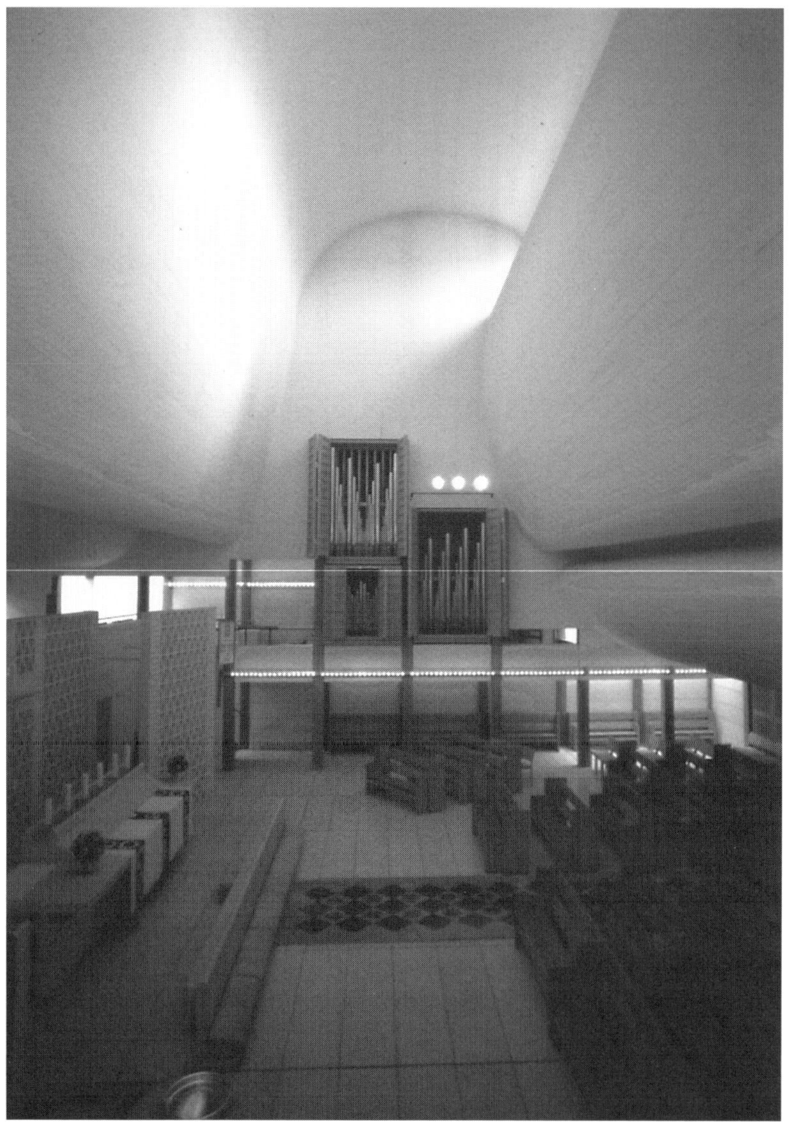

18.4
Bagsværd Church.
Jørn Utzon, 1976.

The famous conceptual sketches published with Sydney link the project both to Utzon's analysis of ancient architectures, represented by a Chinese roof floating above a stone base, and to our experience of nature, of clouds hovering above the sea. This metaphor was not, I think, a conscious inspiration at Sydney, but it was certainly recognized as a valid reading and became operative in later designs. In a competition project for a technical high school in Højstrup (Fig. 18.3) the solidity of the raised platform is heightened by the swelling curves of the lecture theatres, whilst an unrealized plan for a major tourist expansion of Elviria, a coastal town in southern Spain, was structured as vast flights of stepped platforms surmounted by floating, overtly cloud-like roofs. In competitions for theatres in Madrid and Wolfsburg, lightweight roofs and canopies float and flutter above rectilinear platforms that recall the scale of another of Utzon's favourite ancient sites, Persepolis. Finally, in the Bagsværd Church, the platform is implicit rather than explicit, but the connection to nature is made clear in a pair of sketches that show the transformation of clouds into a concrete vault (Fig. 18.4).

Unlike Sydney, the Bagsværd ceiling is a thin concrete structure that gains strength through shape. It offers, Utzon observed, 'the reassurance of something above your head which has been built, not just designed'.[15] Quite how we sense that it is actually doing the job of spanning the space, and is not just a ceiling suspended from hidden structure, is not easily explained. But sense it we can, and this feeling of the palpable reality of everything he built, grounded in a heightened sense of what we now like to term 'materiality', is another key to the power of Utzon's place-making.

In building Can Lis, he used entirely standard materials from the local builders' merchants, but asked that the marks of the circular saw with which the blocks were cut from the ground should be left, not rubbed smooth in the usual way. The bricks and tiles of the Kingo and Fredensborg courtyard houses are again conventional, but thanks to the refusal to allow any window openings in the walls facing the common space, and the accommodation of all penetrations of the roofs in the distinctive cubic chimneys, the result has a monolithic character rare in modern housing.

Like Islamic settlements, the housing groups appear to be made 'in one casting',[16] and like Sydney and Bagsværd, the example of nature is immanent. In 1944, whilst escaping from occupied Denmark by working in Stockholm, Utzon heard a lecture by Aalto in which he proposed a branch of flowering cherry as a model for a housing scheme. Just as all the flowers were the same, but no two were exactly alike due to their different positions, exposure to wind and sun, and relationships to their neighbours, so, Aalto suggested, houses could acquire individuality whilst maintaining an essentially repetitive character. With his courtyard schemes, Utzon achieved this by asking an assistant to sit on the patio of each house in turn, and determine the most appropriate configuration of the enclosing walls in response to sun, wind, views and potential overlooking. The result has the ease and suppleness of a place that has grown slowly over time: organic variation has replaced mechanical repetition as a paradigm for the 'second modernism' of the postwar period.

By embracing nature in place of the machine as a presiding metaphor, and by rejecting the abstractions of space and time in favour of the more concrete qualities of place and occasion, Utzon's work can readily be seen as exemplifying the values inherent in the rejection of the reductive functionalism that was widely, if not always accurately, thought to have characterized the first wave of the modern movement. It would, however, be misleading to try to assimilate Utzon's work too directly to the postmodern discourse about place. Just as a broad measure of agreement can be traced beneath the radically different appearances of the Villa Savoye and Can Lis, so Utzon's work has much in common with Le Corbusier's commitment to biology and to that heroic conception of an ideal Nature that was present in all his work and became increasingly dominant after 1945.

Detachment from the vagaries of the (potentially tubercular!) ground may have been an explicit goal of the Corbusian 'Five Points', but the contact with nature that was denied at ground level was re-established in unmistakably heroic terms on the roof-garden, from where the universal delights of *soleil, espace et verdure* could be enjoyed in all their purity. At their most sublime, the roof gardens offered the experience of what Le Corbusier called 'ineffable space'. The roof-tops of the houses in Algiers, he once observed, gave the 'fortunate Arabs' the pleasures of 'sky, sea and mountains. Beatitudes of space. The power of eyes and mind carries far.'[17] And lecturing in Buenos Aires in 1929 he ascribed moral value to this experience of 'vast space' (*grand large*) by suggesting that 'the eye of man who sees wide horizons is prouder, wide horizons confer dignity.'[18]

Views of broad landscapes feature frequently in Le Corbusier's sketchbooks – a surprising number of early watercolours on this theme are, one recalls, included in the *Album La Roche*[19] – and from the roof-garden of the Palace of the League of Nations project of 1927, configured to address the Alps, to the capture of the Himalayas as part of the Chandigarh Capitol complex, engaging the horizon became fundamental to Le Corbusier's conception of architecture. In a revealing choice of language, the roof-top of the Marseilles Unité is described as a 'fabricated terrain',[20] suggesting something altogether more solid and earth-like than the abstract planes of the 1920s and 1930s – qualities emphasized in the *Oeuvre Complète* by presenting a photograph of the model detached from the Unité itself but set in the context of the landscape against which it was to be measured.[21]

The familiar photographs of the Marseilles roof in use are not as revealing about Le Corbusier's underlying intentions as the account in *Le Corbusier. Les Maternelles vous parlent*,[22] in which the directness of the abstraction from nature of this artificial, child-scaled landscape of ocean, islands and mountains is made abundantly clear. There, a photograph of children at play on '*le territoire de la Maternelle*' is juxtaposed with a seascape. This appears to be a photograph, but could quite possibly be a montage, or at least modified so as to be 'pre-abstracted', and features a lighthouse on a small, rocky island in the middle ground and, beyond, the kind of rugged skyline described in so many

18.5
Utzon sketches.

perspective sketches of *'le grand large'* – emulated directly by Utzon, incidentally, in a 1946 competition for a sports complex in Aarhus.

Le Corbusier frequently implored architects to learn from nature, and few have done so more imaginatively or so extensively as Utzon. For Gyorgy Kepes, this capacity to come to creative terms with nature was fundamental to shaping a world in which we can feel at home:

> If, in the world, man sees around him the rhythm of nature's processes revealed; and if the colours, forms, and movements he sees are expressions of organic events, then his vision is nourished by the 'primal sanities of nature' to use Walt Whitman's words. If the primal sanities of nature can be absorbed through his vision, if man is led to see them, he can reproduce them in the world he shapes for himself.[23]

The exhilaratingly open platform and cave-like shells Utzon designed in Sydney are potent examples of those qualities of prospect and refuge which Jay Appleton believes are archetypal human experiences.[24] By articulating all his public buildings as the interplay between a homogeneous earthwork or platform and roofs or ceilings which variously spring, soar and float above it, Utzon sought to ground his work in our elemental experiences of nature. Walking around his built landscapes we feel of a piece with hilltops and clouds, promontories and caves, *in* a particular place but *part of* a larger, shared world: by extending the discourse of place to embrace the planet, Utzon sought to renew the modernist vision of an emerging world culture (Fig. 18.5). Rooted in diverse ancient cultures, but owing obvious debts to none, Sydney Opera House could, he believed, belong to the world.

Notes

1 See Le Corbusier and P. Jeanneret, *Oeuvre Complète, Vol II, 1929–34* [1935], Zurich: Les Editions d'Architecture, 1995, p.28, for a sketch of a group of villas 'aux environs de Buenos Aires'.
2 A.Smithson (ed.), *Team 10 Primer*, London: Studio Vista, 1968, p.101.
3 Le Corbusier, *Towards a New Architecture*, London: Architectural Press, 1982, p.31.
4 See A. van Eyck, 'Place and occasion', *Progressive Architecture*, September 1962, p.155.
5 This is explicated in S. Menin and F. Samuel, *Nature and Space: Aalto and Le Corbusier*, London: Routledge, 2003.
6 See R. Weston, *Utzon: Inspiration, Vision, Architecture*, Hellerup: Edition Bløndal, 2002, p.371.
7 R.D. Martienssen, *The Idea of Space in Greek Architecture*, Johannesburg: Witwatersrand University Press, 1956, p.3.
8 For a detailed exploration of Wright's possible debts to Mayan architecture, see A. Alofsin, *Frank Lloyd Wright. The Lost Years, 1910–1922. A Study of Influence*, Chicago: University of Chicago Press, 1993.
9 J. Utzon, 'Platforms and plateaus', *Zodiac*, 1962, 10, p.113–41; text reproduced in full in Weston, *Utzon: Inspiration, Vision, Architecture*, p.247.
10 Ibid.
11 K. Frampton, 'Jørn Utzon: transcultural form and the tectonic metaphor', in *Studies in Tectonic Culture*, Cambridge MA and London: MIT Press, 1995, pp.247–98.
12 S. Giedion, *The Eternal Present. The Beginnings of Architecture*, London: Oxford University Press, 1964, p.296.
13 Weston, *Utzon: Inspiration, Vision, Architecture*, p.407.
14 M. Benedikt, *For an Architecture of Reality*, New York: Lumen Books, 1987, p.52.
15 Weston, *Utzon: Inspiration, Vision, Architecture*, p.291.
16 R. Rainer, *Traditional Building in Iran*, Graz: Akademische Druck-u. Verlagsanstalt, 1977, p.29.
17 Le Corbusier, *The Radiant City*, trans. P. Knight, E. Levieux and D. Coltman, London: Faber & Faber, 1967, p.230.
18 Le Corbusier, tr. by Edith Schreiber Aujame. *Precisions. On the Present State of Architecture and City Planning* (Cambridge, MA and London: MIT Press, 1991), p.23
19 5.S. von Moos (ed.), *Album La Roche*, San Francisco: Monacelli Press, 1997; this is a facsimile edition of an album of sketches and watercolours was presented by Le Corbusier to his client, Raoul la Roche, on New Year's Day, 1925.
20 See J. Lucan, 'The search for the absolute', in C. Palazzolo and R. Vio (eds), *In the Footsteps of Le Corbusier*, New York: Rizzoli, 1991, pp.197–208.
21 Le Corbusier, *Oeuvre Complète, Vol. IV, 1938–46* [1946], Zurich: Les Editions d'Architecture, 1995, p.185.
22 Le Corbusier, *Les Maternelles vous parlent*, Paris: Editions Gonthier, 1968, see in particular p.32–3.
23 G. Kepes (ed.), *Education of Vision*, New York: George Braziller, 1965, p.i.
24 See J. Appleton, *The Experience of Landscape*, London: Wiley, 1996.

Chapter 19

The landscape of work

A place for the car

Brian Carter

> The roadmaster turned off Mound Road and stopped at the Tech Center security gate. Though it was still under construction, Will loved this place, loved the way architects … had made you feel as though you were leaving the past behind you when you paused here under the high flat roof that floated over the security gate. Everything was sharp and clean and right. … The uniformed guard waved the Buick through, into a world of orderly engineering and design studios, research laboratories, ponds and fountains, and the auditorium with its shimmering silver-domed roof that gave it the look of a flying saucer poised to take-off. … This was where people were paid to dream and experiment and create, and Will couldn't wait to get inside.[1]

The General Motors' Technical Research Center, designed by Eero Saarinen and arguably the largest and most complex architectural commission in mid-twentieth-century America, demanded the construction of a unique place. Planned to sponsor research, serve as a symbol of corporate prowess and emphasize industry's commitment to advancing technology, the Center was to house one of America's wealthiest industrial corporations. It was also to provide a focus for a company deeply committed to the research, design and manufacture of arguably the twentieth century's ultimate machine – the car. As a result the commission provided an exceptional opportunity for this young Finnish-

American to advance ideas about place, architecture and the machine outlined by Le Corbusier in his influential manifesto 'Vers une architecture' and subsequently reinterpreted within the context of the American mid-west through Frank Lloyd Wright's portrayal of Broadacre City. The project for General Motors was to result in the design of a place based on new interpretations of space, building typologies and ways of working. Indeed, in designing this very particular place the architect collaborated enthusiastically with the client to develop the plan for a vast site, invent materials and formulate alternative systems of construction as an integral part of the design process.

19.1
Site plan of the General Motors' Technical Research Center showing the five groups of buildings set around three sides of the lake. The Styling Dome is at the bottom right of the plan close to the main entrance off Mound Road.

The directors of General Motors first approached Eliel Saarinen – Eero's father – with a request to design a new Technical Research Center in 1945. Before coming to America, Eliel Saarinen had already founded one of the most successful architectural practices in Scandinavia. First established in 1897 with two colleagues in Finland it was a practice rooted in the Arts and Crafts movement, which had gained prominence after successes in several significant competitions and a number of prestigious commissions. However, after being awarded second place in the Chicago Tribune Competition in 1922, Saarinen decided to move with his family to America, where he met George Booth – a wealthy industrialist and the father of one of the students that he was teaching at the University of Michigan. Booth was also committed to founding a school in America that would be rooted in the ideals of the Arts and Crafts movement and, as a result, he commissioned Eliel Saarinen to design a new Academy of Art at Cranbrook near Detroit. For Saarinen this was to be the foundation of a second successful professional career and, with the completion of new buildings at Cranbrook, he was also appointed to be the Academy's first Director. Alongside his work in practice Saarinen created a unique design programme there. It was a programme where

> all work done by the student must be based upon reality, and therefore be a part of life itself, and not upon artificial conditions about which the student can only theorize … there is no assembling of stylistic forms for the solution of a problem, but a dependence upon common sense.[2]

Eero Saarinen had spent much of his first twelve years in his father's studio at Hvitträsk in Finland. 'I practically grew up under his drafting table,' he said, 'and then when I was old enough to get on top, I was drawing on the other end of it.'[3] He was then to spend his adolescent years in the equally lively setting at Cranbrook where design was also the focus.

After graduating in architecture from Yale, and working in New York, Eero returned to Cranbrook in 1936. He taught there and had been working on a series of projects with his father when General Motors asked Eliel Saarinen to

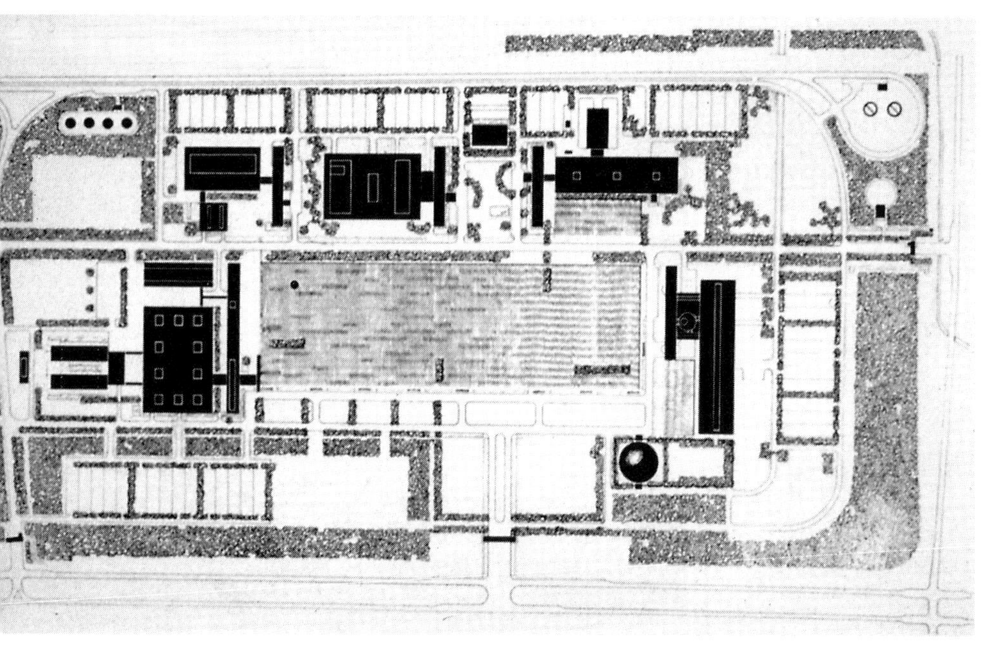

design their new Technical Research Center. A scheme was designed that planned a series of buildings in groups around a large new lake specially formed on the site. Two levels of circulation segregated people and cars, while buildings were connected by pedestrian decks. However, the client put the project temporarily on hold and, by the time they returned three years later, Eliel Saarinen was seventy-five years old, and it was Eero who was awarded the commission. Later Eero noted that, when General Motors first approached his father,

> they probably thought and imagined in their mind that they would get something like Cranbrook. But the problem was a different one. The whole spirit of what they stand for is a different one. The time was a different one.[4]

At the time that he received the commission, Eero was thirty-seven years old and his office was small. However, although the plan that he developed for this vast new complex was clearly influenced by his father's earlier proposal it was also substantially different (Fig. 19.1). It still focused on the creation of distinct clusters of buildings around a newly made lake on the flat 320-acre (130-hectare) site, but Eero increased the lake's size to almost three times the size of the earlier proposal. This 22-acre (9-hectare) expanse of water was rectangular, in contrast to the freer shape proposed by his father, and to be set within a sequence of green spaces formed by extensive new planting. Long avenues,

19.2
One of the long, low office buildings and the Styling Dome seen across a corner of the lake.

landscaped courtyards between buildings and shelter belts were planned across the site, while reflections on the mirror-like surface of the lake were to bring the expanse of the sky down to the ground (Fig. 19.2). These moves created an extended and newly constructed landscape – a contrived natural setting of trees, water and sky. This was to be a place that was conspicuously different from the city and one that also redefined the view of industry – a view where the lightness and precision of scientific research were substituted for the weightiness of manufacturing and where the quiet hum of the car engine replaced the roar of the furnace. It was also to be a different place from River Rouge – that vast industrial complex nearby that had been designed thirty years earlier for Henry Ford by Albert Kahn, one of Eero Saarinen's mentors.

As Eero Saarinen's expansive new lake had the effect of pushing the buildings considerably farther apart, so his plan no longer saw the need to separate cars and people on different levels. As a result the architect created a place where, as distances increased, the pedestrian became virtually invisible and the expanse of the landscape was registered by the scale of the road. Suddenly the car reigned supreme and, as one critic suggested 'Just as the Acropolis was built to be contemplated by a man standing still, Venice to be enjoyed from a drifting gondola, the GM Tech Center should best flash by a Buick window at 35 miles an hour.'[5]

In this plan that described a place to be experienced from the car and viewed at speed the design of the buildings also played an important role. Planned into five distinct groups housing research, process development, engineering, styling and services, they were stretched out so as to frame the lake on three sides. With no building higher than three floors, and organized with extended linear plans and neutrally gridded façades, they emphasized the perspective and exaggerated distance. Both site plan and building design then combined to reference not the density of the traditional city, but the expanse of the natural landscape of the mid-west and that relentless line of the horizon that seemingly extended to infinity.

Discussions of Eero Saarinen's overall plan for General Motors frequently recall Mies van der Rohe's proposals for the new IIT campus in Chicago, which were developed a few years earlier in 1939. The two projects have similarities because both were planned for large sites and to establish new centres for research focused on technology. Both also involved the design of many new buildings that were grouped together to suggest new typologies of place. However, while the *tabula rasa*, created by clearing a run-down section of the city in Chicago to construct a pedestrian-centred campus for the newly constituted Illinois Institute of Technology, can be viewed as a precursor for the radical urban renewal, Eero Saarinen's plan for the General Motors' Technical Center was different. Planned for a large open site 12 miles (19 kilometres) north of Detroit it assumed self-sufficiency for a place of work that was beyond the city, and the creation of a complete environment that assumed movement at speed and individual mobility.

As his father had advocated that the design programme at Cranbrook be based on reality, so Eero Saarinen approached the design of the new buildings for the General Motors' Technical Center with that same search for reality. For this particular architect, that was a reality defined by the activities of his client. He believed:

> General Motors is a metal-working industry; it is a precision industry; it is a mass-production industry. All these things should, in a sense, be expressed in the architecture of its Technical Center. Thus the design is based on steel – the metal of the automobile. Like the automobile itself, the buildings are essentially put together, as on an assembly line, out of mass-produced units. And, down to the smallest detail, we tried to give the architecture the precise, well-made look which is a proud characteristic of industrial America.[6]

Designing the General Motors' Technical Center presented Eero Saarinen with an opportunity to connect architecture, industry and the car in ways that most other architects had only dreamed of. It was an opportunity that he seized with great enthusiasm.

19.3
The precise curtain wall façade provides a backdrop to a sculpture by A. Pevsner.

Between 1948 and 1956 Saarinen designed more than twenty-five buildings for General Motors on the site at Warren. All used metal extensively – for structural systems, cladding, staircases, suspended ceiling systems, office partitioning and furniture. The buildings were rigorously organized on a 5-foot (1.5-metre) grid, thoroughly integrated structural and servicing systems and designed to provide the best possible working conditions for all. Saarinen confirmed that

> the architecture attempts to find its eloquence out of a consistent and logical development of its industrial character. It has been said that in these buildings I was very much influenced by Mies. But this architecture really carries forward the tradition of the American factory building which had its roots in the Middle West in the early automobile factories of Albert Kahn.[7]

Saarinen's enthusiasm for the work of Albert Kahn was founded not only on an admiration for his professional achievements but in close family friendships. Kahn, who was four years older than Eero's father, had played an important role in bringing Eliel Saarinen to Michigan, finding him work in Detroit and encouraging him to build the programme at Cranbrook. At the same time, together with Henry Ford and other industrialists in the region, Kahn had developed an innovative, integrative way of working that enabled him to design large new industrial buildings on a vast scale.

With this inspiration, and his father's encouragement, Saarinen worked closely with his client to develop designs for new buildings that grew out of General Motor's own expertise.

Perhaps the most significant aspect of this was Saarinen's development of the curtain wall (Fig. 19.3). Using metal forming techniques developed by the car industry he was able to design and fabricate extremely thin yet refined curtain-wall systems at a time when few were readily available on the market. In addition, while neoprene gasket glazing was already commonplace in the car industry for fixing windscreens in vehicles, it had rarely been used in the construction of buildings at that time. Combining these two areas of expertise it was possible to design cladding systems that were efficient, quick to build and visually light. The architect and his client perfected these designs through studies of day-lighting and thermal performance, the testing of mock-ups and the construction of full-scale prototypes. These testing sequences, which were everyday routines for car-makers, were virtually non-existent in the construction industry at this time. Enthusiastically adopted by Saarinen, they resulted in the creation of new materials and systems of construction that were immediately put to use in the construction of the new offices and workshops at the General Motors' Technical Center.

19.4
The stainless steel-clad water storage tank standing in the lake creates a landmark of the General Motors' Technical Research Center.

The two most significant structures within the GM Technical Center were also designed to utilize advanced metal technology. The Water Storage Tower and the Styling Dome were emblematic objects within the scheme, with one prominently signing this new place of work and the other signalling the significance of design (Fig. 19.4). Both are conspicuously shaped, constructed using highly reflective metal and sited at strategic points within the overall plan. Both also borrowed from other technologies.

The Dome at the General Motors' Technical Center appeared in the very first designs in 1945. However, in those early proposals it was integrated into the design of other buildings and appeared as a curved form on top of larger flat-roofed buildings. Eero's design transformed that into an emphatic freestanding dome. In his scheme it was also sited adjacent to the main entrance. Constructed as a smooth, silver, metallic, curving form that reflected the sky, it was built within a courtyard enclosed by a wall that was in turn screened by pleached trees. These moves created a conspicuous machine contained within a constructed garden to present an image of a future shaped by technology. They also suggested a temple to the machine, placed at the gate of the Center and designed to be clearly visible to the drivers and passengers in passing cars on Mound Road.

This building provided the client with a large column-free space where the latest models of their cars could be presented. That space also had to have good lighting with uniform levels of illumination from all sides. The open space created by the form of the dome, which had a diameter of 188 feet (57 metres), was ideal and Saarinen was also able to use the form of the dome internally to create a giant reflector of light. The building consists of two thin shells with a 65-feet-high (19-metre-high) outer shell made up of $\frac{3}{8}$-inch-thick (95-millimetre) structural steel plate, reinforced by steel angle stiffeners. Clad with insulation it was covered by a second outer shell of aluminium plates. Detailed like giant reflective shingles, these plates are supported on stainless-steel studs welded to the steel structure. The inner shell, which is non-structural, consists of 12- and 14-gauge perforated sheet metal suspended from the structural steel shell.

Completed in 1954, the Dome is an outstanding example of the innovative use of metals and application of techniques used in both the car and aircraft industries to the design and construction of buildings. It is arguably Eero Saarinen's most successful attempt to integrate modern industrial technology and architecture and effectively captures the spirit of this particular place.

The Water Tower, also built of metal, was sited in the lake – as if to double its height with the reflection. It holds 250,000 gallons (11,365 hectolitres) of water in a stainless steel spheroid tank supported 132 feet (40 metres) up in the air on three circular stainless steel legs, and was built by a contractor who specialized in the construction of pressure vessels. And if the dome places a temple to the car at the entrance to the site of the Technical Center, this tall, sculpted silvery tower forms a second emphatic marker that uses the symbolism of material to create a clear sign of industry in the prairie landscape.

Not all of the technical developments were focused on the use of metal, however. Another collaborative design research project resulted in the manufacture of specially made bricks. As an integral part of his overall plan for the site, Saarinen wanted to create a series of large-scale 'cards of colour'. These would 'sign' the new buildings and provide guidance for visitors in the exaggerated openness of the landscape that he had devised. Like billboards, the walls would introduce glowing colour – selected from a rich palette of red, orange, yellow and tangerine as well as deeper ochres, sky blue, grey and black – against a backdrop of sky, water and the new long glassy buildings that were designed to be light and ephemeral. At a scale commensurate with that of the site they were also to be clearly legible from fast-moving vehicles. To do this the architect proposed large planar walls at the ends of selected buildings that were without openings and constructed in different and specific colours with a finish that would sparkle in the daylight. No such material was available and consequently techniques to manufacture special bricks were developed in close collaboration with scientists from General Motors, who had been working on the development of spark-plug technology. By also involving local brick-makers this collaboration resulted in the production of a range of vibrantly coloured, glazed-face bricks, manufactured specially for the project, which captured the eye as well as the seasonal variations of light and landscape.

There are many other examples of the development of new materials and innovative methods of construction in the Technical Center that resulted from the collaborative research work of Saarinen and General Motors. They included the development of new types of glass, suspended stairs and integrated structural systems designed to house lighting, power and air supplies. So a series of different yet grand sweeping staircases, designed as suspended structures that hovered above the ground, defined the various departments. The design of a spiral stair in the main entrance of the Research Building recalled the spoke wheels of a racing car, while a gently rising dog-leg stair planned over a reflecting pool provided a backdrop for the display of the company's latest cars in the Styling Building. And in the offices themselves illuminated modular ceilings, designed and detailed to incorporate air supply, fire detection systems and internal office partitions, created expansive internal landscapes that replaced the cellular space of the private room and established an alternative setting directed to efficiency and performance in this new place of work. These buildings had a conspicuous thinness and an order derived from the precision of manufacture and the repetition of mass-production that, when combined with the shimmering surfaces of metal and glass, created a complex of buildings that recalled the machine. Described as 'horizontal skyscrapers' these groupings of buildings also integrated offices, research facilities and industrial spaces seamlessly together to create new social landscapes.[8]

The project was eventually constructed at a cost of $100,000,000 – a figure equivalent to around half a billion dollars at the beginning of the twenty-first century. It was dedicated on 16 May 1956. In his opening address, Charles F. Kettering, the Vice-President and Director of Research of General Motors, confirmed that, 'We now have a place where we can make an indefinite number of practice shots; the only time we don't want to fail is the last time we try.'[9]

Eero Saarinen had enthusiastically adopted that same process of design – of making an indefinite numbers of practice shots. Learning from the techniques that were regularly used by his client to design, test and manufacture cars he went on to apply those same approaches in his subsequent work.

Charles Eames noted that the 'industrial research vocabulary and procedures accorded in many ways with Eero's fondness for testing by models, both abstract and concrete' and went on to explain how, for this particular project

> innovative building elements were tested at full-scale, in real conditions, over time. Energy and experience from each stage of construction were fed back to the successive ones, to upgrade the details and materials. Surface finishes were changed and changed again; aluminium glazing strips gave way to precisely detailed neoprene gaskets, as the same new techniques were incorporated in GM's assembly lines. From the beginning ... the modular principle so often taken only as an aesthetic guideline was applied with unprecedented operational thoroughness.[10]

Operational thoroughness, developed in a close collaboration with industrial corporate America, was fundamental to the shaping of this expansive new development. Combined with the traditions connecting art and craft that had been such an integral part of Eero Saarinen's upbringing in Scandinavia, and his subsequent experiences in America, his design for the General Motors' Technical Center resulted in the construction of a strikingly new and radically different place of work.

Notes

1 Bill Morris, *Motor City*, New York: Alfred A. Kopf, 1992, p.39.
2 Anon, 'An announcement of the third post-graduate program at Cranbrook, Architectural Department, *Architectural Record*, June 1933, vol.63, pp.431–2.
3 Eero Saarinen, *The Oral History of Modern Architecture*, New York: Harry N. Abrams Inc., 1994, p.193.
4 Ibid., p.208.
5 Anon., 'Progress report: GM nears completion', *The Architectural Forum*, November 1954, p.118.
6 Eero Saarinen, *Eero Saarinen on his Work*, New Haven: Yale University Press, 1962, p.30.
7 Ibid., p.30.
8 W. Curtis, *Modern Architecture since 1900*, New York: Phaidon Press, 1982, p.267.
9 C. Kettering, Opening address, GM Technical Center, 1956.
10 C. Eames, 'General Motors revisited: a special report', *The Architectural Forum*, June 1971, pp.25–6.

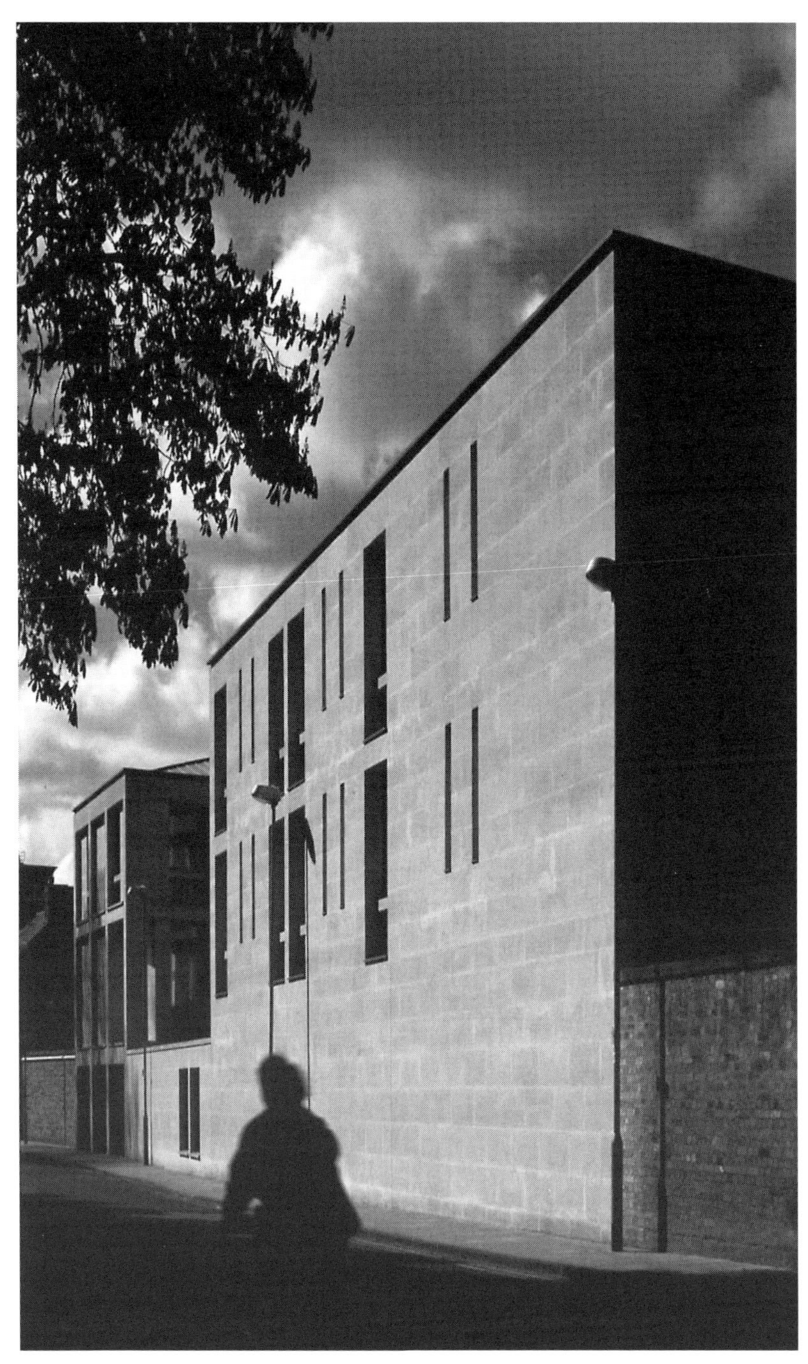

Plate 7
Student accommodation, Pembroke College, Cambridge
Eric Parry Architects, 1997.

Considerate intervention

Chapter 20

Rooted modernity

Reconstructing memory in architecture

Samia Rab

Introduction

Despite the thriving role of history within many schools of architecture, it is still considered an arena for future architects to acquire a fundamental familiarity with 'a repository of both spatial and tectonic typologies available for use and transformation'.[1] Architectural historians are expected to impart insights into the distinct forms, paradigms, hypotheses, positions and 'styles' of architecture. While students of architecture acquire the language, behaviour and culture of their discipline within studios, they are expected to passively receive the different pursuits of past architects. Presenting students of architecture with a pictorial history of their future profession is most certainly a demanding and challenging task. However, it is equally important to induce in architecture students the ability to create buildings that are rooted in the history of a place. While prompting an in-depth understanding of the value of select architectural works of past societies may at best enhance their critical thinking skills, analysing the successful examples of contemporary architecture inspired by history of an individual, a community or a nation can provide a didactic tool to ensure their critical participation with the places in which they will intervene through their designs.

This paper focuses on three contemporary architectural projects from Australia: the Arthur and Yvonne Boyd Art Education Centre in Riversdale near Nowra by architects Glen Murcutt, Wendy Lewin and Reginald Lark (1998); the Uluru Kuta-Tjuta Cultural Centre near Ayers Rock by architect Gregory Burgess (1996); and the Parliament House in Canberra by architect Romualdo Giurgola, of Mitchell/Giurgola & Thorp Architects (1989). In the context of Australia, these contemporary architects have explored a didactic role of memory in designing public buildings that address the following critical aspects of architectural design: a) engagement with the natural landscape; b) commemoration of a historically significant personality; c) instilling a sense of pride in a marginalized group within a society; d) reflection of a multi-faceted and diverse state of a nation.

These three projects are diverse in the purpose they serve and the context of their location. They constitute examples of thoughtful and imaginatively creative attempts to go beyond the mere technology of built form and to search for the means by which a direct relationship can be established between the building, the site, its history, the individual and the community. Collectively architects Murcutt, Burgess and Giurgola have interpreted and transformed the existing attributes of their sites to illustrate a new role for architectural production: understanding the motivations for the varied local characteristics of architecture by actively and critically engaging with the past of a historic personality, a marginalized cultural group and a pluralistic nation.

While dwelling in a place is generally considered dealing with the realms of specificity, the expression of a place's identity may relate to something that is beyond the local. The universal challenge of providing dwelling spaces may be accomplished by retaining memory in place through architecture.

Boyd Education Centre in Riverdale

The design of an Education Centre in Riversdale (NSW), near Sydney by architects Murcutt, Lewin and Lark revives the memory of an eminent Australian artist, Arthur Boyd (1920–99). As noted by Peter Ward, Arthur and Yvonne Boyd had an 'Aboriginal' attitude towards the properties they assembled on the Shoalhaven from the early 1970s to the early 1980s. They believed they held them in trust for the Australian people. In 1993, as an act of determined conservation, they officially donated to the nation their Bundanon properties near the Shoalhaven River, along with the paintings, drawings and ceramics by four generations of the Boyd family.[2] The Bundanon properties are at the centre of a working farm, contain an extraordinary variety of natural and cultivated areas, provide home to a rich variety of flora and fauna, and represent important aspects of Australia's pastoral heritage. Boyd perceived a powerful environmental message in the properties. According to Ursula Hoff, 'the element of destruction in nature itself, the struggle of each live organism against chaos, as well as the threat posed to nature by man's activities are present in [his] Shoalhaven landscapes ... Boyd looks at the scenery with the objective eye of the naturalist, as well as with the anxious care of the conservationist.'[3] Boyd found inspiration in this landscape (natural and cultivated) and placed his studio to the western end of the Bundanon properties. The influence of this landscape is evident in most of Boyd's artwork, produced over the last twenty-five years of his life.

Arthur Boyd's art encompassed two worlds: a weighty European artistic heritage and a new Australian vision, each expressed by the contrast between the calm of the cultivated European landscape tradition and Boyd's interpretation of the native landscape as dark and weird and tormented – 'a native landscape lacking any rules or guideposts', as suggested by Philip Drew.[4] Boyd's art reflected his life, which was similarly divided between England and Australia. This contrast of cultivated and natural landscape is powerfully conveyed by the new Art Education Centre recently completed at Riversdale, which commemorates the life and art of Arthur Boyd (Figs 1.18, 20.1 and 20.2).

The design of this Centre promotes art education for school children and combines a multi-purpose assembly hall, forecourt, amphitheatre and dormitory wing to house thirty-two students. The linear composition of this Centre is divided into three main parts: (a) the entrance porch that leads to (b) the main hall and connects with (c) the dormitories beyond. This composition marks a line of permeable transition between the indigenous 'nature' above and the cultivated 'landscape' below. Each of the three functional zones is connected with a corridor opening towards the surrounding indigenous 'nature'. Each of these three spaces faces the cultivated 'landscape' along the Shoalhaven River. This continuous permeable composition is interspersed with openings that connect by framing contrasting views of both the indigenous 'nature' behind the building and the cultivated 'landscape' below.

The main hall, used for multipurpose activities, is situated on a large terrace that acts as the floating stylobate for the entire building. The hall is flanked on one side with the kitchen and services, and on the other by the landscaped garden and the Shoalhaven River beyond. The façade of the main hall comprises a series of concrete columns and, along with the stylobate, results in an unconsciously classical formality reinforced by the placement of the repetitive rhythm of the riverside elevation. It is a convertible space designed for dining 80 or 100 people, and has also been used for art workshops and concerts. On the east elevation, the doors of this main hall slide back to reveal

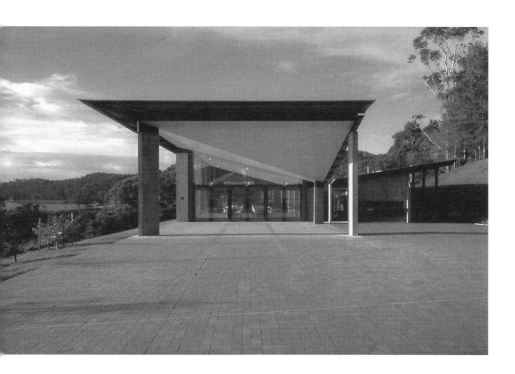

20.1
The underside of the porch roof rushes forward to greet arriving visitors. Arthur and Yvonne Boyd Art Education Centre, Riversdale, Australia (Murcutt, Lewin & Lark, 1998).

the Shoalhaven River glittering in the sunlight. The interior focuses our framed attention to the landscaped garden and the River beyond, connecting and framing the outer landscape to enliven the experience in the interior of the building of being one with the cultivated surrounding (Fig. 1.18). The enclosed serenity of the main hall contrasts dramatically with the form and space of this

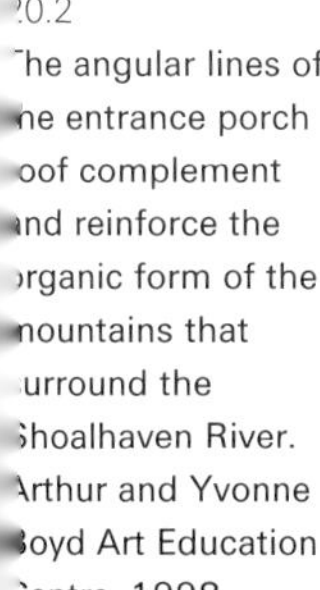

20.2
The angular lines of the entrance porch roof complement and reinforce the organic form of the mountains that surround the Shoalhaven River. Arthur and Yvonne Boyd Art Education Centre, 1998.

porch, which leads us into this space. The hall and its covered extension into the entrance porch form a single large veranda under one roof. The angular lines of this porch roof complement and reinforce the organic form of the mountains that surround the Shoalhaven River (Fig. 20.2). The underside of the roof rushes forward to greet arriving visitors as they pass the sliding doors made of recycled wood and enter the main hall, which is finished plainly in austere grey concrete with grey brick pavers for the floor.

The sloped and geometric roof of the entrance porch inclines towards an atrium and actively reaches out to the landscape. Verandas are transitional devices that constitute an intermediate spatial and climatic zone around buildings that mediates between the inside and the outside and draws its space out into the landscape. Drew has called this intermediate space the no man's land. It is a region of transition between building and nature.[5] Situated between the cultivated homestead landscape and the native bush behind it, the new hall is a perfect metaphor for Arthur Boyd's ambiguous relationship with Europe and Australia. In this context, the veranda seemingly encapsulates Boyd's cultural and artistic predicament. While the adoption of a veranda typology is clearly related to earlier Euro-Australian architectural traditions, this design goes beyond that. The result is a building that heightens appreciation of its surrounding, which addresses its landscape in ways that come as a surprise. Instead of blonding in with the natural and the cultivated environment, the building picks up on the organic lines in the surrounding, abstracting and reinforcing these into geometric and angular forms.

In designing the Arthur and Yvonne Boyd Art Education Centre, the architects Murcutt, Lewin and Lark maintained the duality of the site along with reconstructing Arthur Boyd's painterly devices with which he framed contrasting vistas of Australia's indigenous nature and cultivated landscape. The formal character of the building, its perceptive acknowledgement and reinforcement of the characteristic features of surrounding, and the use of modern materials such as corrugated iron for the roof, is unexpected for the manner in which a site specific solution is explored in contemporary architecture. Despite being modern, the building is rooted in the duality of the natural environment of Australia and evokes the memory of a man who was inspired by this contrast. While dwelling in a place is generally considered dealing with the realms of specificity, the expression of the Arthur and Yvonne Boyd Art Education Centre relates to something that is beyond the local. The universal challenge of providing dwelling spaces is accomplished by retaining the memory of a significant personality in a particular place.

The next example from Australia reveals a different approach in which the architect is simply facilitating the dialogue between a powerful natural site and its indigenous occupants.

'0.3
'he building form
.nd composition
e-enact the
'jukurpa traditional
tory of Liru and
(uniya – involving
iru the Poisonous
Snake and his
attle with Kuniya
he Carpet Snake –
nfolded around
his side of Uluru.
Jluru-Kuta Tjuta
Cultural Centre,
Northern
erritories,
ustralia
NCA, with Gregory
urgess, 1995.

Uluru Kata-Tjuta Cultural Centre

The Uluru Kata-Tjuta Cultural Centre, near Ayers Rock (Northern Territories), celebrates the spirit of the Anangu culture. Uluru (Ayers Rock) is sacred to Anangu, the Aboriginal people of central Australia. It is also an icon for Australians of European origins, embedded deep in the national psyche. To build here, respect for the environment, spiritual as well as physical, was paramount. The Centre was always envisaged as an Anangu place where visitors, *Minga* ('ants'),[6] could be invited to share in Anangu culture. It was also the wish of Anangu that the building design accommodate their re-activation of Dreamtime and express their working together 'as one' with the rangers of the Australian Nature Conservation Agency (ANCA) in the joint management of the World-Heritage-listed Uluru-Kata-Tjuta National Park. The building opened in October 1995 on the tenth anniversary of the Uluru-Kata-Tjuta National Park Title Handback to the traditional owners. Since then, it has been awarded nationally and published internationally for its architectural qualities, environmental sustainability, and effective cross-cultural collaboration.

The design concept was evolved through a collaborative on-site process over a month in 1990 between the Mutitjulu community, ANCA and the consultant team headed by architect Gregory Burgess; a warm trust formed the basis for a successful collaboration. The architect walked the site with the elders of the Anangu tribe community, who mapped and painted stories of Uluru, and engaged in the development of the programme brief development and the precise siting of the building. Drawings of the possible building plan, along with many lively sketches of the way the visitors would move though the Centre, were traced with fingers in the red sand by Anangu (Fig. 1.1).

The Uluru Cultural Centre comprises two serpentine buildings (Fig, 20.3) carefully located with minimum disturbance to its setting, situated about one kilometre to the south of Uluru, amongst the landscape where wider plains (sand dunes, desert oaks and spinifex) meet and mixes with the site character of the Uluru, defined by the mulga, bloodwood, umbrella bush and bearded grass. The building form and composition re-enact the Tjukurpa traditional (law) story of Liru and Kuniya, involving Liru the Poisonous Snake and his battle with Kuniya the Carpet Snake – unfolded around this side of Uluru. In certain features on the Rock, the result of their fatal battle can still be read in the form of subtle rock paintings and low reliefs. Anangu spoke of the two serpentine buildings as representing Liru and Kuniya watching each other warily across the site of their battle.

In the various approaches to the Centre, the two buildings appear as a mysterious undulating presence of skin, sinew and shadow emerging and disappearing, looking, approaching, withdrawing. The architect has transformed and animated red sand, bloodwood and copper, modulating spatial sequences by contrast of scale, of light and deep shadow, of openness and opacity, of movement and stillness, of weight and lightness. Throughout this rhythmic play, an elusive resonance develops between the building, the Anangu past, the landscape and the visitor – a living field for the introduction of the senses to the heart, the spirit and the mysteries of Anangu knowledge and wisdom.

Anangu have enriched the building enormously by superb Tjukurpa paintings on the sand walls, painted tiles and formed glass that, along with ceremonial song and dance cycles, vividly introduce visitors to Anangu perception and culture, before they move off to experience the wider desert landscape. Through its animated relationship with its powerful site, extensive use of sustainable materials, low energy consumption and its sympathetic responsiveness to both people and the environment, the Centre celebrates the spirit of Anangu culture. It embodies traditional Anangu culture but works with and supports the contemporary needs and economic development of the Anangu people. This unique integration of indigenous knowledge of nature and traditional land management with western science has proved highly complementary and successful in practice and an inspiration for other initiatives throughout the world. This subtle structure nestled in the landscape in the shapes of the ancestral snakes continues to inspire and inform visitors about the re-activation of Anangu Dreamtime.

Dreaming, for Aboriginal Australians, points to a concept that symbolically expresses the eternal qualities of life, both as a general concept, and as an issue of immediate significance to human beings. The Dreaming, existing from the beginning of time, is just as relevant in the present as it was in the past, and is vitally important to the future. This is not just a matter of recognizing the importance of the past in the present, in our western Eurocentric sense, but underlines the essential similarity and the essential oneness of all living, natural things, of which human beings are a part: all share a common life essence, a kind of basic identification with the natural environment and all that it contains within. Mythic beings are key figures that provide linkages into the Dreaming as the real source of life. These beings, and their adventures in Dreaming, are the subject matter of myth, song, ritual and art.[7] Aboriginal art is not 'art' per se, as defined by the western canon. It is in fact the ritual of re-activating the Dreamtime with the help of representational images of these intermediary mythic beings. The purpose of these rituals (which resulted in art) was to re-activate the spiritual powers of Dreaming spirits, bringing them into direct relationship with present-day humans, who can then draw on these powers. The artist performed a crucial role, as a re-activator of the creative era of the Dreaming for the real world of human beings now.

By facilitating the re-activation of Dreamtime for the descendents of the Anangu tribe, through the architectural design process, architect Gregory Burgess is not acting like an architect in the Renaissance sense of the word; he is engaged in elevating the past and spirit of a marginalized community. This engagement has resulted in the superb crafting of undulating forms that blend in with the natural setting yet are striking and futuristic. The Uluru Kata-Tjuta Cultural Centre maintains an animated relationship with its powerful site (Ayers Rock) and integrates in its design the Anangu tribe-members' historical knowledge of their 'Dreamtime', a knowledge through which aboriginal artists harnessed and engaged with nature. According to Paul Mammott:

> Whatever the architect's original logic or intent with respect to semiotics, the building has now taken on multiple associations which are being transmitted to the public in their experience of the Centre. Perhaps it can be said that an outstanding attribute of a piece of high quality architecture is its capability to generate and maintain multiple meanings and associations which provide the complexity and intricacy with visual associations.[8]

The Uluru Kuta-Tjuta Cultural Centre collaboratively generated and successfully communicates multiple meanings and associations with the physical, spiritual and psychological characteristics of its site. It can be read as an example of 'architecture IN place', asserting and rehabilitating the local and indigenous (as opposed to introduced and borrowed) perception of Australia's native landscape. The physical embodiment of re-activating the spirit of a place has resulted in a building that goes beyond the 'regionalism of resistance'.[9] It draws upon as a source of inspiration for its formal and spatial composition from the intellect and imagination of a marginalized community; it dwells upon the relationship between a specific people and their perception of a sacred, powerful and an intimidating site; it also animates the imagination of the many visitors who are encouraged to explore their own relationship to this powerful site through the mythic origins of its creation.

The last and third example from Australia explodes its natural setting from within to create a symbol of national identity for a young nation in the contemporary and postmodern world.

Australia's Parliament House at Canberra

The new Parliament House at Canberra, Australian Capital Territory, completed in 1989 by Mitchell/Giurgola & Thorp Architects, embodies a national place for a young nation on a vast sub-continent. It was intended by the architect as a place that functions simultaneously as a 'working' building for the Parliament as well as a symbol of national unity and broad commitment to the postcolonial democratic process.

The functional brief required a building that would last a minimum of 200 years with all materials to be Australian in origin, wherever possible. Among over 4,500 rooms, the brief specifically included the House and Senate Chambers, office suites for Members and Senators, accommodation for the Executive Government, and functional support spaces for the parliamentary departments. All spaces were to be designed to permit large numbers of visitors to witness the workings of Australian democracy without compromising the building's security.

The site of the Parliament House is 32 hectares and the building covers 15 per cent of this area. The huge scale of the Parliament House is achieved with the least visual impact on the physical environment. Its design has responded to massive technological and functional changes required by the Parliament since its completion, and has also been conducive to considerable ongoing improvements towards energy efficiency and environmental sustainability. According to the Secretary of the Joint House Department, Michael Bolton,

> national and international visitor numbers have been three times those projected at the time of its opening, demonstrating the ongoing keen

> interest shown by the public in this national contemporary heritage 'working' building as an expression of Australian culture.[10]

The siting of the building on the Capital Hill at the apex of Walter Burley Griffin's 1912 Plan for Canberra's Centre and the Parliamentary Triangle inherently required close consideration of the surrounding landscape and urban environment within the design process. Dominating Griffin's plan for Canberra was a central artificial lake and a 'parliamentary triangle', in which the most important national buildings were to be placed. The surrounding residential areas had a geometric street pattern, circular and radial in shape, all fitting well into the general topography. According to Griffin,

> the site may be considered an irregular amphitheatre with Mount Anslie at the north-east, flanked by Black Mountain and Mount Pleasant all forming the top galleries; with the slopes to the water, the auditorium – the waterway and flood-basin, the arena; with the southern slopes reflected in the basin, the terraced stage and setting of monumental Government structures sharply defined rising tier on tier to the culminating highest internal hill, Capital Hill; and with Mugga Mugga, Red Hill and the blue distant mountain ranges forming the back scene of the theatrical whole.[11]

The exterior form of the Parliament House follows the natural profile of the Capital Hill. Its curved walls reach to encompass the radial avenues established by the Griffin Plan[12] as the primary axes of the city (Fig. 20.4). This externally site specific response is contrasted with the defined, secure, open internal courtyards with formal and cultivated landscape contained within the House. The architecture's resulting general character conveys the sense of a balanced, horizontal 'nestling' of built forms within a natural setting.

While the formal composition of the Parliament House establishes its links to the existing environmental surrounding, the art projects associated with this building attempt to reconcile the differences between the historical European and indigenous Aboriginal approaches to the production of art. Commissioned works of art and craft from Australian artists working in close collaboration with the architect intentionally create a subtle symbolic sequence of content and meaning throughout the public and parliamentary areas of the building. One of the main commissioned art projects is located in the great forecourt at the entrance of the Parliament House. The wide space of the forecourt lies just across the area designated for protest by citizens and acts as the collection point for visitors and as the parade ground on military and state occasions. It is dominated by the Aboriginal mosaic and a ceremonial pool. The mosaic is

20.4
The curved walls of the Parliament House reach to encompass the radial avenues, established by the Griffin Plan, as the primary axes of the city. The Parliament House, Canberra, Australia.
Mitchell, Giurgola & Thorp Architects, 1989.

designed by Michael Tjakamarra Nelson, an Aboriginal from the Northern territories, and is made of over 100,000 pieces of granite, all chiselled by hand. It is based on the sand-painting tradition of the Warlpiri people in the central Australian desert and depicts a gathering of men from the kangaroo, wallaby and goanna groups of ancestors. The water in the ceremonial pool ripples gently as it flows around the mosaic, representing the sea circling the island of Australia. The stretches of red gravel represent the vastness and dryness of the Australian landscape. They contrast with the whiteness of the arcaded entrance veranda that marks the ceremonial entrance for dignitaries and the main public entrance to the House. The centre door was first unlocked by Her Majesty Queen Elizabeth II on 9 May 1988.[13] The white Italian Carrara marble of the veranda activates the serene and abstracted classicism of the Parliament House main façade and provides an appropriate background for the great forecourt.

The sequence of movement interspersed with the art projects commissioned for the Parliament House quietly 'layers' references to the history of Australia's Aboriginal and European occupation. It reveals aspirations of a new national identity that is grounded in multiple layers of history. This layering of multiple voices is an essential and inseparable element of the Parliament's design and its capacity to 'speak' with conviction to its occupants and visitors.

Conclusion

In conclusion, two comments are relevant: one relates to the kind of self-image/identity that Australians are seeking, and the other relates to the role of history and memory in architectural production.

Irrespective of the recent attempts by conservative politicians to keep Australia in a time warp, there is a contrasting self-image that is being explored in Australian architecture, based on three recognitions:

1. Commemoration of the dilemma faced by Australians of European origins in attempting to assimilate within the overpowering aspects of the indigenous natural environment.
2. A blunt acknowledgement of Australia's brutal past in relation to Aboriginal destruction and decimation, setting in motion a process of reconciliation with the country's indigenous people based on their land rights (wherever retrievable), cultural traditions, and a measure of self-management of their communities and memories.
3. The need to work towards accepting both the pre-colonial and the British colonial eras as legitimate and multiple histories of this young nation-state.

These three projects, as spatially and visually appealing as they may be, pose some of the most intellectually demanding questions for future aesthetic and social historians. My reading of these three projects supports Katherine Fischer Taylor's assertion that 'architecture is at odds with the pictorial orientation of art history'. In teaching architectural history, we need to develop a framework that lets us think with some consistency within and across the many different domains addressed by a building. In order to do so, we will have to ask some tough questions at the level of the entire curriculum: Is history germane to architectural production, or education? Is history an autonomous discipline or is it a support service in architectural education? If the former, is it nonetheless valuable as a source of critical insights into the position of architecture in society? If the latter, is it a trove of available forms, an array of formal paradigms awaiting transformation, a breeding and testing ground for architectural hypotheses? Should historians trace from the past the sequence of 'progressive' development, or should they glance from the present looking backwards in time with contemporary concerns as their acknowledged intellectual baggage?

In 1999, Stanford Anderson of MIT's History, Theory and Criticism (HTC) programme conducted a survey of architectural history courses and programmes within the US. He noted that each of the programmes was:

> marked by accidents of the history and the structure of its home institution, and the proclivities of its key faculty members ... The enduring questions of the proper relation of history to the teaching and practice of architecture remain matters of debate.[14]

The proper relation of history to teaching and practice is established through 'memory', which is our contemporary connection with certain past societies and cultures. Analysing examples that trace the histories of an individual, a people or a nation will provide for students of architecture a point of entry for their engagement with specific 'histories'.

My reading of the three projects by Murcutt, Burgess and Giurgola highlights the importance of an architect's engagement with particular places in commemorating the history of an individual, celebrating the spirit and imagination of a marginalized cultural group, and acknowledging the multi-faceted diversity of a nation in our contemporary and post-colonial world. Buildings or sites have several layers of meaning for an individual, a group or a nation. These three projects reflect efforts to address the challenge of generating and maintaining multiple meanings and associations with both the spiritual and natural characteristics of a specific site. Relationship by harmony or contrast with the environment brings out qualities in the surroundings not easily perceived before. This provides the complexity and intricacy of thought, forms and spaces, as opposed to re-creation of borrowed visual associations.

Notes

1 S. Anderson, 'Architectural history in schools of architecture', *Journal of the Society of Architectural Historians*, September 1999, vol.58, no.3, pp. 282–90, p.282.

2 P. Ward, 'Befitting Boyd's genius', in *The Australian*, 3 May 1999, p.19.

3 U. Hoff, *The Art of Arthur Boyd*, London: André Deutsch, 1987, p.112.

4 P. Drew, 'Arthur's metaphor', *Architecture Australia*, May/June 1999, vol.88, no.3, p.2.

5 Ibid., p.3.

6 The term '*minga*' is translated in English as 'ants'. Anangu are used to observing tourists 'conquering' their sacred site by hiking on a linear trail, appearing from afar like a row of ants slowly heading towards a singular destination.

7 R.M. Brendt and C.H. Berndt with J.E. Stanton, *Aboriginal Australian Art*, French Forest, NSW: New Holland Publishers, 1992, pp.24, 29, 41, 50.

8 P. Mammott, 'Aboriginal signs and architectural semiotics', *Architectural Theory Review*, 1997, vol.2, no.1, pp.56–7.

9 K.L. Eggener, 'Resisting critical regionalim: a post-modern perspective', in S. Akkach, S. Fung and P. Scriver (eds), *Self, Place & Imagination*, Adelaide: CAMEA, University of Adelaide, 1999, p.4.

10 Michael Bolton, submitted statement for required 'User Assessment' for the 1998 Kenneth F. Brown Asia-Pacific Culture & Architecture Award Program, sponsored by the School of Architecture, University of Hawaii at Manoa, Project 2000-24, p.6.

11 W.B. Griffin, quoted in 'The story of Canberra'. Online. Available HTTP: <http://www.tomw.net.au/cnbst3.html> (accessed 14 March 2003).

12 For detailed discussion on the Griffin Plan and the planning of Canberra, refer to: P. Reid, *Canberra Following Griffin: A Design History of Australia's National Capital*, Canberra: National Archives of Australia, 2002; 'Commonwealth of Australia design for the layout of the Federal Capital City', in *Report from the Senate Select Committee Appointed to Inquire and Report upon the Development of Canberra September 1955*. Appendix B, 93–102, 'Copy of Federal Capital Design No. 29', Canberra: National Archives, 1995.

13 *Parliament House Pictorial Guide*, Canberra: Co-communication, 2000, p.3.

14 Anderson, 'Architectural history in schools of architecture', p.290.

Chapter 21

Making our place

The Museum of New Zealand, Te Papa Tongarewa

Michael P. T. Linzey

The Museum of New Zealand (Jasmax Architects, 1998; Fig. 21.1) is one of a number of monuments to culture that have been completed in the Pacific region in recent years. These works signify at least three trends in current thinking. First, that there is rekindled interest in the culture of Oceania, driven no doubt in part by tourism. Secondly, it seems that we have become dissatisfied with the form of imperial mausoleums that once seemed adequate to contain the antipodean culture. Thirdly, there is a surprising expression of confidence, arguably unfounded, that architecture is capable of contributing to the construction of culture in the postcolonial world, or even, as Ian Wedde put it, of 'reporting on the condition of culture' through its formal symbolism.[1]

In this essay I will discuss this apparent confidence in architecture as cultural place-making in terms of C.S. Peirce's theory of the triadic sign. In Peirce's semiology, a sign is said to have three valencies, or three kinds of interest. First, we may have a primary interest in a thing for itself. Secondly, we may have a secondary interest in it, on account of its reactions with other things. Thirdly, we may have a mediatory interest in a thing, in so far as it conveys to a mind an idea about another thing. In so far as it does this, Peirce said, it is a *sign*.[2] For example, a sign-post *marks* its place in the world, *points* a path towards another place, and *says* something about the path or the place. If any one of these component kinds of interest is missing, Peirce argued, if the post is dislodged from its place, or if it is twisted so that it points in the wrong direction, or if the writing is erased

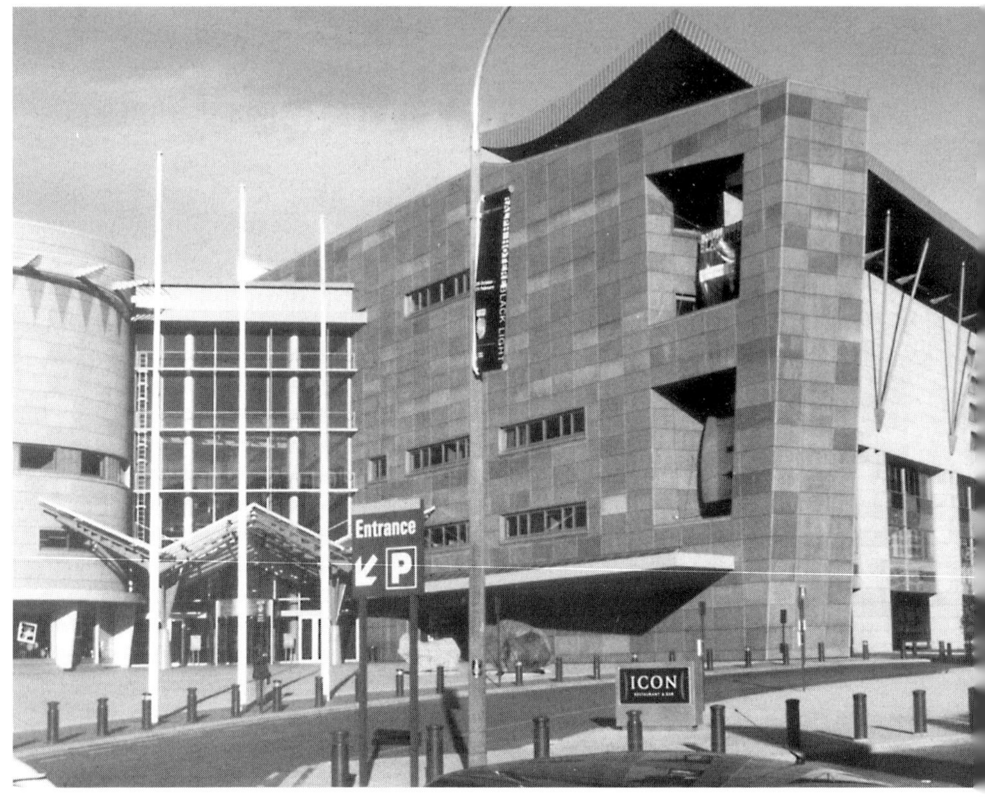

21.1
Te Papa Tongarewa.
Jasmax Architects, 1998.

so that it says nothing, then it ceases to be a triadic sign. Ferdinand de Saussure, on the other hand, represented the linguistic sign in dyadic relational terms of *signifier* and *signified*.[3] I will argue that the dyadic formulation fails to reveal the full empirical meaning of architecture as place-making.

The Museum of New Zealand opened to mixed reviews, 'alternately considered a triumph of design and an architectural turkey; a powerful statement of New Zealand's cultural identity and a discordant mish-mash of competing interests'.[4] Among the new museums this one is generally perceived to be less interesting for architects than Renzo Piano's Tjibaou Cultural Centre in New Caledonia (1998). Nor is it thought to be of the standard of Ashton Raggatt McDougall's glittering new National Museum of Australia that opened in Canberra in 2001. I will argue that the Museum of New Zealand is of particular interest because of a single architectural gesture that it makes. It constructs its place in the world, as Vincent Scully suggested that the ancient temples did, by pointing out a significant orientation in the local geography.[5] It is a vector of cultural construction, a triadic sign.

The Maori version of its name, Te Papa Tongarewa, begins to express this intention of cultural place-making. *Papatuanuku* in Maori mythology is the divine female character of the earth. Her name is complemented by that of *Ranginui*, who is the male principle of the sky. Te Papa Tongarewa therefore means something like 'The Treasures of Mother Earth'. The word for a museum in Maori dictionaries is *whare tongarewa*, or *whare taonga*. This means a house (*whare*) where treasured things (*taonga*) such as greenstone ornaments (*tongarewa*) are stored and displayed. Te Papa Tongarewa means the 'place' or 'ground' or 'site' or even the 'land' of treasures, not referring only to a building that houses culture, but also implicating elements of geography and geopiety in this building's attempt to articulate through its form a national identity and a place for all New Zealanders. The diminutive name, Te Papa, also loosely translates as a geographical reference, meaning 'Our Place'.

This mytho-poetic ground is inscribed in the architecture with a long horizontal element that signifies a particular geographical direction. When visitors arrive at Te Papa they are greeted first by this striking architectural element. A hollow stone wall stands five storeys tall beside the main Cable Street entrance. This vast architectural sign carries on into the interior as a perforated wall, permitting access into the multi-levelled display spaces. A powerful ramping corridor inside the wall itself takes the visitor through the length and height of the building to discover a modern Maori *marae* situated on the roof. And this introduces a second body of references to place-making, for the traditional Maori *marae*, too, uses a pointing element as a vectorial signifier of place-construction. The architects named this horizontal pointing element, which strikes a bold line across the whole body of Te Papa, a 'symbolic faultline'. Effectively it draws the imagination underground, creating a sort of fantasy world in a subterranean realm of geomorphology.

New Zealand is a bicultural country. We have recently decided that the kind of postcolonial culture that we wish to construct in this country will be 'bicultural'.[6] The symbolism of a faultline is a poetic way of saying that two cultures, here nominally designated as Maori and Pakeha, will co-occupy one place and position in New Zealand society. The deep-seated grinding-together of the two cultures, which may also be conceived as Oriental and Occidental, or Oceanic and European, is like different geological formations grinding together along the line of an active fault. Colin James notes that biculturalism is not just a branch of multiculturalism.[7] Multiculturalism, he says, is acceptance that people of minority cultures might maintain their customs, ceremonies and language and that the state might even help them to do that. Biculturalism acknowledges that two cultures stand side by side as equals and command mutual recognition and respect. It is now accepted in New Zealand that whenever a major new development such as Te Papa is undertaken, some need and opportunity will arise for the negotiation of perceived differences in terms of this bicultural treaty.

Biculturalism is not a recent event in New Zealand. It has been a central issue in Maori circles since early in the nineteenth century. For many years it has been expressed in terms of a very strong tradition of architectural place-making. I have explored the bicultural aspect of Maori architecture at length elsewhere.[8] Here I want to emphasize specifically that the *taahu* (ridge-pole) of the *wharenui* (the large meeting house) is a vectorial sign that points to the place of the *marae* (approximately the village or the village square) in terms of geography, economy and cosmology, and that by pointing it also constructs that place. A significant contributor to informing this powerful architectural idea was Te Kooti Arikirangi (?1832–93), whose buildings diverted attention away from the vertical 'pointing' of the early mission churches to the horizontal 'pointing' of the *wharenui* form – turning away, that is, from the hope for transcendental redemption, and towards more of a Nietzschean kind of politically negotiated settlement.

Te Kooti's *wharenui* make an architectural gesture of pointing that is similar in many respects to the faultline gesture at Te Papa. Roger Neich has identified multiple layers of interconnected narratives through which meeting houses point out (and construct) meaningful directions in the world.[9] Neich remarks that the cultural space of the *marae* is specified by narratives that are associated with the orientation of the *taahu*. Several levels of meaning were revealed in stories told to Neich by the owners of one specific house in the Bay of Plenty. They were: a geographical orientation, relating to the openness of the sea in the front of the house and the relative closure of the land at its rear; a techno-economical pointing, pointing out that the sea and the forests at front and rear respectively are valued traditional resources, so that the house in a sense lays claim to these by pointing to them; sociological orientation, in which the house points out the direction from which the canoe immigrants arrived, and in the other direction the retreat and sanctuary of the Tini-o-Toi aborigines (directions of arrival, confrontation and retreat in the sociological and historical space of the tribal *whakapapa*); and finally the *taahu* points out the mythical and cosmological direction of the pathway to Hawaiki along which a spiritual bond is always maintained. Neich argues that the *taahu* is the 'point' of a kind of multilayered narrative space.

According to the architects, the faultline symbolism at Te Papa makes a similar kind of reference to the bicultural condition.[10] The distinctive backbone axis is said to be aligned with the mythical pathway between New Zealand and Hawaiki that is ubiquitous in Maori culture. The same gesture points to the geographical openness of Wellington's harbour, which was a traditional life-line in the colonial connection with Europe. In the other direction it points back to the relative closure of the city grid of down-town Wellington. The latter is designated as a typically Pakeha (non-Maori) form of urbanity. The intended message of Te Papa, perhaps, is that both cultures share the same general orientation within the world, or that we can be so co-aligned.

The axis of the museum also traces the line of intersection of a major tectonic collision-event between the Pacific Plate and the Australian Plate, which geologists now believe was the principle generator of the mountainous topography of New Zealand. There is therefore an additional, 'scientific' reference to place-making – as geological movements forcing a new land up from under the sea. The faultline at Te Papa, then, symbolizes and summarizes a heady mix of political aspiration and poetic intent, physical force and historical narrative. All these meanings are compressed and summarized in a single vectorial gesture – Te Papa is an architectural sign-post.

Admittedly, it is a strange gesture, even by 1990s standards of postmodern architecture. But bicultural architecture in New Zealand has always been susceptible to strange narrative and allegorical gestures of this kind. From the meeting house that Raharuri Rukupo built in 1840–2, Te Hau-ki-Turanga, which is now an exhibit in the museum, to Rewi Thompson's widely published City to Sea Bridge, adjacent to the museum, a bridge that compares itself to Maui's mythical fishing expedition, Maori architects and other New Zealanders who have attempted to address the complex bi-fold condition of the culture of this country seem repeatedly driven to make an architecture that speaks about something else.

Critical responses to these kinds of narrative references are divided between those who are sympathetic to the idea of *allegoria* – works of art and architecture saying something else in addition to what they 'ought' to be depicting – and those on the other hand who are deeply suspicious of what seems to be a reversion to primitivism and an appeal to something like sympathetic magic. Critics are divided between those who can appreciate the symbolism of pointing and those who cannot see the point of any architectural allusion. So the issue for theory is to simplify and demystify as much as possible the issues associated with cultural narrative. A theory of place-making should expose the bare bones and the inevitability of speech-like acts in architecture.

To me it seems that the very simplest way to say everything that needs to be said in this regard is to assert that *architecture is a triadic sign*, and that the division within the critical community is energized by differences and misunderstandings between adherents to Charles Sanders Peirce's triadic semiotic logic and Ferdinand Saussure's linguistic theory of dyadic semiology respectively.[11]

If I appear to be passing too quickly over Martin Heidegger's theory of place-making, or Deleuze and Guattari's theory of transversality (which is explored elsewhere in this volume by Andrew Ballantyne), it is because I hold that Continental theory often complicates the cultural logic of architecture more than the situation warrants. For example there is widespread among critical theorists an implicit assumption of epistemological dualism between intuitions of time and of space, which is made explicit in Kant's *Critique of Pure Reason*.[12] Expressed in semiotic terms, the assumption is that the *temporal* is signified and that the signifier is *spatial*.

Heidegger made a major contribution to theory when he asserted a conjunction between being and time; but then he spent an enormous amount of effort fruitlessly trying to embrace art and space under the same time-privileging phenomenology. 'Building Dwelling Thinking' is a beautiful essay on architecture, but it is thoroughly mystified because of this aspect of its intellectual pedigree. There has not been a thoroughgoing deconstruction of this particular (Kantian) premise, so 'Building Dwelling Thinking' cannot function as a straightforward theory of architectural place-construction.

Andrew Ballantyne exposes a disjunction that is implicit between Deleuze and Guattari in their supposedly empirical theory of transversality and world-making. Transversality is exposed as being at best an *illusion*, the illusory moving image in cinema or the illusion of psychological well-being among the mentally ill, or the further illusion that these two illusions are one and the same.

But a sign-post is not an illusion. Architecture that constructs its place in the world by pointing is not an illusion. A sign-post is a simple empirical fact. Empirical facts, for Peirce, are triadic signs.

A vector, in mathematical mechanics, comprises three spatial properties: length, direction, and *sense* of direction. In architectural terms, the three aspects of place-making are the *mark*, the *cut* and the *saying*. Te Papa marks its place in the Pacific region in the late twentieth century – this is its primary interest. Secondly it cuts a path, and points to an orientation within and through that place. This cut is the secondary interest of the museum in relation to culture and to geography. Thirdly our mediatory interest in Te Papa is conveyed to the mind as an idea about biculturalism. It is what Te Papa says to the people of New Zealand. In so far as it speaks to us, Te Papa is a triadic sign.

Mark possibly derives from the Sanskrit root, *ma*, which means 'laying out the foundation for a house'. Other words that are said to derive from the same root include imagination, measure, mathematics and magic. Architecture makes a mark on the surface of the world.

When we signify by marking we also *cut* the world in various ways – such as the cut of consciousness itself that divides the world between subjectivity and objectivity, between that which marks and what is marked. Architecture also divides the space of the world into front and rear, left and right, up and down. The Latin root for this is *scio*. Hence words are derived from cutting, like consciousness, science, scissors, etc. Cutting is the scientific consequence of every architectural sign.

The third aspect of an architectural sign is to *make a point*, to *say* something. To make a point is to point *something* out, and this *something* is logically distinct from what is pointed *at*. A work of architecture that marks and cuts the world in order to make a point is in this sense an essay, a statement, a sayable thing. Ultimately, it is an allegory.

Equivalent terms in Maori are revealed in words that have the prefixes, *mata-*, *whaka-*, and *kau-* respectively. In what follows I have adhered as closely as possible to Williams' *Dictionary of the Maori Language*.[13]

Mata is the point or the leading part of any body, the face, the eye, the surface. Alternatively it can be a geographical point, a rock or a headland that marks a boundary between fishing grounds. *Mataahi* is the first person slain in a battle. *Mataaho* is the window or 'eye' of a house. *Mataihi* is the gable end 'face' of the house. *Mataihi* serves in Maori as an architectural equivalent of a mark (bearing in mind that in the Maori world architecture is more of a 'living presence' than is the case in Europe).[14]

Secondly the Maori equivalent of the *cut* is approximated by the prefix, *whaka-*, whose meaning is both directional and causative, like a generalized cut. *Whakanoa* is the ceremonial act that divides the profane part of the world from the sacred. *Whakapapa* is a genealogical table that is 'cut and dried' compared to the confused uncertainty of unrecorded lineage. *Whakairo* means to cut incisions into the surface of pieces of wood, in order to make a carved house. More precisely it means to adorn with a pattern, to design, to weave together aspects of a building's design. The *wharenui* is often called *whare whakairo*, meaning a house that is carved and woven in this sense.

Finally the Maori equivalent of the say-ability of the architectural sign is most clearly expressed by the prefix *kau-*. *Kaumatua* is an adult or an elder, so designated as one who has the right to speak on a *marae*. *Kauhimu* is gossip and *kauwhau* is recitation. *Kaupapa* is the plan, the scheme, the brief for a building project. It is what an architectural work *sets out to say*. *Kauhanga* is a specifically architectural term for the space down the centre of a house (that speaks) when it is *tapu*.

In a Maori reading of the architecture of Te Papa, *mataihi* is the face-like *marae* on the fifth floor of the museum, facing the harbour, and designed by Cliff Whiting. *Kauhanga* is disclosed in the powerful ramping corridor that takes the visitor directly to the *marae* along the axis of the faultline. *Whakairo* is the distinctive pattern of the museum that I argue is organized and woven together by this metaphor of the faultline.

Te Papa symbolizes a deep-seated morphological grinding together of two peoples who have equal rights and opportunities in one place. Its apparent liveliness and its success as a constructed place, I argue, can be attributed to its triadic semeiology that is modelled on traditional meeting houses in New Zealand.

Saussure's dyadic formulation of the linguistic sign fails to reveal the full empirical meaning of architecture as place-making. In Heidegger's terms we can say that it causes the relation of *dwelling* not to appear in architecture, or it makes dwelling appear to be deeply mysterious, as indeed it was mysterious for Heidegger himself. If we think about semiology in terms of Heidegger's essay on architecture, then 'building' could be designated to be the signifier term. Building is that physical thing or act which signifies architecture, the relation that architecture makes with the physical world. In the same vein 'thinking' could be the signified term. Thinking is what architecture is really about, the relation that the architectural sign establishes with humans and the human world. Yet there is nothing left in this dyadic formulation that would signify 'dwelling'. Dwelling fails to reveal itself – to Being, to semiology or to Continental theory.[15]

The dyadic model of semiology provides no adequate explanation for the allegorical, indeed for architecture being in the world and at the same time 'saying something else'. When Te Papa is understood in dyadic terms, it is incapable of either contributing to culture or reporting on the condition of culture. In this view there would be no point in imitating a geological faultline in the form of a building.

Conversely, from the viewpoint of C.S. Peirce's triadic and empirical theory of signs, it would be inconceivable for a work of national importance such as Te Papa *not* to make a significant contribution to the culture in which it is embedded. From Peirce's side of this critical and theoretical 'faultine', the allegorical faultline at Te Papa is seen to have been well worth the risk. Peirce's theory of the triadic sign is rigorously logical in the best scientific tradition. It is elegant, spare and to the point. It says much about the logic of architectural place-making, without unduly mystifying the subject. In this attempt to apply Peirce's theory to architecture, admittedly, I have made my task easier by choosing to criticize a work that points overtly, in the manner of a sign-post. Perhaps semeiology will be found to be applicable only for architecture that points. Perhaps on the other hand we will find that all architecture points to the place that it makes in the world, only less intrusively, less diagrammatically can we say, than Te Papa does.

Notes

1 I. Wedde quoted in P. Matthews, 'Te Papa: the remake', *NZ Listener*, 1 December 2001, pp.50–1.

2 C.S. Peirce, 'What is a sign?' MS 404, (1894); published in part in C.S. Peirce, *Collected Papers of Charles Sanders Peirce*, 8 vols, eds C. Hartshorne and P. Weiss, Cambridge MA: Harvard University Press, 1931–58, pp.281, 285 and 297–302.

3 F. de Saussure, *Course in General Linguistics*, eds C. Bally and A. Sechehaye, trans. R. Harris, London: Duckworth, 1983. Roger Neich attempts to apply Saussurian (dyadic as opposed to triadic) semiotic theory to Maori art and architecture, with very limited success, in R. Neich, *Carved Histories, Rotorua Ngati Tarawhai Woodcarving*, Auckland: Auckland University Press, 2001, pp.106–12.

4 R. Kent, 'Museum of New Zealand', *Art AsiaPacific*, 1998, 20, pp.84–5.

5 V.J. Scully, *The Earth, the Temple and the Gods; Greek Sacred Architecture*, New Haven: Yale University Press, 1962.

6 The Treaty of Waitangi was signed in 1840, promising a partnership between New Zealanders and the Crown. Its bicultural implications were ratified in the Treaty of Waitangi Act, 1975, and consolidated in succeeding amendments to the Act. Thelma Rodgers, ('Museum of New Zealand Te Papa Tongarewa, analysis and interpretation for architectural concepts, of the museum institutional concept and organizational structure as published in reports from 1985 to 1989', unpublished B.Arch Research Report, University of Auckland, 1989) discusses the slow and contentious emergence of bicultural concepts in the briefing documents for Te Papa.

7 C. James, 'A bicultural path to a new centre', *NZ Herald*, 7 November 2001.

8 M. Linzey, 'Bicultural architecture: evaluating the contribution of Te Kooti', *In the Making: Architecture's Past*, SAHANZ 18th Conference, Darwin, 2001, pp.101–8.

9 R. Neich, *Painted Histories, Early Maori Figurative Painting*, Auckland: Auckland University Press, 1993, p.229.

10 P. Bossley, *Te Papa, An Architectural Adventure*, Wellington: Te Papa Press, 1998.

11 The less usual spelling of semeiology is adopted here as an indication to differentiate between the triadic formulation of Peirce and the dyadic formulation (and the spelling) of Saussurian semiology. (This spelling convention is often preferred by Peirce scholars.)

12 I. Kant, *Critique of Pure Reason*, trans. J.M.D. Meiklejohn, London: Dent, 1934, pp.41–61.

13 H.W. Williams, *A Dictionary of the Maori Language*, 7th edn, Wellington: Government Printer, 1971. The three key words *mataihi*, *kauhanga* and *whakairo* all appear with the given meanings in the 5th Edition (1917). *Mataaho* meaning 'window', and *whakairo* meaning 'carved, carving, to carve', are recorded in the 1st Edition (1844). The prefix *whaka-*, meaning 'towards, in the direction of', appears in the 3rd Edition (1871). A 1915 version (not a separate edition) of the *Dictionary* includes *whakairo*, meaning 'carve, adorn with carving'. Two years later this is replaced with the fuller meaning, 'ornament with a pattern, used of carving, tattooing, painting, weaving'.

14 M. Linzey, 'Speaking to and talking about Maori architecture', in J.-P. Bourdier and N. Al Sayyad (eds), *Dwelling, Settlement and Tradition*, Lanham: University Press of America, 1989, pp.317–34.

15 M. Linzey, 'Our habit of dwelling – between Peirce and Heidegger', in M.J. Oswald and R.J. Moore (eds), *Reframing Architecture Theory, Science and Myth*, Sydney: Archadia Press, 2000, pp.107–12.

Chapter 22

Architectural spoils

Francesco Venezia and Sicily's *spogliatoia*[1]

Annette Condello

> Perhaps, today, we need to gather the fragments of our present and clumsily construct with them our 'new churches,' as was done in the fifth century, which used fragments of ancient architecture as a construction material that was partly gifted with a discourse.[2]

Sicily's concern with architectural spoils started with its critical reconstruction of cultural fragments from the surplus of wars and natural catastrophes. In 1968 a strong earthquake shook Gibellina, turning the town into a quarry of destroyed fragments. In response to this catastrophe, the Italian government called for architects to prepare experimental projects in the Belice Laboratory of 1980. The old Gibellina no longer exists, a new town having been planned 20 kilometres away,[3] but the ruins are now covered with layers of concrete, in a sculptural intervention designed by Alberto Burri. This is an example of a contemporary preserved fragment; a grounded landscape that provides gestural cavities of collapsed fragments (Fig. 22.1). Some spoils from the ruined town were transferred into new locations, implying certain influences on the collective remains.

If, as Vittorio Gregotti mentions, 'we need to gather the scattered fragments of our present', then what becomes of spoils 'partly gifted with a discourse'?[4] The exploration of this question is set in two Sicilian ghost towns: the new town of Gibellina and Salemi.

22.1
Cretto, by Alberto Burri, old town of Gibellina, Sicily.

The term 'spoil' is perplexing from a contemporary architectural standpoint. Spoil conjures images of rubble, re-use, transformation, or the assimilation of passages. It is problematic when considering how all of these images are manipulated to cover or uncover parts of the building structure, or to support the fabrication of preceding buildings. The word 'spoil' still alludes to the plundering of other cultural fragments that are hidden within the architectural production. It is, perhaps, irrelevant to perceive spoils as being stolen from another place. Instead it is helpful to recognize the positive perception of decontextualized fragments that displace meaning. The process of architectural 'spoliation' offered here is, as the etymology of the term suggests, the undressing of architectural spaces (*spoliatio*). The *spogliatoio* is used in Italian architectural drawings as a space for stripping or uncovering, rather than simply a 'dressing room'. The process of spoliation identifies the unexplored panoply of material and architectural narratives that produce convincing variations of space in relation to the contingent placement of these spoils with new meaning.

In order to identify some of the problems and themes that emerge from the conception of spoils (*spolia*) as a 'positive practice', it is necessary to review other readings about its history in which the architectural spoils have been discussed.[5] The spoils of ancient Rome, such as the Arch of Constantine,

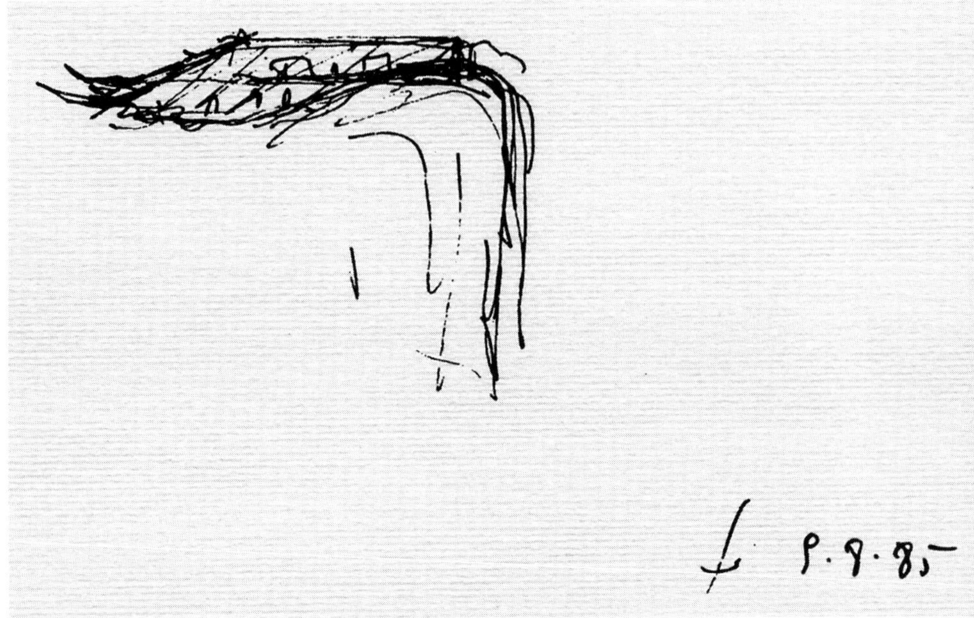

22.2
Sketch of Casa Malaparte by Francesco Venezia.

the renowned example of accumulative spoils, is mentioned by Beat Brenk, who writes 'this triumphal arch was commissioned by someone who clearly intended to use *spolia*. The arch, therefore, is not a precipitous patchwork but a prominent monument of imperial propaganda'.[6] The practice of spoliation indicates a positive measure of architecture, where past and present readings of gestural spoils are incorporated into new buildings. The *spogliatoia* in Sicily will be analysed as a series of grounded compositions,[7] in order to respond to the preceding ideas that inform the variegated placement of spoils dictated by both reconciled spoils and by seismic impact that uproots covered spoils.

To borrow a phrase, 'architecture of spoils',[8] from the architectural critic Marco Frascari and the Italian architect Francesco Venezia, this essay will consider the spoils in the Gibellina Museum and those apparent in the Salemi Theatre, experimental projects stemming from the Belice Laboratory. Venezia's design process is particularly significant in relation to the historical and topographical analysis of these projects, influenced by Adalberto Libera's design of Curzio Malaparte's house (1938–40) located on the Isle of Capri, near Naples (Fig. 22.2).[9] In this context spoliation refers to the improvisational use of materials and ideas, through adjustment of the specific image in question.

Writers have discussed the implications of historical spoils, or *spolia*, of Italy and elsewhere, but many of these studies have disregarded the appropriateness of its positive aspects. They have argued that the historical significance of the plundering of spoils was introduced in the Roman era, displaying a passion for the incorporation of coded meanings into architecture. The incorporation of ancient spoils, through fragments' capacity for significance, is visible in a large number of diverse cultures. Spoils have been captured from battling cities, and were dispersed as powerful gestures through numerous buildings, as a way of preserving significant moments of cultural significance. Many other cities left extensive remains that were later transferred and reused in new structures. This practice of spoliation was widespread from the Byzantine, through the Middle Ages to the Neoclassical period. In constituting architecture as a palimpsest it played some part in forming the architecture of southern Italy.[10] Alan Plattus argues that many historical spoils were taken from distant places, then purposefully reused in new monuments to yield a 'superior *mana* – [to] possess and bring back [trophies]',[11] the cultural energy association of which might be useful to the possessor.

The 'superior *mana*' of spoils is amplified in Dale Kinney's interpretation of *spolia*, where he defines this practice as 'once a powerful gesture to alter the identity of an existing image'.[12] This practice appears in Sicily, specifically in relation to the ancient city of Syracuse. With reference to the Roman writer Marcus Tullius Cicero, Kinney argues that 'the cognate *spoliatio* denoted, with specific reference to works of art and architectural decoration, illegal removing, an ignoble use of the power of appropriation.'[13] Spoils were interpreted as the preservation of specific memories that implied powerful gestures through the reusable capacity of fragments from other buildings. In terms of the discussion here the implication is that architectural *spoliatio* reveals positive and attentive 'powers of appropriation'; a plethora of demonstrative buildings in new contexts.

After the Middle Ages the powerful gesture of the spoil ceased to play an expressive part in architecture and appears tohave been absorbed into an 'illusion' in the Renaissance and Baroque eras. Here the theory of the fragment changes. Architects opted for a more deviant measure of distorting space by using representation as a sign.[14] Through illusion, fragmentation was eclipsed from the panoply of surviving classical models into a controlled manner of disarray. The process of fragmentary architecture reveals historical sources, permitting the analysis of such compositions in specific sites, and structures its intentional accumulation of cultural implications. This theory and practice started to regenerate into fragmentary compositions from the end of the Middle Ages through to Postmodernism. As Inigo Jones and William Davenant wrote in their anti-masque *Salmacida Spolia* (1640): 'the scene was changed into magnificent buildings composed of several selected pieces of architecture'.[15]

In his book *Monsters of Architecture*, Marco Frascari elucidates the definition of the 'architecture of spoils' in relation to the transference of buildings from the past into present forms.

> This is not an architecture of prefabricated romantic ruins, or of postmodern 'instant history', but is a way of producing architecture as the assimilation of prior architectural artefacts. Buildings are cultural texts that are generated by assembling fragments, excerpts, citations, passages and quotations. Every building is then an assimilation and transformation of other buildings. Every architectural piece echoes other pieces into infinity, weaving the fabric of the text of culture itself. The building elements are the joints of the construction of human culture; they are compelling demonstrations of how we inhabit the world.[16]

Frascari's notion of spoils as being fragmentary impactions (or conceptually compacted entities) is perhaps closely linked to a more apparent characteristic, the practice of 'demonstration'. In pursuing a discourse on spoils, Frascari refers to 'monstrosities' (or deformations) that enable the construction of a meaningful architecture unified by specific detailing, 'the margin or joints' that enable a passage of meaning.[17] This forms a base from which to trace the shift in the transformation and assimilation of other buildings into new contexts. Frascari's explanation is realized in Francesco Venezia's compositional method as his reconstructions resonate chthonic images from the topography of southern Italy.[18] In focusing on the 'attentive appropriation' of spoils, its relocation has allowed for a critical discussion of these building elements within the selected works as a series of *spogliatoia* – places of conceptual experimentation with the ground.

Venezia was inspired by the ancient 'spoils of war' and damaged topographies, preparing himself for the design of buildings through meticulous research into the reconciliation of modern works, rather than pursuing postmodern concerns. Venezia derives his inspiration from the Sicilian landscape and from Curzio Malaparte's house. He addresses the potential of the Rationalists and Neorationalists and he reuses their devices as spoliatory traces. Other devices that inform Venezia's architecture include passages from Italian novels such as Alberto Moravia's *Il Disprezzo* and Curzio Malaparte's *La Pelle* (*The Skin*).

The construction of Venezia's Gibellina Museum (1981–7) called for the transferral of the northern façade of the San Lorenzo Palace, a building that had been destroyed by the earthquake, to the new Gibellina town. The façade is subdivided into two opposing segments, and Venezia reconstructed some of the lost symmetry. He mounted the fragment on the internal façade and extended the use of spoils to the floors, reusing stone from the central region of Sicily (Fig. 22.3). This stone is contrasted with the bands of coloured concrete. Venezia's demonstration of the separation of the new and old spoils re-enacts partial secrets from previous buildings, concealing what should not be repeated again – conflicts due to destruction. Within this roofless rectilinear space, a sense of ambiguity plays against the absence of balustrades, recalling the design of Curzio Malaparte's house.

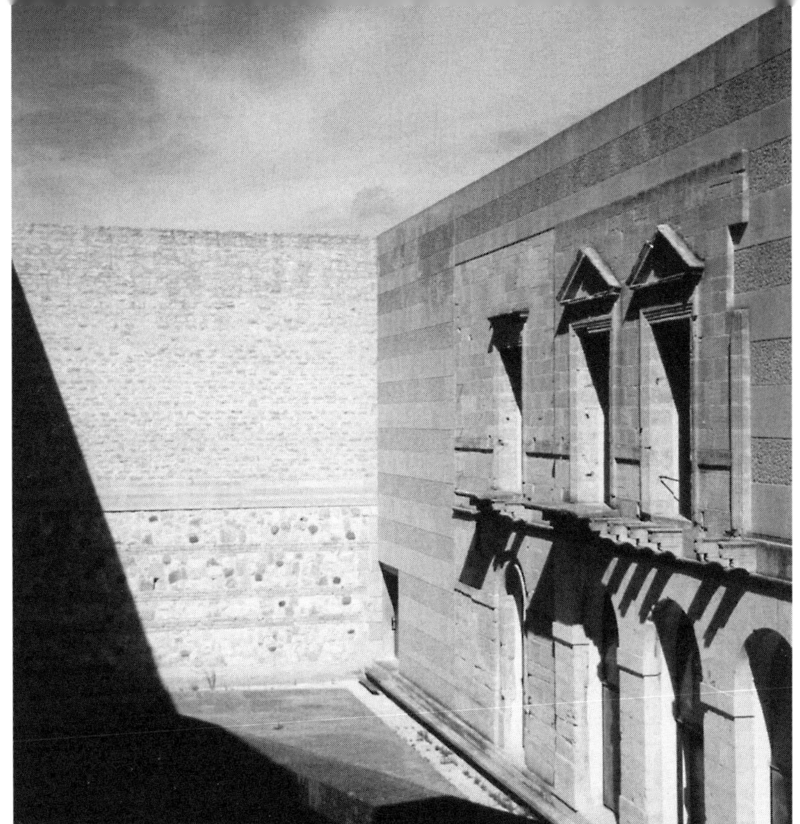

22.3
Old and new spoils, interior/exterior courtyard of the Gibellina Museum, New Town of Gibellina, Sicily.

> From this remote, silent sea the perpendicular rocks of the island seemed to me to be coming upwards in swarms, like arrows, their bare points flashing in the sun. Then all at once, a kind of suicidal exaltation came over me.[19]

Venezia's design approach is a theoretical exploration of the concept of the fragment and its association. The problem of grounding a composition through the incorporation of the fragment is apparent in the Gibellina Museum. Here it is necessary to focus on the original site of the displaced spoil and the spirit or 'mana' of such fragments. In referring to the spirit – or rather, the 'meaning capacity' of the spoil [20] – it has the capacity to speak of other places. These informative devices revolve around the impoverished topography from the traces of standing walls and foundations. The Gibellina Museum amplifies the architectural crisis of fragments, as mentioned in the writings of Manfredo Tafuri, by using the earthquake metaphor.[21] The detailed image of the interval between the new and old spoils within its walls (which incidentally Tafuri used on the cover of his book *The History of Italian Architecture 1944–1985*) provides evidence of prominent transformative architecture. The building offers a summation of Italian architecture, in particular suggesting the possibility of creating 'gestural spoils'.

The spaces within Venezia's Gibellina Museum accentuate images of Curzio Malaparte's house as instances of gestural spoils (Fig. I.19). The walls here seem to have absorbed aspects of the framing of Jean-Luc Godard's film *Le Mepris* (*Contempt*), 1963, an adaptation of Moravia's novel set on the Isle of Capri, in the calm vertiginous spaces they create. The film reveals interior shots of a Roman apartment, which is contrasted with the changing scenes of the disjointed cinematography, *spogliatoia*, illuminating the broken settings of southern Italy. As the film critic Winston Wheeler Dixon writes:

> Life in Le Mepris is conducted in deserted and abandoned studios, and in apartments and villas either rented … or under construction … As Deleuze notes, 'Godard's unfinished apartments permitted discordances and variations, like all the ways of passing through a door with a missing panel … '[22]

Venezia's compositional method allows him to 'distill' each spoil that alludes to the incomplete positions of architectural scenery, expressing the cultural fragments from previous buildings or previous situations, and in this way accumulating monumental memories. His work implies the filmic method of Godard, which may be translated as a culmination of 'disjointed connectedness' and conceptually framing architecture, or a device anchoring the displaced gestural spoil.[23]

Thomas Raff, however, overlooks Venezia's intention for an incomplete construction in the Gibellina Museum, describing it as 'a strangely superficial conception of the historic monument [preserving] only part of an older building, often the façade, while the rest is demolished and replaced by a new structure'.[24] Despite Raff's dismissal of Venezia's technique, he considers this work to be a 'secular architectural relic', projecting the medieval process of *spolia*, which was rejected by neoclassicist critics as a culture of disembodied fragments. The reconstruction is not fragmentary in the pejorative sense of the neoclassicists, but is an attempt to reconstruct a pertinent image of the ground. The museum clearly demonstrates the awareness of the problem of the transferred fragment, through this juxtaposition of old and new spoils within its walls. Although Raff considers Venezia's museum to be an 'undignified manipulation', in the sense of meaningless surface manipulation, I argue that Venezia's engagement in diverse modes of preceding buildings provides a grounded array of gestural spoils.

Another such array is refound in the Salemi Theatre (1983–6), a collaborative work by Francesco Venezia, Roberto Collovà and Marcella Aprile. This open-air theatre is a recollection of the Carmine district of that town. Two terraces occupy the site dividing the sunken auditorium and the square (Fig. 22.4). Demolished walls of a convent building were recomposed into retaining walls, and materials are joined in a complex manner. Spoils were transferred

22.4
View of the auditorium, Salemi Theatre, Sicily.

from the convent and displayed on the ramped stage; pieces of the column appear to be sinking into the cobbled surface (Fig. 22.5). The building is a misprision of an unbuilt project by Giuseppe Terragni for a cinema theatre (1940).[25] These sinking spoils perhaps represent another catastrophic scene waiting to happen, the suspension of time where the building remains as a still object, a roof upturned, or a solidified 'pool of lava'. The open corridor that surrounds the theatre constitutes what could be described as a phantasmagoric race-track, a dreamlike complex consisting of a changing series of *spogliatoia*. The continuous strips of travertine were located at knee height, an ambiguous height demonstrating the converging levels of the absent floor. Towards the auditorium is a pit, or *spolarium* – the place that had been dug on wasteland near the Colosseum – where dead gladiators were stripped of their equipment.[26] This space creates an oneiric composition that transmits a whole range of meanings of spoils. The sequence of paintings by Giorgio De Chirico alluding to *spogliatoia* (such as 'The Gladiators') may be contrasted with the imaginary mannequins within or without dressings rooms. Melancholy, the anxieties, and the manes of the site are evident traits within these passages.

The Salemi Theatre may also be interpreted as an allusion to Malaparte's house, particularly in the configuration of the remnants on the

22.5
Spoils sinking into the ramped stage, Salemi Theatre, Sicily.

stage, recalling the solarium on its roof terrace overlooking the Mediterranean Sea. An accumulation of spoils is layered in deposits within this square, exposing the incomplete states of construction. The difference in this reconstruction is that the appearance of this upturned 'pool of lava' further suggests the surreal charge of the project. The lava layers in the ramped stage suggest this enigmatic play of making apparent the sinking of the columns. These are distinguished from the romantic and picturesque allusions or nostalgic tones that at first appear to demonstrate a metaphysical platform, but reveal more of a psychological frame of the undetected contemplation. Such personal attitudes to the history and architecture of southern Italy are thus revealed. A quasi-excavation remains, creating a landmark for sleepwalkers.

The way in which the placement of the spoil within one or many parts of a building accomplishes meaning thus becomes something other than fragmentary. As geological 'spoil banks' these works evoke the influence of the earthquake metaphor in their poetical constructions, and are appropriate vehicles to explicate an architecture of displacement. Perhaps this practice in which the distortion of the spoil identifies the 'misprision', that is, the anxieties of the architectural influences of preceding architectures, forms a specific southern Italian image.[27] Anxious characteristics develop into complete or incomplete geometries, as a broken interior or exterior.

These constructions respond to both northern and southern Italian crises – political, economic, religious, conflictual and natural – forming into poetical architecture and into complex composite wholes. The Gibellina Museum and the Salemi Theatre both project a desire to renew ground datums for Sicily. Spoliatory constructions may be understood as being revelatory of the gestural space, and may contribute through subsequent constructive acts to the legitimate fabrication of contingent architecture. This discussion of architectural spoils is therefore not to do with the joining of buildings, as Frascari mentions,[28] but the orientation of meaning to justify an imposed order.

This analysis of the preceding examples of Mediterranean architecture focused on the orientation of spoliatory meanings as transferred into gestural buildings, and is based upon a reading of the region's history and contingent geography. The earthquake metaphor becomes critically significant for the analysis of Venezia's reconstructions. Seismic edges seem to 'battle' with each other – in the project they become the poetical battle of the dislocated spoil assimilated over the contested ground of the site. Details are distorted and displaced in subtle spatial gestures that divert and reassemble the spoliated fragments of forms in a passage forming new stages. Such spoliated projects lure the observer to discover, individually, something within the construction. The use of spoils invites the ascription of influential experiences. The *mana* is not only manifest in the configuration of elements, but is realized in the individual's experience of the space, that is, through the establishment of levels of architectural experience articulating another topography. Architectural spoliation can rearrange, transform something, and attentively appropriate elements into specific contexts to accommodate the specificities of a defined programme.

Notes

1 Versions of this paper were presented at the 16th SAHANZ Conference on *Thresholds*, University of Tasmania, September 1999, and at *The Use and Abuse of Antiquity: Interrogating the Classical Tradition* Symposium, University of Melbourne, October 1999. Refer to my unpublished Master's thesis entitled 'Spoliation: The Trapezial Architecture of Francesco Venezia, The University of Western Australia, 2000. This research was supported by the Mrs Jessie Mary Vasey Scholarship (War Widows Guild of Australia), and an Australian Post Graduate Award.

2 V. Gregotti, *Inside Architecture*, Cambridge MA: MIT Press, 1996, p.30.

3 See P.A. Croset, 'Salemi e il suo territorio', *Casabella*, June 1987, vol.536, pp. 18–25.

4 V. Gregotti, *Inside Architecture*, Cambridge MA: MIT Press, 1996, p.30.

5 See B. Brenk, 'Spolia from Constantine to Charlemagne: aesthetics versus ideology', *Dumbarton Oaks Papers* 41, Washington DC, 1987.

6 Brenk, 'Spolia from Constantine to Charlemagne', p.104.

7 The concept of spoils is distinguished from the new deconstructivist simulations, to redefine the 'refounding' of architecture. Instead of discussing the problem of the postmodern or post-postmodern condition of fragmentation and pluralist debates, the following projects uncover the consequent loss of 'depth' in culture. The revisiting nature of spoils, where materials and ideas are expressed and revealed, requires a basis for the legitimizing the fragmentary meanings of the deliberate disarray of projects. Francesco Venezia's projects are places in 'desolation', an architecture that is used to culturally reconstruct contemporary 'stages'. On the notion of 'ungrounding' refer to J. Rajchman, *Constructions*, Cambridge MA: MIT Press, 1998, pp.77–91. For a discussion on 'desolation' and 'the contemporary place' see I. de Sola-Morales, *Differences: Topographies of Contemporary Architecture*, trans. Graham Thompson, Cambridge MA: MIT Press, 1997, pp.65, 103–4.

8 On this see F. Venezia, 'Transfer and transformation. The architecture of spoils: a compositional technique', in *Daidalos*, 1985, vol.16, pp. 91–104; and M. Frascari, 'Carlo Scarpa in Magna Graecia: the Abatellis Palace in Palermo', *AA Files*, 1985, vol. pp. 9, 3–9.

9 See F. Venezia, 'Casa Malaparte a Capri', in *Scritti Brevi 1975–1989*, Naples: Clean, 1990, pp.6–7. Also, see M. Talamona, *Casa Malaparte*, Princeton: Princeton Architectural Press, 1992.

10 A. Plattus, 'Passages into the city: the interpretive function of the Roman triumph', *The Princeton Journal: Thematic Studies in Architecture*, vol.1, Princeton: Princeton Architectural Press, 1983, p.107.

11 Plattus, 'Passages into the city: the interpretive function of the Roman triumph', p.107.

12 D. Kinney, 'Rape or restitution of the past? Interpreting spolia', in S.C. Scott (ed.), *The Art of Interpreting*, Papers in Art History, Vol.IX, Pennsylvania: Pennsylvania State University, 1995, p.58.

13 Kinney continues, '*Spoliatio* was one of the crimes for which Cicero prosecuted Verres on behalf of the province of Sicily', in Kinney, 'Rape or restitution of the past?', p.53.

14 The concern in the late eighteenth century for incorporating spoils into a building established palatial buildings or 'sedate', in the sense of the building being regenerated. In the early nineteenth century spoils were used indiscriminately. As Marco Frascari notes, 'Architectural critics of the Neo-classical era were disdainful of this type of architecture and called it 'fragmentary.'' Frascari reintroduced the idea of the Italian term '*spoglia*' in relation to Carlo Scarpa's reconstruction of the Palazzo Abatellis (1953–5) in Palermo, bombed during the Second World War. See Frascari, 'Carlo Scarpa in Magna Graecia', p.3. Also, refer to T. Raff, '*Spolia* – building material or bearer of meaning', *Daidalos*, December 1995, vol.58, p.70, and D. Vesely, 'Architecture and the ambiguity of the fragment', in R. Middleton (ed.), *AA. The Idea of the City*, London: The Architectural Association, 1996, p.111.

15 Quoted in T.J. Spencer, 'Inigo Jones and William Davenant, *Salmacida Spolia* (1640)', Song IV (lines 436–437), in *A Book of Masques*, London: Cambridge University Press, 1967.

16 M. Frascari, *Monsters of Architecture: Anthropomorphism in Architectural Theory*, Savage MD: Rowman and Littlefield, 1991, p.22.

17 Frascari, *Monsters of Architecture*, pp.16–18.

18 Refer to F. Venezia, *Francesco Venezia: L'architettura, gli scritti, la critica*, Milan: Electa, 1998.

19 The interior courtyard of the Gibellina Museum bears a strong resemblance to Alberto Moravia's description of Malaparte's house as a series of contemplative stages led by following the path that encircles the island, through which he passes as a succession of thresholds. A. Moravia, *Contempt* [originally published in Italian as *Il Disprezzo* in 1954], trans. A. Davidson, London: Prion, 1999, p.196.

20 Refer to O.K. Werckmeister, 'Walter Benjamin, Paul Klee and the Angel of History', ed. K.W. Forster, *Oppositions*, autumn 1982, vol.25 'Monument/Memory', pp. 103–25.

21 See M. Tafuri, *History of Italian Architecture 1944–1985*, London: MIT Press, 1989.

22 W.W. Dixon, *The Films of Jean-Luc Godard*, New York: State University of New York Press, 1997, p.48.

23 Andrew Ballantyne refers to Deleuze in the films of Jean-Luc Godard in his Chapter 12 of this volume.

24 Raff, '*Spolia* – building material or bearer of meaning?', p.71.

25 See F. Venezia, *Indizi e congetture: due corse di progettazione tenuti da Francesco Venezia*, Milan: Cittá Studi Edizioni, 1995, pp.18–21.

26 See D. Kyle, *Spectacles of Death in Ancient Rome*, London: Routledge, 1998, pp.158–9.

27 On 'misprision' see H. Bloom, *The Anxiety of Influence*, New York: Oxford University Press, 1973.

28 Frascari, *Monsters of Architecture*, p.22.

Chapter 23

Horizon in the Hamar Museum

An instrument of architecture and a way of looking at site

Suzanne Ewing

Introduction: inventing place

> Outside, the tree fractures the horizon. Time will allow it to grow and add to its room. The tree mobilises light and casts its shadow on the earth, a realisation of place.[1]

Architect Sverre Fehn suggests that he comes of age 'in the shadow of modernism'.[2] His built work (mainly in Scandinavia) has been described as poetic, sculptural, humanistic, inclusive, and was recognized by the 1997 award of the Pritzker Prize. Following exposure early in his career in the 1950s with the publication of the Nordic Pavilion in Venice, acclaim for his work was consolidated in the 1980s. Norberg-Schulz and Postiglione suggest that 'the belated recognition of Fehn is due to the fact that his works suddenly appear to "adapt" themselves to the international situation and to offer compelling answers to difficult and complex conditions'.[3] The focus of this paper is to generate understanding of the complex condition of 'site' in Fehn's work; a condition that I argue is about inventing place.

Andrea Kahn has suggested that the subject of site has been 'systematically ignored by both architectural and urban design discourse',[4] and is, to some degree, also subject to fabricated dualisms inherent in modernism:

before/after; above/below; new/old; urban/landscape.[5] Kahn observes that we are usually 'in the midst of site' rather than 'hovering over', as in most modernist conceptions, and argues that this is critical to how an architect acts or responds. David Leatherbarrow notes how 'the existence of a defined building site is always taken for granted in contemporary architectural design, yet attempts to understand the reasons underlying its definition are surprisingly rare'.[6] He presents three contemporary partial understandings or assumptions: site as a division of space, site as context and site as real estate. Both Kahn and Leatherbarrow conclude that site in relation to the act of building is always a matter of invention. Kahn develops a model of site constructions in architectural education that acknowledges the interpretative reality of engagement with a particular physical location that is also a conceptual construct. Leatherbarrow explores historic inventions of site in Vitruvius (sites within a potential whole), Alberti (the site platform), Borromini (mediated sites) and the eighteenth-century 'genius loci' where he locates the roots of (modernist) partial understandings of site.

Heidegger's rethinking of the nature of space, place and inhabitation is also relevant. His work from the late 1920s to 1960s freed the question of space from its previous disciplinary boundaries, breaking from a Cartesian ontology of neutral, flattened space (site as a division of space) and reasserting investigation into the spatiality of the world in which we find ourselves, 'the concrete context of actual life'.[7]

Heidegger's concepts of *horismos* and *raum* have been noted as a preoccupation of Fehn's work.[8] The architect claims that his work interprets the site it confronts.[9] An exploration of Fehn's approach to site 'in the shadow of modernism' is offered here through an outline interpretation of one built project, the Hamar Museum, Norway.[10] I aim to show in this essay that 'horizon' is seen by Fehn as critical to understanding the invention of site, surrounding limits and orientation, and marking territory of 'significant opposition'.[11] In his work, implied lines of horizon are fractured and become a conceptual and spatial instrument fundamental to the creation of a room. Rooms, in turn, can potentially be mobilized by light to become realized place. More generally I suggest that practices and possibilities of invention of site deserve closer scrutiny in relation to how place is realized or constructed.

Territory

Confrontation and struggle is a recurrent theme of language used by Fehn in his narratives. When 'acting violently in order to emphasize their latent, secret, hidden qualities',[12] he calls the act of building 'brutal', 'violations'. He writes,

> when I build on a site in nature that is totally unspoiled, it is a fight, an attack by our culture on nature. In this confrontation I strive to make a building in the setting, a hope for a new consciousness to see the beauty there as well.[13]

Analogies with ships and conquest recur as do his diagrams of the line of a boat forging through the sea.

There is resonance here with both Norwegian tradition and Vitruvian identification of sites, as described by Leatherbarrow, where the soil is literally ploughed and cut to mark off a site from its surrounding expanse, and the resulting artefact, a boundary wall, denotes 'not a line but a container symbolically equivalent to the wall of a ceramic jar or vase, a limit that served as a receptacle of civic life, generative and abundant because female'.[14] The horizon 'without' was perceived as an open expanse, an unbounded and formless field, perhaps analogous to the sea. The idea that 'the secret of the boat was to fight the horizon', however, reveals a fabricated modernist dualism of nature versus culture, with an implication that the marking vessel (container, boat, room, architectural space) is the focus in undifferentiated ground, rather than as a balancer of territory enclosed or exposed, within or without.

Fehn understands architecture as 'subject to the layout of the ground', where 'sites ... contain in their profundity the sense of the project, to which the architecture must conform'.[15] This is closest, perhaps, to Leatherbarrow's category of partial understanding of site as context. Fehn also describes site as an archive – in other words something distanced from the present and future, a source of information and knowledge, perhaps to be plundered, certainly to be discovered and not unrelated to the myth of the untouched site identified by Khan, which is often a necessity for modernist intervention.[16] She unravels the myth of the contained and controllable site, that analysis is inconsequential to site definition, as it accepts all given boundaries; that is scientifically objective, a neutral description of data; and that it is only preparatory to design.

The site at Hamar is clearly one that has been previously touched – it is an archaeological site and incorporates additional buildings, remains and artefacts. Fehn's approach of built detachment from these past touchings however invents the site to some extent as untouched territory.

Line

Norberg-Schulz outlines a narrative interpretation of the forming of limits and boundaries in relation to building;[17] first the earth as given territory, secondly the marking or making of lines related to cultivation, and thirdly enclosure, the

23.1
View of external courtyard of Hedmarkmuseet showing highest point of external ramp.
Sverre Fehn, 1967–79.

containing of inhabited space. In Leatherbarrow's Vitruvian ordering of territory, the line of cut ground primarily separated difference (or different presences). The significant opposition noted in relation to Fehn's work is evident in his writings, and in the ordering moves set up between nature and man, earth and sky, boat and sea. Architecture becomes a charged void contained or bounded in opposition to all that surrounds it in nature. Thus the focus is on the line or actual boundary itself (container/boat/room/architectural space) rather than on the differentiated ground and implied activity where it is situated.

The defined limits of the Hamar Museum site stem from previous inhabitation – the previously defined buildings and edges. Where territory is less clearly bound in the semi-enclosed courtyard/ excavation area, a new visitors' ramp is introduced, with the same plan geometry as the remains of an existing boundary wall. The new ramp replicates this wall, yet its location is shifted from the original ground. The ramp contains visitor movement, becomes a line cutting through the invented space bounded by the more solid wings of the museum (Fig. 23.1).

Horizon

Fehn's own writings include reference to the horizon as 'the dramatic confrontation between earth and sky. The point of intersection'.[18] Despite its usual meaning of a circular visual limit, the term horizon is not originally connected to seeing and intuition. 'It means, in accordance with the Greek verb *horizein*, what

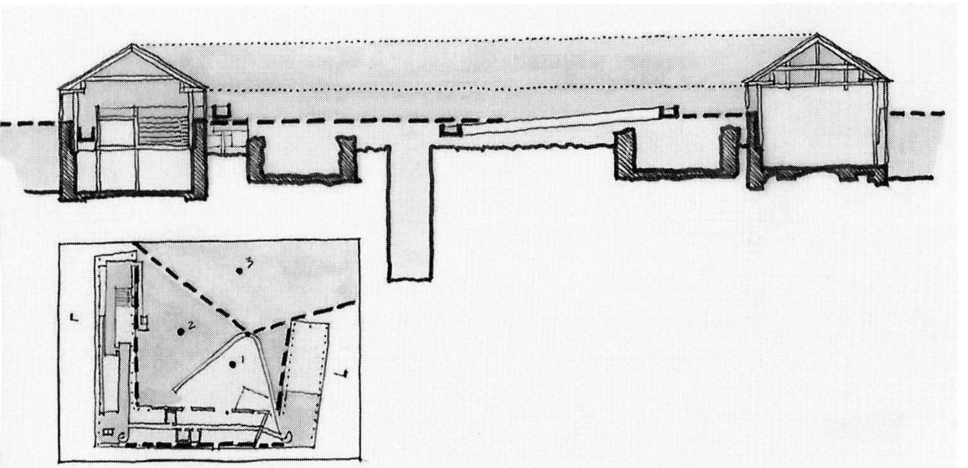

3.2
ketch plan and ection through the arns and ourtyard of Hamar luseum.

limits, surrounds, encloses'.[19] It is 'the *apparent* line that divides the earth and the sky' and it is the aspect of imagined or interpreted horizon which is pertinent to site invention.[20]

Heidegger's shift from the horizon of a mathematician (understanding site as a division of space) posited Time as the transcendental horizon for the question of Being in the 1920s.[21] The horizon of *praesens* (presence, present) is the leading horizon because it is the one which commands all relation to inner-worldly beings of any kind whatsoever, and in this sense it also commands the relation to the *Vorhandenen*, to the merely present being. This thinking developed later in the 1940s,

> the horizon as such is only the side, turned towards us, of an openness which surrounds us and this openness should, as such, be named *Gegnet*, 'region' in the sense of a gathering locus for all extended and enduring things … To experience what 'lets' be – *sein lasst* – horizon leads us beyond such a representational, transcendental-horizon thinking to a waiting that can never be understood as an anticipating because it has no object, a waiting for the opening of the *Gegnet* to which we all belong.[22]

Fehn's interpretation of horizon relates an elemental understanding of human, building and situation, and can be argued to some extent to relate to aspects of Heidegger's philosophical approach to time and being. However, Fehn's imagined horizon is primarily spatial and physical. It is concerned with being rather than merely present being, an experiential connecting horizon, as he explains:

> What was especially lost was the horizon, which human beings forgot with the discovery of the roundness of the earth. And with the loss of horizon we also lost known and unknown space. We have lost the earth underneath the sky and what is beyond ... Let the people in their individual homes own the horizon. Let the apartment roof be the large piazza for the social interaction for a visual conversation with the elements of the sky.[23]

Fracture

I introduced Fehn describing the tree fracturing the horizon. He relates this language of confrontation and struggle to existing patterns in nature. A narrative of pure or original nature is embodied in the line of the horizon where spatial infinity is inferred to be analogous with timelessness and purity, the untouched. Interventions transform, conquer or change and mark both space and time, enabling human inhabitation – the shade of the tree, the support of a column, the corner or edge of a room, the beginning of a building. His architecture attempts to provide 'a horizon for man' so that each project identifies a place in space between earth and sky, *mellomron*, meaning 'the space between' in Norwegian.

Fehn's preoccupation with redefining or revealing the earth underneath the sky can be seen in Hamar where the surface of the earth is revealed as having historic depth. An ordering develops where new 'ground' of contained ramp and route is established between the redefined horizontal datum of the roof and uneven earth remains. Spaces are limited and bounded by the repetitive rhythmic secondary vertical elements. The literal passing or breaking through primary enclosed volumes emphasizes the here and the beyond of the perceived or imagined horizon. Fehn claims that it is in the fracturing of horizon (what limits, surrounds, encloses) that place can be realized.

Instrument

Leatherbarrow compares the modern notions of site with earlier examples, such as Alberti's notion of site platform that may order and limit vertically and Borromini's idea of 'mediating' (the manner in which staged sites influence the external configuration of spaces adjacent to a site). He cites Theo van Doesberg's early modernist experiments with axonometric projection, which aimed to remove the composition from the horizon of perspectival experience, 'which confers frontality on whatever (object or person) reciprocates the "frontalism" of one's body'.[24] This abstraction dislocates from real time, with the potential confusion of horizon and perspective (or vista) as 'a view on reality' rather than understood implicit presence. Fehn's presentation of his own approach refers to horizon as instrument:

> [In those days] the horizon was an instrument of architecture determining the large exterior 'room'. The vista then served the practical purpose of defense, extending no further than the eye could see. The sight on the weapon was an extension of the eye and its view was a definition of mortality ... The conversation with nature was not based on aestheticism or sentimentality, for every opening not only admitted light, but also determined survival in relation to topography.[25]

It is perhaps not surprising that invention of site, a way of realizing place, begins to resonate with instrumental thinking, or military overtones, given the cultural and social context of the twentieth century. 'Survival in relation to topography' recalls the act of building as confrontation with nature. To some extent Fehn does attempt to relocate architecture in time and human experience, with connections to the imagined beyond rather than an abstraction.

The room of the tree: a place on earth

The Archbishopric Museum of Hamar, Norway, 1967–79 – started when Fehn was 43 and completed when he was aged 55 – is built over an archaeological site that was significant in the late Middle Ages because it lay along the Kaumpung trail, which was the route of the Bishop of Hamar's journey to Rome in 1302. The remains of an early nineteenth-century farm structure, resting on the top of the ruins of a medieval fortress demolished in the second half of the sixteenth century, still have some visible traces. The relationship to the existing remains is deliberately detached, thus inventing the literal material of the site as differentiated territory of the past. Conscious exposure effectively reinvents a territory of site as untouched within reconfigured boundaries of the museum. The site is interpreted as a confrontation between old and new, stillness and movement, ground and sky. Location of spaces above or below the historic ground and the gradually sloping floors of interior spaces reinforce shifts of movement that are articulated by materials. These internal constructed horizons are fractured by elements such as stairs or the main ramp in the making of rooms for the occupation of the Museum (Fig. 23.3).

23.3
View of ramp in galleries of the Hamar Museum, understood as an inserted 'horizon' 'the space betwee earth and sky'.

The building was described in the Pritzker Prize proceedings as '[a] suspended itinerary, … overhanging … This confrontation reveals the story of the passing of time, the unchanging pursuit of its course, the confrontation between old and new'.[26]John Hedjuk has described the place as

> [a] site where the frozen earth grips in its vise the retaining and foundation walls of past acts and occurrences. The present archaeologist reveals the earth-encrusted tombs of past joys and of past sadness. We know we are in the presence of an event and we are strangely enough participating spectators. The lake and the mountain are the proscenium.[27]

The simple linear buildings with timber pitched roof and masonry base recall the basic form of Norwegian folk buildings. The museum comprises four main areas: the entrance area, or excavation zone in the central nineteenth-century barn block; the galleries to the north side; the concert hall in the barn to the south-east; and the external courtyard with ramp and excavations.

Spatial organization of the galleries, where the museum of peasant life is housed, emphasizes the linearity of the nineteenth-century low-level barns, perpendicular to the entrance block. Two levels are joined by a sloping concrete floor, which appears to float apart within the barn-like structure, exposing clear differentiation of the building's structure and components of stone, timber post and beam and new roof. Two spaces are composed within the barn. There is an ambiguity between the relative importance of upper and lower levels, one connected with the revealed depth of the earth, the other with the light and rhythm of the sky. The roof construction articulates the sky boundary of the space, derived in part from vernacular construction, yet invented to appear distant as the horizontal of the truss marks a lower boundary. This emphasizes the space beyond and perhaps allows 'conversation with the elements of the sky'.

The entrance area is a fusion of the existing medieval fort walls incorporated into the nineteenth-century farm buildings. The new entrance links to a significant opening on to the external courtyard, with a view of the external ramp that cuts through the external space. The 'ground' is revealed as uncertain, since what is assumed to be 'ground' on entering the building is in fact contradicted by the deepening rough stone trenches that become evident as you move through. It is only at the upper level of the museum that you realize the boundary of this enclosure extends between the nineteenth-century stone walls. The smooth concrete bridge linking the gallery areas to the external ramp and its pivot stair provides a higher datum for the insertion of concrete boxes containing especially valued objects and fragments extracted from the rough ground below. Space appears to be compressed at ground level by the intruding monolithic insertions, allowing only

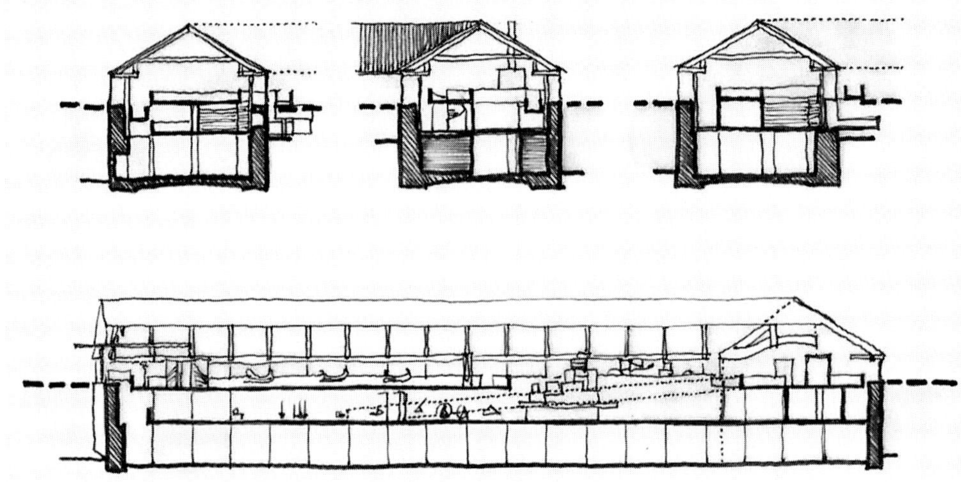

23.4
Sketch sections through the galleries of the Hamar Museum showing the implied horizon in relation to spaces 'realised'.

limited glimpses beyond. The focus becomes the cave-like quality of the excavated ground area that appears to be stepped on and filled in. This recalls the underground feeling of the Venice Pavilion and, more tenuously, the monumental shards of the towers of Oslo Town Hall. A similar preoccupation can be seen in Fehn's 1965 competition project for a church in Honningsvåg, North Cape.

Materials are used to orient the human experience in relation to both ground and sky. Throughout the building the fundamental relationship of being 'above' accentuates the experience of being 'below'. Within the stone walls of the museum the transition between above and below is always related to penetrating light and concrete finish, seen in the stairs, the ramp. The highest part of the walls, in the central entrance block, relates to the highest point of the ramp within the external courtyard. Fehn's conceptual 'point of intersection' in this building relates not to the horizontals of the existing stone walls or roof structure but to the inserted routes of platform, ramp and stairs. All below is treated as part of the earth: dark, cave-like, rough terrain. Above is evenness, a consistent timber articulation and rhythm. Participation in moving through these spaces is participation in the division between above and below, earth and sky. At the moment where the ramp penetrates the building at high level, vertical proportions and vertical elements invert the spatial horizontality of the other areas of the building.

Two less apparent spaces (a space above and a space below) are created by the bold introduction of the ramp in the external courtyard area. The ground of existing material becomes read as one area bounded by the wings of the farm buildings/museum, within the wider context of the lake and mountains beyond. This is overlooked when moving down or up the ramp. On arrival at the lowest level, the hub of the archaeological site, a more interior space related to the entrance level of the museum is experienced, enclosed by the ramp's turn itself. This 'space below' is however not an enclosed fortress-like space, but one where the beyond (i.e. the wider archaeological site, the experienced occupation of the museum wings and wider landscape) is emphasized by the marking presence of the ramp structure. 'The project culminates in the development of a route that, uncoiling itself in space, seeks to discover a new horizon'.[28] It is only from the ramp's highest external point that the wider landscape in which the museum is sited is revealed. The occupied horizon of the route of the ramp is effectively also revealed at this point as a line cutting through territory.

The plan geometry and form of the ramp refer directly to the existing remains of the external walls of the fortress. Its fundamental shift is from being a protective boundary separating within from without, to being an open route – a contained fracture. The ramp physically completes a spatial journey around the museum, and is fundamental to reinventing the perceived boundaries of the new museum site. The ramp's slope by definition is about movement and the oscillating relationship between suspended route and historic ground. It can therefore also be seen as the point (or line) of intersection between the two 'rooms' of the courtyard. The ramp's puncture of the building adjacent to the spiral stair from ground to hall is highlighted as significant on the site models/drawings and can be interpreted as a vertical pivot or fracture. It is the place of both real spatial shift, from the end of the linear barn to the outdoor *raum*, and of interpreted historical shift, where the enclosed spaces of the museum, as defined by previous military and agricultural use, are transformed into a new horizon of a route. This is itself a shifted remnant, no longer the line of a protective wall but a viewing platform.

There is some relationship to Heidegger's concept of *raum*, 'making room' here. Kenneth Frampton links Louis Kahn and Sverre Fehn to Heidegger's distinction between evenly divided and distant space.

> What the word for space, *raum*, designates is said by its ancient meaning. *Raum* means a place cleared or freed for settlement and lodging. A space is something that has been made room for, something that is cleared and free, namely within a boundary, Greek *peras*. A boundary is not that at which something stops but, as the Greeks recognized, the boundary is that from which something begins its presencing. That is why the concept of *horismos*, that is the horizon, the boundary. Space is in essence that for which room has been made, that which is let into bounds.[29]

It can be argued that the ramp at Hamar acts, it occupies a *raum*, a made room, yet also itself becomes a boundary of sorts allowing the external courtyard to be

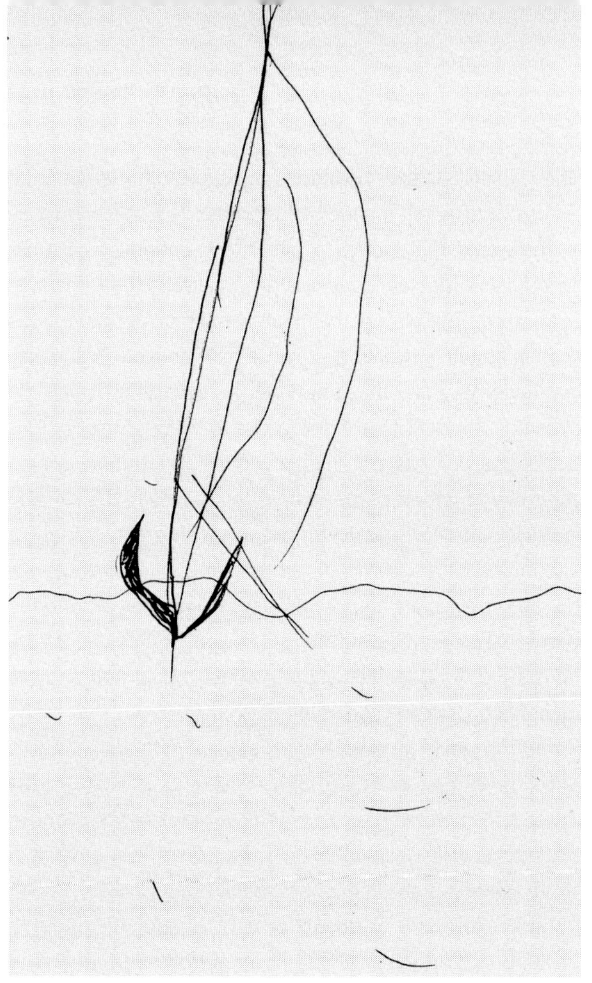

23.5
Sketch of boat forging through th[e] horizon of the sea, by Sverre Fehn.

understood as a series of overlapping spaces. As the shadow of the tree realizes a place on earth (or makes a place real), the impact of the ramp within the building and the courtyard gives the internal and external spaces their 'being'.

Conclusion: constructing place 'in the shadow of modernism'

It is argued here that the territory of the site at Hamar is reinvented as untouched despite the existing historic material of the ground that is integral to its existence, and thus to some extent is in concurrence with modernist myths related to site. However, the insertion of new layers of ground enables the resulting place to seem to develop a series of new relationships relating to space 'above' and 'below' in an eloquent manner. The articulation and manipulation of concrete and light within these new vessels or lines of occupation emphasizes a charged void between earth and sky, a positioning of experience in relation to the visible horizon bounded by the rebuilt stone and timber structure and also to the horizon in terms of imagined boundary. The imagined boundary of the site has some overlap in plan with the existing boundary walls of previous built form. In the external courtyard this shifts to emphasize new orientation and experience of new and old, as a line inserted into free terrain rather than a bounding within or without. To some extent the ramp places the visitor outside or beyond an interpreted sequence of history. A fracture is interpreted at the point of pivot of the ramp's junction with the upper-level walkway and the spiral stair, vertical fixing point of the platforms of the interdependent museum spaces. Fehn has manipulated the horizon in terms of physical limits and orientation of experience, and has used horizon as an instrument of orientation, movement and engagement in this built project. The literal 'realizing of the place' is finally a process of participation on location in the reinvented site.

Reworked definitions of site can be understood and interpreted both as a subject and a relationship fundamental to the making process. Site is not a lesser part of design but clearly a less articulated aspect of the design process. Questioning modernist site analysis myths of the untouched or hovered over sites allows exploration of issues of perception, interpretation, representation, and understanding working design practice. The argued premise that sites are always a matter of invention needs to be restated.

Notes

1 C. Norberg-Schulz and G. Postiglione, *Sverre Fehn Works, Projects, Writings 1949–1996*, New York: Monacelli, 1997, p.243. See also S. Fehn, 'L'albero e l'orizzonte' ('The tree and the horizon'), *Spazio & Societa*, 1980, vol.10, pp. 32–55; P. Cook, 'Trees and horizons: the architecture of Sverre Fehn', *Architectural Review*, August 1981, pp. 102–6; P.O. Fjeld, 'The fall of horizon', in *Sverre Fehn: The Thought of Construction*, New York: Rizzoli, 1983; R. Weston, 'A sense of the horizon', *Architects Journal*, 19 November 1988, pp. 38–46; S. Fehn, 'Above and below the horizon', *Architecture & Urbanism*, January 1999, no.1, p.340.

2 From award speech by Sverre Fehn '…about Sverre Fehn', *Sverre Fehn Pritzker Architecture Prize Laureate*, Los Angeles: The Hyatt Foundation, 1997. Also available HTTP: <http://www.pritzkerprize.com/svbio.htm>

3 Norberg-Schulz and Postiglione, *Svehre Fehn*, p.19.

4 A. Khan, 'Overlooking: a look at how we look at site or … site as "discrete object" of desire', in D. McCorquodale, K. Ruedi and S. Wigglesworth (eds), *Desiring Practices*, London: Black Dog, 1996, pp.174–85.

5 A. Roy, 'Traditions of the modern: a corrupt view', *Traditional Dwellings & Settlements Review*, 2001, vol.12, no.11, pp. 7–19.

6 D.Leatherbarrow, *The Roots of Architectural Invention, Site, Enclosure, Materials*, Cambridge: Cambridge University Press, 1993, p.7: 'we have largely missed the creative aspect of site definition and the architect's responsibility to "invent" the site of any design project'.

7 M. Villela-Petit, 'Heidegger's conception of space', in C. Macann (ed.), *Critical Heidegger*, London: Routledge, 1996, pp.8, 138, 145, 154.

8 K. Frampton, 'The constructive thought', in Norberg-Schulz and Postiglione, *Svehre Fehn*, pp.253–5.

9 Norberg-Schulz and Postiglione, *Svehre Fehn*, p.59.

10 The building has been well documented, see C. Norberg-Schulz and G. Postiglione, *ibid*, pp.129–44, with bibliography of articles 1975–1994 on p.138; also 'Hamar Bispegard Museum', *GA Document*, 1984, no.11, pp. 72–81; R. Weston, 'Nordic light', *Architects Journal*, 30 September 1987, pp. 25–9.

11 Norberg-Schulz and Postiglione, *Svehre Fehn*, p.19.

12 Norberg-Schulz and Postiglione, *Svehre Fehn*, p.59.

13 Fehn, '...about Sverre Fehn'.

14 Leatherbarrow, *The Roots of Architectural Invention*, p.34.

15 G. Postiglione, 'Mellom jord og himmel: between earth and sky', in Norberg-Schulz and Postiglione, *Svehre Fehn*, p.58. The importance of site ground to project can be seen in many of Fehn's early schemes including a project for a Craft Museum in Lillehamer: 'The unwillingness to compete with the Folklore Museum which comprises mostly small wooden structures, unequivocally expresses their confidence that the specificity of a site resides in its historical consciousness and in the traces that have accumulated throughout time.' (Norberg-Schulz and Postiglione, *Svehre Fehn*, p.65).

16 Andrea Kahn, in 'Overlooking: a look at how we look at site', re-examines modernist assumptions and associated processes related to architectural design: 'intersecting trajectories of representation, analysis and design practices' Yet models of normative undertaking of unthinking 'site analysis' continue to permeate architectural education at all levels. There have been tendencies in educational discourse to treat site in a reductionist manner, focusing primarily on appearance, 'the assumption that the visual characteristics of the given site in the design studio have consequential impact on the creative potential of the pupils' .

17 Norberg-Schulz and Postiglione, *Svehre Fehn*, p.8.

18 Norberg-Schulz and Postiglione, *Svehre Fehn*, p.248.

19 F. Dastur, 'The ekstatico-horizonal constitution of temporality', in C. Macann (ed.), *Critical Heidegger*, London: Routledge, 1996, p.164.

20 D. Veseley in 'Introduction', *eric parry architects*, EU: Black Dog Publishing Ltd, 2002, p.6 describes 'The deeper meaning of horizon has its origin in the experience of the imaginary line where the earth meets the sky. The nature of this imaginary horizontal line is revealed in its power to define the boundary of our visible world as well as in the invitation to transcend this boundary', concluding that horizon is significant in its ability to preserve constancy of human situations.

21 Dastur, 'The ekstatico-horizonal constitution of temporality', p.166.

22 Ibid.

23 Norberg-Schulz and Postiglione, *Svehre Fehn*, p.42.

24 Leatherbarrow, *The Roots of Architectural Invention*, p.12.

25 Norberg-Schulz and Postiglione, *Svehre Fehn*, p.243.

26 Fehn, '... about Sverre Fehn'.

27 Quoted in writings on Fehn in Norberg-Schulz and Postiglione, *Svehre Fehn*, p.257.

28 Postiglione in Norberg-Schulz and Postiglione, *Svehre Fehn*, p.58 on Hamar and the Wasa museum competition project.

29 Heidegger 1954, quoted in Macann, *Critical Heidegger*.

Bibliography

Aalto, A., *Experimental House, 1953*, reprinted in Aalto, *Experimental House*, (Alvar Aalto Museum: Jyväskylä, 1985), unpaginated.

Aalto, A., *Experimental House*, Muuratsalo 1953, (Jyväskylä: Alvar Aalto Museum, 1985), unpaginated.

Alofsin, A., *Frank Lloyd Wright. The Lost Years, 1910–1922. A Study of Influence* (Chicago: University of Chicago Press, 1993).

Anderson, D., *Identity and Ecology in Arctic Siberia*, (Oxford: OUP, 2000).

Anderson, E. N., *Ecologies of the Heart: Emotion, Belief and the Environment*, (Oxford: OUP, 1996).

Anderson, S., 'Architectural history in schools of architecture', *Journal of the Society of Architectural Historians*, Vol. 58, No. 3, September 1999, pp. 282–90.

Appleton, J., *The Experience of Landscape*, (1975), revised ed. (London: Wiley, 1996).

Appleton, J., 'Landscape and architecture', in B. Farmer and H. Louw (eds), *Companion to Contemporary Architectural Thought*, (London: Routledge, 1993), pp. 74–7.

Appleton, J., 'Prospects and Refuges Re-visited', *Landscape Journal*, vol. 3, no. 2, 1984, pp. 91–103.

Arnheim, R., *The Dynamics of Architectural Form*, (Berkeley, Ca.: University of California Press, 1977).

Arnheim, R., *The Power of Center*, (Berkeley, Ca.: University of California Press, 1988).

Bachelard, G., *The Poetics of Space*, (trans. M. Jolas, 1964), (Boston: Beacon Press, 1958), orig. pub. as *La poétique de l'espace* (Paris: Presses Universitaies de France, 1958).

Bakhtin, M., *The Dialogic Imagination*, (Michael Holquist ed; trans. C. Emerson and M. Holquist), (University of Texas Press, Austin and London, 1981).

Ballantyne, A., *What is Architecture?* (London: Routledge, 2002).

Barthes, R., *Le Plaisir du texte* (Paris: Éditions du Seuil, 1973) (trans. R. Miller), *The Pleasure of the Text* (New York: Farrar, Straus and Giroux, 1975).

Bateson, G., *Steps to An Ecology of Mind* (New York: Chandler, 1972).

Benedikt, M., *For an architecture of reality* (New York: Lumen Books, 1987).

Berleant, A., 'The Idea of a Cultural Aesthetic,' *The Great Book of Aesthetics: Proceedings of the XVT International Congress of Aesthetics* (Tokyo, Japan: forthcoming).

Berleant, A., *Living in the Landscape: Toward an Aesthetics of Environment* (Lawrence: University Press of Kansas, 1997).

Berleant, A., *The Aesthetics of Environment* (Philadelphia: Temple University Press, 1992)

Berleant, B. 'The aesthetics of art and nature', in S. Kemal and I. Gaskell, *Landscape, Natural Beauty and the Arts*, (Cambridge: CUP, 1993).

Bhabha, H.K., *The Location of Culture*, (London: Routledge, 1994).

Birksted, J., (ed.) *Relating Landscape to Architecture*, (London: Spon, 1999).

Bloom, H., *The Anxiety of Influence*, (New York: OUP, 1973).

Bonsdorff, P. von (ed.), *Ymparistoestiikan Polkuja* (*Paths of Environmental Aesthetics*) (International Institute of Applied Aesthetics Series, Vol. 2, Jyväskylä: Gummerus Kirjapaino Oy, 1966), p.130.

Bord, J. and C. Bord., *Sacred Waters: Holy Wells and Water Lore in Britain and Ireland*, (London: Paladin Grafton Books, 1986).

Borsi, F., *Leon Battista Alberti*, (Oxford: Phaidon, 1977).

Bossley, P., *Te Papa, An Architectural Adventure*, (Wellington: Te Papa Press, 1998).

Bourdieu, P., *Pascalian Meditations*, (Cambridge: Polity Press, 2000).

Bourdieu, P., *Distinction*, (Cambridge: Harvard University Press, 1984) and (London: Routledge, 1989).

Bourdieu, P., *Outline of a Theory of Practice*, (Cambridge: CUP, 1977).

Bourdieu, P., *Pascalian Meditations* (Cambridge: Polity Press, 2000).

Brady, E., 'Imagination and the Aesthetic Appreciation of Nature,' *Journal of Aesthetics and Art Criticism*, Vol.56, No: 2, 1998, pp.139–47,

Brady, E., *Aesthetics of the Natural Environment*, (Edinburgh: Edinburgh University Press, 2003).

Brady, E.,'The Aesthetics of the Natural Environment,' in V. Pratt et al., eds, *Environment and Philosophy* (London: Routledge, 1999).

Brendt, R .M., C. H. Berndt, and J. E. Stanton, *Aboriginal Australian Art*, (New Holland Publishers, 1992)

Brenk, B., "Spolia from Constantine to Charlemagne: aesthetics versus ideology," *Dumbarton Oaks Papers* 41, Washington District of Columbia, 1987, pp.103–9.

Brook, I., 'Can "Spirit of Place" be a Guide to Ethical Building?' in W. Fox (ed.), *Ethics and the Built Environment*, (London, Routledge, 2000), pp. 139–51.

Burgess, R., 'The State and Self-Help Building in Pereira, Colombia', PhD thesis, University College London, 1990.

Calthorpe, P., and W. Fulton, *The Regional City*, (Washington: Island Press, 2001).

Calvino, I., *Invisible Cities*, (trans. Harcourt Brace Jovanovich Inc.) (London: Picador, 1979).

Campbell, D., 'Land of the Twee', in *The Guardian*, 8 July 2002,, pp. 12–14.

Carter, P. and Jackson, N., 'An-aesthetics', in S.Linstead and H. Hopfl, *The Aesthetics of Organisation*, (London: Sage Publications, 2000), pp.180–3.

Casey, E.S., *Getting Back into Place*, (Bloomington: Indiana University Press, 1993).

Casey, E.S., *The Fate of Place: A Philosophical History*, (Berkeley: California University Press, 1998).

Chakrabarty, D., 'Modernity and Ethnicity in India,' in D. Bennett (ed.), *Multicultural States Rethinking Difference and Identity*, (London: Routledge, 1998).

Chakrabarty, D., 'Of Garbage, Modernity and the Citizen's Gaze', *Economic and Political Weekly*, 7–14 March, 1992, pp. 541–7.

Chakrabarty, D., 'Postcoloniality and the Artifice of History: Who Speaks for "Indian" Pasts?', *Representations*, 37, Winter 1992, pp. 1–26.

Chambers English Dictionary. Chambers Cambridge 1988, 1989.

Chambers, I., *Migrancy Culture Identity*, (London: Routledge, 1994).

Chattopadhyay, S., *Depicting Calcutta*, PhD Thesis, University of California, 1997.

Chaudhuri, S. (ed.), *Calcutta The Living City, Volume I: The Past*, (Oxford: OUP, 1990).

Cheney, J., 'The Journey Home' *An Invitation to Environmental Philosophy*, ed. A. Weston, (Oxford: OUP, 1999), pp.141–67.

Cobb, E., *The Ecology of Imagination in Childhood*, (Dallas: Spring Pub., 1993).

Colin, R. and R. Slutzky, 'Transparency: Literal and Phenomenal', Perspecta 8 1963, pp 45–54.

Colloredo-Mansfeld, R., 'Architectural Conspicuous Consumption and Economic.

Cook, P. 'Trees and Horizons: The architecture of Sverre Fehn', *Architectural Review*, August 1981 pp.102–6.

Cook, R., *The Tree of Life* (New York: Avon, 1974).

Coraghessan Boyle, T., 'Greasy Lake,' in *The Granta Book of the American Short Story*, ed. Richard Ford (London: Granta Books, 1993), p.555.

Crinson, M., *Empire Building, Orientalism and Victorian Architecture*, (London: Routledge, 1996).

Cronin, R., *Imagining India*, (London: Macmillan Press Ltd., 1989).

Croset, P. A., 'Salemi e il suo territorio,' *Casabella* 536, June 1987, pp.18–25.

Crowe, N., *Nature and the Idea of a Man-Made World*, (Cambridge: M.I.T, 1995).

Cuff, D., and R. Ellis (eds.), *Architects' People*, (New York: OUP, 1989).

Currie, G., 'Realism of Character and the Value of Fiction', in J. Levison (ed.), *Aesthetics and Ethics: Essays at the Intersection*, (Cambridge: CUP. 1998), pp.161–81.

Curtis, W., *Modern Architecture since 1900* (New York: Phaidon, 1982).

Darke, J., 'Women and the Meaning of Home' in Gilroy, R. and Woods, R. (eds) *Housing Women*, (London: Routledge, 1994), pp.11–30.

Dastur, F., 'The ekstatico-horizonal constitution of temporality' in Macann, C. (ed.) *Critical Heidegger* (London: Routledge, 1996).

Davies, D., 'Christianity: the Sacred and Ritual in Theology and Religious Studies', eds. Holm and Bowker, *Themes in Religious Studies: Sacred Place*. (London: Continuum, 1994), p.52.

de Saussure, F., *Course in General Linguistics*, (eds) C. Bally and A. Sechehaye, (trans.) R. Harris, (London: Duckworth, 1983).

De Sola-Morales, I., *Differences: Topographies of Contemporary Architecture*, trans. G. Thompson, (Cambridge: MIT, 1997).

Deb, C., 'The "Great houses" of Old Calcutta,' in, S. Chaudhuri (ed.), *The Living city, Volume 1: The Past*, (Oxford: OUP, 1990), pp. 56–63.

Deleuze, G., and F. Guattari, *L'Anti-Oedipe; Capitalisme et schizophrénie t. 1* (Paris: Minuit, 1972), (trans) H.R. Lane, R. Hurley and M. Seem, *Anti-Oedipus; Capitalis and Schizophrenia volume 1* (New York: Viking, 1977).

Deleuze, G., and F. Guattari, *Mille plateaux; Capitalisme et schizophrénie t. 2* (Paris: Minuit, 1980). (trans) B. Massumi, *A Thousand Plateaus; Capitalism and Schizophrenia volume 2* (London: Athlone, 1987).

Deleuze, G., *Empirisme et subjectivité: essai sur la nature humaine selon Hume* (Paris: Presses Universitaires de France, 1953), (trans) C.V. Boundas, *Empiricism and Subjectivity: An Essay on Hume's Theory of Human Nature* (New York: Columbia University Press, 1991).

Deleuze, G., *Pourparlers 1972–1990* (Paris: Minuit, 1990), (trans) M. Joughin, *Negotiations* (New York: Columbia University Press, 1997).

Deleuze, G., *Proust et les signes*, (Paris: Presses Universitaires de France, 1972) translated by Richard Howard, *Proust and Signs*, (London: Athlone, 2000).

Der Ryn, S. V. and S. Conran, 'Make Nature Visible', *Ecological Design*, Island Press, 1996, pp.160–72,

Despres, C., 'The Meaning of Home: Literature Review and Directions for Future Research and Theoretical Development', *Journal of Architectural and Planning Research*, 8 (2), 1991, pp.96–115.

Dixon, W.W., *The Films of Jean-Luc Godard*, (New York: State University of New York Press, 1997).

Dodson, S., 'Playing for keeps in the cyberland of Norrath,' *Guardian Weekly*, 28 March – 3 April 2002, p. 23.

Dovey, K., 'Home and Homelessness' in Altman, I. and Werner, C. M. (eds), *Home Environments*, (New York: Plenum Press, 1985), pp.33–64.

Downing, F., *Remembrance and the Design of Place* (College Station: Texas A and M University Press, 2000).

Dramstad, W. E., J .D. Olson, and R. T. T. Forman, *Landscape Ecology Principles in Landscape Architecture and Land-Use Planning*, (Harvard: Island Press, 1996).

Drew, P., *Architecture Australia*, May/June 1999, Vol. 88, No. 3 .

du Gay, P., et al. (eds), *Identity: a reader*, (London: Sage, 2000).

Duncan, J. S. 'The House as Symbol of Social Structure: Notes on the Language of Objects Among Collectivistic Groups' in Altman, I. and Werner, C. M. (eds) *Home Environments*, (New York and London: Plenum Press, 1985), pp. 33–151.

Dunnet, N., and A. Clayden, 'Resources: The Raw Materials of Landscape' in M.H Roe and J.F.Benson, *Landscape and Sustainability*, (London: Spon Press, 2000), pp.179–201.

Eagleton, T. *The Idea of Culture*, (London: Blackwell, 2000).

Eggener, K. L., 'Resisting Critical Regionalim: A Post-modern Perspective', in S. Akkach, S. Fung and P. Scriver (ed) *Self, Place & Imagination*, (Canberra; CAMEA, 1999).

Eliade, M., *The Sacred and the Profane*, (trans. W. R. Trask, 1959), (New York: Harcourt Brace Jovanovich, Publishers, 1957).

Eliot, T.S., 'Little Gidding', *Four Quartets*, (London: Faber & Faber, 1986).

Elliott, A., *Concepts of the Self*, (Cambridge: Polity, 2001).

Etzioni, A., *The Spirit of Community: Rights, Responsibilities and the Communitarian Agenda*, (London: Fontana Press, 1995).

Fehn, S., 'Above and below the horizon', *A&U* no.1 (340) January 1999.

Fehn, S., 'L'albero e l'orizzonte' (The Tree and the Horizon), *Spazio & Società* 10:1980 p.32–55.

Fehn, S., ' ... about Sverre Fehn', *Sverre Fehn Pritzker Architecture Prize Laureate*, (Los Angeles: The Hyatt Foundation, 1997)

Feuilherade, P., 'Med TV: 'Kurdistan in the sky'', *World Media Watch* at www.bbc.co.uk, 23 March 1999.

Fjeld, P. O., 'The Fall of horizon' in *Sverre Fehn: The Thought of Construction*, (New York: Rizzoli, 1983).

Foster, D. W. 'Survival Strategies of Low-Income Households in a Colombian City', PhD dissertation, University of Illinois, 1975.

Frampton, K., 'The Constructive Thought', in Norberg-Schulz, C. and Postiglione, G., *Svehre Fehn works, projects, writings 1949–1996*, (New York: Monacelli, 1997), pp. 253–5.

Frampton, K., 'Jørn Utzon: Transcultural Form and the Tectonic Metaphor', in *Studies in Tectonic Culture* (Cambridge, MA and London: MIT Press, 1995) pp. 247–98.

Frampton, K., *Modern Architecture: A Critical History*, 3rd ed. (New York: Thames and Hudson, 1992).

Frampton, K., *Studies in Tectonic Culture*, (Cambridge: MIT, 1995).

Frascari, M., 'Carlo Scarpa in Magna Graecia: The Abatellis Palace in Palermo,' *AA Files* 9, 1985, pp.3-9.

Frascari, M., *Monsters of Architecture: Anthropomorphism in Architectural Theory,"* (USA: Rowman and Littlefield, 1991).

Freud, S., 'The 'uncanny', in J. Strachey, A. Freud, *The standard edition of the Complete Psychological works of Sigmund Freud*. Vol. XVII, (London: The Hogarth Press and the Institute of Psycho-analysis), 1st ed., 1955, pp 218- 56.

Gallagher, S., and J. Shear (eds), *Models of the Self*, (Thorverton: Imprint Academic, 1999).

Gans, H., *The Urban Villagers: Group and Class in the Life of Italian-Americans* (1962), (New York: Free Press, 1982).

Gellner, E., *Reason and Culture: The historical role of rationality and rationalism*, (Oxford: Blackwell, 1992).

Genosko, G., 'The Acceleration of Transversality in the Middle' in Hypersurface Architecture edited by Maggie Toy (London: Wiley, 1998) pp. 32–7.

Genosko, G., 'The Life and Work of Félix Guattari: From Transversality to Ecosophy', in Guattari, *The Three Ecologies*, (London: Athlone, 2000), pp. 106–59.

Genosko, G., 'Transversality' in *Félix Guattari: an Abberant Introduction* (London: Continuum, 2002) pp. 66–121.

Gibson and Ward, *Courage Remembered*, (HMSO 1989).

Gibson, J. J., *The Senses Considered as Perceptual Systems* (Boston: Houghton Mifflin, 1966).

Giddens, A., *The Constitution of Society: Outline of the theory of structuration*, (Cambridge: Polity Press, 1984).

Giddens, A., *The Consequences of Modernity* (Cambridge: Polity Press, 1990).

Giedion, S., *The Eternal Present. The Beginnings of Architecture* (London: OUP, 1964).

Gillis, J. R., *A World of Their Own Making*, (Oxford: OUP, 1997).

Godard, J.-L., *Le petit soldat*, [1960] screenplay trans, Garnham, N. as *Le petit soldat: a film by Jean-Luc Godard* (New York: Simon & Schuster, 1967) p. 39.

Goodman, N., *Ways of Worldmaking* (Indianapolis: Hackett, 1978).

Gothein, M. L., *A History of Garden Art, Volume 1*, (London: Dent, 1928).

Gough, K. and Kellett, P., 'Housing Consolidation and Home-based Income Generation: Evidence from Self-Help Settlements in Two Colombian Cities', *Cities: International Journal of Urban Policy and Planning*, 18 (4), 2001, pp.235–47.

Gough, K., 'From Bamboo to Bricks: Self-Help Housing and the Building Materials Industry in Urban Colombia', PhD thesis, University College London, 1992.

Gowing, L., (ed.), *The Critical Writings of Adrian Stokes. Vol. 1 1930–1937; Vol. II 1937–1958; Vol. III 1955–1967*, (London: Thames & Hudson, 1978).

Gregotti, V., *Inside Architecture,* (trans. Wong and Zaccheo), (Cambridge: MIT, 1996).

Guattari, F., 'Psychanalyse et transversalité', 1964, *Revue de psychothérapie institutionelle,* no. 1 (trans) R. Sheed, 'Transversality', in *Molecular Revolution* (Harmondsworth: Penguin, 1984).

Guattari, F., *Chaosmose* (Paris: Galilée, 1992) (trans) P. Bains and J. Pefanis, *Chaosmosis: an Ethico-Aesthetic Paradigm* (Sydney: Power, 1995).

Guattari, F., *Les trois écologies* (trans. I. Pindar and P. Sutton) (Paris: Galilée, 1989); (London: Athlone, 2000).

Gudeman, S. and Rivera, A., *Conversations in Colombia: The Domestic Economy in Life and Text,* (Cambridge: CUP, 1990).

Guilford, J. P., *The Nature of Human Intelligence*, (New York: McGaw Hill, 1967).

Gullestad, M., 'Home Decoration as Popular Culture: Constructing Homes, Genders and Classes in Norway' in del Valle, T. (ed.), *Gendered Anthropology*, (London: Routledge, 1993), pp. 128–61.

Habermas, J., *The Theory of Communicative Action* (London: Heinemann, 1984).

Hagan, S., *Taking Shape: A New Contract between Architecture and Nature*, (Oxford: Architectural Press, 2001).

Häring, H., 'Formulations Towards a Reorientation in Applied Arts', *Bauwelt,* 1927, vol. 49, p.1211.

Harries, K., *The Ethical Function of Architecture*, (Cambridge: M.I.T., 1997).

Harvey, D., *Justice, Nature and the Geography of Difference*, (Oxford: Blackwell, 1996).

Haskins, S., *Mary Magdalene* (London: Harper Collins, 1994).

Heidegger, M., *Being and Time*, (trans. J.Macquarrie and E. Robinson), (New York: Harper, 1962); (trans. by J. Stambaugh) (Albany: State University of New York Press, 1996).

Heidegger, M., and K. Jaspers, *Martin Heidegger and Karl Jaspers: Briefwechsel*, Biemel and Saner (eds), (Frankfurt: Vittorio Klostermann, 1990).

Heidegger, M., 'Why Do I Stay in the Provinces?', (trans. by T. Sheehan), T. Sheehan, (ed.) *Heidegger: The Man and the Thinker*, (Chicago: Precedent, 1981) , pp.27–8.

Heidegger, M., *Poetry, Language and Thought*, (trans. A. Hofstadter), (New York: Harper and Row, 1971, 1977).

Heidegger,M., 'Building Dwelling Thinking', in *Martin Heidegger: Basic Writings*, ed. by D. Farrell Krell, (London: Routledge, 1993), pp. 347–363.

Hepburn, R., 'Landscape and the Metaphysical Imagination' *Environmental Values*, 1996, Vol.5, pp.191–204.

Hepburn, R., 'Restoring the Sacred: Sacred as a Concept of Aesthetics' in *The Reach of the Aesthetic* (Aldershot: Ashgate, 2001), pp.124–7.

Hepburn, R., *The Reach of the Aesthetic: Collected Essays in Art and Nature*, London: Ashgate, 2001), pp.124–5.

Hertzberger, H., A. van Roijen-Wortmann and F. Strauven, *Aldo van Eyck, Hubertus House*, (Amsterdam: Stichting Wonen, 1982).

Hester, R.T., ' Sacred Structures and Everyday Life: A Return to Manteo, North Carolina', in D. Seamon (ed.), *Dwelling, Seeing and Designing: Toward a Phenomenological Ecology.* (SUNY 1993).

Hildebrand, G., *The Wright Space. Pattern and Meaning in Frank Lloyd Wright's Houses*, (Seattle: University of Washington Press, 1991).

Hoff, U., *The Art of Arthur Boyd*, (London: André Deutsch Ltd, 1987).

Holl, S., *Anchoring*, (New York: Princeton Architectural Press, 1989).

Holm, J., and J. Bowker, *Themes in Religious Studies: Sacred Place*. (London: Continuum, 1994).

Holston, J., 'Autoconstruction in Working-Class Brazil', *Cultural Anthropology*, 6 (4), 1991, pp.447–65.

Hume, D., *A Treatise.of Human Nature* (London: 1739), L.A. Selby-Bigge and P.H. Nidditch (eds) (Oxford: Clarendon, 1978).

Hunt, J.D., and P. Willis, P. (eds) *The Genius of the Place. The English Landscape Garden 1620–1820*, Cambridge, MA (London: MIT, 1988).

Huttman, E., 'The Homeless and "Doubled-Up" Households' in Arias, E.G. (ed.), *The Meaning and Use of Housing: International Perspectives, Approaches and Applications*, (Aldershot: Avebury, 1993), pp.457–78.

Icduygu, A., D. Romano, and I. Sirkeci, 'The Ethnic Question in an Environment of Insecurity: The Kurds in Turkey', *Ethnic and Racial Studies*, vol.22, no.6, 1999, pp.991–1010.

Ingold, T., *The Perception of the Environment: essays in livelihood, dwelling and skill*. London: Routledge, 2000).

Irigaray, J., 'Creating another space – outside any framework. The opening of openness', in *Elemental Passions*, trans. J. Collie and J. Still, (New York: Routledge, 1992), pp.59–64.

Irigaray, L., 'Place Interval: A Reading of Aristotle, Physics IV' in *An Ethics of Sexual Difference*, (trans C. Burke and G. C. Gill), (Ithaca: Cornell University Press, 1993), pp.47–59.

Jackson, J. B., *A Sense of Place, a Sense of Time*, (New Haven: Yale, 1994).

Jacobs, J., *The Death and Life of Great American Cities* (1961), (London: Penguin, 1994).

Jacques, D., 'Memory and Value' in J. Woudstra, and K. Fieldhouse, *The Regeneration of Public Parks*, (London: Spon, 2000), pp. 22–30.

James, C., 'A bicultural path to a new centre,' *NZ Herald*, 7 November 2001.

James, W., *A Pluralistic Universe*, (New York: Longmans, Green & Co., 1909).

Kahn, L.I., *Writings, Lectures, Interviews*, A. Latour (ed.) (New York: Rizzoli, 1991) pp. 293, 296.

Kant, I., *Critique of Pure Reason*, (trans.) J. M. D. Meiklejohn, (London: Dent, 1934).

Karjalainen, P. T., 'Place and Intimate Sensing,' *Nordisk Samhällsgeografisk Tidskrift* [*The Nordic Journal of Social Geography*], 27 (1998).

Karjalainen, P. T., 'Real pace Images', in *The City as Cultural Metaphor*, ed. A. Haapala (Lahti, Finland: International Institute of Applied Aesthetics, 1998), pp. 95–101.

Kaviraj, S., 'Filth and the Public Sphere: Concepts and Practices about Space in Calcutta', *Public Culture*, 10, part 1, 1997, pp. 83–113.

Kellett, P. and Napier, M., 'Squatter Architecture: a Critical Examination of Vernacular Theory and Spontaneous Settlement with Reference to South America and South Africa', *Traditional Dwellings and Settlements Review*, 6 (2), 1995, pp.7–24.

Kellett, P. 'Voices from the Barrio: Oral Testimony and Informal Housing Processes in Latin America' *Third World Planning Review*, 22 (2), 2000, pp.189–205.

Kellett, P., 'City Profile: Santa Marta, Colombia' *Cities: International Journal of Urban Policy and Planning*, 14(6), 1997, pp. 393–402.

Kellett, P., 'Cultural Values and Housing Behaviour in Spontaneous Settlements', *Journal of Architectural and Planning Research*. 16 (3), 1999, pp. 205–224.

Kent, R., 'Museum of New Zealand,' *Art AsiaPacific* 20, 1998, pp. 84–5.

Kepes, G., ed. *Education of Vision* (New York: George Braziller, 1965).

Khan, A, 'Overlooking: A look at how we look at site or ... site as "discrete object" of desire' in McCorquodale, Ruedi, Wigglesworth, *Desiring Practices*, (London: Black Dog, 1996).

Kinney, D., 'Rape or Restitution of the Past? Interpreting Spolia,' ed. S. C. Scott, *The Art of Interpreting*: Papers in Art History, Vol.IX, (Philadelphia: Pennsylvania State University Press, 1995), pp. 52–67.

Kite, S., 'Introduction' to *Stones of Rimini* in A. Stokes, *The Quattro Cento and Stones of Rimini*, (Pennsylvania: Pennsylvania State University Press, 2002).

Kitwood, T., *Concern for Others*, (London: Routledge, 1990).

Klaufus, C., 'Dwelling as Representation: Values of Architecture in an Ecuadorian Squatter Settlement', *Journal of Housing and the Built Environment*, 15 (4), 2000, pp. 341–65.

Kostoff, S., *The City Shaped: Urban Patterns and Meanings through History*, (London: Thames and Hudson, 1991).

Krier, R., *Urban Space* (London: Academy Editions, 1975).

Kristeva, J., 'Holbein's Dead Christ', M. Feher, R. Naddaff, N. Tazi, *Fragments for the History of Human Body, part one*, (New York: Zone, 1989).

J. Kristeva, *Black Sun: Deprsession and Melancholia*, trans. L. S. Roudiez. (New York: Colombia, 1992), orig. pub. *Soleil noir, dépression et mélancolie*, (Paris: Editions Gallimard, 1987), and in Finnish as *Musta aurinko, masennus ja melankolia*, Finnish trans. M. Siimes, P. Sivenius, (Helsinki: Nemo, 1999).

Kunstler, J. H., *The Geography of Nowhere: The Rise and Decline of America's Man-Made Landscape*, (New York: Touchstone, 1993).

Kyle, D., *Spectacles of Death in Ancient Rome*, (London: Routledge, 1998).

Laanemets, M., 'Places That Remember,' in Kaia Lehari and Virve Sarapik, eds., *Koht ja Paik / Place and Location* (Tallin: Estonian Academy of Arts, 2000), pp.73–5.

Langer, S. K., *Philosophy in a New Key*, (Cambridge: Harvard University Press, 1993).

Lansing, S. J., 'Balinese Water Temples and the Management of Irrigation,' *American Anthropologist* 89, 1987, pp. 326–41.

Le Corbusier and P. Jeanneret, *Oeuvre Complète, Vol II, 1929–34*, (Zurich: Les Editions d'Architecture, 1995), [orig. pub. 1935].

Le Corbusier, *Couvent Sainte Marie de la Tourette built by Le Corbusier*, L'Arbresle, (L'Arbresle: Dominican Convent of La Tourette: Photocopied Pamphlet, *c*.1999).

Le Corbusier, *Journey to the East* (Cambridge: MIT, 1987).

Le Corbusier, *Le Modulor* (Paris: Editions de l'Architecture, 1950).

Le Corbusier, *Modulor 2* (London: Faber and Faber, 1955), [originally pub. as Le Corbusier, *Le Modulor II* (Paris: Éditions d'Architecture d'Aujourd'hui, 1955)].

Le Corbusier, *Oeuvre Complète Vol. V, 1946–1952* (Zurich: Les Editions d'Architecture, 1995), [orig. pub.1953].

Le Corbusier, *Oeuvre Complète, Vol. IV*, 1938–46, (Zurich: Les Editions d'Architecture, 1995), [orig. pub.1946].

Le Corbusier, *Precisions. On the Present State of Architecture and City Planning*, (trans. E. Schreiber Aujame), (Cambridge: MIT, 1991).

Le Corbusier, *The Radiant City* (London: Faber & Faber, 1967).

Le Corbusier, *Vers une architecture* (Paris: Crès, 1923), (trans. F. Etchells), *Towards a New Architecture* (London: Architectural Press, 1987).

Le Corbusier, *When the Cathedrals were White: A Journey to the Country of the Timid People* (New York: Reynal & Hitchcock, 1947).

Le Corbusier. *Les Maternelles vous parles* (Paris: Editions Gonthier, 1968).

Leatherbarrow, D. and M. Mostafi, 'Opacity'", AA files 32, p 59.

Leatherbarrow, D., *The Roots of Architectural Invention, Site, enclosure, materials*, (Cambridge: CUP, 1993)

Leccese, M., and K. McCormick (eds), *Charter of The New Urbanism*, (New York: McGraw-Hill, 2000).

Lefebvre, H., *The Production of Space* (Oxford: Blackwell, 1991).

Linzey, M., 'Bicultural architecture: evaluating the contribution of Te Kooti,' *In the Making: Architecture's Past*, SAHANZ 18th Conference, (SAHANZ Darwin, 2001), pp. 101–8.

Linzey, M., 'Our habit of dwelling–between Peirce and Heidegger,' in M. J. Oswald and R. J. Moore, (eds), *Reframing Architecture Theory, Science and Myth*, (Sydney: Archadia Press, 2000), pp. 107–12.

Linzey, M., 'Speaking to and talking about Maori architecture,' in J.-P. Bourdier and N. Al Sayyad, (eds), *Dwelling, Settlement and Tradition*, (Lanham: University Press of America, 1989), pp. 317–34.

Little, A., *The Politics of Community: Theory and Practice*, (Edinburgh: Edinburgh University, 2002).

Lloyd, D., *Battlefield Tourism: Pilgrimage and Commemoration of the Great War in Britain, Australia and Canada 1919–1939*, (Oxford: Berg, 1998).

Losty, J.P., *Calcutta City of Palaces, A Survey of the City in the Days of the East India Company 1690–1858*, (London: The British Library Board, 1990).

Lucan, J., 'The Search for the Absolute', in C. Palazzolo and R.Vio, (eds), *In the Footsteps of Le Corbusier* (New York: Rizzoli, 1991), pp. 197–208.

Lynch, K., *The Image of the City*, (Cambridge: M.I.T, 1960).

Lyotard, J.-F., 'Ylevä ja avantgarde', J. Kotkavirta, E. Sironen, *Moderni / Postmoderni*, (Helsinki: Tutkijaliitto, 1986).

Macann, C. (ed.) *Critical Heidegger*, (London: Routledge, 1996).

Madanipour, A., Cars, G., and Allen, J., (eds), *Social Exclusion in European Cities* (London: Jessica Kingsley/Routledge, 1998).

Madanipour, A., *Design of Urban Space* (Chichester: Wiley, 1996).

Madanipour, A., Hull, A. and Healey, P. (eds), *The Governance of Place* (Aldershot: Ashgate, 2001).

Madanipour, A., *Public and Private Spaces of the City* (London: Routledge, 2003).

Malaparte, C., *La Pelle* (originally published in 1949), (Milan: Arnoldo Mondadori, 1991).

Mâle, E., *The Gothic Image* (1910), (New York, Harper and Row, 1972).

Malkki, L., 'National Geographic: The Rooting of Peoples and the Territorialization of National Identity among Scholars and Refugees', in *Culture, Power, Place*, A. Gupta and J. Ferguson (eds), (Durham: Duke University Press, 1997).

Mammott, P. 'Aboriginal Signs and Architectural Semiotics,' in *Architectural Theory Review*, Vol. 2, No. 1, 1997, pp. 56–7.

Marinetti, F.T., *Mafarka the Futurist: An African novel* (originally published in 1909), trans. C. Diethe and S. Cox, (London: Middlesex University Press, 1998).

Markovicz, D.M., *Martin Heidegger, Photos 23 September 1966 / 17+18 Juni 1968*, (Frankfurt: Vittorio Klostermann, 1985).

Marks, M., *Deleuze* (London: Pluto, 1998).

Martienssen, R. D., *The Idea of Space in Greek Architecture* (Johannesburg: Witwatersrand University Press, 1956).

Massey, D., 'A Place Called Home?', *New Formations*, vol.17, 1992, pp.3–15.

Matoré, G., *L'Espace Humain* (Paris: La Columbe, 1962), pp.22–23.

Matthews, P., 'Te Papa: the remake,' *NZ Listener*, 1 December 2001, pp. 50–1.

McEwan, I. K., *Socrates' Ancestor*, (Cambridge, MA: MIT, 1993), p.53.

Menin, S. and F. Samuel, *Nature and Space: Aalto and Le Corbusier*, (London: Routledge, 2003).

Menin, S., 'Relating the Past: the Creativity of Sibelius and Aalto', *Ptah*, (Helsinki: Alvar Aalto Foundation), 1, 2001, pp.32–44.

Merleau-Ponty, M., *Phenomenology of Perception*, (London: Routledge, 1962).

Merritt, R. K., 'From Memory Arts to the New Code Paradigm: The Artist as Engineer of Virtual Information Space and Virtual Experience,' *Leonardo* 34, 5 (2001), p.405.

Miller, D., *Modernity: An Ethnographic Approach. Dualism and Mass Consumption in Trinidad*, (Oxford: Berg, 1994).

Milton, K., *Loving Nature: Towards an Ecology of Emotion*, Routledge 2002 p.104.

Minh-ha, T., 'Other than Myself/My Other Self', in G. Robertson et al (eds), *Travellers' Tales*, (London: Routledge, 1994), pp.9–26.

Minsky, M., *The Society of Mind* (London: Heinemann, 1987).

Moe, R. and C. Wilkie, *Changing Places: Rebuilding Community in the Age of Sprawl*, (New York: Henry Holt, 1997).

Moles, A., *Histoire des Charpentiers* (Paris: Librairie Gründ, 1949).

Moravia, A., 'Contempt' (originally published in Italian as *Il Disprezzo* in 1954), trans. A. Davidson, (Wales: Prion, 1999).

Moreland, J., *New Milestones, Sculpture, Community and the Land*, (London: Common Ground, 1988).

Morley, D., *Home Territories*, (London: Routledge, 2000).

Morris, S., *Daidalos and the Origins of Greek Art*, (Princeton: Yale University Press, 1992),

Mosquera, G. *Morfologia, Desarrollo y Autoconstrucción en Cali: Diagnostico Preliminar*. Programa de Estudios de Vivienda en America Latina (PEVAL), Medellin, 1983.

Mumford, E., *The CIAM Discourse on Urbanism, 1928–1960*, (Cambridge: MIT, 2000).

Nair, P. T., *Calcutta Tercentenary Bibliography*, vols. 1 and 2, Calcutta: The Asiatic Society, 1993).

Nancy, J.-L., *The Inoperative Community*, (trans P.Connor), (Minneapolis: University of Minneapolis Press, 1991).

Neich, R., *Carved Histories, Rotorua Ngati Tarawhai Woodcarving*, (Auckland: Auckland University Press, 2001).

Neich, R., *Painted Histories, Early Maori Figurative Painting*, (Auckland: Auckland University Press, 1993).

Norberg-Schulz, C. and Postiglione, G., *Sverre Fehn works, projects, writings 1949–1996*, (New York: Monacelli, 1997).

Norberg-Schulz, C., *Architecture: Meaning and Place*, (New York: Rizzoli, 1986).

Norberg-Schulz, C., *Existence, Space and Architecture*, (New York: Praeger, 1971).

Norberg-Schulz, C., *Genius Loci; Towards a Phenomenology of Architecture*, (New York: Rizzoli, 1984).

Norberg-Schulz, C., *New World Architecture*, (New York: Princeton Architectural Press, 1988).

Norberg-Schulz, C., *The Concept of Dwelling*, (New York: Rizzoli, 1985).

Norberto, B., *Liberalism and Democracy*, (London: Verso, 1990).

Norst, M. J., 'Biedermeier', in J. M. Ritchie (ed.), *Periods in German Literature*, (London: Oswald Wolff, 1966), pp. 147–70.

Ockman, J., *Architecture Culture: 1943–1968*, (New York: Rizzoli, 1993).

Oliver, P., Davis, I. and Bentley, I., *Dunroamin: The Suburban Semi and its Enemies*, (London: Barrie and Jenkins, 1981).

Ontiveros, T., *La Casa de Barrio: Aproximación Socioantropológica a la Memoria Espacial Urbana*, (Venezuela : Sección de Estudios Urbanos, Universidad Central de Venezuela, 1989).

Ott, H., *Martin Heidegger: A Political Life*, (trans. A. Blunden,) (London: Fontana, 1994).

Packard, V., *The Hidden Persuaders* (1957), (London: Penguin, 1981)

Peattie, L. R., 'Aesthetic Politics: Shantytown Architecture or New Vernacular?', *Traditional Dwellings and Settlements Review*, 3 (2), 1992, pp. 23-32.

Peirce, C. S., 'What is a sign?' *MS 404*, (1894), reprinted in C. Hartshorne and P. Weiss (eds) *Collected Papers of Charles Sanders Peirce*, 8 vols., (Cambridge: Harvard University Press, 1931–58).

Pérez-Gómez, A., 'The Space of Architecture: Meaning as Presence and Representation', in *Questions of Phenomenology: Phenomenology in Architecture, A&U* July 1994, Special Issue, p.13.

Perrin, N., *Introduction* to Dennis Stock, *New England Memories* (Boston: Bullfinch Press, 1989).

Petit, J., *Le Corbusier lui-même*, (Geneva: Rousseau, 1970).

Petzet, H-W., *Encounters and Dialogues with Martin Heidegger*, (London: University of Chicago Press, 1993).

Pinkney, T., *Women in the Poetry of T. S. Eliot. A Psychological Approach*, (London: Macmillan Press, 1984).

Plato, *Timaeus and Critias*, (trans. H. D. P. Lee) (Harmondsworth: Penguin, 1965), pp.70–1.

Plattus, A., 'Passages into the City: The Interpretive Function of the Roman Triumph,' *The Princeton Journal*: Thematic Studies in Architecture 1, *Ritual*, 1993, pp. 93–115.

Porphyrios, D., *Sources of Modern Eclecticism: Studies on Alvar Aalto*, (London: Academy, 1982).

Porteous, J. P., 'Intimate Sensing,' *Area* 18, pp. 250–1.

Porter, R., (ed.), *Rewriting the Self: Histories from the Renaissance to the Present*, (London and New York: Routledge, 1997).

Proust, M., *A la recherche du temps perdu*, 12 vols. (Paris: Grasset, 1913–27); (trans. S. Moncrieff, A. Mayor and T. Kilmartin, rev. ed. D. J. Enright, *In Search of Lost Time* 6 vols. (London: Chatto & Windus, 1992).

Pugh, C., 'Squatter Settlements: Their Sustainability, Architectural Contributions and Socio-Economic Roles', *Cities: International Journal of Urban Policy and Planning*, 17 (5), 2000, pp. 325–37.

Raff, T., '*Spolia* – Building Material or Bearer of Meaning,' *Daidalos* 58, '*Memoria*,' December 1995, pp. 65–71.

Rainer, R., *Traditional Building in Iran* (Graz: Akademische Druck-u. Verlagsanstalt, 1977).

Rajchman, J., *Constructions*, (Cambridge: MIT, 1998).

Rand, A., *The Fountainhead* (New York: Bobbs Merrill, 1943).

Rapoport, A., 'A Critical Look at the Concept "Place" ', in R. P. B. Singh (ed.), *The Spirit and Power of Place*. Human Environment and Sacrality', (Varanasi: Banaras Hindu University Press, 1994), pp. 31–45 and in D. Benjamin, (ed.) *The Home: Words, Interpretations, Meanings and Environments*, (Aldershot: Avebury, 1995), pp. 25–52.

Rapoport, A., 'Cultural and the Urban Order', in J. Agnew, J. Mercer and D. Sopher (eds), *The City in Cultural Context*, (London; Allen and Unwin, 1984), pp. 50–75.

Rapoport, A., *House Form and Culture*, (Englewood Cliffs: Prentice-Hall, 1969).

Rapoport, A., 'Spontaneous Settlements as Vernacular Design' in Patton, C. V. (ed.), *Spontaneous Shelter: International Perspectives and Prospects*, (Philadelphia: Temple University Press, 1988), pp. 51–77.

Rapoport, A., *The Meaning of the Built Environment: A Non-Verbal Communication Approach*, (London: Sage, 1982).

Rapoport, A., 'Thinking about Home Environments: A Conceptual Framework' in I. Altman and C. M. Werner (eds), *Home Environments*, (New York: Plenum Press, 1985), pp. 255–86.

Rapport, N. and A. Dawson (eds), *Migrants of Identity*, (Berg: Oxford, 1998).

Rauch, E.M., *The Adventures of Buckaroo Banzai across the Eight Dimension*, (Century City, Ca.: Twentieth Century Fox, 1984).

Réau, L., *Iconographie de l'art Chrétien Volume 3.2*, (Paris: Presses Universitaires de France, 1957).

Reid, P., *Canberra Following Griffin: A Design History of Australia's National*, (Canberra: National Archives of Australia, 2002).

Relph, E., *Place and Placelessness* (London: Pion, 1976), pp.42–3.

Richards, J. M., *Memories of an Unjust Fella*, (London: Weidenfeld & Nicholson, 1980).

Richards, S., *Le Corbusier and the Concept of Self*, (New Haven: Yale, 2003).

Richardson, M., 'The Spanish American (Colombian) Settlement Pattern as a Societal Expression and as a Behavioural Cause' in Walker, H. J. and Haag W. G, (eds) *Man and Cultural Heritage*, (Baton Rouge: Louisiana State University, 1975).

Riesman, D., et al., *The Lonely Crowd: A study of the changing American character* [1950], (New Haven: Yale, 1963).

Roche, A. V., *Provençal Regionalism* (Illinois: Northwestern University Studies, 1954).

Roe, M. H., and J. F.Benson, *Landscape and Sustainability*, (London: Spon, 2000).

Rotondi, P., *Il Palazzo Ducale di Urbino. La sua Architettura e la sua Decorazione*, (London: Alec Tiranti, 1969).

Rowe, C., 'La Tourette' (1961), *Mathematics of the Ideal Villa and Other Essays*, (Cambridge: MIT, 1976).

Roy, A., 'Traditions of the Modern: A corrupt view' in *Traditional Dwellings & Settlements Review* Volume XII no.11, 2001, pp. 7–19.

Saarinen, E., *Eero Saarinen on his work* (New Haven: Yale University Press, 1962).

Safranski, R., *Martin Heidegger: Between Good and Evil*, (Cambridge MA: Harvard University Press, 1998).

Said, E., *Orientalism*, (Harmondsworth: Penguin, 1995).

Sainte Theresa, 'The Philosophical city of Rabelais and St Teresa', *Literature and Theology* 13, 2 (1999), pp.111–26.

Samuel, F., 'A Profane Annunciation; The Representation of Sexuality in the Architecture of Ronchamp' *Journal of Architectural Education*, 53, 2, (1999), pp.74–90.

Samuel, F., 'Le Corbusier, Rabelais and Oracle of the Holy Bottle', *Word and Image*, 17, 4 (2001), pp. 325–38.

Schafer, E. H., 'The Conservation of Nature under the T'ang dynasty,' *Journal of the Economic and Social History of the Orient*, 5 (1962), pp.280–1 cited in Yi-Fu.

Schildt, G., *Alvar Aalto Own Words*, (New York: Rizzoli, 1998).

Schildt, G., *Alvar Aalto: The Decisive Years*, (New York: Rizzoli, 1986).

Schildt, G., *Alvar Aalto: The Mature Years*, (New York: Rizzoli, 1992).

Schürmann, R., 'Reiner Schürmann's Report of His Visit to Martin Heidegger', (trans P. Adler), *Graduate Faculty Philosophy Journal*, vol.19, no.2 – vol. 20, no.1, 1997, pp.67–8.

Scott Fitzgerald, F., 'The Crack-up' (1936) in *The Crack-up with other pieces and stories* (Harmondsworth: Penguin, 1965).

Scully, V., 'The Architecture of Community', in Peter Katz, *The New Urbanism: Toward an Architecture of Community*, (McGraw-Hill: New York, 1994).

Scully, V., *Louis Kahn*, (New York: Brazillier, 1962), pp.114–21.

Scully, V., *The Earth, the Temple and the Gods; Greek Sacred Architecture*, (New Haven: Yale University Press, 1962).

Searle, J., *Mind, Language and Society: Philosophy in the real world* (London: Wiedenfeld & Nicolson, 1999).

Sennett, R., *The Uses of Disorder: Personal Identity and City Life* (1970), (London: Faber & Faber, 1996.)

Serenyi, P., 'Le Corbusier, Fourier, and the Monastery of Ema,' *Art Bulletin*, XLIX, 1967, pp. 277–86.

Sharr, A. and S. Unwin, *Heidegger's Hut*, ARQ, vol.5, no.1 Spring 2001, pp.53–61.

Shepheard, P., 'Introduction to *Modern Gardens*' in J. Birksted,. (ed.) *Relating Landscape to Architecture* , (London: Spon,1999), pp. 17–38.

Shumaker, S. and G. J. Conti, 'Understanding Mobility in America: Conflicts between Stability and Change' in I. Altman and C. M.Werner, (eds) *Home Environments*, (London: Plenum, 1985), pp. 237–53.

Slessor, C., 'Rural Mission', *Architecture Review*, March 2001, pp 54–61.

Smith, C., *Architecture in the Culture of Early Humanism. Ethics, Aesthetics and Eloquence 1400 – 1470*, (Oxford: OUP, 1992).

Smithson, A. (ed.), *Team 10 Primer* (London: Studio Vista, 1968).

Spencer, T.J., *A Book of Masques*, (London: CUP, 1967).

Sperber, D., *Rethinking Symbolism*, (Cambridge: CUP, 1975).

Steiner, G., 'An Almost Inebriate Bewitchment: Review of Young J., *Heidegger, Philosophy, Nazism*', *TLS*, 15 August 1997.

Stenros, A., 'Orientation, Identification, Representation: Space Perception in Architecture', in Aura, Alavalkama, and Palmquist (eds), *Endoscopy as a tool in Architecture*. Proceedings of the 1st European Architectural Endoscopy Association Conference, Tampere, 25–28 August 1993, (Tampere: Tampere University Press, 1993), p.76.

Stokes, A., 'Form in Art', in M. Klein, P. Heimann and R. E. Money-Kyrle, (eds), *New Directions in Psycho-analysis. The Significance of Infant Conflict in the Pattern of Adult Behaviour*, (London: Tavistock Publications, 1955).

Storr, A., *The School of Genius*, (London: André Deutsch, 1988).

Strati, A., *Organisation and Aesthetics*, (London: Sage Publications, 1999).

Fehn, S., ' ... about Sverre Fehn', *Sverre Fehn Pritzker Architecture Prize Laureate*, (Los Angeles: The Hyatt Foundation, 1997).

Swan, J., (ed.), *The Power of Place: Sacred Ground in Natural and Human Environments*. (London: Gateway Books, 1993).

Swan, J. A., *Sacred Places: How the Living Earth Seeks Our Friendship*. (New York: Bear & Co, Inc. 1990).

Tafuri, M., *History of Italian Architecture 1944–1985*, (London: MIT, 1989).

Talamona, M., *Casa Malaparte*, (New York: Princeton Architectural Press, 1992).

Thayer, R. L, *Gray World Green Heart: Technology, Nature, and the Sustainable Landscape*. (London: Wiley, 1994) .

Thompson, I. H., *Ecology, Community and Delight: Sources of Values in Landscape Architecture*, (London, Spon, 2000).

Tillotson, G. H. R., *The Tradition of Indian Architecture: Continuity, Controversy and Change since 1850*, (New Haven: Yale University Press, 1989).

Tiptree, J. R., 'The Psychologist who Wouldn't do Awful Things to Rats' in D. Hartwell and K. Cramer, (eds), *The Ascent of Wonder. The Evolution of Hard SF*, (London: Orbit, 1994).

Tschumi, B., *Questions of Space* (London: Architectural Association, 1990), Scruton, R. *The Aesthetics of Architecture* (London: Methuen, 1979).

Tuan, Y.-F., *Space and Place*, (Minneapolis: University of Minnesota Press, 1977).

Tuan, Y.-F., *Topophilia: a study of environmental perception, attitudes and values*, (New York: Columbia University Press, 1990).

Tuan, Y.-T., 'Place: an experiential perspective.' *The Geographical Review*, 65, 2 (1975), p. 151.

Tuan, Y.-F., 'Rootedness versus Sense of Place', *Landscape*, no.25, 1980, pp. 3–8.

Turner, J. F. C., 'The Fits and Misfit's of People's Housing', *RIBA Journal*, 81 (2), 1974, pp. 14–21.

Turner, J. F. C., 'The Squatter Settlement: an Architecture that Works', *Architectural Design*, 38 (8), 1968, pp. 355–60.

Turner, T., 'Hyperlandscapes', *Landscape Design*, 304, October 2001, pp. 28–32.

Turner, T., *City as Landscape: A Post-Postmodern View of Design and Planning*. (London: Spon, 1996).

Utzon, J., 'Platforms and Plateaus', *Zodiac* 10, 1962, pp. 113–41.

Van Eyck, A., 'Place and occasion'. *Progressive Architecture*, September 1962.

Van Eyck, A., 'The Medicine of Reciprocity Tentatively Illustrated,' *Architects Yearbook*, no 10, London, 1962, pp. 173–8.

Van Eyck, A., 'Towards a Configurative Discipline,' *Forum* 3, August 1962, pp. 81–93.

Van Eyck, A., *Works*, ed. Vincent Ligtelijin, (Basel: Birkhäuser, 1999).

van Pelt, R. and Carroll William Westfall, *Architectural Principles in the Age of Historicism* (New Haven: Yale, 1991).

Venezia, F., *Indizi e Congetture: Due corse di progettazione tenuti da Francesco Venezia*, (Milan: Città Studi Edizioni, 1995).

Venezia, F., 'Transfer and Transformation. The Architecture of Spoils: A Compositional Technique' in *Daidalos* 16, 1985, pp. 91–104.

Venezia, F., *Francesco Venezia: L'architettura, gli scritti, la critica* 114, (Milan: Electa, 1998).

Venezia, F., *Scritti Brevi 1975–1989*, (Naples: Clean Pub., 1990).

Venturi, R., *Complexity and Contradiction in Architecture*, 2nd ed. (New York: Museum of Modern Art, 1977).

Venturi, R., D. Scott Brown and S. Izenour, *Learning From Las Vegas*, (rev. ed.) (Cambridge, MA: MIT Press, 1977).

Veseley, D, 'Introduction', *eric parry architects*, (London: Black Dog Pub., 2002).

Veseley D., 'Architecture and the Ambiguity of the Fragment,' ed. R. Middleton, *AA. The Idea of the City*, (London: Architectural Association, 1996), pp.109–21.

Vetlesen, A. J., *Perception, Empathy and Judgement: An Inquiry into the Preconditions of Moral Performance*. (Philadelphia: Pennsylvania State University Press, 1994).

Vidler, A., *The Architectural Uncanny*, (Cambridge: MIT, 1994).

Villela-Petit, M., 'Heidegger's conception of space' in C. Macann, (ed.) *Critical Heidegger*, (London: Routledge, 1995), pp.8, 138, 145, 154,

Virtanen, P., 'The Role of Customary Institutions in the Conservation of Biodiversity: Sacred Forests in Mozambique.' *Environmental Values* Vol. 11, No: 2, 2002, pp. 227–41.

Viviescas, F., 'Myth of Self-Build as Popular Architecture: the Case of Low-Income Housing in Colombian Cities', *Open House International*, 4, 1985, pp. 44–8.

Viviescas, F., *Urbanización y Ciudad en Colombia: Una Cultura por Construir en Colombia*, (Bogota: Foro Nacional por Colombia, 1989).

von Moos, S. (ed.), *Album La Roche* (San Francisco: Monacelli Press, 1997).

Voragine, J. de., *The Golden Legend Volume 1* (Princeton: Princeton University Press, 1993).

Walden, R. (ed.), *The Open Hand: Essays on Le Corbusier*, (Cambridge: MIT, 1977).

Ward, P., 'Befitting Boyd's genius', in *The Australian*, 3 May 1999, p. 19.

Welch, 'Aesthetics beyond Aesthetics: Toward a New Form of the Discipline,' *Literature and Aesthetics*, October 1997, pp. 17ff.

Welch, W., *Undoing Aesthetics* (London: Sage, 1997).

Werckmeister, O .K., 'Walter Benjamin, Paul Klee and the Angel of History,' in K.W. Forster (ed.), *Oppositions* 25, Monument/Memory, Fall 1982, pp.103–25.

Weston, A., 'Before Environmental Ethics', A. Light and E. Katz (eds), *Environmental Pragmatism* (London: Routledge 1996), pp.152–66.

Weston, R., 'A sense of the horizon', *Architects Journal*, 19 November1988, pp. 38–46.

Weston, R., 'Nordic Light', *Architects Journal*, 30 September 1987, pp. 25–9.

Weston, R., *Utzon: Inspiration, vision, architecture* (Hellerup: Edition Bløndal, 2002), p. 247.

Whitehand, J., *The Making of Urban Landscape* (Oxford: Blackwell, 1992).

Whyte, W. H., *The Organization Man*, (New York: Doubleday Anchor, 1956).

Wiesenfeld, E., *La Autoconstrucción: Un estudio psicosocial del significado de la vivienda*, (Caracas: Universidad Central de Venezuela, 2001).

Williams, H.W., *A Dictionary of the Maori Language*, 7th edn., (Wellington: Government Printer, 1971).

Wilson, C. St. John, 'The Natural Imagination. An Essay on the Experience of Architecture', *The Architectural Review*, vol. 185, no. 1103, 1989, pp. 64–70.

Wilson, C. St John, 'Functionalism and the Uncompleted Project', *Functionalism – Utopia or the Way Forward*, (Jyväskylä: Alvar Aalto Symposium, 1992), pp.163–70.

Winnicott, D. W., *Home is Where we Start From: Essays by a Psychoanalyst*, (Harmondsworth: Penguin, 1986).

Winnicott, D. W., *Maturational Processes and the Facilitating Environment*, (London: Hogarth, 1965).

Winnicott, D. W., *Collected Papers: Through Paediatrics to Psychoanalysis*. (London: Tavistock, 1958).

Winnicott, D. W., *Playing and Reality*, (Harmondsworth: Penguin, 1972).

Winnicott, D. W., *The Child and the Family* (London: Tavistock Publications, 1957) [Harmondsworth: Penguin, 1991].

Wollheim, R., (ed.), *The Image in Form: Selected Writings of Adrian Stokes*, (Harmondsworth: Penguin, 1972).

Young, R. J. C., *Colonial Desire: Hybridity in Theory, Culture and Race*, (London: Routledge, 1995).

Index